Nonalignment and the Afro-Asian States

NONALIGNMENT AND
THE AFRO-ASIAN STATES

G. H. JANSEN

FREDERICK A. PRAEGER, *Publishers*
NEW YORK · WASHINGTON

Published in the United States of America in 1966
by Frederick A. Praeger, Inc., Publishers
111 Fourth Avenue, New York 3, N.Y.

© 1966 by G. H. Jansen, London, England

Library of Congress Catalog Card Number: 66-15450

Published in Great Britain by
Faber and Faber Limited
under the title of
Afro-Asia and Non-Alignment

Printed in Great Britain

Contents

Contents

8

Contents

Introduction and Acknowledgements

This work is not an impartial, objective account of the recent historical scene in the Afro-Asian region: partly because I do not believe that impartial, objective history is possible, and partly because I do not think it desirable for an Asian writer to be impartial on such a subject at this stage in history.

It is a tract for the times which has been written principally for Afro-Asian readers. I naturally hope that no Afro-Asian government will prevent them from reading this account, but I am not over-optimistic on that score.

The approach in this book to its subject, Afro-Asia and Non-alignment, is not even broadly Afro-Asian. It is that of an Indian observer. This has perhaps, or almost certainly, led to partisanship. I attempted to avoid its more crude manifestations but if it is there the charge is cheerfully accepted: I would not have it otherwise. Nor am I an impartial Indian observer of Indian policy. Till about 1960 Indian policy was national and, more or less, bi-partisan: it is so no longer.

Much of the information incorporated in this work has been received at first hand in writing or by word of mouth from officials and diplomats of several governments, most of them Afro-Asian, but some also from outside the area. The documents seen also came from a variety of national sources. I would have liked to have thanked all helpers by name but I cannot do so. Not that any dark secrets were revealed, but much of what was imparted was in the well-defined journalistic category of 'not for attribution'.

The reader will notice that, in many cases, the volume of information on what transpired in the private sessions of conferences decreases for their more recent meetings. The explanation is that even the most friendly or garrulous official is more relaxed about a conference held five or six years ago than about one held more recently.

I have to render thanks to many institutions and people.

Walid Khalidi provided the occasion for my first writing on this subject, and subsequently urged me to expand it into what has become this book—may he go and do likewise. If he is the godfather

11

Introduction and Acknowledgements

of this book, its godmother is Elizabeth Monroe. She gave to it, most generously, far more than it deserved in terms of time and energy and enthusiasm.

Albert Hourani made possible the writing by suggesting the one place where it could have been done—Oxford in vacation—and he then made possible my stay there. I thank St. Antony's College for the hospitality it offered me through its Middle East Research Centre.

The Government of India enabled me to attend some of the Afro-Asian conferences I have written about. For that I am grateful, and also for its long-suffering patience during the years when I was one of its servants.

My newspaper, *The Statesman* of Calcutta and New Delhi, gave me the chance to be present at yet other of these conferences. For those opportunities and for his understanding of a journalist-temporarily-turned-author, I wish to thank the Editor.

The late Jawaharlal Nehru, with his usual generosity to writers, gave me some of his time to discuss the subject of the book. I do not think that he would have been irked by any criticism of his policies, though some of his followers might be so.

B. Shiva Rao, of New Delhi, not only introduced me to journalism but, many years later, was generous in providing material.

Dr. Appadorai and the Indian School of International Studies, New Delhi, were also most helpful and co-operative; as was Wilfred Lazarus of the Press Trust of India, who in spite of being a journalistic colleague remains a friend.

Najla Izzedin of Beirut, Guy Wint of Oxford and Gordon Addenbrooke of East Hendred read the typescript and made many useful suggestions and corrections.

Without the friendly good cheer and hospitality provided me at Oxford by Nancy and Granville Austin, I would probably have abandoned the whole project after the first week.

Susan Ellis and Gillian Ellicott of Oxford, and Rosette Nuwaisser of Beirut, struggled heroically to reduce my handwriting to typescript; and Joan Kirman of St. Antony's was of invaluable assistance in many ways.

And to Rupa Jansen goes thanks for more than can be said.

G. H. J.

Prologue

This is a study of how in the twenty years since World War II the newly independent countries of Asia and Africa, more especially of Asia, came together and dealt with each other after a century of deliberate separation by the imperial powers of Europe. For the new states this was a process of rediscovery, even of genuine discovery, for they had been thoroughly isolated from each other by inclusion in strictly isolated imperial systems.

This coming together may broadly be called the Afro-Asian movement. Within this large and diffuse movement there were crests, nodal points or foci of interest that were the Afro-Asian conferences.

When people think of the Afro-Asian conferences it is the names 'Bandung' and 'Belgrade' that usually occur to them, and no others. That is a pity, because the first, the biggest and the best of these gatherings was held earlier and elsewhere. This was the Asian Relations Conference that met in New Delhi in March 1947. It was supposed to be an unofficial conference dealing, in scholarly fashion, with subjects of cultural and economic interest, but since the moving spirit behind it was Mr. Nehru, and since he had just become the first Prime Minister of India, its deliberations had a strong bias towards anti-colonial politics.

The countries of South and South-East Asia were on the threshold of freedom in 1947 and there is about this conference, as no other, an air of blissful dawning, of naïve and innocent enthusiasm. This is seen in its membership: for the first and the last time the Central Asian Republics of the Soviet Union, Tibet, and the Jews of Palestine were invited. In all there were twenty-eight countries represented, but this figure would rise to about thirty-five if one took the Arab League observer as representing all its members. Its conclusions are noteworthy for two things. It rejected as impractical the idea of an 'area of immobilisation' in Asia in the event of war. This was, in fact, the first tentative suggestion of neutralism. And it tried to set up a continuing organisation for inter-Asian co-operation, which, largely because of rivalry between India and China, was ineffectual from the outset and gently faded away over the years. No other conference has

13

even attempted to create a permanent body to carry on the work of unifying Afro-Asia.

The heroes of this first conference were the Indonesians, who had some difficulty in getting to it from their embattled country. It was the final attempt by the Dutch to knock out the young republic that prompted Mr. Nehru to call the next meeting, also in New Delhi, in January 1949.This, not Bandung, was the first gathering of the new, independent governments of Afro-Asia (one can say 'Afro' as well as 'Asia' for this time Ethiopia was present in addition to Egypt). It was indeed an Australasian assemblage for Australia and New Zealand attended with Australia playing a leading part in the proceedings—another invitation that was never repeated. The conference, in workmanlike fashion, dealt with the single subject of the Dutch attack, and made detailed and specific proposals which probably prodded a reluctant Security Council, that is to say its Western members, into really putting pressure on the Dutch.

Since no further large-scale formal gatherings were held for another five years, the practical co-operation between the Afro-Asians in international affairs was maintained only through the Afro-Asian group at the United Nations. There, and especially on the Korean problem, the Afro-Asians were able to exemplify the policy of non-alignment, which had been first formulated by Mr. Nehru in 1946, and which was now gaining adherents from the new Afro-Asian countries. Though non-alignment in essence is nothing more than a desire to exercise an independent judgement on questions of foreign policy, it was viewed, incorrectly, as a product of, and an abstention from, the antagonisms of the Cold War. The countries of Afro-Asia opted for non-alignment for a wide variety of reasons, in order to serve their own special national interests; diversity of origin produced shades of difference in the practice, to which different labels such as neutralist, uncommitted and non-aligned may be applied.

Since 1950, and down to the present time, the one factor in common between several Afro-Asian governments has been that in foreign affairs they practice non-alignment, in one or another of its varieties. That non-alignment should serve as almost the sole link between them has tended to give this policy an exaggerated importance in the estimation of the Afro-Asian states.

The intermediate period of five years—1950 to 1955—was marked towards its end by two developments that were equally important and unfortunate for Afro-Asia. After Stalin's death in 1953 had produced a real softening, even then evident, in Russia's policy, Mr. Dulles, just a little later than was necessary, began building barriers against Russia's southward expansion in West Asia, in the Baghdad Pact, and against that of China in East Asia, through SEATO. The restraining of China had begun in another way, too. Mr. Nehru had got it to accept publicly, and as widely as possible, the Five Principles of Peaceful Co-existence, the Panchsheel, that was supposed to impose on it a moral code.

The vague aura of religiosity that hung over Panchsheel unfortunately blurred the clear outlines of non-alignment, for there is no real or necessary connection between the two concepts.

By chance the Prime Ministers of Burma, Ceylon, India, Indonesia and Pakistan decided to meet together in Colombo in April 1954, and after discussing the peace settlement in Indo-China at great length they accepted, as an afterthought, an Indonesian suggestion for a large Afro-Asian conference. This led in April 1955 to the Bandung meeting.

At Bandung the two policies, of pacts and Panchsheel, clashed headlong. The result was a draw. 'Colonialism in all its manifestations' was denounced, in terms that some interpreted as referring to the old colonialism of the West and others insisted on applying to the new colonialism of World Communism. Pacts were said to be good if they were for self-defence, but bad if they served the interests of great powers. It was on these equivocations that the vast myth of the Bandung Spirit was based.

Yet this myth became a factor of considerable importance in world affairs when, in the years 1955–8, the Communists placed themselves alongside the non-aligned in accepting, not so much non-alignment, as the idea of peaceful co-existence that had been grafted on to it. Their chosen instrument was the self-styled Afro-Asian Solidarity Movement that held a profusion of unofficial Afro-Asian conferences.

By this time even heretically Communist Yugoslavia had become a member of good standing in the non-aligned club, and it was she and the United Arab Republic who sponsored the third large Afro-Asian Conference, that of the Non-aligned Heads of States or Governments at Belgrade in September 1961.

Though the liberation of Africa was the biggest happening in the Afro-Asian world since Bandung, Africa was inadequately represented at Belgrade, as it had been at Bandung also. This came about because the Congo crisis had split the new African states into antagonistic groupings one of which, the six-nation 'Casablanca Group', imposed its veto on most of the twenty-one countries of the 'Monrovia Group'.

The Afro-Asian non-aligned countries that numbered about a dozen at Bandung had now increased to some thirty-five. From these a selection of twenty-three Afro-Asians, plus Yugoslavia and Cuba, was made for Belgrade. The conference met at a time of high tension soon after the building of the Berlin Wall, and its most significant decision was a call for peace and negotiations issued directly to President Kennedy and Mr. Khrushchev.

Largely under Yugoslav impulsion, the idea was somewhat belatedly accepted that, for the developing countries, their economic problems were at least as important as those of freedom from imperialism. Accordingly a wide range of developing countries—mainly Afro-Asian and non-aligned but also including some aligned nations, and representatives from Europe and Latin America—met in Cairo in July 1962. The understanding of common economic problems reached at this meeting is likely to have more far-reaching effects than will be achieved by most of the purely political conferences.

The first use that Africa made of its new-found independence was to split itself into contending groups. But because of Africa's strong continental feeling—a sentiment that is almost completely absent in Asia—it decided to heal these self-inflicted wounds, and all its independent states met at Addis Ababa in May 1963. There they rejected the fervid slogans of total and immediate unity, but set up a single African co-ordinating organisation that already has some signal achievements to its credit. The African states thus attained a degree of formalized unity that the Afro-Asians as a whole and the non-aligned were neither able nor willing to achieve.

At this conference Africa was to be seen, self-confidently on its own, pulling away easily and naturally from Asia. The Afro-Asian movement as such had achieved its purposes and had worked itself out as a political driving force. It continues for the most part merely as a loose, convenient framework within which joint consultations may be held from time to time.

Apart from the unfolding of linear developments in time, there would seem to be three themes or patterns implicit in the turbid events of these twenty years in Afro-Asia, on which there is some comment in this book.

The first of these is the role of morality in politics. The Afro-Asian movement, and even more so its offshoot non-alignment, and still more so the commandments of Panchsheel, all self-consciously and

16

Prologue

deliberately produced standards of judgement and principles of political conduct. Yet, applying these very criteria to the policies and conduct of their creators in Afro-Asia, one sees that the Afro-Asians have failed twice over to meet the test of truth and courage. On the first occasion they were confronted with a problem from another continent, the crisis in Hungary; on the second, with a major Asian problem, the India-China dispute. This latter failure became evident at the Second Colombo Conference of December 1962 where, though only six countries were present, they discussed this momentous crisis involving one thousand million people and the future of the continent. In their proposals they deliberately refused to pass judgement on the rights and wrongs of the case, and subsequently failed even to defend the correctness of their findings.

The second theme is that of the intertwining of the Afro-Asian feeling and the policy of non-alignment. Afro-Asia gave birth to non-alignment and in its exuberant youth this policy clothed itself in the highly-coloured garb of Panchsheel. The assertive Chinese stripped this away. For a time the two trends ran parallel, with neither impinging much on the other. But more recently Afro-Asia, symbolised by 'Bandung', and non-alignment, under the banner of 'Belgrade', have become openly competitive, mainly because of Russia's and China's search for allies in their ideological dispute. It is this tussle, alien to Afro-Asia's interests, that produced the Second Belgrade Conference of the non-aligned in Cairo in October 1964 and the Second Bandung Meeting in June and October 1965.

The third theme is the contrast between illusion and reality in international affairs. After their separation, the long-lost Afro-Asian brothers threw themselves into each other's arms. This was inevitable and even necessary and desirable. Only a little later, after the emotional reunion, did they discover that during the separation they had grown apart.

The first big conference, in New Delhi, was fired by little beyond sentiment and the fresh feeling of freedom, though the first ominous drum-beats of later antagonisms could just be heard.

At Bandung the Afro-Asians came together, quite simply, as members of the same continents against their present or former rulers from another continent; and at this meeting the wave of sentiment barely managed to wash over the rocks of reality.

Later, at Belgrade, there was a greater degree of sophistication for, this time, the Afro-Asians met as exponents of a distinctive approach to the Cold War conflicts between the other continents. Despite a more selective membership—itself a concession to reality—the conference had to be forced by India to admit that real, primary importance had to be given to world problems over less really urgent protests against colonialism.

At New Delhi it was apparent that merely to be parts of the same continent was not enough when it came to evolving common policies; Bandung showed that joint participation in the same anti-colonial struggle was not a very strong link; and at Belgrade it was clear that similarity in foreign policy did not necessarily mean friendship.

The hard reality of separate national interests ultimately asserted itself against all these illusions.

One noteworthy characteristic of these conferences is that while the geographic area covered by them expands, their membership contracts. Only Asia, with Egypt, was represented at New Delhi, but over thirty countries attended; Bandung took in Asia and Africa but only twenty-nine governments were represented; while at Belgrade, which included Asia, Africa, Europe and Latin America, there were twenty-five delegations. Only in the more recent meetings, when all independent Africa and parts of Latin America were brought in, has there been a really wide expansion of membership.

There would have been no Afro-Asian movement, and therefore, most probably, no policy of non-alignment if Europe had not left its empires in Asia and Africa to go back home. Matthew Arnold once wrote the elegy of the age of faith, but if in the following quotation, from 'Dover Beach', one substitutes the words 'European rule' for the word 'faith', what he said is perfectly applicable to the political happenings of the last twenty years in Afro-Asia:

> The sea of faith
> Was once, too, at the full, and round earth's shore
> Lay like the folds of a bright girdle furl'd;
> But now I only hear
> Its melancholy, long, withdrawing roar. . . .

The background music to this book, faint but persistent, is that 'melancholy, long, withdrawing roar'.

CHAPTER I

Early Contacts Between the Nationalist Movements

The Afro-Asian movement had its official birth in a hotel suite in San Francisco in June 1945, during the conference at which the United Nations Organisation was also brought to birth. But the initial contacts between nationalist movements that led up to this act of creation went back over a period of forty years. These had had, of necessity, to be private and non-official and somewhat clandestine; and they were mostly between the nationalist movements in Asia, for, till the end of World War II, Africa remained the Dark Continent of colonialism. In view of the multiplicity of Afro-Asian contacts and meetings after 1947, it is surprising how few and how fugitive these earlier connections were. There were two good reasons why contact was intermittent.

One was imposed isolation. The European Powers that enforced this had the means to make it effective. Britain, France and Holland alike applied all over Asia a deliberate policy of divide and rule. By 1850 the European conquest of Asia was complete, or at least by that date Asia had accepted the crushing superiority of Europe: the subsequent military campaigns were no more than mopping-up operations. Not for two generations did the Asians, numbed with defeat, shake off the fear and the feeling of impotence. In the meantime, the restive and resentful Asian masses were tightly bound to distant metropolitan countries in Europe, and were thereby cut off from all possible subversive links with one another. This imperial precaution was no more than elementary. Its result was that there was far less travel and trade between the countries of Asia in 1900 than there had been in 1700.

Hence the Indian people were completely integrated into a British system of administration and a British code of law. They bought goods manufactured in Britain and sold their raw materials to that country. They were educated in English, which meant not only that they were steeped in English thought but that news of the rest of the

19

world—even of the rest of Asia—came to them, suitably filtered, through London. If they wished to acquire higher learning they had to go to Britain and to travel there by British shipping lines. In the last resort, if they wished to visit the Asian colonies of other imperial systems, and they were at all politically suspect, the police could step in and forbid them to do so. The same held good for the Asian subjects of France and Holland. Reins to guide and restrain, blinkers to constrict vision, three separate sets of harness, were all securely buckled on.

Asian nationalist leaders knew, of course, what had been done and was being done to their continent. As Pandit Nehru wrote in 1944: 'Then came the British and they barred all the doors and stopped all the routes that connected us with our neighbours in Asia.'[1] British historians have written that an 'object of British policy' was to snap the links between India and all her neighbours. This isolation, they were honest enough to admit, was 'a recent and entirely novel feature in the history of India'.[2]

To a certain limited extent the peoples of Asia and Africa are still in isolation wards, with British or French matrons sitting by the doors. Even now it is easier and quicker to travel from East to West Africa, or from an ex-French to an ex-British colony within West Africa, via London and Paris, than directly. Till very recently a telephone call from Lebanon to Cyprus, which on a clear day can be glimpsed from the hills behind Beirut, had to travel 6,000 miles through Paris and London, simply because Lebanon had been French and Cyprus British. What are now merely curious anomalies were once, not so long ago, standard practice for every sort of communication between the peoples living in the vast area between Manila and Jakarta in the east and Rabat and Leopoldville in the west.

Nevertheless, because of a small but vital section of the Afro-Asian peoples, this divisive, Euro-centric system was to prove self-defeating. This element was the stream of young men who perforce had to go to the imperial capitals for their higher education. For some time these young men were even encouraged to do so, in the expectation that they would be so overawed by the spectacle of imperial power at its very source; so absorbed intellectually into the culture pattern of the metropolitan country, that they would be rootless when they went home, and so all the more likely to be efficient cogs in the colonial machine. This happened in many cases but, after 1920, the future leaders of independent Asia and Africa found the universities of Britain and France convenient places in which to meet and to plot and plan with fellow 'colonials'.

For English-speaking British subjects, these centres of cross-pollination were Oxford and Cambridge and, above all, the London School of Economics during the time when the powerful, slightly warped intellect of Harold Laski dominated that institution. Mainly because of his leftist, anti-imperial ideas, brilliantly and mordantly presented, the London School was much more of a centre of colonial protest than were the older universities. Though the Indian majlis at Oxford and Cambridge were centres for all Asian students, and not merely Indians, the fact was, and is, that the young men who went to Oxbridge were more likely to end up as administrators or prosperous professional men than as jail-birds. Jawaharlal Nehru is the most outstanding of the relatively few exceptions to the rule that the subtle, casual seduction of Oxford and Cambridge works in favour of the Establishment, native or foreign.

Outside the cloisters and the common rooms there was in London a second very significant rallying point for young Asians and Africans which, in a way, was even more important than the London School of Economics; for here there were not only discussion but first steps towards positive action. This was the India Institute as embodied in its Secretary-General, V. K. Krishna Menon, who took it over and revitalised it in 1924. To its grimy offices off the Strand came young men from many colonial possessions and, once there, they readily submitted to the forceful leadership and the strange, magnetic spell of Mr. Menon. He would, by turns, lecture them on liberation and left-wing socialism and then lash them with his sarcastic tongue; he gave little but demanded much, and usually got it. Besides hundreds of young Indians who worked for the India Institute, there were also Indonesians like Subandrio, now Foreign Minister of his country, and his wife; Africans like Jomo Kenyatta, Prime Minister of Kenya; U Pe Kin of Burma, where he was several times cabinet minister, and Wickramasinghe, later one of the founders of the Lanka Lama Samaj party in Ceylon. There were many young Arabs, too; for the Institute, while working mainly for India, worked for Arab national causes also. So behind their leader, a latter-day Pied Piper, these young Asians would speechify, demonstrate and march in processions, address envelopes, distribute leaflets, and make endless cups of English tea. This was the first, beneficent, impact of Mr. Krishna Menon on the Afro-Asian movement; a quarter of a century later his impact on it was to be more profound but also more malign.

Early Contacts Between the Nationalist Movements

Across the Channel in Paris the Sorbonne and the cafés of the Quartier Latin provided the same sort of common meeting ground for the future nationalist leaders from the French colonies in Indo-China, North Africa and West Africa.

Paradoxically, because of the very success of the European powers in blocking direct connections between their colonies, it was in the imperial capitals and through the imperial languages that young Afro-Asians pooled their ideas for the great counter-attack on Europe.

The second reason for the comparative paucity of preliminary contacts between the Afro-Asian nationalists is to be found in the nature of nationalism itself. Like mysticism, like all schemes of salvation, whether they be private or public, nationalism is a self-centred, inward-looking emotion. 'Internationalism can indeed only develop in a free country, for all the thought and energy of a subject country are directed towards the achievement of its own freedom . . . it becomes an obsession,' Mr. Nehru very rightly remarked.[3] Caught up in the exaltation of fighting their own particular enemy, or else because they are too hard-pressed, nationalists can spare little time or sympathy for others even if they are attacking the same enemy from another flank. Because of this preoccupation we shall see that though Afro-Asian nationalism was aroused and active from 1900, it remained split into separate nationalisms for virtually another twenty years. Only after World War I did the sense of involvement in a single, common struggle bring about some relations between them, but even then not many.

Afro-Asian protest, from the turn of the century, not only found expression in political activity but also, and equally, found outlet in armed rebellion. Viewing the continent as a whole one sees Asia, from the Yellow Sea to the Mediterranean, seething and heaving in violent revolt that was suppressed in one area only to break out in another.

The rebellion of the Egyptian Army under Orabi in 1881 was a very early, and isolated, manifestation. But while the Abyssinians were defeating the Italians in 1896 the Filipinos were fighting the Spaniards and, three years later, the Americans. After the Boxer Rising in China in 1900 came two climactic events in the Far East. In 1902 a European power deigned to contract an alliance with an Asian country—the Anglo-Japanese Treaty of 1902. In 1904–5 the Japanese inflicted crushing defeats by land and sea on another European power, Russia. That event sent tremors of delight and vicarious pride

rippling across the entire continent. In 1906, and for two years thereafter, the French had a rebellion on their hands in Indo-China; the
first bomb was thrown in India in 1907. In the following year it was
the turn of Persia where Tsarist Russia helped the Shah brutally to
crush a nationalist uprising. In 1911 the Kuomintang overthrew the
Manchu regime that had become subservient to the West, while in
the same year the Arabs set aside their opposition to the Ottomans
to join them in fighting the Italians in Libya. The greater violence of
World War I, the first great European civil war, overlaid these
sporadic outbursts, but they reappeared with great frequency immediately after it came to an end. That suicidal blood-letting had
'deglorified' Europe in Asian eyes and had also compelled the
colonial governments to make promises of self-government, soon to
be broken. An aroused and angry Asia pressed home the knife and
pulled the trigger with greater confidence than before.

In 1919 Turkey expelled the European armies from Asia Minor. In
1920 there was widespread rebellion in Iraq, and in 1921 in Egypt.
Syria's turn followed in 1925-6, while in the latter year the Indonesians in Java rose against the Dutch, and simultaneously the Riff
tribesmen battled heroically against France and Spain in Morocco.
After a long drawn-out struggle, Peking fell to the Kuomintang in
1928. The British and the French faced uprisings in Burma and Indo-
China in 1930-1 and the same two powers had to fight again in 1936,
the French in Syria and the British in Palestine. In the latter territory
a bitter struggle against the Arabs went on till 1939 and the outbreak
of World War II.

As before, global conflict blanketed the nationalist uprisings,
though there was one massive outburst of violence in India in 1942.
After the War there was, comparatively speaking, less armed protest
in Asia, but only because it was by then evident that the nationalists
were on the point of achieving a victorious breakthrough on the
political front. And at this point it would be appropriate to turn back
and review the political activities of the nationalist movements in
Asia, both on their own and in association with each other.

There is romance, and something too of pathos, about the earliest
inter-Asian links—an impression of hesitant hands reaching out to
touch in the darkness of the colonial night. In 1871, for instance, an
appeal for help against the Dutch was addressed from the Sultan of
Atjeh, at the northern tip of Sumatra, to the Turkish emperor at
Constantinople. No help was sent, of course, but one cannot but
wonder how the message from the jungle-covered hills and the steam-

ing rice-fields ever reached the marble palaces beside the Golden Horn; and what the Shadow of God on Earth, already dubbed the Sick Man of Europe, would have thought if he had set eyes on these fierce co-religionists of his, armed with their serpentine kris and ready to die for the faith against the infidel.

Islamic fellow-feeling was certainly the basis for that particularly improbable connection; it was the principal, though not the only, motive for the next inter-Asian episode. This was the founding in Paris in 1884 of a secret society by the Egyptian reformer Muhammed Abduh and the Persian-Afghan Jamaluddin Afghani, a mysterious, restless, intellectual incendiary. The society had branches in Tunis and elsewhere, but is remembered because of a magazine it published called *The Indissoluble Link* that was, alas, all too soluble, since it closed after eighteen issues. The approach was Pan-Islamic, but its objective was as much nationalist as religious—to rouse the Muslim peoples against their foreign rulers, especially against Britain, that chief 'enemy of the Muslims'—a danger as much for its military as for its religious penetration. The British took the periodical seriously enough to ban it from all their colonial possessions, but its message lived long after it.[4]

The next manifestation of Asian nationalism was more decorous; this was the formation of the Indian National Congress in 1885. Impeccably clad in top hats, frock-coats and cautious liberal sentiments, its founders were reformists basically loyal to the British Crown. The meetings began with the singing of 'God Save the Queen'; yet even these men, at their very first meeting in 1885, deprecated the annexation of neighbouring Burma to the British Empire. Repeating this sentiment in 1892, they found it especially deplorable that the conquest should be carried out with Indian money and resources: they felt so strongly on the subject that they passed resolutions on it five times before 1902. In 1904 they likewise condemned the British expedition to Tibet, but by that time such sentiments were no longer exceptional, for the pace of nationalist protest was quickening across the entire continent.

The ensuing period, 1900 to 1914, was above all the time when Asian nationalists built up the machines and the political parties later to be employed in the big battles of which the opening skirmishes had begun. The Indian National Congress proceeded on its orderly, organised way, and was joined in 1907 by two Egyptian parties, the Party of the People, founded by Egypt's greatest nationalist leader, Sa'd Zaghlul, and the Party of the Nation under Mustafa Kemal.

Early Contacts Between the Nationalist Movements

Five years later, in 1912, on the far side of Asia, the semi-nationalist Sarekat Islam rapidly picked up a large popular following in Indonesia, while in West Asia in the same year was born the body that has been described as the first genuine political Arab organisation.

This was the clumsily-titled 'Ottoman Party of Administrative Decentralisation' started in Cairo by Syrians living there. It had branches in other Arab towns, such as Beirut, but there is no evidence of any working co-operation with the Egyptians in whose country it had its headquarters. This strange circumstance provides a suitable starting point for a brief consideration of the origins and early years of Arab nationalism—an exercise that reveals the narrowness and selfishness of nationalist movements that has afflicted not only the Arabs but all Asians down to the present time.

The first assertions of a distinct Arab political personality were, like those of the Indian National Congress twenty-five years earlier, restrained and 'loyal'. These came from secret and semi-secret groups started in Constantinople itself. Yet even these first clarion calls 'did not strike a response among all who spoke Arabic', as a contemporary scholar puts it with gentle obliquity.[5] The Arabs subsequently to be known as Lebanese struck off on their own; and so did the Syrians. Hence when a body calling itself the Arab Congress met in Paris in 1913, its membership of twenty-five was composed of twenty-three Syrians and two Iraqis.

Small wonder, therefore, that the Egyptians remained the great abstainers from Arab nationalism for another thirty years. In 1911 a Syrian delegation led by Shukri al-Assali came to Cairo and met the Egyptian nationalist leaders, of whom the best known was Ahmad Lutfi al-Sayyed. History is a repetitive process; the Syrians of 1912 put forward a proposal that later Syrian delegations suggested in 1958 and 1963; this was that the movements in the two countries should merge, with the Syrians providing the men and the Egyptians the money.[6] In 1912, as in 1958 and 1963, the Egyptians said 'no', and two years later, in 1914, the Egyptians were able to boast their own parliament, even though it was one with truncated powers.

Simultaneously, larger and more generous Pan-Asian sympathies were at work. It has already been noted that the Arab nationalists sank their quarrels with their Turkish rulers to help them in fighting the Italians in Libya (one of the Arab volunteers was Abd al-Rahman Azzam, later the first Secretary-General of the Arab League). This campaign, and the Balkan Wars of 1912 to 1913 involving Turkey, stirred the Muslims of Indonesia and, Mr. Nehru noted, roused 'an astonishing wave of sympathy' in the Muslims of India. He went further: 'All Indians felt that anxiety and sympathy'; an India medical mission was sent to Turkey 'and even the poor subscribed'.[7] Thus even before World War I Asian nationalism carried within itself the centrifugal and centripetal forces that have tugged at it ever since.

During the between-war years of the 20's and the 30's, political activity by the Asian nationalist movements was, as might have been expected, as continuous and intense as their military action. Conferences and manifestoes, strikes and campaigns of civil disobedience became part of the accepted pattern of life in Egypt and the Arab countries, India and Burma, Indonesia and Indo-China. Two further important political parties were established: the Wafd, under Zaghlul and Mustafa Nahas in Egypt in 1919, and the Nationalists under Sukarno in Indonesia in 1928.

We can only pick out the highlights of this busy, turbulent period, especially those that reveal an increasing measure of practical co-operation between nationalists. One of these produced a strange cultural confrontation.

Soon after World War I Asian nationalism threw up two archetypal figures in Kemal Atatürk and Gandhi, who in themselves epitomised two contrasting ways of meeting the politico-cultural challenge of Europe. To use the definitions of Arnold Toynbee,[8] Atatürk was a 'Herodian' who believed, with the Japanese, that the West could only be beaten with its own weapons wielded by a thoroughly westernised Asia. The 'Zealot' Gandhi rejected the West and all its works, turning his back on the industrial revolution and the machine age, propounding his belief that the East could only find strength to hold its own by returning to its ancient, well-tried traditions and its spiritual past.

Atatürk, who can claim the dubious privilege of being Asia's first modern republican dictator (the first of a long line), is a much over-rated figure whose superficial reforms have not gone very deep even in his own country. Gandhi, on the other hand, not only converted the Indian National Congress from an upper-class debating society into a strongly-organised mass movement; he also had a profound effect on every aspect of modern Indian life and thought. Yet it was the approach of Atatürk rather than that of Gandhi that was ultimately adopted by all the Afro-Asian nationalists, who worship the gods of industrialisation, military power and the authoritarian state. This has been so even in India, where the Congress Party itself used Gandhi's discipline of non-violent non-co-operation merely as a tactical weapon against the British Raj. One further paradox remains to be noted: Atatürk deliberately cut Turkey from its Asian roots, so that when it returned, reluctantly, to the Asian political scene it did so as an intensely conservative and divisive force. Gandhi, by contrast, launched India into the broad mainstream of Asian national feeling to which it gave leadership and cohesion.

The contrasting policies of these two leaders impinged on each other only on one curious topic. Since the early years of the century the devout Muslims of India had succumbed to the spurious idea of Pan-Islamism, which the deplorable Sultan Abdul Hamid had concocted as a means of holding together the ramshackle Ottoman Empire. Thus impelled, they expressed great concern, soon after World War I, lest the Caliphate of Islam, a purely Turkish institution, should be endangered by the European powers then occupying Turkey. To generate a feeling of Hindu-Muslim unity in India, Gandhi threw the full weight of the Congress Party behind the Khilafat Movement, and this strange aberration became for some time a central issue in Indian politics. It faded away, to an accompaniment of shamefaced embarrassment when Indians discovered that the real enemy of the Caliphate was Atatürk himself; he finally abolished it in 1924.

Mr. Nehru himself has written[9] that the Congress Party was long engrossed in internal politics and began to take an interest in foreign affairs only after 1920. For this broader outlook Mr. Nehru was himself responsible—perhaps even more so than Gandhi. Certainly the Party's resolutions read like a chronology of Asian nationalism during this period. In 1920 it resolved on co-operation and, in particular, friendly relations with all neighbouring countries. In 1922 congratulations were sent to the Turkish nation on its recent victories; the resolution of the moment declared that unless the 'jaziratul-Arab is freed from all non-Muslim control there cannot be peace and contentment in India'. Sympathy for Egypt was expressed in 1924, and in 1927 the Congress Party called for the withdrawal of the Indian troops then being used against nationalists in China, Mesopotamia and Persia. In 1928 the Indian movement was officially linked with that in the rest of Asia by means of a resolution that 'the struggle of the Indian people for freedom is part of the world struggle against imperialism', with which contacts should be established. In the following year the Party expressed 'anxious concern' at 'reactionary attempts to put an end to the reform introduced by King Amanullah' in Afghanistan.

27

Early Contacts Between the Nationalist Movements

With the world clearly drifting towards war, a separate Foreign Department was set up within the Congress Party Secretariat in 1936, a year when its interests were particularly complex and widespread. The League of Nations was condemned for its impotence in the face of Italian aggression in Ethiopia, and greetings were sent to the Spanish people fighting General Franco. The thorny problem of Palestine received attention, too, on the lines of condemning partition and asking the Jews not to let themselves be exploited in the interests of British imperialism. Much the same note was struck again, in 1939, when Congress expressed admiration for the courage and sacrifices of the Arabs. The Jews, it said, by relying on the British armed forces to advance their special interests, had aligned themselves with British imperialism. The solution offered by the Indian Party was a democratic state in Palestine 'with adequate protection for Jewish rights'.[10]

It was not only a matter of passing pious and well-meaning resolutions: within the limits of its means and power the Congress Party also took action. To support the Chinese in their war against Japan, a boycott of Japanese goods was called for in 1936. In November 1937 Chu Teh, the redoubtable general of the Chinese Communist Army, wrote to Mr. Nehru asking for financial and medical assistance, as also for volunteer fighters from India. The Congress despatched a medical mission, and a letter from Mao Tse-tung in May 1939 thanked Mr. Nehru on the arrival of the ambulance at Yenan, the Communist headquarters.[11] In view of recent happenings, it is ironic that this Indian assistance should have been sent directly to the Chinese Communists, and not to the official Chinese Government of the time.

In writing of the Congress Party's Pan-Asian and international interests, Mr. Nehru showed a quiet pride which is entirely justifiable, for few, if any, other nationalist movements had such wide-ranging sympathies. 'No other nationalist movement of a subject country came anywhere near this: and the general tendency in such other countries was to keep clear of international commitments,' he remarked. He was particularly proud of the fact that Congress resolutions referred to the danger of Fascist dictatorship long before the appeasers in the West woke to it. For all this activity he himself was mainly responsible, because Gandhi was far more of an internationalist, a believer in world brotherhood, than a mere Asian. Yet the Mahatma, despite his doctrine of non-violence, expressed admiration in 1925 for the embattled Riff tribesmen in Morocco.[12] When he

28

was on his way to the First Indian Round Table Conference in London in 1930, the Egyptian leaders of the Wafd met his ship at Port Said, and he told them of his sympathy for their struggle: a jerky, flickering film was made of this meeting between the frail Indian, clad in his homespun cotton drapes and the burly, tarbooshed Egyptians. Despite a good deal of persuasive pressure exerted on him by the Zionists, including the philosopher Martin Buber, the Mahatma remained firmly opposed to the idea of a Jewish state.[13]

But he looked beyond Asia: 'How can we have Asia for the Asiatics unless we are content to let Asia remain a frog in a well?' he asked.[14] What he wanted was not 'isolated independence' but a 'voluntary interdependence . . . a federation of friendly, interdependent states'.[15]

The strong Asian bias in Mr. Nehru's internationalism was almost wholly due to the deep impact made on him by one particular event—his attendance at the Congress of Oppressed Nationalities in Brussels in February 1927. Though the organisation that actually sponsored this historic meeting was non-Communist, there is little doubt that it was in fact what would nowadays be called a 'Communist front', discreetly manipulated from the rear. The pages in his *Autobiography* in which he describes the event make curious reading because of his partial denial, yet partial admission, that the Congress was Communist-run: this ambivalence always marked Nehru's attitude towards the Communists.[16] He was more frank in a confidential report in which he referred, critically, to 'the possibility that Russian foreign policy might influence it'.

At Brussels were gathered 175 delegates representing 134 organisations and 300 visitors from India, China, Syria, Arabia (Palestine and Egypt), Korea, Indonesia, Indo-China, Annam, Japan, North and South Africa, North and South America and almost every European state. Among the Afro-Asians present and later to become famous were Nehru, representing the Congress Party, Mohammed Hatta, later Vice-President of Indonesia, Ho Chi Minh, now President of North Vietnam, Léopold Senghor, now President of Senegal.

Even across the waste of years one can, on reading the conference records, sense something of the excitement, earnestness and exaltation with which the downtrodden of the earth came together for the first time to share their sufferings and their hopes. On the third day of the meeting, for example, 'the leader of the recent Syrian revolt and two generals from the Cantonese army', fighting the Peking regime, joined the gathering and were given a tremendous reception.

Early Contacts Between the Nationalist Movements

The noise from the wings was one of thunder over Asia. There is about it an air of amateurish spontaneity. The Congress flag was displayed but, confessed Mr. Nehru, 'the charka (on it) could not easily be reproduced in the short time we had'. There were other oddities: the languages of the conference were English, French and German with some Arabic and Chinese; but the use of Hebrew had to be stopped because 'few understood it'.

In his speech Mr. Nehru made a slashing, frontal attack on British imperialism in India for plunder and repression. But one of the main points he stressed had a Pan-Asian slant. 'On account of India, other lands have suffered and suffer still' through the use by the British of Indian troops against other nationalist movements. He named the countries: 'China, Egypt, Abyssinia, the Persian Gulf, Mesopotamia, Arabia, Syria, Tibet, Afghanistan and Burma . . . it is a horrifying list'; some of the names in it still figure as battle-honours on the flags of Indian regiments. Therefore, he concluded, 'it is important for you if we win freedom, not only internal freedom but freedom also to make connections with our neighbours and other lands as we wish'. In his words one can hear the Asian nationalists beating against the dividing and distracting walls erected between them by Europe.

After six days of almost continuous meetings, the Congress produced forty resolutions of which perhaps the most important, from the purely Asian point of view, was one issued jointly by the Indian and Chinese delegations. In this, after referring to their 'cultural and intellectual isolation', they resolved to 'co-ordinate their struggle' 'so that by simultaneously engaging British imperialism on two of its most vital fronts', the hard-pressed nationalists in China could be helped. There was, as might have been expected, a resolution on the establishment of a permanent world organisation linking up all the forces opposed to imperial and colonial oppression. The final manifesto ended with this rousing peroration: 'The oppressed and enslaved nations which represent the overwhelming majority of mankind, like the proletariat, can conquer the world, the world of the future. Oppressed Peoples and Oppressed Nations, unite!'

Mr. Nehru, in the report that he made to the annual Congress Party meeting in 1928, reveals that for all his enthusiasm he had not lost his acute political insight. He made the point that co-operation between the oppressed peoples is easier than between the oppressed and the working class in the oppressor country, which was contrary to one of the main themes of the conference. Their interests would coincide, he said, only if nationalist movements clearly stood 'for the economic liberty of the masses'.

Or again, following up an idea advanced by a speaker from Mexico, Mr. Nehru prophesied that the 'great problem of the near future will be American imperialism'. Not until the Cairo Preparatory Conference of 1961 was there further contact between Afro-Asia and Latin America. On that occasion Cuba expatiated on the dangers of dollar imperialism.

Mr. Nehru, convinced of the great importance of the meeting, strongly recommended that the Congress Party should affiliate with the permanent organisation to which it gave birth, the League against Imperialism. He thought that this body could play a big role in the future as a 'a League of Nations of Peoples, a truer one than the League of Governments which sits at Geneva'. The party was affiliated to the former League and in 1927 and 1928 contributed $250 to its funds.[17]

In his report Mr. Nehru made three points that have since become familiar. Talking of the possibility of war, he said that every effort should be made to prevent it for if that happened 'our best laid plans for our national betterment will break down': he used that argument many times after 1928.

Secondly, he remarked that the Brussels Congress was viewed with consternation by the foreign and colonial offices of the colonial powers. They have registered the same alarm over every Afro-Asian conference since.

Thirdly, the nationalist leaders at Brussels, Mr. Nehru noted, were 'anxious for closer bonds, especially with the Chinese', but 'nothing practicable could be suggested'. The failure, or reluctance, to set up a continuing permanent organisation has also been a common feature of every other Afro-Asian meeting despite similar enthusiasm for the idea.[18]

The organisers of the Congress treated Mr. Nehru with great deference. He was named as one of the honorary members of the Presidium along with Madame Sun Yat-sen, George Lansbury, Einstein and Upton Sinclair. But it was not long before the doctrinaire Communism of these sponsors broke through the anti-colonial façade when, in 1929, they denounced Gandhi for 'betrayal of the cause of workers and peasants', and ordered Mr. Nehru to dissociate himself from a compromise offer that Gandhi had just made to the British. Mr. Nehru indignantly refused, and in 1930 issued a curt directive to the Congress Party secretariat: 'No further communications are to be sent to the League against Imperialism from this office.'

Early Contacts Between the Nationalist Movements

Yet the Brussels Congress had achieved its main purpose through the impression that it had made on the mind of Mr. Nehru: he admitted that it gave him a new insight into the problems of other colonial countries, a new vision that this was a single world-wide struggle. He himself saw the Bandung Conference as in direct line of descent from this Brussels meeting.

Against this wider Afro-Asian scene it might be useful to glance briefly at two smaller regions within it, to see whether nationalist co-operation was any easier of achievement on a more limited scale.

Co-operation should have presented no great difficulties to the Arab countries of West Asia, since their struggle was identical in aim and they were united in race, language, religion, culture, as well as being geographically contiguous. However, throughout the 1920's, Egypt, the biggest of these states, insisted on maintaining its individuality. After the Paris Peace Conference in 1919, when other Arab delegations suggested a working alliance to Sa'd Zaghlul, he replied that 'our problem is an Egyptian problem and not an Arab problem'. And in the early 1920's when Abd al-Rahman Azzam (later to be the first Secretary-General of the Arab League) made much the same proposal, Zaghlul's scornful retort was that zero plus zero would still only add up to zero.

Only in the 1930's did Egypt show any real interest in the Arab movement. It has been suggested that its new attitude was due to failure by the then Egyptian royal family to establish a new Caliphate, and to a belief that what would not be achieved through religion could perhaps be attained politically. Egypt set about calling Arab conferences in Cairo and several new magazines were started, propounding the Arab idea. Yet even in 1938 Egypt's most famous intellectual, Taha Husain, while advocating educational, economic and even military unification of the Arab countries, still insisted that Egypt had its own personality which should be preserved, not diluted. In 1963 President Nasser confessed that this strain of thought was still dangerously strong in Egypt.

It took the monstrous injustice and the growing menace of the situation in Palestine to pull the Arabs together. In the middle of the long Palestine rebellion a conference of 400 Arab leaders met at Bludan in Syria to discuss Palestine: its president was an Iraqi and the vice-presidents were an Egyptian senator and the Greek Orthodox Bishop of Hama. Here was a striking display of Arab unity of feeling, but it had little direct impact on Palestine itself.

In the late 1930's and during World War II, Arab unity became a fixed principle in the programmes of many political parties and groups in Egypt, Syria and Iraq, and this common Arab aspiration seemed to come to fruition with the founding of the Arab League in 1945. But the League failed dismally to meet the challenge of Zionism and imperialism in Palestine, and at least in the realm of political action, has not yet recovered from that shattering experience.[19]

Mr. Nehru made his first direct contact with Arab nationalism, an association that was to be of great importance in the years that followed, when he paid two brief visits to Egypt in 1938; a Wafd Party delegation toured India in the next year. The Iraqi leader Chaderchi invited Mr. Nehru to his country in 1938, on the plea that the nationalist campaign 'must not be considered in separate units'. But it is noteworthy that the Egyptian leader Nahas, though speaking of nationalist co-operation, inserts the rider 'while safeguarding our respective independence'.[20]

Much the same attitude of 'thus far but no further' is to be found in the relations between the nationalist movements in India and Burma in the years between the wars. Of all India's neighbours, Burma was perhaps the only one that defied the dictum of Anatole France and entertained really 'neighbourly' feelings for the larger country across the frontier, despite differences of race, language and religion. Unlike Ceylon, Burma was, till 1935, administratively a part of India, and in the absence of a university in Rangoon most young Burmans had their higher education at the University of Calcutta— a very vocal centre of Indian nationalism; in 1919 there were no less than 875 young Burmese in Calcutta.

The biggest obstacle to friendly feelings between India and Burma was the presence of a large Indian community there (this was, and is, true also of Ceylon, Malaya and to a lesser extent, Indonesia). Whether as a labourer, or bureaucrat, or, above all, as a money-lender and absentee landlord, the Indian in Burma was both feared and despised. Burmese nationalist feeling at times seemed to be as much anti-Indian as anti-British; unlike the secular Indian movement it had, and still has, strong religious roots in Buddhism.

After 1920, when Burmese nationalism got off to a rather late start, the more radical wing always maintained contact with the National Congress Party in India—a policy that both sides openly accepted as two-faced. Thus over the years, and especially around 1930, Burmese nationalists joined the Indians in protesting at the proposed separation of Burma from India not because Burma really felt itself to be a part of India, but because the Burmese feared that they would be isolated from the bigger and stronger Indian national movement, and might be deprived of the constitutional advances which the movement was wringing from the British. The Burmese nationalists simultaneously tried to persuade the British to keep Burma politically abreast of India, and to induce the Congress Party not to try and hang on to Burma. They succeeded in this dual approach, and it was after the administrative separation of 1935 that Indian and Burmese nationalism, now at a respectable distance, co-operated closely. After 1938, the younger and still more activist party, the Dobama Asiayone or the Thakins, of which U Nu was a member, sent a delegation to the annual meetings of the Indian party. The fourth annual conference of the Thakins in 1939 copied the Congress Party programme in its entirety. The Japanese conquest of Burma in World War II unfortunately brought this realistic and fraternal association to an abrupt end.[21]

Japan's victories over Russia in 1904 had thrilled the whole of Asia, but thereafter it turned its back on Asia to seek the strange gods of westernisation. Sun Yat-sen said, in 1922, that Japan had missed its chance of creating Pan-Asia when, in World War I, it joined the Western Allies; if, instead, it had joined the Central Powers, all Asia would have revolted under its leadership. Whether this was true or no, Japan's shamelessly aggressive policy towards China from 1931 onwards, culminating in open, large-scale war and the rape of Nanking in 1938, made it impossible for any Asian nationalist to take Japan's slogan of 'Asia for the Asiatics' seriously. Once again it was the psychological impact of swift and seemingly effortless military victories in World War II—over the British at Singapore and in Burma, against the Dutch in the Indies and the Americans in the Philippines—that had lasting importance, because the feats destroyed once and for all the myth of the innate superiority of Occident over Orient.

The Japanese conquests brought into existence the Greater East Asia co-prosperity scheme, in which Asian territories were supposed to be free and equal partners of Japan in the great task of world conquest. They were endowed with constitutions, declared independent and their 'governments' then concluded treaties of alliance with Japan. All this play-acting culminated in the Assembly of Greater East Asiatic Nations in Tokyo in November 1943. Present were the 'Presidents' or 'Prime Ministers' of China, India, Thailand, Burma and Manchukuo, who struck a minor blow for nationalism when they jointly challenged the Allies to declare their war aims for Asia.

Early Contacts Between the Nationalist Movements

In fact, these countries were never treated as anything but conquests by the Japanese. For instance, the Japanese detached a portion of eastern Burma and handed it over to Thailand without even informing the Burmese 'government'. In the tussle in Japan between politicians and diplomats, some of whom perhaps dreamt the Asian dream, and the soldiers, who merely wanted secure bases and sources of raw materials, the arrogant soldiers always won. Only incidentally, and as a consequence of the swiftness of their final collapse, did the Japanese give any real assistance to Asian independence, and that too in only one of the former colonies, Indonesia.[22] Throughout their Asian domain they administered the grim but useful lesson that imperialism is not a western monopoly.

A happier wartime development was the cordial, if rather tenuous relations that war produced between the Kuomintang in China and the Congress Party in India. When war broke out in Europe, Mr. Nehru was actually in Chungking visiting Generalissimo and Madame Chiang Kai-shek. Even after the outbreak of hostilities had made communications difficult, the Central Executive Committee of the Chinese party somewhat unrealistically proposed co-operation through the exchange of professors, tourists and Buddhist groups, and also of intelligence. The Chiangs, and Gandhi and Mr. Nehru kept in touch, and when the former visited India in early 1942, when the Japanese were advancing on India's frontiers, the Chiangs put the case for India's freedom to their British hosts. The Generalissimo also sent several messages to President Roosevelt with intent to reinforce the American leader's pleas to Mr. Churchill that an independent India be brought in promptly on the Allied side, but to no avail: the Prime Minister had already declared that he had no ntention of presiding over the liquidation of the British Empire.[23]

In this rapid survey of the preliminary and unofficial contacts between the nationalist movements of Asia and Africa, it is necessary to glance briefly at the latter continent, and especially at the activities of nationalist movements in its sub-Saharan Negro territories. One great difference between African and Asian nationalism is immediately apparent: from the very start African nationalism was co-ordinated on a continental scale in a manner unknown in Asia. The first Pan-African Congress was held as far back as 1919, and in 1920 a National Congress of West Africa, bringing together the British territories of Nigeria, the Gold Coast, Gambia and Sierra Leone, met at Accra.

In his *Autobiography* President Nkrumah brushes aside these and other early gatherings as of small account, but they must have fostered some habit of nationalist feeling and thinking on a continental scale. He himself was inclined to date the truly effective beginning of Pan-Africanism from the Fifth Pan-African Congress held in Manchester in 1945, which, unlike its four predecessors, was not solely 'composed of middle-class intellectuals and *bourgeois* Negro reformists'. Among the 200 delegates were representatives from the United States and the West Indies as well as from many African colonies, including Nkrumah for the Gold Coast, Wachuku from Nigeria and Kenyatta from Kenya.

In the following year the gulf between English-speaking and French-speaking Africa was bridged when Nkrumah visited Paris to meet the French West African members of the National Assembly such as Senghor and Houphouet-Boigny, now President of the Ivory Coast. In the course of long discussions, they planned, according to Nkrumah, a movement for the Union of West African Socialist Republics. As a result of this meeting, the French West African representatives attended a West African conference in London in 1946; a West African secretariat established in London in 1947, 'drew in all Africans and West Indians'. After Nkrumah's departure from London no more is heard of Pan-African activity there or in Paris; only in 1958 did he call the first official Pan-African Conference in Ghana.

In contrast to these direct, working relationships between the African nationalists, the links between African nationalism and Asian nationalism as a whole were in the realm of inspiration and ideology. President Nkrumah writes that when working out the plan of action for his party he asked himself 'how is it possible . . . for a revolution to succeed without arms or ammunition? After months of studying Gandhi's policy, and watching the effect it had, I began to see that when backed by a strong political organisation it could be the solution to the colonial problem.'[24] That the connections between nationalist Africa and Asia were not closer at this juncture can be attributed not merely to distance and limited resources; it was also at least partly due to the presence in Kenya and East Africa of a large colony of Indian business men and, in West Africa, of 'Arab' —Syrian and Lebanese—traders, who were not liked because of their wealth, their business practices and their support of the political *status quo*. These two communities remain a continuing problem to this day.

In drawing the distinctions between the strong, practical continental feeling in African nationalism, and the comparative weakness and haziness of such a feeling in the nationalism of Asia, one must note that demands for a specific Pan-Asian organisation were nevertheless frequent.

The former Aga Khan called for an Asiatic Federation in 1918, and at the annual sessions of the party the President of the Indian National Congress made the same demand in 1922 and 1926 and 1927. In the latter year the Japanese were hosts at Nagasaki to a Pan-Asiatic Conference of Chinese, Indians, Filipinos and Koreans. In 1928, the Congress Party actually adopted a resolution for the creation of a Pan-Asian Federation by 1930.

What impelled these serious-minded and responsible leaders to demand that an illusion become reality? Was it the impulsion of an Asian feeling? Is there such a thing as Asianism?

'Pan-Asianism'—like 'the spiritual East'—is in origin a European concept; Asia found both notions flattering, adopted them and developed them as its own. What is worse it tried to fit itself to these second-hand, ready-made ideas.

If 'the spiritual East' was produced by a sense of religious doubt and inferiority in Europe, 'Pan-Asianism' was the product of a sense of political guilt and, in turn, an outcome of fear. Over and over again we shall see Europe recoiling in quite unnecessary alarm from this bogey of its own creation. In this feeling there are echoes of 'the Yellow Peril', which itself taps older atavistic European fears, born of memories in the collective unconscious, of the tribes erupting out of the eastern steppes, of the Turks at the gates of Vienna and the Moorish thrust turned back only at Tours. Many times in the period under examination we see European (and American) policy towards the Afro-Asian movement generated by the belief that once Asia were to free itself from the grip of Europe it would unite and take revenge.

When 'realistic, materialistic Europe' saw Asian ghosts as real things, Asia, understandably, did likewise, and married the concepts of Asianism and the spiritual East. In the first years of the century the Japanese artist Okakura Kakuzo proclaimed that: 'Asia is one . . . not even the snowy barriers can interrupt for one moment the broad expanse of love for the Infinite and Universal which is the common thought—inheritance of every Asiatic race . . . and distinguishing them from the maritime peoples of the Mediterranean and Baltic who love to dwell on the particular and to search out the means, not the ends, of life.' Sun Yat-sen, in 1924, said that the independence movements in Asia could only succeed if 'all Asiatic peoples unite and stand as one', which they should do because Eastern civilisation was superior to the 'scientific utilitarian' West in its 'humanity, justice and morality'. Nevertheless, he added, the East must learn something of Europe's 'military culture'.

Something of the same sagging of the flabby flesh of rhetoric on the hard bone of fact is to be found in Rabindranath Tagore. His essays, and the speeches he made during his travels, are full of spiritual Asianism but in the end he concludes that 'because we are Asiatics a protest again Europe seems to be in our blood'. And the key word is 'protest'.

For Mr. Nehru, too, reality has the last word. In 1949 he said that 'there are many factors that join the countries of Asia together, apart from geography', and he goes on to list four: the experience of colonial domination by Europe; the process of 'finding oneself' after that experience; the fear that freedom may be lost to Europe once again; and common economic needs.[25] The first three are, of course, facets of the same thing, anti-colonial feeling—that is, the real, and the only real, basis of Asianism.

In a speech a year later Mr. Nehru frankly accepted this fact: 'There is such a thing as Asian sentiment. Perhaps this sentiment is merely the outcome of the past two or three hundred years of European influence in Asia. Personally I do not believe that any profound difference exists between the Orient and the Occident. Such differences as can be accounted for by history, tradition and geography exist even among the Asian countries and, in fact, even within the same country.'[26]

These references to history and tradition serve as reminders that Asia is divided by the very influences that have made it great— its religions, its rich cultures, its ancient empires. China, India, Persia, Arabia are proud of the distinctive and unique contributions they have made to world civilisation, and are not ready to merge them in an Asian blur.

This is why Pan-Asian talk by the Asian nationalist leaders is always vague, with no great force of conviction behind it. It never even amounted to a very palpable political myth; even the half-hearted references die away after 1950.

One of the last attempts to revive it was made by the late K. M. Panikkar in his brilliant but perverse work *Asia and Western Dominance*, published in 1953. He admits to the negative origin: 'Asianism is exclusively the counterpart of the solidarity of European feeling.

Before the end of the nineteenth century there was no such feeling.'
He admits, too, that there is an 'unbridgeable gulf between the
Chinese Confucian and the Indian Brahmin'. But he then tries to
argue that this gulf is confined to the upper class and that 'there is a
community of thought and feeling between the common peoples of
India and China'.[27] This is leftist romanticism; for if Asianism is a
reaction to the West it mut be confined to the Asian *élites* who alone
have a Western background.

There is no real reason why Asia should be half-ashamed to admit
that its continental feeling is the outcome of politics. But, as we have
seen, the reluctance exists. No doubt it stems from the overlap; the
concepts of 'Asianism' and 'the spiritual East'; spiritual people ought
to have spiritual, as well as political, motivations.

No such confusion afflicts the strong continental feeling that prevails in Africa. And this is so because, broadly speaking, the peoples
of Negro Africa are of the same race, with the same colour and cast
of features. The absence of ancient religions and literary languages
is a blessing in disguise. The absence of remembered history, of
warring kings and 'battles long ago' is perhaps the greatest asset of
all. For Asian nationalism the real question is: what unites a Filipino
and a Syrian? For Africa one has to ask: What divides a Liberian
from a Kenyan?

This chapter has outlined the emergence of the nationalist movements in Asia and Africa and the first tentative and unofficial contacts they established during the period of their struggle for freedom.
We must now survey their first attempts at co-operation as governments when Asia attained independence soon after World War II.
The scene shifts to the west coast of the United States of America.

NOTES TO CHAPTER I

1. Nehru: *The Discovery of India*, London, 4th ed., 1956 (1st ed., 1946),
   chap. 5, p. 6.
2. *Cambridge History of India*, vol. I, p. 52.
3. Nehru: *op. cit.*
4. C. C. Adams: *Islam and Modernism in Egypt*, London, 1933, chap. 3;
   and A. Hourani: *Arabic Thought in the Liberal Age, 1798–1939*,
   London, 1962, pp. 109–20.
5. Hourani: *op. cit.*, p. 285.
6. Information provided by Miss Afaf Lutfi al-Sayyed.
7. Nehru: *op. cit.*, chap. 7, p. 10.
8. Toynbee: *Civilisation on Trial*, Oxford, 1948, chap. 10.
9. Nehru: *op. cit.*, chap. 9, p. 1.
10. Chakrabarty and Bhattacharyya: *Congress in Evolution*, Calcutta, for
    the texts of these resolutions.

11. Nehru: *A Bunch of Old Letters*, 1958, pp. 261, 385.
12. *Young India*, Feb. 1925.
13. *Harijan*, 26th Nov. 1938.
14. *Harijan*, 24th Dec. 1938.
15. Nehru: *op. cit.*; and P. F. Power: *Gandhi on World Affairs*, Washington, 1960, chaps. 4 and 5.
16. Nehru: *An Autobiography*, London, 1936, chap. 23.
17. *James Maxton Papers*.
18. *Indian Annual Register*, 1927, vol. I, pp. 204–5, and vol. II, pp. 152–9, for Nehru's speech and report. Also Eudin and North: *Soviet Russia and the East*, Stanford, 1957, pp. 265–6; and Brecher, M.: *Nehru, A Political Biography*, London, 1959, pp. 109–15, 341.
19. Hourani: *op. cit.*, pp. 291–323; and A. G. Chejne, 'Egyptian attitudes towards Pan-Arabism', *The Middle East Journal*, Washington, summer, 1957.
20. Nehru: *A Bunch of Old Letters*, pp. 291, 312, 313.
21. J. F. Cady: *A History of Modern Burma*, Cornell, 1958, chaps. 6 and 12.
22. F. C. Jones: *Japan's new order in East Asia*, Oxford, 1954; and W. H. Elsbree: *Japan's Role in South-East Asian Nationalist Movements 1940–45*, Harvard, 1953; and H. Toye: *The Springing Tiger*, London, 1959, chap. 5.
23. Nehru: *The Discovery of India*, chap. 7 and *A Bunch of Old Letters*, pp. 390, 405, 476, 494.
24. Kwame Nkrumah: *The Autobiography of Kwame Nkrumah*, London, 1957, Preface and chaps. 3 to 5.
25. *India's Foreign Policy: Selected Speeches of Jawaharlal Nehru, 1946–1961*, New Delhi, 1961, p. 261.
26. Nehru, *op. cit.*, p. 265.
27. K. M. Panikkar: *Asia and Western Dominance*, London, 1953.

The best general survey of the period dealt with in this chapter is to be found in Jan Romein's *The Asian Century*, London, 1962.

CHAPTER II

The First Official Links

The first formal proposal that a full-scale Asian conference should be held was made on the opposite side of the globe from Asia. The idea came from 'many of the Asian delegates' to the United Nations Conference on International Organisation, held in San Francisco between 2nd April and 20th June 1945; they suggested to Mrs. Vijayalakshmi Pandit, leader of the unofficial Indian delegation, that her brother Jawaharlal Nehru 'should take the lead in summoning such a conference in Asia'.[1]

The Asian conference was planned as an alternative to the conference which they were attending, and at which the structure of the future world organisation was decided, because they feared that the new United Nations would end up, like the old League of Nations, as nothing more than a White Man's Club.

Fifty nations were represented at San Francisco and, of these, twelve were from the Afro-Asian area: China, Egypt, Ethiopia, India, Iran, Iraq, Lebanon, Liberia, the Philippines, Saudi Arabia, Syria and Turkey. But of these China, Ethiopia, Liberia, the Philippines and Turkey were not fired by Asian sentiment for some years to come, leaving an Asian group of seven, of whom five were Arab countries that had special reasons for disliking the League of Nations or anything that smacked of it.

That League had started with a membership of forty-two with China, India, Persia, Siam, Japan and Liberia representing Afro-Asia. Later Afghanistan, Ethiopia, Iraq, Turkey and Egypt were added—Egypt in 1936, when the League was paralysed by Italy's conquest of Ethiopia. That failure to halt European aggression in Africa was only one of the reasons why the Arabs were suspicious of the League. Apart from the fact that its deliberations had been dominated by Britain and France, the League was for them associated with the mandates system whereby, after World War I, four Arab countries, Palestine, Iraq, Syria and Lebanon, became thinly disguised colonies of Britain and France.

41

The First Official Links

Because of apprehensions born of past experience, the Egyptian delegation put forward a whole series of amendments to the proposals of the Dumbarton Oaks Conference which provided the basic working papers at San Francisco. The Egyptian amendments were designed to secure guarantees that the British military occupation of Egypt should not be legitimised, that regional Arab military agreements should be considered legitimate, that the powers of the General Assembly should be increased as against those of the Security Council, and that the latter body should have fourteen and not eleven members. As none of these amendments was included in the final United Nations Charter, Arab fears of the new organisation seemed well founded.[2]

Arab doubts found ready acceptance with the unofficial Indian delegation. India's attitude towards the League had long been one of scepticism. The 'Indian' delegations to that body had been strictly official, and wholly unrepresentative of national opinion. This practice continued with the Indian delegation to San Francisco itself; for instance, the secretary and the military adviser were Britons. Hence the need for an unofficial nationalist delegation that operated outside the conference. Both Gandhi and Mr. Nehru had spoken disparagingly of the League, criticising, among other things, its lack of interest in colonial problems and its failure over disarmament. The United Nations trusteeship system seemed to be a continuation of the mandates system, and the veto idea repeated the weakness that had destroyed the League. For all these reasons India was receptive to the idea of an Asian alternative.[3]

The ideas thrown out at San Francisco were reported back in India to Mr. Nehru by Mrs. Pandit and Mr. B. Shiva Rao, another member of the Indian delegation. Mr. Nehru picked them up and amplified them. In his public speeches in the latter half of 1945 he advocated a Federation of Asian States. The lines along which he was thinking are indicated in a long interview that he granted to Mr. Shiva Rao; it appeared in *The Hindu* of Madras and the *Manchester Guardian* on the 25th December 1945. This statement is important because in it, for the first time, Mr. Nehru tried to formulate his Pan-Asian ideas in detail; it is also interesting because from it we can see which of these ideas he held to and which he later discarded.

Mr. Nehru began by telling Mr. Shiva Rao that an Asian Federation was 'a possibility in the near future'; it depended on the effectiveness of the United Nations. If this body was not effective, large groups would form in Asia 'for their own protection against outside

aggression', for unity against war and also against 'economic penetration'. For these reasons, as also because of old cultural bonds, he
predicted with confidence that 'a closer union of the countries border-
ing on the Indian Ocean both for defence and trade purposes is
almost certain to emerge'. There would also be 'co-operation in
foreign policy'. At this point he mentioned the likelihood of calling
an Asian conference, for which his choice of venue was India. In that
first conference no definite and precise conclusions were likely to be
reached. The conference would not have a racial approach 'nor will
it be opposed in any way to America or the Soviet Union or any other
power or group of powers'.

Significant here, apart from the sweeping certainty, is the bracket-
ing of America and Russia, the reassurance to the West, and, of
course, the mention of joint defence; this was evidently much in his
thoughts at that time and, in view of later developments, is a collec-
tor's item.

Though Mr. Nehru's reference to the Asian conference was tentative, he began actively working for it, and during a visit to Bombay
shortly afterwards, he collected Rs. 100,000 for its budget. He did
more: he carried the idea to South-East Asia during a visit there in
March 1946, and reported on his return that Aung San, the Burmese
leader, favoured it, and that Sukarno of Indonesia had independently
expressed approval.

In the following month, April 1946, the definite planning of the
conference was taken in hand in New Delhi by the Indian Council of
World Affairs (ICWA).[4] This body, modelled on the Royal Institute
of International Affairs, was chosen possibly because Mr. Shiva Rao
was one of its influential members, but more likely because it was
non-partisan and unofficial. The reasons why Mr. Nehru preferred
this non-political sponsorship are to be found in current political
developments in India. At these we must glance, for a few months
later they were to impinge on the calling of the first Asian conference.

When the British Labour Government came to power in July 1945,
a reasonably certain assumption was that India would achieve independence some time during its five-year term of office. But the pace
greatly quickened after decisive happenings in India in February 1946.
These were the mutinies in the Indian Navy, the refusal of some
squadrons of the Indian Air Force to take action against the naval
vessels, and signs of disaffection in the Indian Army. Having lost
its grip on the Indian armed forces Britain lost its capacity to hold
down India or to keep possession of it any longer. At the end of

March 1946 a Cabinet Mission arrived in India in what was the last attempt to achieve a united and independent India; it departed at the end of June with nothing really decided. In the middle of August 1946 there followed the great Calcutta killing of Hindus and Muslims, repeated in East Bengal in October, and in Bihar in November—each event marking a quickening swing of the pendulum of communal violence.

In the midst of this ugly shambles, the sixty-year struggle of Indian nationalism bore some fruit when the Congress Party, on 1st September 1946, joined what was called an Interim Government, and Mr. Nehru became Vice-President of the Viceroy's Executive Council (that is, *de facto* Prime Minister), and Member for External Affairs and Commonwealth Relations (that is, *de facto* Foreign Minister). A month later, in October, the Muslim League also joined the Interim Government, and then began the prolonged, searing deadlock that could but result in the division of India ten months later. In December, the Assembly that was to draw up free India's constitution somewhat desultorily began its work. In February 1947 the final British decision to quit India not later than June was announced. Lord Mountbatten, the last British Viceroy, whose chief task was liquidation, arrived the day before the first Asian conference opened, on 22nd March 1947.

It is nothing short of astonishing that during these twelve months, in the midst of all this momentous and bloody confusion, Mr. Nehru was able to spare time for preparing the conference; the measure of how important he thought it was the amount of time and attention he gave to this task. Political developments influenced the conference. At first, it had to be run by a non-governmental organisation; because when work began on it, in April, the government was still the British Indian Government and no one knew whether there would be one or two governments in independent India, or when independence would come. Later, after Mr. Nehru became Foreign Minister in September, he was in a position to take full charge of the conference; the government put its weight behind it and preparations were speeded up. Nevertheless the fiction was maintained, and still prevails, that the Indian Council of World Affairs was arranging an unofficial gathering of scholars to discuss Asian culture.

The first formal contact between the ICWA and Mr. Nehru was an exchange of letters in April to May 1946, in which the latter wrote: 'I understand that your Council proposes to take the initiative in convening an Asian conference. I am glad of this.'

44

This was the first known use of the title 'Asian' for the conference. In a preliminary note from the ICWA about the meeting, the word 'Asiatic' is struck out and 'Asian' written in. Before Mr. Nehru wrote his letter, the Council was trying to choose between three titles: the Inter-Asiatic Relations, or Welfare, or Contact conference. The press was given the first formal announcement about the conference on 1st May.

On the 31st August the Council set up an organising committee and a working committee with Mr. Nehru as chairman of both. When he joined the Interim Government, Mrs. Sarojini Naidu succeeded him on the former, of which he continued to be honorary president.

A week later Mr. Nehru's foreign ministry was officially informed of the conference, and at the end of September impatience got the better of him and he asked the organisers for weekly progress reports. In January 1947, he made the official presence further felt when he suggested that one of the senior officials of the External Affairs Ministry, Mr. Humphrey Trevelyan, should attend the Executive Committee meetings. It is significant that while Trevelyan was to attend meetings only 'if and when necessary' an Indian official, H. Dayal, was 'to attend all your meetings'.

Invitations were sent out early in September 1946. After much anxious deliberation the Council had decided on three types of invitees: a joint delegation of sixteen scholars from each country, individual scholars, and four observers from each government. According to the ICWA,[5] 193 delegates attended with thirty-nine governmental observers. This is incorrect, and is part of the 'cultural' façade. Many of the delegates were officials (India alone had six cabinet ministers among its 'unofficial' delegates), and a truer count would be about 150 non-officials and eighty officials.

According to the original listing, thirty-two countries were to be invited; of these, six Arab countries—Syria, Lebanon, Transjordan, Saudi Arabia, Yemen and Iraq—did not accept individual invitations. The delegation from Singapore was merged with that of Malaya, while the United States Occupation Authorities in Japan refused to allow that country to participate. Later additions were the three Indo-China states, Cambodia, Cochin-China and Laos taken as a unit, and Armenia and Georgia. The final count was twenty-eight countries with observers from the United Nations, the Arab League, and the Institutes of International Affairs or Pacific Relations from Australia, Moscow, London and New York. Listed with these foreign observers was the representative of the India Institute, London, Mr. V. K. Krishna Menon.

The process of getting the invitations delivered was complicated by one of the chief characteristics of Asia in the age of European imperialism—the difficulty of inter-Asian communication. The first replies took a full three months to come in. It was understandable that the invitations to Tibet and Bhutan should, in the final stages, be carried by postal couriers on horseback, or that the delegates from Turkmenistan and Kirghizia should arrive one day after the conference ended. But it is surprising that the invitation to China should not have been received 'because of some postal mishap': the Indian Council of World Affairs was reduced to asking the Indian Foreign Ministry to ask the British Ambassador in Nanking to persuade the Chinese Government to send observers. (One doubts whether the Chinese Government accepted this correct but improbable explanation; in the event it sent eight delegates and one governmental observer.)

The diplomatic machinery of the British Government was resorted to by the Indian Council not only to extend the invitations but also to provide information on institutions and persons to whom invitations should be sent. (India, at this juncture no more than a self-governing territory, actually had no diplomatic representatives of its own. Only eight consuls or consuls-general were resident in India, of whom only one, from Nepal, was resident in New Delhi.)

It is difficult to resist the conclusion that British diplomatic representatives, in some areas of Asia at least, did their best to render the invitations abortive. The Council played into their hands by its pedantic suggestion that invitations should be extended to institutions comparable to the Indian Council of World Affairs. It was thus all too easy for Her Britannic Majesty's ambassadors in the Arab countries to reply, with straight-faced honesty, that nothing comparable existed; though the British Ambassador in Iraq revealed that this was no more than a manœuvre in the astonishing statement that 'the Ambassador cannot think of any expert in Iraq who might qualify for an invitation'. Equally astonishing was the *naïveté* of the Indian Council in believing that the British would be willing to further a gathering of their erstwhile colonial subjects. From the United Nations Mrs. Pandit reported complaints by the Arab representatives that their governments had not received their invitations, so duplicates were sent to her to distribute.

In November, Mr. Krishna Menon complained that the Soviet Central Asian Republics had likewise not received their invitations; these he issued himself through Mr. Molotov, who 'warmly welcomed' the idea of the conference, as well as he might. In November, Mr. Menon also reported that the Moroccans particularly wanted to come and should be asked since 'they have a national liberation movement like ours'. But later in the month the conference secretariat decided not to invite Morocco, Tunisia and Libya, in order 'to keep the conference restricted to Asian countries'.

The same narrow, exclusive Asianism—Afro-Asianism still being some years away—emerges in the refusal to invite the Pan-African Congress, that had held its fifth meeting in 1945, and in the intimation to the Natal Indian Congress, given on Mr. Nehru's advice, that no group from South Africa could attend. This concentration on a narrow target may have been prudent, but it reveals a lack of vision.

By the middle of December 1946 the ICWA discovered that, whether it liked it or not, it was involved in politics: the mere act of inviting governments to send observers produced this result. A Council note of this period concedes that Tibet was one of the first countries invited, but goes on to argue in ungrammatical embarrassment, that since China is 'rather anxious that Tibet should not come independently we should rather not press Tibet coming in'. But these second thoughts were too late; whether because of the 'postal mishap' over the invitation to China, or because Tibet's pony-post was functioning unusually efficiently even in the depth of winter, Tibet's acceptance was already on its way and was received on 31st January 1947, a mere six months after its despatch through the high Himalayan passes.

A note from Mr. Nehru in December also reveals complications arising from inviting Ho Chi Minh to represent Vietnam; because he was engaged in a dispute with Cochin-China, the President of that country could not be asked, though the King of Laos and the King of Cambodia were eligible. All four were eventually invited. And then there was Siam, consistent in its reluctance to be Asian; the Siamese had to be persuaded to attend.

There are two anomalies in the composition of this first Asian gathering, and an attempt must be made to explain them: the presence of the Soviet Central Asians and the absence of the Arabs. When asked today about the massive Soviet representation (nine out of twenty-five countries) the scholars of the Indian Council blandly reply that since the conference was meant to cover the whole of Asia, and since the Central Asian Republics were, and are, a part of Asia, they were invited. But this is disingenuous. Bandung was also supposed to comprise the whole of Asia, but the Soviet states were not invited.

It is safe to guess that these invitations were the result of Mr. Nehru's influence. In his early and enthusiastic writings about Russia, he is especially complimentary about the work of modernisation that the Russians had carried out in hitherto backward parts of Asia. Further, as a historian, he may well have been influenced by the ancient links between India and the part of the world that was the homeland of the Moghul dynasty. And as 'a lover of words and phrases' he, or anyone else for that matter, would have been interested to meet, for the first time, travellers from Merv and Bokhara and Samarkand.

The only rational explanation for the absence of the Arab states is that, having suggested the conference in the first place, they were indignant at receiving their invitations late, and so stayed away in a huff. But a less rational explanation is more plausible: they could not be bothered to attend; for the Arabs have always been and still are, careless in their international public relations. Though the organisers were punctilious in inviting both Arab and Jewish representatives from the then embattled land of Palestine, even from there the Arabs did not come, leaving the field open to the Zionist representatives. Nor did the few Arabs who did attend do much good. The Egyptian delegation was led by a member of the Muslim Brotherhood, which was fanatically anti-Indian, and the solitary observer from the Arab League, who was meant to represent the seven other Arab states, knew no English and so could have understood very little of what was said.

The various drafts for the agenda of the conference contain one point of interest—the initial prominence given to the question of joint defence and its later disappearance. We have already seen that in December 1945 Mr. Nehru spoke of defence co-operation between the countries of the Indian Ocean area as a virtual certainty. In early May 1946 a letter from Mr. Shiva Rao, giving Mr. Nehru's ideas on the agenda for 'the Inter-Asian' conference, says that 'the agenda should not only include but give first place to defence and security problems of the Indian Ocean area'. This was done, and the preliminary eight-point agenda mentioned this as the first item. Later in May, however, Mr. Nehru must have changed his mind, for a Council letter dated 27th May presents a revised agenda with no mention of the defence item.

The Council, in its volume on the conference,[6] gives a general explanation for this change, and a slightly more precise one in a private note: 'Defence questions were excluded because the defence of Asia is bound up with world security, and discussions on it would be unreal without the representatives of the U.S.A., U.S.S.R. and Britain.' That this hard fact should have been realised in time is hardly surprising; the cause for surprise is that Mr. Nehru did not see the point earlier. Perhaps the responsibility of office and power had begun to cast its shadow before.

Arranging this conference was a big task for the Indian Council. It was at this time only three years old, and even the backing of the Government of India did not greatly add to its financial or human resources. It had to depend on a small, temporarily-hired staff working in a few, overcrowded offices. This was the first large international conference ever held in Delhi, and every aspect of it—procedure, protocol and hospitality—presented problems that were new and unforeseen. The conference was carried through thanks to the energy and devoted enthusiasm not only of the Council staff but of a large number of volunteer helpers. The ladies of Delhi society made a particularly effective contribution. There was, necessarily, much amateur improvisation but this, if anything, only added to the feeling that the event was something new and important and exciting. For the organisers and for the participants coming to Delhi from the four corners of Asia, the dawn was a good one in which to be alive.

For Mr. Nehru the Asian Relations Conference was unique in a very special way. It was the only major Asian conference that he actively wanted; he subsequently attended all the others, the only Asian leader to do so, but he went with ever-increasing reluctance, as we shall see. He not only wanted this meeting but he, personally, worked for it, at home and abroad, in the midst of a hundred other distracting calls on his time. The future of India was being discussed; the country was scarred with massacres; and he had just become the chief executive in the vast, groaning machine that is the Government of India and that was utterly unfamiliar to him; yet he made time to attend the conference's committee meetings and pushed, prodded and enquired into minor details of organisation, as was his wont. He must have wanted something very definite and something very important from the conference. What could it have been?

Speaking in August 1946 of the objectives of the conference, Mr. Nehru said: 'We have no doubt that, if we do meet, the conference will not put an end to the world's troubles. The conference will help to promote good relations with neighbouring countries. It will help to pool ideas and experience with a view to raising living standards. It will strengthen cultural, social and economic ties among the peoples of Asia. The data papers presented to the conference will constitute valuable documents and the discussions on them will, we hope, throw out correct suggestions for firm policy.'[7] The surprising omission here is that he does not express the hope that the conference would speed the process of liberation in Asia: his silence may have been due to a cautious desire not to give the impression that the conference was going to be wildly denunciatory, partly also to a conviction that once India was free the independence of the rest of South and South-East Asia would follow as a matter of course.

No doubt he wished to stimulate a resurgence of Asian pride, an increase in continent-wide self-confidence, through the renewal of former friendly ties: but he had a further end in view. Throughout the conference his main preoccupation was the creation of a permanent organisation to carry on the conference's work—a development that might be expected to lead to the Asian Federation to which he had long attached importance. Writing about the future of India and Asia when in jail early in 1945, he had noted that:[8] 'If people are foolish enough to avoid world unity and some world organisation, then vast supernational regions, each functioning as one huge state but with local autonomy, are very likely to take shape. For the small national state is doomed. It may survive as a cultural, autonomous area but not as an independent political unit.' The 'correct suggestions for firm policy' that he hoped would emerge from the conference must have been relevant to some such idea, because the permanent organisation for which he pressed so hard was conceived as more than a mere continuation of the conference. It is in the conference's reaction to this idea that we find its principal short-term significance.

NOTES TO CHAPTER II

1. B. Shiva Rao, in conversations with the author and in notings in the files of the Indian Council of World Affairs, New Delhi.
2. *Egypt and the United Nations*, Carnegie Endowment for International Peace, New York, 1957.
3. *India and the United Nations*, Carnegie Endowment for International Peace, New York, 1957, chap. 1.
4. Indian Council of World Affairs: *Asian Relations: Proceedings and Documentation of the First Asian Relations Conference*, New Delhi, 1948, p. 2.
5. *Op. cit.*, p. 8.
6. *Op. cit.*, p. 4.
7. *Op. cit.*, p. 14.
8. Nehru: *The Discovery of India*, chap. 10, p. 11.

CHAPTER III

Dawn: The Asian Relations Conference, New Delhi, March 1947

The international fiesta that was the Asian Relations Conference marked the apex of Asianism, for never again was there to be such a gushing outflow of the Asian spirit, pure and undefiled. The fruit began to rot even as it ripened and perhaps the decay set in because it ripened so fast. The expressions of suspicion uttered at the conference were real enough, however, to prevent the enthusiasm from becoming too cloying and were, perhaps, the most significant pointers to the future. To the participants and spectators, the Delhi Conference was like a door slowly swinging open on to vast, inspiring vistas; vast they certainly proved to be though at times also drab and dispiriting.

The setting of the conference was itself historically symbolic. It took place within the grey, crumbling walls of the Purana Qila, or Old Fort, constructed in the sixteenth century by one of Delhi's Muslim rulers on the site of an earlier Hindu Delhi. The grim warlike past met the peaceful present when the spectators streamed up through the steep, narrow, cobbled gateway built just wide enough for a single file of horsemen. The 'building' of the conference was no building at all, but an immense 'pandal' or marquee roofed with long, narrow strips of orange-coloured cloth held up on tall bamboo poles. It had to be so, for no building in Delhi was of the dimensions, 400 feet long and 300 feet wide, required to accommodate the throngs that attended: 10,000 persons were present at the opening and 20,000 at the closing plenary sessions.[1] The political leaders claimed to speak for the people and for once the people were present, in person. Three thousand six hundred and thirty persons paid for their seats at prices ranging from fifty rupees (£3 10s. 0d.) to one rupee (1s. 4d.). With the increasing formalisation of the conferences, public participation in them shrinks; there was room for perhaps 500 people in the public galleries at Bandung, and for less than 100 at Belgrade.

The fan-shaped marquee was set on the gentle slope of a natural

51

amphitheatre, the whole structure focusing the eye downwards on to a two-tiered rostrum at its bottom. On this sat the President, Mrs. Naidu of India, Mr. Nehru and the leaders of the twenty-eight delegations. Behind them was a huge map topped with a red neon sign saying ASIA. This was flanked by the flags of eighteen countries, for some of the countries represented had not as yet an official flag; India's was still the Union Jack. Some of the crests of the countries were also symbolic concoctions rather than correct heraldry.

Now that Afro-Asia provides half the membership of the United Nations, it is odd to recall that at Delhi only eight of the delegations represented members of the world body. Most of the delegations were small—after India's fifty-one, the next largest were Indonesia's twenty-five, and Burma's seventeen. Among the Indians were two future presidents of the republic and a future president of the United Nations General Assembly. There were also six cabinet ministers, and while a few of the other delegations were also led by official dignitaries, most were headed by scholars or educationists, so that the 'cultural' façade was more or less maintained.[2]

The status of some of the delegations was conditioned by politics.[3] The Chinese had, in February, officially protested at the invitation to Tibet; thus while the Tibetans began the conference as 'delegates' they ended it not as 'observers', as the Chinese wanted, but as 'representatives'. The boundary line on the big map of Asia dividing Tibet from China was at the same time erased—an early foreshadowing of India's disastrous complaisance over Tibet. A lighter note had been introduced by the French Government, that coupled a protest at the invitation to the Vietnamese with a query why France should not have been invited as a government with special interests in Indo-China. A few days before the conference began, the Indian Government hurriedly asked the Indonesian Government not to send an 'official' delegation as it had intended to do, because the conference was not official; in the event the Indonesian group was political, if not officially so; it represented all parties, including the Communists.

The cloven hoof of politics kept appearing beneath the trailing robes of culture, to the great embarrassment of the Indian Council of World Affairs. Ten days before the conference it felt obliged to issue a communiqué stating that the conference would 'deal mainly with cultural, economic and like subjects'. Even this reassurance was not sufficient to allay the mistrust of the Muslim League, which boycotted the conference as an attempt by 'the Indian Hindu Congress' to spread its influence abroad; the allegation was that in attempting this it had 'beguiled' Muslim countries into attending. Mr. Nehru himself had long been aware that the meeting had acquired a dual nature, for in January he had told the ICWA that 'the participation of representatives of governments in this conference gives it a certain official flavour although the conference is meant to be completely non-official'.

Hence it was in an atmosphere charged equally with innocent enthusiasm and ambivalent politics that the Asian Relations Conference began its work on the morning of 23rd March 1947, with a meeting of its steering committee. After settling various details of organisation this body took two important decisions.[4] The first was that the conference would not adopt resolutions, but would merely accept a report embodying the consensus of opinions expressed in the various discussion groups into which it was to be divided. The second decision set up a sub-committee of fifteen persons 'to consider the advisability of establishing a permanent institute'.

This last was a piece of skilful politicking. A continuing organisation of some sort was of deep interest to Mr. Nehru, who attended this committee meeting 'by special invitation'. This item, nevertheless, had not been included on the preliminary outline agenda of the conference, presumably because so specific an objective might have frightened off some of the governments invited. By dealing with the item in this fashion, as merely something to be considered, it was, innocuously introduced on to the conference agenda by a side entrance, if not through the back door. And even this, as we shall see, was not the whole truth of the matter. Furthermore five of the fifteen members of this sub-committee were Indians, including Mr. V. K. Krishna Menon, now accepted as a delegate representing India. The work of this sub-committee, the only part of the conference that met in secret, will be considered later in this chapter.

That evening, after the worst heat of a Delhi summer's day had passed, the opening plenary session[5] met before the assembled thousands. Mr. Nehru's speech, eloquent but balanced, provided a most effective introduction and is as noteworthy for what he did not say as for the points he made. 'What has brought you here, men and women of Asia?' he began by asking, and answered by saying that it was 'some deeper urge' that had impelled them to accept the invitation that 'some of us, greatly daring' had issued. He went on to talk of Asia, liberated from Europe, as a great new factor in the world which would break down the dividing walls: 'we look at each other again and meet as old friends long parted'. He spent some time

Dawn: The Asian Relations Conference, New Delhi

describing Asia's ancient cultural ties as a process of interflow, each region or country giving as well as taking. Therefore in the new Asia 'there are no leaders and no followers'. 'In this atomic age' Asia would have to play her part in securing peace in 'One World' and because of that the conference could not be a Pan-Asian movement directed against Europe or America, while at the same time 'we do not intend to be the playthings of others'. He was the only speaker to make even passing reference to Africa.

Although modest in his references to India's role in convening the conference, because the idea of it 'arose simultaneously in many minds and in many countries of Asia', he was sure of its importance: 'the mere fact of its taking place is itself of historic significance . . .' 'this occasion is unique in history . . .' 'a landmark which divides the past of Asia from the future'.

Mr. Nehru made two references to the idea of inter-Asian co-operation. Asia, he said, should work for the larger ideal of 'One World' 'and not for any grouping which comes in the way of this larger world group. . . . But in order to have "One World" we must also in Asia think of the countries of Asia co-operating together for that larger ideal.' In this fairly typical synthesis of contradictions he seemed, in the end, to leave the door open for a smaller grouping. To that he referred when he said, 'I hope that out of this some permanent Asian Institute for the study of common problems and to bring about closer relations will emerge; also perhaps a School of Asian Studies.' He had in mind a purely academic institution, a 'school', as well as a larger, non-academic body.

Notably missing from his speech was any reference to non-alignment—all the more remarkable because early in September 1946 he had made clear that freedom from entangling blocs was to be a principal element in free India's foreign policy. Perhaps he thought that even after seven months this idea would be too novel and controversial to recommend to the conference. Equally noteworthy is the fact that his speech was not directly or strongly anti-colonial. 'The old imperialisms are fading away,' he said. With an almost contemptuous wave of the hand he did something worse than attack them; he pronounced a valediction.

Following Mr. Nehru the flood gates of oratory were opened by the Conference President, Mrs. Sarojini Naidu, a prominent figure in the national movement and a minor poet in the ripest Edwardian manner. Using expansive gestures and every cliché known to poetic diction she invoked the spring, dawn, morn, stars and moon: only the fact that all this poured from her *extempore* redeemed it from total banality. She also spoke, alas, of Asian politics, of how 'you and we together may dream a common dream of our Asia and how our Asia can redeem the world'. Yet even she came down to earth for long enough to deride the idea of 'a conspiracy of Asian people against Western civilisation'.

In the speeches, mercifully brief, of the other representatives, certain common themes recur; Asia is awake and experiencing a new birth of freedom; it was once united culturally and should be so again; it is a continent of peace and is concerned and fearful at the prospect of a new world war; what the countries of Asia need are a realistic outlook and hard work: 'we have used enough words about Asian unity. Now let us act,' as the Vietnam representative said.

Only one speaker referred at all precisely to the possibility of political, as opposed to cultural, unity in Asia. This was Mr. S. W. R. D. Bandaranaike of Ceylon, who hoped that the conference would lead to 'a federation of free and equal Asian countries'. Ten years later, when he was Prime Minister of Ceylon, we find him still hoping for this end and still with no result.

In his speech Mr. Nehru had referred to the Soviet Central Asian Republics as having 'so many lessons to teach us'. Their representatives certainly agreed, for their speeches unanimously lauded the Great October Revolution and 'Soviet power' that had brought them such great advantages, especially in education. This was for them a super propaganda opportunity and they seized it with both hands.

All was not unadulterated sweetness and love during the opening plenary session. The representative of the Palestine Jews, Dr. Bergmann, had spoken of the Jews 'as an old Asian people' now at last returning to their homeland. He also hoped 'that Palestine . . . will not go the European way of solving, so to speak, problems by dispossessing populations', though that is precisely what his people did to a million Arabs just a year later. An Egyptian woman delegate was given the opportunity to reply by Mr. Nehru, and denied the Jews' right to claim Palestine as their home. When Dr. Bergmann sought to answer her, Mr. Nehru refused to grant him the floor, and after a brief, angry exchange with the chair, Dr. Bergmann and his delegation walked out. Some of the Indian delegates hurried after them and persuaded them to return, and Dr. Bergmann even shook hands with the observer from the Arab League. This must have been one of the last occasions on which Zionist and Arab leaders experienced that minimal degree of physical contact.[6]

Mr. Nehru, in closing remarks referring to this incident, said that issues involving two countries should not be discussed and that India's policy was that 'Palestine is essentially an Arab country and no decision can be made without the consent of the Arabs'. His remark presaged the future, for in many subsequent conferences Israel's presence—or rather non-presence, for she was never invited again—became a source of discussion and even controversy. Though a small country she remains an irritant—a splinter in Asia's thumb.

After the opening plenary session the conference split into five groups which met privately. The official volume on the conference gives a summary of the opening statements and of the discussions on their reports which, when adopted, became the equivalent of conference resolutions. Comparison with the verbatim text of the discussions shows that the printed text is a reasonably full and fair summary of what was actually said—the first and last time that the private discussions of an Asian conference were made publicly available, and the more remarkable because some of the talk was brutally frank.

Group A dealt with only one topic, 'National Movements for Freedom'; this had three subdivisions, one of which referred to the 'extent and limitations of co-operative action' between Asian countries, but only in 'the non-political sphere'[7]. Although this was by far the most important of any of the topics discussed it was, oddly enough, taken up only on the sixth day of the group discussions and then for only two sessions in the course of a single day. This summary treatment was possible because the problems of only five South-East Asian countries were raised, the Arabs remaining silent even after the chairman had asked if there were any other problems for discussion.

One finds a clear distinction between the approach of countries already or soon to be free, such as China and India, and those still fighting for their freedom, like Indonesia, Vietnam and Malaya. The latter wanted the former to take action in their support by granting them recognition, supporting their cause in the United Nations, granting them financial and military assistance and denying transit to the ships and planes of the colonial powers. To the obvious irritation of the others the independent countries displayed singular caution in giving firm commitments; the report refers only to the requests, and to pledges of 'moral support' in response.

Mr. Nehru was perhaps the most cautious of all, and to a quite unnecessary degree. In a reference to the war in Indo-China he did not see, the summary says, how the Indian Government could be expected to declare war on France (a course no delegate had suggested). That was not the way to proceed, he went on: by such precipitate action they were likely to lose in the long run. Any wise government would try to limit the area of conflict. Pressure could not be exercised by governments through public meetings, he concluded— an unduly superior attitude for a government that had been in office for only seven months.

India also came in for criticism because its troops had been used against nationalists in Burma, Ceylon, Malaya and Indonesia. This was an unjust criticism—and Indian delegates, including Mr. Nehru, had no difficulty in rebutting it, pointing out that they had always opposed this practice, and had stopped it altogether as soon as they had the power to do so.

In addition, both India and China were accused by Burma of taking over the European practice of 'brown exploitation'. Ceylon, moreover, alleged 'economic and demographic' 'aggression' by 'their big brothers like China and India'.[8] Both these small countries also commented critically on the behaviour of local Indian and Chinese communities. India did not reply, but the Chinese delegation countered with a claim that its nationals were being unfairly treated in Burma.

Except for urging removal of these political injustices, the group could not produce any precise or practical suggestions as to how the liberation of the rest of Asia could be helped forward. Sensing this deficiency, a delegate from Malaya produced the idea of what he called 'a neutrality bloc'. This is of the greatest interest not only as a foreshadowing of the non-aligned 'area of peace', of which so much was to be heard later, but also because on this first presentation the Asian Relations Conference rejected it and, for good measure, did so with a certain degree of scorn.

The Malayan delegate was Mr. John Thivy, an Indian lawyer who had setttled in Singapore. During the war he had participated in the anti-British movement led by Subash Chandra Bose, and he was later to take Indian nationality. He was then appointed Indian Ambassador to several countries, including Syria and Italy.

Mr. Thivy broached his idea thus (to quote the summary): 'He suggested the formation of a neutrality bloc to refuse assistance of raw materials, arms, dockyards, etc., in the event of a crisis. He was very earnest about this proposal, he said, because with no army, navy or air force this seemed the only way to ensure the effectiveness of Malayan independence.[9] While, as a summary, this is not inaccurate, the verbatim report (which does not seem to be a word-for-word account) adds interesting sidelights and suggests something of the quality of the discussion.

Mr. Thivy: The other countries must adopt a neutrality bloc. He realized that the conference was not competent to take decisions but he wished to appeal to the various Asian countries to adopt a neutrality bloc and refuse to assist by raw materials, dockyards, arms, etc. He pointed out that Malaya was a small country having no air force, army or navy. Thus to effect her independence he considered the neutrality bloc as the only way. He believed that Asia could be demobilised and consequently world wars could be prevented.

Justice Kyan Myint (Burma): India having become over-cultured is perhaps soft. You need a core of hardness—and India has never been hard—to survive. But after many centuries of suffering India has out of sheer necessity become hard. I believe that of Asian countries only India can really produce enlightened persons whom we call future Buddhas.

Mr. Thivy: A neutrality bloc is meant both to prevent assistance reaching alien powers in their suppression of freedom struggles and to immobilise the areas covering the territories of Asia in the event of a possible world war. With these words 'neutrality bloc' would be given a dynamic force and not just a passing idea.

A Malayan delegate: What help can we get from other Asian countries? We want you to particularise because if you would only say 'moral aid' we do not know what you mean by 'moral aid'. Otherwise we should go back to our countries and say—'well, we have a vague notion that we all want to unite and fight but nothing tangible has been proposed'.

An Indonesian delegate: We from Indonesia, who have come fresh from the battle front, we hope and sincerely trust that you will make some contribution to the fight which is still going on in Vietnam and Indonesia.

In the report this was reduced to a single sentence, 'A delegate from Malaya suggested the formation of a Neutrality Bloc in Asia.'[10] The discussion on the report that followed at this stage is of sufficient interest to be given in the verbatim version that is slightly more detailed than that given in the published volume.

Mr. J. A. Thivy, Malaya: Mr. Chairman and friends, I would refer you to page 2, paragraph 4 last sentence of the report which runs:
'A delegate from Malaya suggested the formation of a neutrality bloc in Asia'.

If the alphabetical order had given me the chance to speak before the delegate from Indonesia I would have clarified this point. I had already felt that a mere statement like this that 'a delegate from Malaya suggested the formation of a neutrality bloc' would mean that we want to start a movement.

It is not that at all. When this suggestion was brought forward at the group meeting it was clearly indicated that the idea of this neutrality

Dawn: The Asian Relations Conference, New Delhi

bloc was to prevent aggression by alien powers that dominate certain portions of South-East Asia and also to prevent a world war. It was something active in that sense. If you will see page 3, an Indian delegate (Mr. Nehru) pointed out that short of a declaration of war it was difficult to visualise what form such help can take except moral support. . . . It was with a view to meeting this point that the idea of a neutrality bloc was suggested and I would suggest that after the words neutrality bloc in Asia put a comma and add these words 'both to prevent assistance reaching alien powers in their suppression of freedom struggles and also to immobilise the areas covering the territories of Asia in the event of a possible war'. With these words neutrality bloc would be given dynamic force and not be just a passing idea.

Chairman: Does everybody agree to this amendment?

Mr. K. Santhanam (India): What is the meaning of the words 'immobilising in the event of a world war?'

Mr. Thivy (Malaya): We in Asia are, as far as strength in warfare is concerned, weak. We have no control over seas, land and also air. But what we can do is to prevent the active use of our land, say, for example, aerodromes, dockyards, and also prevent our man-power from being used in a world war and also prevent our soldiers from fighting against freedom, and also by various devices we should prevent the use of our raw materials from being used for war purposes. These are active ways by which we can boycott the efforts of imperial countries dominating subject peoples as also prevent a world war.

Mr. Santhanam: But we may be attacked. You cannot immobilise. You must adopt active resistance. I think there is something in the suggestion, but it depends on the nature of the world war. For example, the United Nations may declare a war against an aggressive country; then we cannot be passive spectators of such a war.

A delegate from Burma: If we are attacked we will fight.

Mr. Thivy (Malaya): You know that in the last war there were certain countries like Turkey which maintained neutrality.

Mr. Santhanam: That may be applicable in the case of certain countries but you cannot make a general proposition like that.

Mr. Thivy (Malaya): I leave it to the House, but I feel strongly that we must do something definite in preventing war. It is not only for the United Nations Organisation to decide whether it should declare a war or not; we want peace, to have the opportunity for progress in agriculture, industry and whatever else it may be, and we can actively take steps by joint action among the nations of Asia by preventing our territories, our man-power and our resources from being used by a foreign country in the prosecution of war.

Mr. K. Santhanam: I suggest that the delegate's remarks may be incorporated in the report but no amendment need be made.

Secretary (Dr. Appadorai): With the consent of the chairman, may I say this: The word 'immobilisation' mentioned by the delegate is not clear to some of those who are present and the chairman would like him to explain more clearly whether he wants 'immobilisation' in the

59

event of a world war or irrespective of the nature of the war and the place from which the world war comes.

Mr. Thivy (Malaya): The mere fact of any country being neutral means that its territory, its people and its resources are to that extent immobilised. That prevents anything from going out of that area and also prevents any other aggressive nation from using that territory. To that extent, if we can adopt this on the whole of Asia, so much that if from the West any nation wants to come right through to the East and attack some country in the East, then all the waters, lands, railways, including man-power and material resources, will be denied to that power which chooses to come from the West to the East. In that sense the area is 'immobilised'.

Mrs. Vijayalakshmi Pandit (India): Sir, I am afraid I cannot accept the suggestion of the honourable delegate for the simple reason that it is extremely vague. He says that if armies want to pass from the West to the East in the prosecution of some war, you can immobilise your resources against them and by non-co-operating you can prevent the war. In some small way India has just done that. Throughout the period of the last war, India attempted to non-co-operate with British imperialism in the prosecution of the war. (Cheers.) But she was unsuccessful in the sense that she was unable to stop the war because this is not something which can be done in this fashion. It raised our morale and was certainly a gesture, but it cannot stop wars. Therefore what is the point of talking in a strain which we know we cannot implement. I think there should be a distinct clarification before we can accept this amendment. (Cheers.)

Mr. Raschid (Burma): I would like very warmly to support the remarks which Mrs. Pandit just now made, and I would like to offer a word of explanation. Before drafting the report, I gave this matter some thought and it was at the suggestion of the delegate who has spoken that this was incorporated, but I myself was very vague as to what he meant. Now that he has clarified his point, I would like definitely to oppose the suggestion. It would have been possible, perhaps, to consider a Defensive Union, but that is very different from what he has suggested —a neutrality bloc especially when he suggests neutrality in the form in which he has defined it. I am afraid the whole thing is going to be absolutely impossible to work. Some of us who do not think in terms of non-violence, but believe in some other ideology, would be prepared to fight. That is why I was careful to underline the suggestion made by Pandit Jawaharlal Nehru that the extension of areas of conflict is a serious matter and it cannot be dealt with lightly. It is easy to say that if India, or Burma, or any other Asian country was free and then there was a war, that country could avoid it by neutrality. That is more easily said than done. If a free country tries to stop or refuse giving a certain amount of help in a war of domination it would mean that it might be attacked. So the whole thing cannot be treated in that light-hearted manner. It is so inter-related and has to be considered on a wider basis. I am afraid putting the thing in a narrow way will lead to further complications. I would therefore draw the attention of the House to the fact that we have already referred to the unanimity in the group that as far as any domination is concerned, all Asian countries should deny supplies to the armies and use of transport and aerodromes. I think we should leave it at that stage and therefore I would like to oppose the proposals of the Malayan delegate.

Chairman: Since there are arguments on the subject of the amendment, the amendment will not be made in the text and the text will be preserved as it is.

Mr. Thivy's suggestion deserved closer and more sympathetic attention than it received. Its Indian critics were caught in a confusion of terms between 'neutrality' and the new, emerging idea of 'neutralism' which is hinted at in Mr. Thivy's word 'immobilisation'. The Burmese criticism confuses 'neutralism' with 'non-violence'; and this particular confusion has dogged the idea of neutralism ever since, not least in India.

The Indonesian delegate did what he could to muddy the waters of neutralism still further by confusing it with Asianism, another long-continuing error. 'The concept of an Asian bloc had been condemned when the Japanese mooted one such some years ago,' he said. 'The idea continued to stand condemned. The aim of an effective inter-Asian co-operation cannot be the formation of a neutral bloc,' which is exactly what it did become in a few years' time.[11]

From this loose thinking it is almost a relief to turn to the blunt assertion of the Vietnam delegate that 'what was needed in Asia was not a neutrality bloc but a fighting federation.[12]

That the Indian delegates should not have seen the practical value of Mr. Thivy's idea is particularly surprising, for Mrs. Pandit was even then one of India's chief spokesmen on foreign affairs. And the more so because Mr. Nehru, as has been said, had enunciated the principle of non-alignment in his first speech as Prime Minister in September 1946: this very important pronouncement had either not been read or not understood by the Indian delegates.

Above all, both the Indian and the Burmese speakers, for all their brave words about 'fighting', seemed to be suffering from a lack of national self-confidence, a carry-over from the time of imperial military dominance.

Fortunately there was at least one Indian delegate who took Mr. Nehru up by saying that 'there were various degrees and methods in which countries can help others without actual declaration of war': moral support was not the only alternative to the declaration of war.[13] The Indian Government itself recognised this when, during the

Indonesian crisis in late 1948, it followed Mr. Thivy's suggestion and denied transit rights to Dutch ships and planes.

Some of the general characteristics of the work of this group, the most important one of the conference, are salient and significant. For one thing, from the outset it quickly brushed aside the pretence that the conference was not supposed to deal with politics; and despite the chairman's appeal for restraint, many hard things were said. These criticisms were directed mostly at India and, to a lesser extent, at China. The delegates of the smaller countries took almost too literally Mr. Nehru's remark that the old imperialisms were fading, and saw the danger to themselves coming from new Asian imperialisms, despite all the fine talk in public about Asian feeling. The Arabs and the Soviet Central Asians were strangely silent, apart from a single, brief, irrelevant intervention from each group. Certain divisions, which continued and deepened with the succeeding conferences, had already become apparent—divisions between the big countries and the small countries, and between the impetuous, such as Indonesia, and the cautious, such as India. By and large, this first discussion of their political problems on an international level by Asia's leaders was disappointingly thin in content, largely because there was too much individualistic nationalism and not enough Asianism.

In the meantime Group B had been discussing Racial Problems and Inter-Asian Migration, topics that also produced plain speaking. As with the Freedom Movements, the discussions were confined to South and South-East Asia and specifically to the Indian community in Ceylon, Burma and Malaya and the Chinese in the two latter countries. The delegates of these host countries bitterly criticised these immigrants for their lack of loyalty, their refusal to assimilate, and their refusal to use their wealth, in philanthropy or investment, in the countries where they made it. All this made still more acute the fear of the hosts that they would be numerically swamped by the outsiders. The Burmese delegate expressed this feeling with brutal directness: 'Burma was between two great powers. It was terrible to be ruled by a Western power, but it was even more so to be ruled by an Asian power. Burma was naturally frightened by the possibility that British imperialism may be substituted by an Indian or a Chinese imperialism.'[14]

Indian and Chinese delegates agreed in deploring the isolationism and the parsimony of their countrymen abroad, but beyond that point their opinions diverged. The Indians said that it was official policy to encourage Indian settlers to abandon Indian citizenship and loyally to assume local citizenship, which should be freely granted. Because, in Chinese law, citizenship could not be abandoned but merely remained dormant, the Chinese delegate said that their settlers who wished to remain foreigners should be allowed to do so, but should be accepted only so long as they were economically useful: the Chinese Government would neither ask for nor extend to them any special privileges.[15]

The contradiction between a total ban on immigration and the maintenance of Asian goodwill was noted, and quota systems were suggested as a compromise.

Once again the report made few if any practical proposals for the solution of these problems; and these are as alive and as thorny today as they were in 1947. That there should be a simple nationality law, that people should be given the right of choice, and that there should be no racial discrimination—these were the rather obvious suggestions made in the report.

The report on the discussion by Group C[16] on 'the transition from Colonial to National Economy' was so vague and platitudinous that the group itself protested; but it was constrained to accept the *rapporteur*'s judgement that it had not, in fact, produced any 'large or striking programmes'. Mr. K. M. Panikkar deplored the lack of any reference to the need to eliminate, or at least control, foreign capital; and the Burmese and Indonesian delegates suggested that this reticence was because foreign capital in South-East Asia was Asian—Indian or Chinese. But another Indian delegate said that since there was, in fact, no alternative to foreign borrowing the only question was one of control. Mr. Krishna Menon, stressing the urgent need for industrialising Asia, pointed out that this was possible only if Asia were to sell its raw materials to Europe in exchange for capital goods: 'I cannot discover the frontier that divides Asia from Europe'; economic isolation could lead to the greater danger of forming economic blocs'.[17] Several speakers had referred to the desirability of an Asian economic organisation, especially Mr. Bandaranaike; but because of a sharp divergence of view the group finally was 'by consensus of opinion, of the view that the immediate possibility was no more than an exchange of ideas among various countries'.[18] In short, Asia was no more ready for a separate economic organisation of its own than for one dealing with politics.

The only other interesting points to emerge were a vague distrust of indigenous capitalists and a lively fear that perhaps with their help foreign capital would cleverly assume local colour (this has happened and is one aspect of what was later called 'neo-colonialism'). It was even suggested that an Asian body should be set up to control the profits on foreign capital.

Most of the speakers on 'Agricultural Reconstruction'[19] made the same points: they spoke of the preponderance of agriculture in their economies, and its present backward state, with such low productivity that even basic food supplies were inadequate. The Palestine Jews and, naturally, the Soviet Central Asians spoke at length about the need for land reform, urging measures adopted by one or the other. But when one speaker replied that what the Asian peasants wanted was land for themselves and not state tenancy or collective farms, the delegate of Soviet Azerbaijan, beating a hasty retreat, agreed! The report mentioned the need for 'fundamental land reforms and linking up ownership and cultivation in the same hands';[20] this has since become almost a cliché in the policies of most Asian governments.

The discussions on 'Industrial Development'[21] made one principle quite clear—that the future course of Asia was towards socialism, with the state controlling all key industries as well as the import of foreign capital; the latter was a subject of much anxious debate. Discussion of planning was introduced, but to this only India had any contribution to make. This difference between her concern and that of most Asian countries continues to the present time. The delegates and the report[22] did well to bring out and deplore 'the complete domination' . . . 'of transport and communications in Asia' . . . 'by non-Asian nations'.

The Soviet delegates and the Palestine Jews turned this discussion to such good propaganda effect, that the report began by singling out, as prominent exceptions to 'the low measure of industrialisation' in Asia, 'the Asian Republics, Turkey, parts of Palestine and parts of the Middle East'. Even now the Asian republics are not heavily industrialised: Israel is lightly industrialised and Turkey's few, inefficient and badly-planned industries are a warning rather than an example. For governments, too, it pays to advertise.

This axiom was even more obvious in the discussions on 'Labour Problems and Social Services'.[23] At this point the imaginary gap between the Asian republics and the rest of Asia proved wide: the delegates of the former gave a wholly laudatory picture of their conditions, while the latter, more honestly, were concerned as to how the prevailing unsatisfactory state of affairs could be improved. In consequence, the report is full of flattering references to the Soviet republics.

The biggest outburst of Asian feeling occurred in the discussions on 'Cultural Problems'.[24] Besides assigning a variety of cultural tasks to the proposed Asian Institute, speakers from India, Ceylon, China, Palestine, Egypt, Siam, and Afghanistan put forth proposals for common Asian science institutes, scholarship schemes, academies, an inter-university organisation, an Asian broadcasting station and a physical culture association. In contrast to this visionary talk, there was a general feeling that an artificial or 'constructed' common language for Asia was not a practical proposition, and that English would still have to be used for some time; on this, even the delegate from Soviet Georgia agreed. Only the Indian delegation tried to work out a definition of fundamental Asian values; but it sought to include so many qualities ('faith in the unity of mankind') that the definition became too vague, and the line of enquiry was not pursued.

In 'the Status of Women' group[25] all the speakers, mostly women, indulged in much bragging about the advances achieved by their sex in their respective countries; and it is surprising that the report, after all, reiterated the need for political and economic equality. It is only fair to add that the report recommended the abolition notably of polyandry, but also of polygamy, which two male delegates from Burma and Cochin-China, greatly daring, defended as an expression of man's 'generosity' and 'fantasy'.[26] The most real sign of sex equality was the disapproval which many women delegates showed of special political concessions for separate feminist movements; and when the inevitable suggestion was made for an Asian women's organisation, this was naturally rejected, though it was agreed that Asian women should keep in touch on their special problems.

These group discussions, which lasted for eight days in all, have been described not only because this was the first time that Asian representatives were dealing with the full range of Asian problems— political, economic, cultural and social—but also because many of the delegates were distinguished personalities from whom original ideas might have been expected. The expectation was not fulfilled, for, apart from a certain acidity in the political discussions, little originality or intellectual vigour was shown in the handling of the other topics; consequently the reports are remarkably bland and anodyne. Some of the participants seem to have felt that they were beating the air and tried to cast the reports in the form of definite resolutions, upon which the participating governments were expected to act.

But though many delegates supported this move, the ICWA Secretariat succeeded in imposing the steering committee's decision that there should be no resolutions, except on one subject. This lack of clear decisions undoubtedly helped to give the conference a vague and indeterminate air; and this, in turn, was probably the reason why, despite its importance, it had so few after-effects.

The mass enthusiasm generated by the closing plenary session certainly suggested otherwise.[27] After the announcement that Mahatma Gandhi would address the session, the conference was transformed into a large public meeting. Twenty thousand people edged and elbowed their way into the marquee, most of them the common folk of Delhi who certainly did not pay for their tickets. They sat on the floor, in the aisles, or wherever they could find space, in stifling heat and under a thin pall of dust. Mr. Nehru's impatient attempts to quiet and control them produced the opposite effect: for to be shoved or pommelled by Mr. Nehru was an honour, and people pushed forward to receive it.

On the rostrum, beneath the map and the flags, alongside Mr. Nehru sat Dr. Sutan Sharir, Prime Minister of the Provisional Indonesian Government, for whom a special plane had been sent and who, the day before, had been reunited with his tall, blonde Dutch wife after an enforced separation of six years. But though he was a centre of interest he was no Mahatma. The Mahatma was the real focus of attention. Scorning a chair, he squatted cross-legged on a mattress placed on the wall of the rostrum, like some fragile brown insect pushing out of the white cocoon of his loose draperies, immobile and aloof. Amid the panoply of young, assertive and not very non-violent nationalism—the flags, the clamant symbols and the bellowing loudspeakers—this exponent of a creed of spiritual anarchy in fact harmonised with only one part of the spectacle, the deep bank of flowers at the foot of the rostrum.

Dr. Shariar made a carefully-worded speech calling for 'firm, definite action' that would at the same time be 'palatable to other peoples'. 'The Asian sentiment' must be 'preserved as a holy flame' lighting the way to 'One Asia' and 'One World'.

The Mahatma's speech, delivered in a soft, indistinct voice, was a quiet chat by an old man, meandering and full of small, irrelevant, details redolent of the past. When he finally got round to talking about the conference he advised the delegates to see the real India of the villages—those 'dung heaps' inhabited by 'miserable specimens of humanity' who, nevertheless, possessed nothing less than 'the con-

66

centrated essence of wisdom'. 'The West is today pining for wisdom. It is despairing of multiplication of atom bombs'; and Asia must not imitate the vices of the West, 'its gunpowder and atom bomb'. Rather Asia must conquer the West through love; and this it could do because its true greatness was in the teachings of its prophets, from Moses and Zoroaster to Mohammed. And, he added pityingly, he told them this 'in order to hearten you'. Here, in truth, was an undeceived critic of everything the conference stood for.

It was a scene of strong, piercing incongruity. Two totally contradictory doctrines of how Asia could find itself and then face the challenge of the West—that of the Herodian and that of the Zealot, the Kemalist and the Gandhian—met face to face for the first and last time. At this historic encounter on the threshold of Asian independence, each respectfully noted the other's presence and then went his own way—Gandhi to his death and his followers to oblivion while the modernising nationalists took the winding road that led, among other places, to Bandung and Belgrade.

Even his chosen successor, Mr. Nehru, parted company with Gandhi when in his closing speech he said, 'I want my country to be industrialised.'[28] But though this meant that Asia would take many things from the West its peoples 'had to find ourselves again'. The conference, said Mr. Nehru, would be a landmark in history because henceforth the centre of events would be shifting away from Europe —to America on one side, and to Asia on the other.

Looking to the future, Mr. Nehru and other speakers referred optimistically to the Asian Relations Organisation (ARO) that the conference had decided to establish. The Chinese delegate invited the conference to meet in China in two years' time. It only remained for Mrs. Naidu, on the wing again, to produce a rousing peroration on how 'we have founded today a new world brotherhood . . . a federation of free peoples' in which 'we have emerged as pure gold, the gold of Asian consciousness, of wisdom . . . culture, service . . . and the oneness of man'.

Why should these bright hopes have proved so illusory, these visionary gleams so fugitive? The proceedings of the conference itself, in public and private, provide the material for the answer. But before going into that, it would be appropriate to take one last, backward look at the Asian Relations Conference as a whole.

The proceedings show that it was essentially a South and South-East Asian conference. The organisers had first thought that they should confine it to this region,[29] and they might as well have done so, because Afghanistan, Iran, Egypt and the Arab countries (sadly under-represented) contributed little. The Palestine Jews had their say on nearly every topic, as did the Soviet Central Asians, but the latter did so with such well-drilled unanimity that it is not surprising that they were never again invited. The conference was not very prescient, for there was only a single reference to Africa, made by Mr. Nehru, and only two—from him and Mahatma Gandhi—to the atomic age.

Mr. Nehru's approach to this first conference was completely consistent with his attitude to all such conferences later on. Now, as afterwards, he insisted that the conference was not directed against any race or region, in other words, Europe; that it ought not to deal with bi-lateral internal disputes; that among the participants there were no leader and no followers. This last point was stressed by so many of the Indian delegates that it should have disposed of the suspicion that through the conference India was trying to assert its title to continental leadership.

If each of the Afro-Asian conferences can be said to have a distinct character, then in each case this was a dual personality. Each of them raised one issue that was the main centre of interest, that caused divisions and delays, and caught the newspaper headlines at the time. These controversial, topical issues are now almost completely forgotten, while in retrospect the conferences have developed a deeper resonance on a longer wavelength that is still audible. Their short-term and their long-term impact have always been quite different, so different in fact that sometimes the topical issue has prevented the conference from exercising a long-term influence. This was the case in Delhi.

We have seen that on the opening day the steering committee had by sharp practice slipped on to the agenda the idea of a permanent organisation. The committee had gone even further in prejudging this issue—a fact that was revealed when the group discussing Race Relations tried to pass a formal resolution. The conference secretariat was then compelled to bring out into the open the minutes of the steering committee in which it decided against resolutions, 'except possibly in respect of the establishment of a permanent institution for carrying on the work of the Asian Relations Conference'.[30]

But if the hosts, and especially Mr. Nehru, thought that they could edge the conference into agreeing with his pet idea, the proceedings in the sub-committee set up for the purpose must have proved disillusioning.

Dawn: The Asian Relations Conference, New Delhi

From a reading of the private files of the Indian Council of World Affairs, one is led to believe that real thinking on the form of this new organisation began only on the 4th March, less than three weeks before the conference began. The names suggested for it were the Asian Council of World Affairs, the Council of Asian Relations and the Institute of Asian Relations. The final working paper in these files bore the last title. The organisation it envisaged was purely academic and non-political, and its constitution was to contain a rule that as a body it would not express any opinion on Asian or international affairs. Its activities were to consist of research and publication, and the arranging of lectures, discussion groups and periodic conferences. It was to have a library, reading room, information services and a language section for inter-Asian relations. National units of the parent body were to be started, and the institute as such was to become active when a minimum of six such units had been formed. Each unit was to be independent. The secretariat of the institute was to consist of six officers with a budget of Rs. 75,000 to 100,000. The initial non-recurring expenditure on buildings and library was estimated at Rs. 500,000, to be raised through public subscription.

This project was undoubtedly the work of the Indian Council of World Affairs—a notoriously cautious, even timid, body—because this institute would have been merely the Council writ large. It is not certain that this was the suggestion made to the delegates, because so harmless a proposal would hardly have resulted in the opposition actually aroused.

The first meeting of the sub-committee[31] to enquire into 'the advisability of a permanent institute' met on the 25th March, two days after its appointment, with fourteen representatives present. From the start there was sharp difference of opinion as to whether any central organisation should be formed. In favour were India (represented by Mr. Krishna Menon), Ceylon, Burma and Iran. Opposed were China, Afghanistan and the Philippines. The objections raised were that the time was not yet ripe for such a development, that the parent organisations represented had to be consulted before a commitment could be made, and, finally, that the delegates present at the conference were perhaps not fully representative of their countries or governments. It is ironic that this last objection was raised by the Chinese delegation, which represented only the Kuomintang: they suggested waiting for the more representative second conference, to be held in China, before taking a final decision. Since the discussions were inconclusive, the sub-committee appointed two sub-sub-committees, one from those in favour and the other from those against, presumably to clarify the proposals and counter-proposals.

This unusual procedure did not get the sub-committee any further when on the 27th March it met for the second time. There was still no agreement, for China and the Philippines were still opposed. So also was one of the Indian delegates, Pandit H. Kunzru, the then President of the ICWA, who agreed that it would entail 'enormous expense', and that it was better to have nothing than to have an organisation dominated by one government. This political consideration proved decisive.

Faced with this deadlock Mr. Nehru wheeled his biggest gun into position, no less a weapon than Mahatma Gandhi, who, very frail and obviously rather bewildered, was brought in to speak to the delegates on the 1st April while they were discussing 'Labour Problems'. The Mahatama's remarks[32] on the subject deserve to be quoted in full as an example of what happens when a saint operates politically. He began by saying that 'some parts of the question of an Asian institute were discussed by Pandit Nehru with me yesterday ... this is a question after my heart—whether I think an institute should be formed'. But it was not long before he was speaking of the relation of Man with God, whether God was knowable and what were His attributes. His conclusion was: 'He is knowable, but knowable only to the extent that our little intellect would allow us. If He is unknowable then, of course, there would be no God. For me He is there. I came to recognise that He was best represented by the word Truth. Hence I would say to you, gentlemen from different parts of Asia, having come here and with eagerness, that you should meet yearly or once in two or three years'—surely the most splendid *non sequitur* in recent political, or theological, discussion.

Despite this intervention, or perhaps because of it, only an uneasy and ineffectual compromise was finally achieved. The third meeting of the sub-committee, was held, informally, at Mr. Nehru's house, with him presiding. Ten people were present, six of them Indians, with the representatives of China, Burma, Iran and the Philippines—a packed group with eight to two in favour from the start. Here it was agreed that some kind of continuing body 'would be helpful', but that it would be non-official; hence 'the idea of establishing a permanent institute to carry on the work of the Asian Relations Conference was suggested and supported'. Yet the main problem remained —whether or not there should be a centralised secretariat within the permanent organisation; though how there could be one without the other it is difficult to see. Since there was no agreement on this point, it was decided instead to suggest a provisional general council that would decide on the form the institute should take. In short the question was merely transferred to another body and the decision on it postponed.

When the proposed provisional general council was announced[33] this was hailed by the plenary session, though not by the Chinese delegate, as 'the foundation of a durable organisation'. It was nothing of the kind, and there was no excuse for this misunderstanding. The official announcement, it is true, did not say that the council had yet to decide on the form of the organisation; but, at the same time, it did not give this council any other precise functions beyond 'such action as it may consider necessary from time to time for the progressive development of the organisation'. It was an unwieldy body of thirty delegates representing twenty-two countries, including seven of the Central Asian Republics. Everybody wanted to believe that the conference had produced something concrete, so they believed this, even if it had not materialised. This self-deception was repeated after other Asian conferences.

The Asian Relations Organisation was to be a much less academic body than the working papers had envisaged. It had as one of its objects 'the study and understanding of Asian problems and relations in their Asian and world aspects', but its other two objectives were 'to foster friendly relations and co-operation' and 'the progress and well-being of the peoples of Asia'. These might have developed into the political and economic aspects of an Asian federation.

This development never occurred, because the organisation was foredoomed to failure. Its final form had yet to be decided—by a council unable to meet with any frequency because its delegates had to come from twenty-two countries: it had its first and last meeting on the day after the ending of the conference, so even its provisional constitution was never framed.

After this inauspicious beginning, it is surprising to find that the Asian Relations Organisation maintained a shadowy, halting existence till as late as June 1955, when the Bandung Conference finally put an end to it.[34] As many as six national units were actually established, in Burma, Ceylon, India, Israel, Malaya and Nepal. By the end of 1947, however, the Central Office in New Delhi was reduced to three small and shabby rooms, and its 'staff' consisted of an Honorary President (Mr. Nehru), an Honorary Secretary, an

Honorary Joint Secretary, a part-time accountant and a full-time clerk and messenger-boy. Propped up by the ICWA on one side and by UNESCO on the other, it was able to arrange, in December 1952, one seminar on 'The Position of Women in South Asia', but that was its last activity. In that year it was unable even to spend the grant-in-aid accorded to it by the Indian Government. At the time of its dissolution its assets were listed as : six chairs (one broken), two tables, one typewriter and two filing cabinets. Thus this first, and only, attempt at organising unity between the free countries of Asia came to a dreary end, 'not with a bang but a whimper'.

If circumstances had been ideal, the Asian Relations Organisation might have grown into something very large and important. In the event it was no more than a nut crushed between the jaws of a steel press closing under the weight of immense events—the rivalry between India and China, the Communist revolutionary take-over in China, the suspicion of India in South and South-East Asian countries, and the rending apart of British India into India and Pakistan.

India may not have wanted to see herself as a rival to China; but China, even Kuomintang China, had, more realistically, accepted the rivalry as inevitable, and on the matter of the Asian Relations Organisation acted as if the rivalry existed. She was clearly quite determined that nothing permanent should emerge from the Delhi Conference, for any body that resulted from this meeting would inevitably be under the Indian aegis and would be sited in and staffed by India. This was why her delegates suggested that the question be decided at the second conference; for it was to be held in China, and there, out of diplomatic politeness, the delegates would have had to accept the offer (which China would certainly have made) to play host to the headquarters. The Delhi Conference decided that there should be two general secretaries, one Indian and one Chinese, but the Chinese was never appointed; and the secretariat was thus deprived of a larger representative character.

It is only fair to point out that the Nanking regime in 1947 and 1948 was hardly in a position to spare time and resources for such external matters as the holding of an Asian conference; for it was then in the process of losing the mainland to the advancing Communists. After the Communist victory, the Chinese People's Institute of Foreign Affairs in Peking did put out a feeler—admitting that 'so far no steps have been taken to consider the affiliation of the institute with the Organisation' in Delhi, and suggesting that 'for the present' the two bodies might exchange publications. This lukewarm approach was probably due to the orthodox Communist belief, held till about 1952, that the newly-independent Asian states were all puppets of the West; and by 1952 the ARO was quite dead.

The ARO could have been kept alive in India, in defiance of the Chinese attitude, if Mr. Nehru had so wished. But after the conference he displayed only minor and desultory interest in the organisation. Considering his earlier enthusiasm for the project, this represents a complete and abrupt reversal in his attitude. The only possible explanation is that at that meeting his Asian enthusiasm suffered a rude shock. For a sensitive man the barely-concealed suspicion and hostility of Burma, Ceylon and Indonesia must have been most distressing. It had already been made plain to him that aloofness was to be Burma's official policy. In a broadcast from Delhi in January 1947, Burma's first nationalist leader, General Aung San, had spelled out his ideas of an Asian Commonwealth: 'while India should be one entity, and China another, South-East Asia should form an entity on its own; and then finally we should come together in a bigger union', and 'there was still a long way to go' before that stage. Faced with the hostility of China, the suspicion of South-East Asia, and the indifference of the Arabs, India had no bricks with which to build any kind of Asian structure.

In the next few years, India and China were alike preoccupied. India had little time or energy left over from the task of keeping her head above water, after the massacres and the immense exchanges of population that accompanied partition. Even on the day that Gandhi addressed the conference twelve people were killed and thirty-seven injured in Calcutta, and during the closing plenary meeting the rumour ran through the crowds that violence had started in Old Delhi, three miles away. The other Asian countries were justified in waiting to see what would emerge in the sub-continent from all these bloody happenings. And by the time that the dust had settled the impulse for the Asian Organisation had ebbed away.

The short-term significance of this conference is in the attempt to create the permanent organisation. The sound and fury roused by this project obscures the conference's long-term importance, namely, that for the first time in history the continent of Asia, a resurgent Asia, had come together. Perhaps the significance of this historic event was blurred by the fact that the conference, through excess of caution, offered little support, except in words, to those Asian countries, Indonesia and Vietnam, which were in the thick of their struggle for freedom.

Thus while this first, most single-minded, and most enthusiastic, of the Asian conferences had little lasting impact on Asia, and is barely remembered, it had a considerable negative effect on Asia, for after it Mr. Nehru was most reluctant about every other large Asian gathering; and his hesitancy probably delayed for some years the holding of these conferences.

The Asian Relations Conference may have been no more than a large grin without a Cheshire cat attached. But the Western Press ran true to its later form in reflecting alarm and expressing wariness. The *News Chronicle* of London[35] wrote that 'a certain nervousness has been apparent in European capitals lest some conspiracy for an anti-Western bloc was being hatched; nothing is further from the minds of those sponsoring this Conference'. The *New York Times* gave a warning that 'the Western World will do well to watch carefully' what was happening in Delhi since 'it may have large potentialities'. And *The Times* of London was even more minatory: 'the world has a new force to reckon with the awakened spirit of Asia'. From these and similar press comments one gathers the impression that the first coming together of Asia was not considered by the West to be a welcome development. The Russians, meanwhile, could not resist putting the conference into their particular Cold War frame; for *Izvestia*[36] noted that the decision to have a permanent organisation produced a negative reaction from countries in the American sphere of influence. This is factually true, but at this time had not the sinister implication that *Izvestia* tries to give to it.[37] It was four or five years before the United States joined the ex-colonial powers of Western Europe in automatically expressing alarm whenever the countries of Africa and Asia held a conference.

The Delhi Conference and that at Bandung have one important factor in common: they taught the same lesson, though they are eight years apart and belong to two different historical epochs. Delhi was held before the Cold War impinged on Asia; Bandung came at a time when the Cold War in Asia itself was reaching one of its climaxes, and its debates were a reflection of the larger struggle. Yet on both occasions, if for quite different reasons, the Asian states failed to reach basic agreement; because geography is not enough. For Asian countries, at least, being part of the same continent does not bring about common policies. This had been proved true of other continents, of Europe and of South America, but independent Asia believed that it was different, and only with reluctance learnt that it was not. 'Thus quick, bright things come to confusion.'

NOTES TO CHAPTER III

All references, unless otherwise stated, are to the volume produced by the Indian Council of World Affairs, *Asian Relations: Proceedings and Documentation of the First Asian Relations Conference*, New Delhi, 1948.

1. pp. 10, 11.
2. pp. 264–79.
3. Indian Council of World Affairs files.
4. p. 12.
5. p. 16 *et seq.*
6. Press reports.
7. p. 71 *et seq.*
8. pp. 73 and 74.
9. p. 76.
10. p. 81.
11. p. 86.
12. p. 89.
13. p. 89.
14. p. 90 *et seq.*
15. p. 96.
16. p. 97.
17. p. 107 *et seq.*
18. p. 113.
19. pp. 127–8.
20. p. 128 *et seq.*
21. p. 148.
22. p. 150 *et seq.*
23. p. 153.
24. p. 157 *et seq.*
25. p. 187 *et seq.*
26. p. 208 *et seq.*
27. pp. 231–2.
28. p. 234 *et seq.*
29. p. 248.
30. pp. 4 and 5.
31. p. 197.
32. ICWA files.
33. p. 175 *et seq.*
34. p. 255 *et seq.*
35. ICWA files.
36. Issues of these papers dated 26th Mar. 1947.
37. Issue dated 31st May 1947.

(blank)

INTERLUDE I

The Landslide of Power in Asia

'When ancient empires are uprooted the ground shakes,' said Mr. Nehru at the Asian Relations Conference. And in the twenty months between it and the next Asian gathering, the Conference on Indonesia in New Delhi in January 1949, there was a great uprooting and a mighty shaking of the earth in Asia. In some areas the tree of imperial power was removed entire, in others it was merely shaken, to crack and fissure the ground around it. A second conference was imperative if only because large areas of the continent were still struggling, violently, to be free.

On the positive side there was, in South Asia, a massive landslide of power as a result of which nearly five hundred million people gained independence. This came to India and the new state of Pakistan in August 1947, to Burma in January 1948, and to Ceylon in February 1948. Though carried through peacefully and with goodwill on both sides the mere size of this operation inevitably produced a complex of problems.

In India during the months following independence, the chief internal preoccupation was the framing of a democratic republican constitution. Until this was completed in 1950, India remained a dominion, though after June 1948 under the first and last Indian Governor-General. Simultaneously, the multitudinous anachronistic princely states were being absorbed into a unified modern India. A somewhat similar integration of states produced the Federation of Malaya during 1948.

There is, unfortunately, much to record on the negative side during this period. The partitioning of the sub-continent produced communal violence on a monstrous scale; perhaps half a million people were killed, and ten million fled in panic from one state to the other. The resulting bitterness led to the assassination of Mahatma Gandhi in January 1948.

Another legacy was the dispute over the state of Kashmir. Kashmir would certainly have joined Pakistan if the Governor-General, Mr.

Jinnah, had not made a hasty grab for it. In consequence, from October 1947 onwards, there was undeclared war between India and Pakistan.

Pakistan suffered a grievous blow, from which it has never quite recovered, in the death in September 1948 of Mr. Jinnah—the hard, cold driving force that created that country.

Death took an even heavier toll of the national leadership in Burma when, in July 1947, General Aung San and six of his colleagues were shot during a cabinet meeting.

In West Asia things were going badly for the Arab states. In the teeth of their vehement protests and against the vote of most of the Asian states, the United Nations in November 1947 decided on the partitioning of Palestine after the termination of the British mandate. This took place in May 1948. The state of Israel proclaimed its existence forthwith, and maintained itself despite attacks from the armies of the neighbouring Arab states. This defeat not only brought the Arab League into disrepute; because of the League's failure to produce any kind of military co-ordination between its members, it also created a deep-seated bitterness against the Arab governments among the younger generation of Arabs, especially the officer corps; and this has been the root cause of continuing turbulence in the area. This bitterness has been kept alive by the presence in the Arab countries of a million Arab refugees driven out of Palestine by the victorious Zionists. An initial expression of this frustration was the first of many military coups in Syria in March 1949.

It was in 1948, too, that another partitioning of an Asian country, Korea, took place, an operation as pregnant with dire possibilities as that of Palestine.

During this period the first campaigns of the long-drawn-out war between France and Vietminh under Ho Chi Minh were fought in Indo-China. Though this was an anti-colonialist struggle, in this case the Vietminh effort was also part of a larger Communist push in Asia and this was directed even more against the newly-independent states than against the imperial powers.

In March 1948 a conference of 'the Progressive Youth of Asia' was held in Calcutta. Here it was decided that the co-operation between the Communist parties and the nationalist movements, which had prevailed since the end of World War II, should be terminated. According to Communist dogma, the new states were not truly independent, and were in fact more dangerous than the colonial system because under a façade of freedom they remained willing lackeys of the imperialist West. The Communists presumably calculated that because these new governments were not yet stabilised they could be overthrown through determined military action by the Communist parties. It was a total miscalculation.

In India the Communist Party tried to set up a Communist base, an Indian Yenan, in the Telengana area of Hyderabad; in Indonesia the Communists struck at Madium in West Java; guerrilla war broke out in the jungles of Burma and Malaya, and the Hukbalahaps increased their pressure in the Philippines. Every one of these rebellions was broken by the nationalist governments: with brutal swiftness in Java, rather more slowly in India, and only over a period of years in Burma, Malaya and the Philippines. Only against the colonialist French did the Communists eventually achieve a partial victory; and this owed much to the swift southward advance across China of the Communist armies during 1948, and their subsequent total take-over of the mainland. During this period, however, Europe was fighting in Indonesia its most vigorous and desperate rearguard action.

When Dr. Sharir attended the Asian Relations Conference as Indonesian Prime Minister, the relations between his country and the Dutch were governed by the Linggadjati Agreement signed in November 1946. This Agreement implied the *de facto* recognition of the Indonesian Republic of Java and Sumatra, and incorporated a plan for an interim semi-independent government of the future United States of Indonesia—semi-independent because the republic was supposed to consult with Holland on foreign policy matters. On this basis the Arab governments in March 1947 granted the republic full *de jure* recognition.

The Dutch had no real intention of making the agreement work. This became apparent when they started conferring 'freedom' on the groupings of the other Indonesian islands. In July 1947 they tired even of the pretence, and attacked the republican areas in what was delicately called a 'police action'. India and Australia brought the matter before the United Nations and the Security Council demanded a cease-fire.

With this demand the Dutch complied on the 5th August because by that time they had already occupied the most important parts of the Republic in Java and Sumatra. A second agreement, signed in January 1948 aboard the American transport *Renville*, reaffirmed the principles of Linggadjati, but in effect consecrated the *de facto* position produced by the police action. It was at this moment, when the Republic had its back to the wall, that the Indonesian Communists

F   81

struck at Madium in September and received their just deserts.

Hardly had the republic recovered from this treacherous stab in the back before the Dutch attacked again in a second 'police action'. On the night of 18th to 19th December Dutch paratroopers captured the republican capital, Jogjakarta; and leading members of the Government, including President Sukarno, Prime Minister Hatta and Dr. Ali Sastroamidjojo, were arrested and interned on a remote island. In the following two weeks the Dutch were able to take over the main towns and roads in Java and Sumatra, but an alternative republican government continued to function in the highlands of Sumatra and from India. This was the situation at the end of 1948, which provides the background for the next Asian conference.

CHAPTER IV

The Spur of Indonesia: the Second New Delhi Conference, January 1949

The conference on Indonesia held in New Delhi in January 1949 is another of the Asian conferences which has been forgotten—not least in Indonesia itself. At the time it was seen clearly for what it was, 'the first Asian Political Conference', as the Syrian representative put it, or as more explicitly described by General Romulo, 'the first inter-governmental conference on the political level to be held in Asia'.

If Mr. Nehru felt impelled to call a conference on a problem that the Security Council had been handling for six months, he did so partly to assert the right of the voice of Asia to be heard on Asian questions; but he acted partly also because the Security Council, or rather the Western Powers that dominated that body, were not prepared to take really firm action against Holland. The reasons for this soft handling are plain; the Western European Union was in the process of being institutionalised as the North Atlantic Treaty Organisation; and the United States at this delicate juncture did not want to give the impression that it was pressing heavily on the European colonial governments that had just become its allies.

Consequently when the Dutch took their first police action in July 1948, the Security Council merely asked them to cease-fire but rejected a Russian resolution, supported by India, that Dutch troops should be ordered back to their original positions. This timidity virtually amounted to encouragement to the Dutch to launch their second police action on the 19th December to finish off the Republic. Six days later the Security Council demanded the abandonment of the police action and the release of the interned Indonesian leaders. Once again a demand for the withdrawal of Dutch troops, sponsored among others by Russia and China, did not succeed because the Western Powers would not support it. Having gained their military objectives the Dutch complied with the cease-fire, but only after a further week's delay. Small wonder that the emergency government of Indonesia, functioning from Sumatra, described the Security Council as 'impotent' to offer more than a committee of good offices, and that Mr. Nehru should say, on the 3rd January 1949: 'We have to confess with sorrow that the attitude of some powers has been one of tacit approval or acceptance of this aggression.' The Security Council added insult to injury when, on the 18th January, it decided that the Indonesian Republic was not 'a nation' within the meaning of the Charter.

In contrast to United Nations inaction, several Asian states had taken such practical measures as they could to help Indonesia and to hinder the Dutch. Saudi Arabia, Pakistan, Ceylon, India and Burma had closed their ports and their air-space to Dutch ships and planes even before the convening of the conference. This was an effective hindrance to air communication on the eastward route from Holland, and thus did Mr. Thivy's 'area of immobilisation' come into effect.

The Indonesian struggle stirred Asian sentiment very deeply at this time. It was approximately for Asia what Algeria subsequently was for the Arab countries. It must be remembered that by January 1949 the Indonesians' fight against the Dutch had been going on for very nearly three and a half years, ever since the first proclamation of the Republic in July 1945. Furthermore the action of little Holland—trying, with considerable brutality, to retain its colonial empire at the same time as the mighty British Empire was being dissolved—appeared especially foolish and infuriating. For the Muslim countries, the Arab states and Pakistan, there was the added consideration that Indonesia was, in terms of population, the largest Muslim state, from which large numbers of particularly devout believers made the annual pilgrimage to Mecca.

India, on its own, felt a special involvement in the Indonesian struggle. Its sentiments may have been due in part to ancient cultural links between the two countries, and partly perhaps to the personal friendship between Mr. Nehru and Mohammed Hatta, who was Indonesian Prime Minister in 1948, which dated from their meeting at the Brussels Congress in 1927.

Almost the first foreign policy decision of the Interim Indian Government in September 1946 was the withdrawal of Indian troops from Indonesia where, as part of the Allied forces of occupation, they had clashed with the nationalists. After the Dutch imposed an air and sea blockade on the Republic, Indian planes, flying by night, slipped past the Dutch Air Force carrying food, medicines, clothing and per-

The Spur of Indonesia: the Second New Delhi Conference

haps arms to the beleagured republicans in Jogjakarta. The pilot of one of these blockade-runners was Mr. D. Patnaik, lately Chief Minister of the State of Orissa. Mr. Hatta flew out in one of them on a secret visit to India, listed as a crew-member under the pseudonym 'Abdullah'. All-India Radio in New Delhi was almost the sole link between the scattered areas held by the Republic, and not only carried special programmes but functioned as the official 'freedom radio' of the Republic. When in the autumn of 1948 the second Dutch police action seemed imminent, Mr. Nehru invited the Republic to set up a government-in-exile in India, if need arose.[1] The offer was not accepted; but for some months in early 1949 New Delhi was the second capital of the Republic and the prime source of its financial support.

It was a very angry Mr. Nehru who issued the invitations to the conference on the 31st December 1948. Revealing this in a public speech two days later, typical of the informality of protocol then prevailing, he stigmatised the Dutch action as 'the most naked and unabashed aggression'.

Invitations went to twenty countries and the list is as interesting for its omissions as for the inclusions. The Soviet Central Asian Republics were not asked, nor was the Communist regime under Ho Chi Minh in Vietnam. This was not for want of trying on Vietnam's part, for in New Delhi it was canvassing vigorously for admission to the conference. Supported by Burma, this request from Vietnam was discussed at an informal meeting of the delegates, which decided that only internationally recognised governments should participate. International legalities apart, the international Communist movement had also made it amply clear, through the Madium uprising in September if in no other way, that despite its anti-colonialism it was not friendly to Asian nationalism.

There was only one outright refusal to attend. This came from Turkey, which replied that, though sympathetic to Indonesia, as an European state it had no right to a place at the conference. At least one Turkish opposition group, the Nation Party, strongly criticised this decision. By not even sending an observer, as it had done to the Asian Relations Conference, Turkey severed its official links with the Afro-Asian movement—only restored, briefly and unfortunately, for the Bandung meeting.

Thailand at first, on the 9th January, refused to attend, but changed its mind a week later, and the Thai Deputy Foreign Minister conceded that this was done only in response to strong urging by the

85

Press and the public. From official sources it can be learnt that Thailand and an equally hesitant Nepal were also 'persuaded by the fact that the United States was satisfied that the conference was not directed against any group of powers and might be useful'. Both countries only sent observers. China, too, was represented only by an observer. She may have responded in this way first, because she was the only invitee who was a permanent member of the Security Council—and in the Council, the Indonesian question was still *sub judice*; secondly, because of her domestic preoccupations and, thirdly because, as before, she could not raise any great enthusiasm for yet another diplomatic initiative by India, whom she still regarded as an unwanted newcomer to the international scene.

The additions to the membership were the new state of Pakistan and the Arab states, which this time attended in force, perhaps because they were the first to grant full *de jure* recognition to the Indonesian Republic, and perhaps because the Palestine debacle had taught them that their only real friends were in Asia and that it was worth while to cultivate them. The really surprising new invitees, however, were Australia and New Zealand, for their presence involved an extension of the basic continental principle.

Australia fully deserved to be invited, for she had from the start played an active and positive role in the Indonesian question. After World War II, and at least in part because of it, Australia had broken out somewhat from its antipodean isolation to realise that it was, so to speak, in the bottom right-hand corner of the Asian picture. Whether or not because a Labour Party government was in power in Australia, Australian dock workers boycotted Dutch ships; and it was on an Australian request that the Security Council first discussed this issue. Thereafter, at the United Nations and elsewhere, Australia gave the Indonesian Republic solid backing, and she agreed to attend the New Delhi Conference as a full member while New Zealand, more cautiously, was represented by an observer.

In Australia itself opinion on this issue was far from unanimous. Press comment from the opposition suggested that, by attending, Australia would be by-passing the United Nations and opposing the United Kingdom and the United States, and that for this reason the Australian delegates ought not to have full plenipotentiary powers.[2] After this assertion had been rejected, the charge was made that Australia's acceptance showed 'incredible' recklessness or *naïveté*, since Mr. Nehru was trying to detach Australia from the West, and that the Government was playing into his hands. It is greatly to the

The Spur of Indonesia: the Second New Delhi Conference

Australian Government's credit that, despite this strong opposition at home, it took a leading part in the New Delhi meeting, and thus made it the one and only Afro-Austral-Asian Conference.

It will be observed that, despite the urgency of the situation in Indonesia, the conference met only on the 20th January, three weeks after the issue of the invitations. Though this delay was considerably shorter than that experienced before the Asian Relations Conference, it was still unduly long: and this was mainly because the host country, India, had not yet full diplomatic representation even in Asia. Thus the invitations to the Arab governments were issued *en bloc* at a meeting in Cairo between the Indian Ambassador there and the governments' representatives to the Arab League. And, as we have mentioned, some acceptances came in only after reassurances about the conference's intentions had been given to the West.

Indeed the Western governments were even more dubious and fearful of this conference than they had been of its predecessor, for this, after all, was an official gathering. There is ample testimony, official and non-official, to these nursery horrors. An official publicity directive issued by the Indian Government on the 17th January had this to say: 'The United Kingdom and United States attitude—the initial nervousness was the result of apprehension that after this first meeting the Asian countries might learn to work together in matters of common interest and thus break away from the tutelage of Western powers. The exchange of views with both governments has secured their general goodwill. Had the conference been designed to discuss or devise something hostile to the United Kingdom we should not have invited Australia and New Zealand.' There is impatience behind the tart wording, and not overmuch sympathy for a British Government that discerned in the calling of the conference a situation that 'is dangerous and difficult'.[3] The *New York Times* declared pontifically[4] that foreign diplomats in New Delhi had impressed on Mr. Nehru the view that an anti-Western bloc would be disadvantageous and would create a cleavage in the United Nations.

If one is to trust the word and judgement of so staunch a friend of the West as General Romulo of the Philippines, this fear had even infected the United Nations which, at this juncture, one must take as being synonymous with the representatives of Western governments. On the 18th January the General said that the Indonesian debate in the Security Council was resumed in order to try to obtain positive results, to save the Council's prestige and 'thus take the wind out of the sails of the conference'. He noted 'mistrust' of the con-

The Spur of Indonesia: the Second New Delhi Conference

ference at United Nations, and the belief that 'an Asian bloc was in the offing'. And this New Delhi Conference, one must remember, was merely an Asian riposte to a flagrant attack made by a European power on a government that it had itself recognised, in breach of two solemn international pledges and of orders from the United Nations.

To soothe the West Mr. Nehru could no nothing, whether in private or in public, except repeat what he had often said before and was to reiterate even more often in the future: 'We have been opposed to joining any bloc for any hostile purpose. We can hardly therefore think of encouraging the formation of a new bloc of nations. This conference is not opposed to any country or people. It is not anti-European or anti-American or anti-Western.'[5] These reassurances finally induced the American representative on the Security Council to state that his government viewed the conference 'with sympathetic interest'.[6]

It is surprising that Asia was so tolerant and so understanding of this absurd trepidation. After centuries of political domination and of racial exclusiveness practised by Europe in Asia, Europe was now afraid and indignant at the remote possibility that Asia might do the same. Western Europe was grouping itself into NATO, but it was impermissible that independent Asia should do likewise. One can still hear quite distinctly the huffing and puffing—'this is a wicked animal, when it is attacked it defends itself'.

It might be argued that in sponsoring this second conference Mr. Nehru seemed to have overcome the reluctance for Asian gatherings produced in him by the previous conference. This is not necessarily so. For one thing, this conference was not his idea. In his speech to the opening session the Burmese delegate said: 'It gives me no end of pleasure to see that the suggestion made by my Prime Minister, Thakin Nu, to call a conference of this kind has been accepted by the Honourable Pandit Jawaharlal Nehru with enthusiasm and with an intuitive perception of Asia's needs.' Though quaintly worded, this claim is accurate, though one might query the 'enthusiasm', for Mr. Nehru said that the proposal came from U Nu 'shortly after the Dutch aggression', on the 19th December, which means that he took ten to twelve days to act on it. For another thing Mr. Nehru had not been averse to calling, or accepting suggestions that he call, Asian conferences or group meetings for one particular purpose—in this case Indonesia. He did much the same thing in November 1956 because of the Suez-Hungary crises. It was the large Asian conference with indeterminate objectives that he had come to mistrust.

88

The Spur of Indonesia: the Second New Delhi Conference

This was a brisk and businesslike conference from beginning to end. The diplomatic corps and the press were admitted to the opening session but the public was excluded. Mr. Nehru set the tone in a pointed, dignified speech of about ten minutes' duration. The conference, he said, must concentrate on the Indonesian issue; by doing this, it would help the Security Council; it would supplement not supplant its efforts. The conference met in no spirit of hostility or racialism. According to him, it had three tasks: to make proposals to the Security Council; to suggest to the Council what action it should take if either party failed to act according to its recommendation; 'to devise machinery and procedures by which the governments represented here today can keep in touch with one another for purposes of mutual consultation and concerted action for the achievement of the purposes for which this conference has met'. This scrupulously circumscribed reference to a continuing body after the second conference is a far cry indeed from Mr. Nehru's wide-ranging ideas for an Asian Institute before the first conference. Only at the end did he permit himself a touch of flagrant oratory when he said that the conference could give a lead 'if we fashion ourselves in accordance with the old spirit of Asia and hold up the torch of truth and peace to a war-distracted world'.

The Afghan, Filipino and Syrian representatives noted that the conference was the first of its kind; and from the Afghans, Yemenis and Ceylonese came assurances that it was not directed against any race or bloc. The Pakistan representative (Sir Mohammed Zafrullah Khan) made the interesting point that present at the conference were seventeen members of the United Nations, plus one soon to be admitted, forming thirty per cent of the membership of that body. Dr. J. W. Burton, for Australia, referred to the 'duty to advise' after 'grave errors' had been committed, but said that the conference should not try to take 'reprisals' but only 'rectify a mistake'.

Special note should, perhaps, be taken of this statement by Mr. S. W. R. D. Bandaranaike of Ceylon: 'We are not met here to decide whether or not a wrong has been done. We are met here as those who, convinced that a wrong has been done, wish to discuss it.' His words are quoted because of the glaring contrast they offer to the attitude adopted by his wife at the Colombo Conference in December 1962, which was called to consider another act of aggression. But in January 1949 non-alignment had not yet come into play. After a morning of speech-making the conference went into closed session on the afternoon of the 20th January. The conference had before it three

89

sets of proposals about the action it should take on the Indonesian problem. The first comprised four general ideas laid down by Mr. Nehru at the time of issuing the invitations. These were as follows: a Dutch withdrawal to the lines held before the campaign, an enquiry into the aggression, 'stoppage of all aid in any form to Holland', and creation of conditions in which the Indonesian Republic could function. The Burmese delegate had suggested a seven-point plan including a Dutch withdrawal and the release of the Indonesian leaders, immediate *de jure* recognition by 'all Asian governments', the lifting of the Dutch blockade, a widened range of sanctions against the Dutch, an appeal to the United States to withhold all aid to Holland, and a watch-dog committee to supervise implementation of these and the Security Council's resolutions. An even more elaborate proposal embodying twelve points was put forward in a 4,000-word memorandum prepared by the Indonesian Finance Minister and five Indonesian ambassadors who had gathered in Delhi. Among other demands, this called for the formation of an interim government by the 1st March, the transfer of sovereignty and the withdrawal of all Dutch troops by the 1st September, and a general election for a constituent assembly by the 1st June, with political and economic sanctions to be applied in case of non-compliance.

Because these various proposals overlapped, and because the delegations from the outset had the same general approach, broad agreement on what they should recommend was reached by the end of the first private session.[7] The cessation of hostilities and the release of the Indonesian leaders was common ground—Australia and Ceylon emphasised the prime importance of restoring the authority of the Republican Government, while Pakistan and Australia suggested that the need to lift the Dutch blockade immediately should be stressed. Egypt and Australia said that there should not be any vagueness in the recommendation relating to the control by the interim government of the Indonesian armed forces, since otherwise this would work to the advantage of the Dutch. Ceylon felt that the dates suggested for elections in the Indonesian memorandum were 'optimistic'.

The conference felt that there was sufficient congruence of views to justify the setting up of a drafting committee consisting of India, Australia, Ceylon and Pakistan—all members of the Commonwealth.

On the 21st January there took place one session of the full conference, for two and a half hours, and two meetings of the drafting committee, one of which went on for three hours. In all of these the work of formulation went quickly.

The Spur of Indonesia: the Second New Delhi Conference

The chairman of the drafting committee (Mr. G. S. Bajpai of India) reported to the full session that Australia had suggested that the resolution should ask the Dutch not to set up new puppet regimes in Indonesia. Ceylon felt that there was not much danger of this. Australia then explained that Dr. Hatta himself had voiced this fear and was strongly of the view that this step should be prevented. Pakistan and the Philippines supported this contention and Ceylon withdrew its objection.

There was much discussion at this session on whether there should be a reference to, or even a threat of, further action by the governments if the Security Council resolutions were not implemented. The consensus was against any direct reference to Article 41 of the Charter, which covers sanctions, as had been requested in the Indonesian memorandum, but thought that there should be only a tactful mention of the possibility.

Pakistan proposed that the conference resolution should be addressed to the Security Council, and Australia suggested that the Security Council be told that it ought to insist on the implementation of its resolutions.

The expression of these views on Indonesia took up part of the two-and-a-half-hour session of the full conference on the 21st, after which a totally different subject, that of a permanent organisation, was discussed. Before considering the debates on the latter subject it would be useful to see what the conference did finally recommend on Indonesia, its ostensible *raison d'être.*

Having received its final directives from the full conference on the 21st, and having held two meetings on that day and a further one on the 22nd, the drafting committee completed its labours, which were promptly approved by the conference and cabled to the Security Council on the night of the 22nd January.

The resolution on Indonesia was one of three passed by the conference and is itself in three parts, of which the core is Section 1A, printed in full on pages 408ff.[8] In it the conference picks its way, delicately and cautiously, through the various proposals placed before it. Of these proposals, the demand for the immediate release of the Indonesian leaders and the lifting of the blockade was naturally accepted without demur; so was the demand for the withdrawal of Dutch troops from areas occupied after the 18th December; but where the Indonesia memorandum asked for this to be completed by the 1st March the resolution fixed the 15th March; the same date, two weeks later than in the Indonesian request, was set for the formation of an interim government. A longer delay was accorded for the constituent assembly election—Ceylon's point was well taken—which was set for the 1st October instead of the 1st June as suggested in the Indonesian memorandum; the final transfer of power was put back from a suggested 1st September 1949 to the 1st January 1950. No precise date was fixed for the final withdrawal of troops. The Australian request that no new puppet ('regional') governments be formed was included.

Any threat of sanctions under Article 41 was wholly omitted, Section B of the resolution simply left it to the Security Council to take action under 'its wide powers' in case of non-compliance; and the spur was applied to that dilatory and complaisant body by asking it to report to the General Assembly in April.

This resolution was admittedly a compromise—but a forceful one, for it retained the substance of all the principal demands of the Indonesians. Just how strong it was is seen when it is compared with the resolution that the Security Council finally passed, six days later, on the 28th January. This asked for the release of the leaders, established a United Nations Mediation Commission and, with a total lack of realism, asked that Indonesia be granted independence by the 1st July 1960 at the latest. What the Council would have decided without the prodding and stiffening from New Delhi is difficult to imagine. For its efforts the Asian Conference received the thanks of the head of the emergency government of the Indonesian Republic in Sumatra.

We now turn to the real, long-term issue discussed at the conference which was not the Indonesian crisis: that was only the immediate cause and was of short-term interest. The major question was the formation of a permanent Asian organisation, as it had been for the previous conference. Asia had already failed once in this endeavour, for by January 1949 it was already clear that the Asian Relations Organisation was not going to amount to anything. Asia was determined to try again.

The matter loomed large even in the opening speeches and was given as much prominence, if not more, than the subject of Indonesia. Mr. Nehru, under Anglo-American pressure, had reiterated that a bloc was not in process of formation; but perhaps because of that very pressure, openly applied, to which as a proud man he had never taken kindly, he returned to the idea in his speech. If, he asked, the countries of the American continent and of Europe had 'created machinery for the protection and promotion of common interests' was it 'not natural that the free countries of Asia should begin to

92

think of some more permanent arrangement than this conference, for effective mutual consultation and concerted effort in the pursuit of common aims', without hostility and to strengthen the United Nations? Why, in other words, should America and Europe say to Asia 'don't do as we do'?

Pakistan hoped for further conferences on common problems; while Syria welcomed 'a regional and Asian permanent understanding'. General Romulo of the Philippines proposed 'a small permanent Secretariat in New Delhi, maybe, or Manila' to implement the conference proposals from which 'we shall be able to evolve a potent permanent organisation of Asian states functioning as a regional body'. This was Yemen's idea, too: 'a Union of Asiatic states to make a machinery for consultation, for study and for co-operation in all problems' but which would not be a bloc. Not at the conference but at a public speech in Delhi, Mr. Bandaranaike returned to his pet idea of a 'mutual defence scheme' for South-East Asia, comprising India, Burma, Ceylon, Pakistan and Indonesia, countries which had in common parliamentary democracy and also, perhaps, socialism.

With this degree of public commitment to the idea there was, naturally, a great deal of talk about it in the private sessions. While the Indonesian problem took up one such session and part of another, discussion on the permanent organisation went on during the rest of the second and for the whole of the third and fourth private sessions on the 22nd January, the last of which occupied five and a half hours.

Mr. Nehru's ideas on this matter did not envisage the setting up of any special separate organisation: he suggested a consultative committee drawn from the permanent representatives at United Nations headquarters in New York, or composed of the ambassadors of the Asian governments in New Delhi. He preferred the latter, since not all governments were yet represented at the United Nations. This was not good enough for some delegations, who wanted a permanent secretariat to handle the process of consultation; their governments, they said, would have hesitated to come to this conference if they had thought that it was not going to lead to future co-operation on all matters. The most enthusiastic delegation in this group was the Philippines supported, a little more cautiously, by Syria, Yemen and Burma; they wanted a permanent secretariat located in New Delhi. Iran, Australia and Ceylon were the most prominent of those opposed to the idea; Ceylon perhaps because Mr. Bandaranaike wanted a limited arrangement confined to the South-East Asian region. These delegations said that the invitation to the conference had only mentioned the Indonesian question and so they could not commit themselves on a new issue. The convener, Mr. Nehru, accepted this as a valid objection. Iraq was sympathetic to the idea but confessed that it would have to get fresh instructions from home: Egypt was lukewarm. Faced with this sharp difference the four observer countries, China, Nepal, Thailand and New Zealand hurriedly reaffirmed their purely observer status. The only compromise suggestion came from Australia, to the effect that the area concerned was so large that perhaps more than one centre for consultation could be established. This found no support; so a Lebanese proposal that the matter be dealt with in a separate resolution was accepted.

This merely said, 'The conference expressed the opinion that participating governments should consult among themselves in order to explore ways and means of establishing suitable machinery, having regard to the areas concerned, for promoting consultation and cooperation within the framework of the United Nations.' This recommendation was to be sent to the governments attending, and they were to be asked to give their views on it.

This limp phraseology makes it clear that the idea had been talked out in the private sessions. Several reasons can be given as to why, once again, Asian unity could not be formalised. The proposal by Mr. Nehru initiating this discussion was itself lukewarm; China, the largest Asian country, was silent on the sidelines; the subject had not in fact been mentioned in the invitation but had developed its own momentum during the conference; the Australian Government, under fire at home, could not in this impromptu fashion move any deeper into an Asian involvement; Egypt probably saw in the proposal a likely competitor with the Arab League which was under her leadership; and, of course, the precedent of the Asian Relations Organisation was hardly inspiring. Lastly, the fears and suspicions of the Western governments, which would have been reawakened if a permanent organisation had been established, must have been an additional inhibiting factor. Whatever the reason, the discussion on the main issue was as fruitless and indecisive as the discussion on the immediate topic had been clear and fruitful.

That Mr. Nehru was not too disturbed by this outcome may be inferred from his closing speech, in which he congratulated the conference for having 'wisely concentrated' on one issue—Indonesia. Its resolution on that subject was the only feasible action it could have taken, since 'this is not a matter of emotion but of cold and calculated thought'—a remark which indicates a substantial change in his approach to Asian and nationalist issues since the Asian Relations Conference.

General Romulo, the chief protagonist of the permanent organisation, pressed the idea even in his farewell speech; he hoped that the conference (which ought to be the first of many) might yet lead to a permanent regional association. But this was the trumpet call of retreat. More interesting was the General's summing-up of the meeting. At its beginning he advanced the theory that the conference had met 'to strengthen the forces of democracy, to prevent other ideologies from capturing the faith of Asia by default', and at its end he believed that it had produced 'an Asian front against Communism' —an objective and a result that would have surprised most of the other participants. A confirmed Cold War crusader, the General finally found the fortress he was looking for in the South-East Asia Treaty Organisation, six years later. General Romulo made much the same assessment of the aims and achievements of the Bandung Conference; and this is perhaps the first example of how participants at the Afro-Asian conferences saw in them, and took from them, only what fitted into their own narrow special frame of reference.

The reaction of the West to the conference was, naturally, one of relief, and it was much praised. Complimentary epithets like 'efficient', 'dignified', 'purposeful', 'moderate', 'mature' were all used. Though one American paper added[9], hopefully, that the meeting had produced two separate groupings, one East Asian and the other West Asian, the private discussions, with their link-up of the Philippines and some Arab states, produced directly opposite evidence. Despite the testimony of the bland third resolution, Western sources continued to assert that a regional organisation would 'almost certainly emerge in the near future'.[10] For this reason, the most sapient remark on the conference would seem to be a comment from a correspondent in New Delhi: 'The only actual Asian bloc today is that which may exist in the minds of Western observers.'[11]

The Communist section of the West insisted on remaining not merely suspicious but overtly hostile to the conference's efforts. While it was in progress the Russian information service, 'Tass', said: 'This conference is a preparation for the creation of an alliance' similar to the Western Union. Its deliberations would 'by no means contribute towards a correct solution of the Indonesian problem in the spirit of international democratic principles'. After it was over 'Tass', determined to slay its private demons, brushed aside the resolutions and asserted that the 'real' purpose of the meeting was 'the hatching behind closed doors of a military alliance' for checking 'the Communist danger'. No results would be achieved. The first resolution was so drafted as to 'ensure that Holland would retain its rule over Indonesia'; nothing more was to be expected from a gathering of 'reactionary elements', it concluded in scorn. From various motives, there was at this time, and till 1954, a common European front against Asia.

Mr. Nehru had suggested that the permanent organisation might take the form of a Consultative Committee of Permanent Representatives at United Nations headquarters, and it was there that the next Asian initiative on Indonesia took place. This meeting was an altogether curious affair. The gathering was summoned on the 4th March 1949 by the indefatigable General Romulo, and was attended by seventeen of the nineteen governments that had met in New Delhi; Ceylon and Nepal were absent because they were not yet United Nations members. The representatives talked for two hours in a suite in the Waldorf Astoria Hotel, and announced the following day that nothing had been decided, since they had to await instructions from their home governments. They confessed that they had been embarrassed by the release of the news of their deliberations. If any action had emerged from this inconclusive and furtive meeting, it would mark the beginning of the Afro-Asian group in the United Nations, but nothing further transpired.

It was in New Delhi, once again, that the Afro-Asians made their last direct intervention on Indonesia. This came on the 13th April, eleven weeks after the conference, and was the product of strong feeling against the inaction of the Security Council which during this period had done little or nothing to get its resolution implemented, weak though it was; the Indonesian leaders, for instance, were still held in internment. The ambassadors of ten countries met in Mr. Nehru's office, and U Nu, who happened to be visiting India at the time, was also present. The absentees were Ethiopia, Iraq, Lebanon, Saudi Arabia, Syria, Yemen, the Philippines and New Zealand, and in all cases this was because they had no diplomatic representation in New Delhi.

After a single long session, it was resolved that the Indonesian situation should be raised by their Permanent Representative at the United Nations in the General Assembly, and that the Dutch refusal to comply should be condemned. Secondly, the governments were asked to examine a proposal, to be sent to the Security Council, asking that economic sanctions be applied against the Dutch and that all transit facilities by land, sea or air be denied to the Dutch. Ceylon was the only country unwilling (and that only in a partial degree) to fall in with these proposals; her representative said she was ready to deny facilities for the transit of troops and war material, but nothing further. Egypt made the sensible suggestion that each government should also apply pressure on the great powers who were responsible for hamstringing the United Nations.

A third item which was discussed, but was not mentioned in the resolution issued after this meeting, was a request for financial aid for Indonesia. Before the meeting the Indonesians had submitted a shopping list amounting to Rs. 46 million for rice, textiles, medicines, administrative equipment for twelve ministries, transport and communications. Hard-headed Indian officials had trimmed this down to Rs. 12 million. But the meeting could do no more than refer back even this smaller request to the governments. The Australians revealed that they had already stock-piled large quantities of textiles and medicines in Indonesia.[12]

The decisions of this meeting did, of course, reach governments other than those attending and, through them, the Dutch: that was the intention. Whether this warning that the Afro-Asians were now seriously considering sanctions, from which they had refrained so far despite Indonesian requests, had any effect or not, the Dutch entered into serious negotiations with the Indonesians. Three weeks later it was agreed that the interned leaders would be released, that the Republican Government would return to Jogjakarta, that an interim government would be formed and no other puppet regimes would be established.

Subsequent negotiations produced a broader agreement by which partial sovereignty was transferred to a United States of Indonesia on the 27th December 1949. This was four days before the deadline fixed by the New Delhi Conference, four months later than the date requested by the Indonesians, and ten years in advance of the time-limit suggested by the Security Council. Indonesia became a full member of the United Nations in September 1950.

Two countries played a leading part throughout this Indonesian episode of the Afro-Asian movement—Australia and India. Australia's role was perhaps the more noteworthy because that Government had to face strong domestic opposition to its policy on this issue; whereas in India political and public opinion was in full support of Mr. Nehru's initiatives. Despite this fact, subsequent differences in foreign policy, and also the difference of race, precluded Australia from any further part in the official Afro-Asian movement. There were many people on both sides who regretted this, but it was probably inevitable.

In international affairs there is, of course, no gratitude: but India received from Indonesia even less than might have been expected. In official Indonesian histories of the struggle for freedom, these international gatherings, which had an undeniable influence on the course of events, are deliberately played down. And the very degree of assistance afforded by India to Indonesia has produced in Indonesians only a feeling of resentful obligation. Honourable exceptions are President Sukarno, Dr. Hatta and Dr. Sharir. But the average Indonesian talking to the average Indian refers more often to Indian troops being used by the British against Indonesian nationalists in 1945 and 1946 than he does to the help given by India, directly and through the Asian conferences, in 1947 and 1949. Asian Big Brothers are no more liked than Big Brothers elsewhere.

Six years and four months after the New Delhi Conference on Indonesia, the next full Afro-Asian conference was held at Bandung. The reasons for this gap must be examined, not only because of its length but also because in January 1949 the expectation was all to the contrary.

After two Asian conferences had been held in the space of twenty months even the ebullient General Romulo was not being over-optimistic when he predicted that they would be the precursors of a series of regional meetings, but there were none.

One possible reason is that after the freeing of Indonesia at the end of 1949, the impetus of liberation in Asia slackened. By then the main areas were independent, leaving only some tidying up on the peripheries, in Malaya and Indo-China. And the outcome in both cases was inevitable—in Malaya because the British, by their record and pledges, could not stay, and in Indo-China because the French could not win.

But, granted that anti-colonialism is a powerful generator of Afro-Asian sentiment, why did not the Afro-Asians show as much interest in Indo-China as they did in Indonesia—as they do today in far-distant Angola? Why were not Afro-Asian conferences called to support and publicise the Indo-Chinese cause during the long five-year war against an European colonial power?

The Afro-Asians did not bring the Indo-Chinese struggle before

the United Nations, though they were asked to do so.[13] This attitude
is in striking contrast to the action taken there by the Afro-Asians
against the same colonial power, France, in respect of the freedom
movements in its North African colonies. From 1951 onwards the
Afro-Asians put increasing pressure on France at each successive
General Assembly session on behalf of Tunisia, then Morocco, and
then Algeria. And the fighting in Tunisia and Morocco, compared
with the large campaigns in Indo-China, were mere tea-parties and
certainly not 'threats to peace'. Only when in 1954 Indo-China
became an *international* question did the Asian leaders discuss it,
at the Colombo Conference of April 1954; as long as it remained
a straight fight between the Indo-Chinese and the French, contrary to
every precedent, they simply ignored this anti-colonial struggle.

The reason for this strange conspiracy of silence can only be that
the independent Asian governments recognised that the Indo-Chinese
movement was, at least in its leadership, Communist; and the world
Communist movement was still hostile to the new Asian states and
remained so till early 1954. India had trouble with the Communist
movement in Telengana till 1951, and Burma, Malaya and the Philippines struggled with Communist guerrillas throughout this period.
They could hardly be expected to give official support to a movement
that was allied with their own domestic enemies.

So with the one big remaining colonial problem in Asia put into
quarantine by the Asians themselves, and with the colonial problems
of Africa not yet acutely prominent, the anti-colonial impetus behind
the Afro-Asian movement no longer operated, at least not in sufficient strength to produce conferences.

The internal preoccupations of the new states was another reason
for diminished Asian enthusiasm. It was a discovery common to all
of them, that independence brought more problems, not fewer, and
they conserved their energy for the long, sustained, unspectacular
effort which the struggle for freedom had not required.

Lastly, India, or rather Mr. Nehru, who had played host to the
first two Asian conferences, was clearly less enthusiastic for further
meetings. In the space of a little over three years his attitude towards
the Asian movement shifted, as we have seen, from federalist unification, before the first conference, to co-ordination through the Asian
Relations Organisation, to inter-governmental consultation, as suggested at the Indonesian Conference. What were the reasons for the
reluctance of the key-figure in the Asian conference scene?

We may recall that he had always mentioned the necessity for an

Asian grouping as an alternative to a world organisation. If the
United Nations was not effective, he had said, regional alliances
might replace it. The United Nations record on Indonesia was not
encouraging, but it showed some disposition to act, and was almost
too ready to take action during the Korean crisis from 1950 onwards.
On other issues also, in the early 1950's, it was not wholly ineffective.
Above all it was clear that it would not function as a White Man's
Club, ready to push aside the Afro-Asians or to ignore them; a
separate Afro-Asian association was accordingly less urgent and
necessary.

Further, since the West perhaps irrationally feared the coming together of the Afro-Asians, it was undesirable to add to this alarm,
for politically and, even more, economically, the principal links of
Afro-Asia were still with the West.

Finally, Mr. Nehru scarcely concealed his impatience with the
anti-colonial hangover. India had been the coping-stone of the imperial arch; and once it had been removed, imperialism in Asia, and
even in Africa, was really at an end; therefore the liberation of other
colonial possessions was certain, and merely a matter of time. The
imperial tide was on the ebb, though some of the waves would occa-
sionally surge back towards the shore. When that happened, when
the Dutch took action in Indonesia or, later, when the Anglo-French
attack on Suez occurred he was to react strongly. But, as his speeches
show, he was basically aware that the old empires were moving out;
that was the great historic fact of the age, the geologic change in the
balance of power between the continents. Here was the root of his
reluctance to get too deeply involved in a movement which, in many
countries, was based on the premise that imperialism was a continuing danger. To be too deeply involved would embarrass him as a
practical politician, disturb him intellectually as a student of history,
and repel him as a fastidious man with no taste for angry shouting of
slogans over imaginary dangers. Because India, that is, Mr. Nehru,
was diffident about Asian conferences, because India could hardly be
left out of Asian conferences, the holding of such conferences by
those eager for them was subject to considerable delays.

Fortunately for the Afro-Asian movement, large international conferences were not its only form of manifestation. Many problems
raised by Afro-Asia in the years between 1949 and 1954—for example, the issues of Korea and North Africa—were not handled by
such gatherings, but they were dealt with by the United Nations,
where Afro-Asia had become a forceful presence. During this period

The Spur of Indonesia: the Second New Delhi Conference

the sustaining element of the movement was the Afro-Asian group in New York; and it is to that body that we must now turn.

When the two continents again meet face to face at Bandung, after an interval of years, they will wear a political aspect very different from that which they showed at the two Delhi meetings. The relentless intrusion of the Cold War involved military and political counter-moves, membership of pacts and the policy of non-alignment. Apart from the cessation of conferences, the years between 1949 and 1954 were a period of great fermentation and change for Afro-Asia.

NOTES TO CHAPTER IV

1. L. K. Rosinger: *India and the United States*, New York, 1950.
2. *Sydney Morning Herald*, issues of 5th and 8th Jan. 1949.
3. *Economist*, London, 8th Jan. 1949.
4. *New York Times*, 22nd Jan. 1949.
5. Speech to Indian Journalists Association, 16th Jan. 1949.
6. *Security Council Record*, 401st meeting, 17th Jan. 1949.
7. Information on what transpired in the private sessions has been obtained from a variety of official sources which wish to remain anonymous.
8. *See* Appendix A.1.
9. *New York Herald-Tribune*, 24th Jan. 1949.
10. *The Times*, London, 23rd Jan. 1949.
11. *New York Times*, 24th Jan. 1949.
12. The same sources as Note 7 above.
13. Ellen J. Hammer: *The Struggle for Indo-China*, Stanford, 1954. Note on p. 201 quotes a five-point programme presented to the earlier Asian Relations Conference by the Vietnamese and Indonesian delegations asking, *inter alia*, for the raising of the Vietnam question in the Security Council, immediate recognition of the two governments, joint action to prevent reinforcements reaching East Asia, and medical aid and volunteers.

CHAPTER V

The Afro-Asian Group in the United Nations

The Afro-Asian group in the United Nations was born shortly after 6 p.m. in a penthouse apartment at 817 Fifth Avenue, New York, on the 5th December 1950. The score of diplomats who met on that wintry evening to talk about events over their whiskies were not the usual caucus group in which most of the United Nations' work gets done. Their meeting was an anxious and urgent conclave, for what they discussed were questions of war and peace, and of life and death, being decided at that moment in fierce battles among the icy hills of North Korea.[1] Behind that meeting to consider the Korean crisis lay not only the sentiment of the Afro-Asian movement but, more directly, the urgings of a British and of an American diplomat, in addition to the pushing power of the Communist Chinese armies.[2]

The partitioning of the Korean peninsula into Russian and American zones of influence was one of the results of Russia's four-day war against the Japanese just before their capitulation. The independent governments that developed in the zones separated by the 38th Parallel were, naturally, Communist in the Russian north and non-Communist in the American south. In December 1948 the United Nations recognised only the southern regime and a United Nations Commission which had watch-dog duties, and of which India was a member, was installed. In September 1949 the Commission had warned the world of the possibility of a civil war and in the middle of June 1950, after a tour by its members, including the Indians, along the 38th Parallel, it noted and reported increased military activity to the north. When fighting began on the 25th June it was, therefore, in a position to issue an authoritative finding, with Indian concurrence, that hostilities had started with an attack from the north.

Consequently the two Afro-Asian countries which were then members of the Security Council, India and Egypt, had no hesitation in voting, along with seven other members, for a resolution which stated that North Korea had committed aggression, and called on it to cease fire and withdraw. Yugoslavia abstained on this vote and Russia was absent. India and Egypt were sufficiently convinced to abstain on a more mildly worded Yugoslav resolution, and this was defeated. It should be noted that this first, crucial resolution was passed in a mere matter of four hours, whereas in many other cases of equally clear aggression the Council has failed to issue a condemnation even after weeks, months or years. The Council is evidently malleable when pressure is applied by a great power.

The first example of Afro-Asian independence of judgement on a really vital Cold War issue came two days later. On the 27th June India and Egypt both abstained, for lack of instructions, on a second resolution which empowered the United Nations to give military assistance to South Korea. At one stage the Indian and Egyptian representatives were in adjoining booths outside the Council chamber desperately trying to contact their capitals by telephone, and wits suggested that they were switched in to one another. On the 30th June the Indian representative announced that India accepted the resolution as 'it was opposed to any attempt to settle internal disputes by resort to aggression'. The Egyptian, however, announced that he would not support it and gave two reasons: the conflict under consideration was only a phase in the struggle of world blocs (which, evidently, was of no direct concern to Egypt), and earlier examples of aggression against member states had not been acted upon by the United Nations. This was obviously a reference to the creation by the United Nations, against Arab opposition, of the state of Israel, whose very existence was in the eyes of the Arabs a continuing act of aggression. This was, then, an example of non-alignment inspired by pique or resentment, a negative *quid pro quo*.[3]

India's doubts about the United Nations' action in Korea began to emerge in September; a Congress Party resolution of that date laid down that 'while aggression had to be resisted in Korea the objectives of the United Nations should be clearly stated'. On the 15th September the United Nations' commander, General MacArthur, in a brilliant exposition of the strategy of the indirect approach, had left-hooked his forces ashore at Inchon in a movement that compelled the rapid evacuation of South Korea by the invaders. By the end of the month his forces were lined up along the 38th Parallel awaiting approval to cross it and thus attempt to reunify Korea by United Nations' military action.

To the great irritation, and even the anger, of the Western Powers, India opposed this step on the grounds that although it made sense militarily, it was politically wrong and unwise; for it would mean that the United Nations was acting in the same way as the North Koreans, and might well prolong and enlarge the conflict. India abstained on the resolution of the 7th October that authorised the crossing; only one other Afro-Asian, Indonesia, did so, all the others giving approval, including even the Arabs. To consolidate this 'victory' the United States pushed through the 'Uniting for Peace' Resolution, which authorised the General Assembly to mount Korea-type operations whenever required in the future, by-passing the Security Council and the power of veto in it. Once again in the voting India was the only Afro-Asian to abstain (along with Argentina). She believed that without the veto (which implies unanimity among the great powers) on questions of war and peace, the United Nations would become a mere weapon for one side or the other in the not-so-Cold War. The argument was valid; but the 'liaison officers', better and more accurately known as 'the arm-twisters', of the United States delegation had done a good job on the Afro-Asians and made them toe the line. After these two acts of lonely defiance, a storm of protest blew about the head of the Indian representative. He was singularly fitted to weather it.

Sir B. N. Rau was not only recognised as the father of the Afro-Asian group at the United Nations, he was during the first important weeks and months of its existence the embodiment of the best that it claimed to stand for: independence and honesty of judgement coupled with integrity of purpose. A civil servant and jurist of distinction, he had already made a major contribution as the chief architect of the Indian and Burmese constitutions. The clarity of his mind was reflected in an almost superhuman precision of expression. More important than these were his personal qualities of character. Sir B.N., as he was affectionately called, would never condescend to any expression of anger, nor was there in his calm mien any of that sanctimonious holier-than-thou attitude to which some of the Afro-Asians were later so prone; serenity was part of the man. Small and neat and white-haired, he was a birdlike figure. Long after his untimely death, the epithet used of him at the United Nations was 'saintly'—a word not often found on the cynical lips of international civil servants who are, and have to be, in the best and worst sense of the words, worldly-wise. He was a good man; and because of this links of personal regard and respect were maintained even among his most bitter antagonists—a factor that was to be important in the next few weeks.

The Afro-Asian Group in the United Nations

'Let your language be soft but make your facts deadly,' was one of Sir B.N.'s admonitions; and throughout October he followed it, warning the United Nations, now advancing triumphantly through North Korea, against approaching the Chinese border, lest this provoke a Chinese riposte. That, of course, happened in late November and early December, when Chinese 'volunteers' with savage strength sliced through the United Nations' lines. It was when these armies were reeling back in defeat that the Western representatives turned to Sir B.N. The feeling of these spokesmen of great powers that they could do this without fear of reproaches, or an 'I told you so', was perhaps the sincerest tribute they could pay him.

The first feeler towards friendship came from Mr. George McGhee, a United States Assistant Secretary of State, who saw Sir B.N. on the 13th November. By this time the first faint doubts of the wisdom of crossing the 38th Parallel were stirring uneasily in Western minds. Mr. McGhee asked why India and the United States could not get together more often; he handsomely conceded faults on both sides; Sir B.N. wrote, 'finally admitted the fault perhaps was on their side rather than ours'—as did most of Sir B.N.'s interlocutors. In a great burst of confidence Mr. McGhee went so far as to say that 'there is no reason why we should not consult India as fully as we consult the United Kingdom in all matters'. The one jarring note in this warm-hearted encounter was Mr. McGhee's reference to the decision of the United States at last to grant India aid.

When Anglo-American representatives next saw Sir B.N. they had much less flattering unction to lay unto their souls. This was in the last days of November and the first week of December. It was by now clear that, for the first time, an Asian antagonist had inflicted a decisive defeat on American arms, that all of North Korea would be lost, perhaps much of South Korea, too. In this situation, Sir B.N. was invited to rally Asian opinion in support of an appeal to the Chinese, asking them not to cross the 38th Parallel. The Western envoys hoped that the Chinese might show their fellow Asians a respect they had not paid to the world organisation that had refused to admit them to membership.

The envoys who repeatedly urged this action on Sir B.N. were Sir Gladwyn Jebb, the British Permanent Representative, and Mr. Ernest Gross, his American counterpart. This approach must have been a difficult one for Sir Gladwyn, whose ability was matched only by his arrogance. It was Sir B.N.'s personal qualities that encouraged such contacts, and made them easier.

The Afro-Asian Group in the United Nations

It was much the same with the Afro-Asians, for they, after all, had parted company *en bloc* with India on two decisive votes. Yet they responded to his invitation to the fateful meeting on the 5th and, without further reference to their governments, agreed with him that an appeal should be issued to China not to cross the 38th Parallel southwards. It was made the next day, the 6th December 1950, and was ignored by the Chinese; but that action by fourteen Afro-Asian representatives was the real beginning of group action by them in the United Nations. Sir B.N. describes it thus: 'That appeal, which was direct and sincere, had a powerful effect on public opinion here and elsewhere, and it gave the first indication to a distracted world that the countries of Asia had taken the initiative—as they would be immediately concerned—to prevent the outbreak of hostilities in the East, which might ultimately envelop the entire world.'

A hectic week followed at New York. No sooner had the Chinese crossed the Parallel than a six-Power resolution was introduced in the General Assembly to ask Peking to withdraw its forces from North Korea: Russia had already vetoed this in the Security Council. In Sir B.N.'s words the passing of this resolution 'would have been followed by another naming Chinese as an aggressor, which would have meant war between the United Nations and China, with the possibility of the Soviet Union joining China—in short a world war; and a good many delegations besides those of Asia felt that immediate action of some kind was necessary if only to stave off the six-Power resolution. Such was the position on the afternoon of the 11th December when the Asian delegations met to consider what to do'.

They decided to do two things. Thirteen of them sponsored a resolution creating a three-man committee to be composed of Sir B.N., Mr. Entezam of Iran and Mr. Lester Pearson of Canada, 'to determine the basis on which a satisfactory cease-fire in Korea can be arranged'. Simultaneously twelve Afro-Asian states (the Philippines having dropped out) sponsored a second resolution recommending that an unnamed number of governments should 'make recommendations for the peaceful settlement of existing issues'. It was understood that the governments would be China, Russia, the United States, the United Kingdom, France, Egypt and India. In short the Afro-Asians proposed one specific and one general line of action, and by this burst of group activity adroitly edged out the six-Power draft.

The two resolutions were tabled on the 12th December and the first was approved by a vote of fifty-two to five (the Communist

countries) with one abstention (Nationalist China). The second resolution was not pressed to the vote at this time because the sponsors
learned, somewhat to their dismay, that the Western Powers would
not support it. The unedifying manœuvres that lay behind this move
are best described in Sir B.N.'s own words. After explaining that the
two resolutions were 'the logical consequence' of the Afro-Asian
appeal to China, since 'the move for peace having once been started
could not be halted without betraying the hopes and aspirations of
the vast numbers who supported it', he writes:

> At this point I would say a word about the attitude and activities of
> the United Kingdom and some other European delegations. Although
> in private conversation these complained bitterly of the manner in which
> the United States had handled the situation, and although they urged
> us to do what we could to slow down if not halt the drift to war, when
> it came to speaking in committees or to voting, they followed the United
> States line. It became obvious to us that United States pressure was too
> great for them, and they were unable to act independently and according
> to their own better judgement.
> As regards the two Asian resolutions, the original draft was in the
> form of a single resolution. We clearly understood from the United
> Kingdom delegation that they would support them, whether separate
> or combined, as they agreed with the principle underlying them. The
> United States delegation, with which we repeatedly conferred on the
> day the Asian delegations were drafting the resolutions, promised full
> support to the first as well as (according to our understanding) to the
> second if the two were separated. Had we proceeded with the original
> single resolution, there might have been an end to the unity of the Asian
> delegations, as the Philippines were vehemently opposed to the second
> part while Pakistan, Egypt and some others were in two minds. To
> obtain the maximum support, therefore, we agreed to the splitting up
> of the resolution, but the next morning the United Kingdom delegation
> informed us that they could not possibly support the second resolution,
> which accorded exactly with a change in attitude of the United States
> delegation also. We therefore went ahead with the first resolution only,
> which was carried by an overwhelming majority. Although it fell a good
> deal short of the objectives which we had in mind, it did give us a
> breathing-space, and whatever may be its ultimate fate, in the larger
> context of world history, it will be recognised that a sincere and deter-
> mined effort was made by the Asian countries in the interests of peace.
> The United States attitude throughout this Korean business has left
> us with few illusions, if we ever had any, regarding United States policy
> which has been changeable and uncertain in the extreme, and has been
> conditioned by a bewildering variety of factors. In the first place there
> has been the fluctuating situation on the Korean battlefield, in the second
> place, the pressure of Republican opinion, in the third place, the general
> world situation. When the war situation has gone well, the Americans

have been tough in the extreme; when it has gone badly, they have talked of flexibility and peaceful settlement. Indeed, before the Asian resolutions were moved, Gross told me that the United States were actually considering making an approach to the U.S.S.R., to help them in securing a cease-fire. The Chinese, on the other hand, began not unreasonably, but they have been getting progressively more and more uncompromising. The one anxiety of most European Missions is to prevent United States involvement in a long and costly war in the Far East, leaving them exposed to the Soviet colossus in the West. But beyond pointing out that the real enemy is Russia, which can be tackled only in Europe, they have done little to stave off the threatening cataclysm in the East.

In view of these subsequent changes of attitude one cannot but wonder whether the original appeals by the American and British representatives were not motivated by something more than alarm; whether they were not an attempt to put China in the wrong with the Asian 'neutralists' and thus strengthen the case against her in face of world opinion. If such was the Western intention, the Chinese did what they could to help it along.

Soon after the Christmas recess on the 3rd January 1951, the Indian representative reported that the three-man commission had been unable to achieve progress towards a cease-fire because the Chinese, as might have been anticipated from the negative Communist vote, had refused co-operation. The Afro-Asian resolution, according to them, was 'illegal' and 'a trick' to cover up the United Nations' military defeats. There was nothing further the Afro-Asians could do to delay the six-Power resolution calling for a cease-fire and withdrawal by the Chinese; this was then passed.

The Chinese reply this time was not flatly negative, and in the next fortnight a bitter wrangle developed between India and the United States on its interpretation, with the latter claiming that the Chinese answer was, in effect a 'complete rejection' and India arguing that it had not slammed the door on negotiations. This was the prelude to a final clash between India and the United States.

As had been predicted by Sir B.N. a month earlier, the six-Power resolution was the prelude to another, condemning China as an aggressor, and a move towards this developed in late January. Once again the Afro-Asians attempted to baulk it. By their earlier initiative they had already gained time, more than a month, for the cooling of tempers, during which period the military situation had also become less desperate for the United Nations' forces in Korea: a vote now would not be taken in a highly-charged atmosphere, against the background of retreating American troops fighting desperate rear-guard battles.

The Afro-Asian move took the form of a revival of their second resolution, the proposed seven-nation commission this time being given two different tasks—the elucidation of the controversial Chinese reply, 'and the making of any incidental or consequential arrangements towards a peaceful settlement of the Korean and other Far Eastern problems'. The resolution was, of course, defeated, but it attracted six additional affirmative votes, and it split the opposition, with fourteen countries abstaining.

That was the last united effort of the Afro-Asians concerning Korea. Four days later, under maximum American pressure, the United Nations condemned China as an aggressor. India and Burma voted against and six Afro-Asians abstained: Saudi Arabia voted as 'not participating'.

Five months later, when the United Nations voted, on the 18th May 1951, to place an embargo on the export of strategic materials to Communist China it was, again, a depleted Afro-Asian group that abstained: Afghanistan, Burma, India, Indonesia, Pakistan and Syria.

The first two months of the Afro-Asian group's existence, December 1950 and January 1951, were undoubtedly its 'finest hour'. Sir B.N. rightly remarked that it would go on record 'that when the world had been marching toward disaster, most of the Asian powers had done all they could to halt the march. They might fail: but the true failure would have been a failure to try'. This period gave it a moral stature and political impetus that endured for several years.

But as the voting record shows the 'group' acted as a group only at a moment of real crisis and only on its own resolutions; on those sponsored by others, such countries as Lebanon, Iran, Iraq and Saudi Arabia could not resist Western pressure.

A more significant pointer to the future was India's frequent isolation from the group which at other times she led. Only Indonesia joined her in abstaining on the resolution that approved the United Nations' crossing of the 38th Parallel, and she was quite alone in her abstention on the 'Uniting for Peace' resolution.

This was not a distressful circumstance, for during this period the Indian delegation under Sir B. N. Rau's leadership, and because of it, gave a superb demonstration of what later came to be known as non-alignment—the judging of each issue separately and honestly on its own merits. Following a straight path down the middle, India condemned the North Korean aggression but also disapproved of the United Nations' forces attacking north across the 38th Parallel and of the Chinese doing likewise southwards. In later years when India's non-aligned course was dubious and wavering, it would be recalled, by others and by Indians, that there was this crisis during which 'neutralism' was positively practised, and was clearly and openly seen to be practised.

Before tracing the subsequent history of the Afro-Asian group at the United Nations, an answer should be given to the question why Sir B. N. Rau called the group into existence at all, since there was no absolute political necessity for it and since this was his personal initiative, taken by him in New York without instructions from New Delhi. Here one comes up against the strange, sad fact that while Sir B.N. was universally respected at the United Nations, Mr. Nehru did not accord to him the respect and confidence that he gave to later Indian representatives. Mr. Nehru seemed unable to forget that he had been a servant of the British Raj. Thus we find Sir B.N. asking for 'greater discretion' to be left to him and giving a long and almost apologetic explanation of how and why the group came into existence. 'The circumstances which led to this action have not been fully understood in India,' he writes; and since he is addressing Mr. Nehru it is clear that by 'in India' he means in Mr. Nehru's mind. He then goes on to describe how desperate and urgent the situation was in New York, how the other Asian representatives took the responsibility of acting without instructions from home and how much credit this had brought India: 'I daily receive dozens of letters and telegrams urging India to continue her efforts for peace.' And in conclusion he uses the ultimate argument of the good bureaucrat—that a line of retreat is open: 'I trust . . . that you will agree that we have not attempted to do more than we should or could have done, and that without shirking our inescapable responsibilities, we have taken all reasonable steps to safeguard fully our own position through this intricate labyrinth of discussions and negotiations.' There was then this melancholy personal reason behind Sir B.N.'s action—that an initiative taken in concert with other Afro-Asian countries would be more likely to gain the approval of New Delhi than one taken by him alone. Since his own views did not carry their full weight with Mr. Nehru, the Indian diplomat needed the added weight of Afro-Asian support, particularly at this juncture, to counteract the pro-Chinese reporting from the Indian Ambassador in Peking, Mr. K. M. Panikkar, to whose views Mr. Nehru, unfortunately, attached much importance. A man of considerable cleverness and erudition, Mr. Panikkar, after lengthy analysis, reached the conclusion, at about this time, that Chinese Communism would never become doctrinally dogmatic.

Sir B.N. had bigger reasons for promoting the Afro-Asian group. There was, as we have seen, the suggestion in this sense from the Western Powers; there was also the feeling, as he put it, that 'the responsibility for interpreting the viewpoints of Peking and Washington to each other was too grave for any one country to shoulder', a burden of responsibility and modesty that Mr. Krishna Menon did not feel at a later stage in the Korean episode.

China's attitude towards this Indian initiative was completely consistent with its subsequent behaviour. In 1950, with a completely unnecessary show of belligerence, its troops had 'liberated' Tibet in a way that India, all too meekly, accepted. At the commencement of that year's General Assembly India, as usual, led the fight for Communist Chinese representation in the United Nations. Just before the Afro-Asian initiative, Sir B. N. Rau tried to see General Wu, the Communist Chinese representative who had been invited to the United Nations to present China's case, but the General 'could not give him any time'. Once the Afro-Asian resolution was passed it was fiercely attacked by Peking. Peking, however, responded more mildly to the stronger Western resolution of the 13th January 1951. In short, India's self-assumed role of mediator on China's behalf earned it nothing but contempt, and even hostility, from China.

Two years later, when the Indian delegation made its next major intervention on Korea, it was under very different leadership and its liaison with the Afro-Asian group was the opposite of what it had been in 1950 to 1951. In June 1951 the Russians opened the way to negotiations on Korea; these began at Panmunjon in October. A year later the talks reached deadlock on the issue of the disposal of Korean prisoners of war in United Nations' hands. It was Mr. Krishna Menon who put forward an Indian formula in November 1952, and he, then and later, had little time for, or patience with the Afro-Asian group, a sentiment that its delegation leaders soon heartily reciprocated. This mutual distrust and dislike did not openly affect the group's policy, but only because of a continuing loyalty by the other delegates to the memory of Sir B. N. Rau. Accordingly the Indian resolution was not co-sponsored by any of the Afro-Asians, though some delegation leaders had expressed their willingness to do this. Mr. Krishna Menon made a gesture in their direction when for over two hours he talked to them about his resolution; but really he told them nothing, leaving them, almost certainly deliberately, less enlightened about it than before he spoke.

To a large extent Mr. Krishna Menon's motives in excluding the Afro-Asians from his move were as personal as those of Sir B. N. Rau when he drew them in. There is, first, the difficulty of personality. Intensely individualistic, with a capacious, lightning-swift intellect, Mr. Krishna Menon is virtually incapable of persuading or cajoling others because he can never see the necessity for it. Secondly, this initiative came at a delicate point in his career. He had just ceased being an official diplomatic representative and had not yet become a political leader: it was desirable that he should bring off an international settlement to enhance his prestige and, understandably, he had no desire to share the credit. Lastly, it may be said in his defence that delicate negotiations lay behind his resolution, and for reasons of security he could not share these secrets with many people: the Indian delegation itself, including its nominal leader, Mrs. Pandit, was kept as much in the dark on his ideas and intentions as were the Afro-Asians.

Once again, as with Sir B.N.'s first resolution, this Indian move was accepted by the West and angrily rejected by the Chinese Communists and their Russian allies. In one of his most vulpine attacks Mr. Vishinsky scathingly referred to Mr. Krishna Menon as 'that pathetic man'; after this the Indian representative called a press conference and launched a verbal onslaught on the United States.

Mr. Krishna Menon's secretiveness and his highly personal interpretation of non-alignment had a shattering impact on the Afro-Asian group from which it never really recovered. Never afterwards did it act as a group on any important Cold War issue. It continued to meet frequently, and to sponsor resolutions jointly, but these were on anti-colonial issues, such as Tunisia or Algeria or South Africa's apartheid policy, that were obvious points of common interest. Apart from this the group meetings kept the idea of Afro-Asia alive—a very important function; but for the most part the meetings were confined to the exchange of ideas and information, and did not attempt the formulation of group policy: from these gatherings the members emerged to vote separately, as the voting record clearly reveals. The continuous publicity given to the group's activities has concealed the fact that from the start it has been and is still the least cohesive of all the groups or caucuses in the United Nations.

In 1949, before the joint action on Korea, the Afro-Asians were unable, despite joint discussions, to evolve a common policy line even on a straightforward colonial issue like the disposal of the former Italian colonies. Syria and Egypt wanted the immediate, and India the 'almost immediate', independence of Libya, but not so the others. When Eritrea was granted autonomy Burma said it would have to become a self-governing unit, Pakistan suggested independence, Iraq proposed self-determination and Egypt reluctantly accepted, and Saudi Arabia indignantly rejected, the final resolution. Thus not even the smaller Arab caucus within the group was united.[4]

Once the group was constituted on an *ad hoc* basis, following its Korean resolution in the Fifth General Assembly of 1950, the number of identical votes cast by its members increased only slightly; but there was a considerable increase in its 'solidarity'—that is, members abstained rather than vote against the majority of the group.[5] This was a gain, but a negative one, and bears no relation to major Cold War issues. This is shown when the colonial and non-colonial votes of the group are considered separately. On 56 non-colonial votes taken up to 1955, the Soviet group reached unanimity within itself 56 times, West Europe 35 times, the Latin Americans 26, the Commonwealth 15 and the Afro-Asians only 9 times. Smaller caucuses within the group reached a much higher measure of agreement. On these non-colonial issues the Arabs were unanimous 33 times and India-Burma-Indonesia as often as 44. On colonial questions the Afro-Asian record is rather better. On 30 such issues the Soviets were unanimous 30 times, the Afro-Asians 17, West Europe 5, Latin American 4 times and the Commonwealth once. Here the Arabs agreed 29 times, and India-Burma-Indonesia 28. The conclusion is inescapable: the group is effective only on colonial questions; on non-colonial issues it has fewer agreements and more disagreements than any other group.[6] It was a symbol of Afro-Asian co-operation that the group was important in the years 1949 to 1955, but it is important to remember that it was little more than a symbol.

NOTES TO CHAPTER V

1. Information supplied by Mr. Rajeshwar Dayal, who was in 1950 India's alternative Representative on the Security Council.
2. Much of the information in this section comes from the papers of Sir B. N. Rau.
3. Carnegie Endowment for International Peace: *Egypt and the United Nations*, New York, 1957, chap. 4, entitled 'The Phase of Indifference and Resentment'. The Egyptian authors say: 'the position of Egypt on the Korean problem represented the culmination of this phase'.

The Afro-Asian Group in the United Nations

4. G. M. Dib: *The Arab Bloc in the United Nations*, Amsterdam, 1956, chap. 4C.
5. T. Horet: *Bloc Politics in the United Nations*, Harvard, 1960, pp. 87–90, for statistics on this point. A lively and penetrating study is also to be found in J. Maclaurin: *The United Nations and Power Politics*, London, 1951, chap. 5.
6. R. E. Riggs: *Politics in the United Nations*, Illinois, 1958, chap. 2.

CHAPTER VI

Pacts and Panchsheel, 1949 to 1954

N on-alignment: it was this new, hard growth within the larger, amorphous body of Asianism that tied India and Burma and Indonesia together as a coherent caucus within the Afro-Asian group.

A definition is the first necessity. Non-alignment is the desire and ability of an independent country, or more accurately, of a country that truly feels itself to be independent, to follow an independent policy in foreign affairs; it is the desire and ability to make up its own mind, to take its own decisions or not to take them, after judging each issue separately and honestly on its own merits. It seems strange that anything so simple, indeed obvious, should have been so misunderstood till one realises that much of the misunderstanding is and was wilful and deliberate. Some of this misunderstanding, per- haps, was due to perplexing changes in the designation of this new policy. It was first called 'neutrality', then 'dynamic neutrality', which passed into 'positive neutralism' that later became 'uncomit- ted' and finally 'non-aligned'.

Non-alignment and India have an especial association. It is gener- ally believed that Mr. Nehru conceived the idea and was the first Asian leader to apply it consistently in his country's foreign policy. At first India was almost alone in taking this line, particularly at the United Nations, as we have seen; but other Afro-Asian states adopted the approach, at first gradually, then more rapidly, so that practically all these countries now are, or claim to be, non-aligned in their foreign policies. This claim has not affected India's position as the fount and origin of non-alignment. To get to the roots of this political phenomenon, that developed with such extraordinary speed in the comparatively short space of seventeen years and gave Afro-Asianism a new basis, one must study the origins of India's foreign policy— that is to say, of Mr. Nehru's thinking on foreign policy.

It has often been said, not least by Mr. Nehru himself, that inde- pendent Indian India began its foreign policy in 1946–7 with a clean slate on which anything might be written. In terms of policy commitments this is true, but it is not true in any wider sense; for India, like every other country, was conditioned by a variety of inescapable limitations. India, and Mr. Nehru, were conditioned by geography, which gives India a central position on the Asian mainland and so predisposes it towards a continental Asian feeling. Geography has also given India a large, compact bulk within clearly-defined natural frontiers that eliminate territorial ambitions. India was conditioned by ancient history, in which she had developed ties of religion and culture with East, South-East and West Asia, and by modern imperial history and a non-violent nationalist movement, which impelled her towards anti-colonialism and anti-racialism, which made her apprehensive and suspicious of the return of imperialist influence through such things as pacts and military alliances, and which inclined her towards peaceful compromise settlements. Indian policy was conditioned too by India's poverty, which could only be overcome by large-scale long-term development. It was influenced also by the fact that India emerged into a world situation in which two super powers and their junior partners were contesting for world supremacy with bitter and barely-restrained antagonism in a cold war. There was, lastly, the massive and malign influence of India's own squabble with Pakistan. These were the given factors of geography, history, economics and politics: they do not include religion, to which has been attributed a spurious influence on Indian foreign policy.

Under the multiple impact of these pervasive forces, it is not surprising that India's foreign policy sprang fully developed from the mind of Mr. Nehru, like Minerva from the brow of Jupiter, and was enunciated in his very first pronouncement as *de facto* Prime Minister of India. In a radio speech on the 7th September 1946 he listed all its main elements: 'we propose, as far as possible, to keep away from the power politics of groups, aligned against one another, which had led in the past to world wars and which may again lead to disasters on an even vaster scale'; anti-colonialism and anti-racialism were likewise clearly indicated; along with the friendship for the Commonwealth, for America and for Russia; he desired close ties with Asia and especially with China; India, no longer 'a satellite' or 'a plaything' was going to make 'the history of our choice'.

But since India's foreign policy of non-alignment is, to an extent not found in any other large country, the inspiration of one man, Mr. Nehru, it is not wholly the product of vast impersonal forces. His personality, his vision, background and foibles, impinged on it, too, and helped to mould it.

Mr. Nehru was a proud man and an intellectual, and was proud of his intellect. Accordingly he strongly resisted any attempt to make him yield his right of individual judgement through blind obedience or subservience to the judgement of other leaders, even if they were leaders of large and powerful countries. 'I am not prepared even as an individual, much less as the foreign minister of this country, to give up my right of individual judgement to anybody else in other countries. That is the essence of our policy.'[1] And that is the essence of non-alignment. He was also a man of fastidious sensitivity who found the Cold War, 'this exhibition of mutual abuse', 'more degrading' than actual war. Over and over again he was wont to lament that 'we are being coarsened and vulgarised all over the world' by its practices, and he wonders 'whether anything of value in life will remain for sensitive individuals'.[2]

Though in his emotions Mr. Nehru was buoyantly optimistic, his cast of mind and his foreign policy analyses were darkly gloomy. His view of a whole series of crises was apocalyptic; war for him was always just round the corner. Since he cared for peace, since it was according to him constantly endangered, he worked hard to preserve it, even if his interventions were unasked for and unwelcome. His personal negativism gave to his policy a positive content of peaceful endeavour; it was understandable that caricaturists should replace the rosebud in his buttonhole with an olive branch.

Next to colonial experience, perhaps the strongest influences on Mr. Nehru's thinking on foreign policy were the events in Europe in the 1920's and 1930's, and the analysis given of them by the intellectual British leftists in the group around Harold Laski and the *New Statesman*. These influences were directly personal, for he visited Europe during this period, seeing Moscow in 1927 and Spain during the Civil War in 1938, and his writings at the time show how deeply moved and impressed he was by Europe's travail. His mental affinity with the English leftists and the climate of opinion reflected by the Left Book Club strengthened two political attitudes which are to be found in his later policies: these are a condescending attitude towards 'immature' America, which is too rich and powerful for its own good, and a tendency to give Russia the benefit of the doubt. It was easy to slip into the latter habit of thought between the Wars. Then, it was the Western capitalist-fascist countries that were on the offensive, in Ethiopia, in Spain, in Sudetenland and Austria—all with the acquiescence, even connivance, of the appeasing Western democracies.[3] It is difficult now, after the take-over of Czechoslovakia, after the Berlin blockade and Korea and Budapest, to think of Russia as a quiescent power; but in the 1930's she was on the defensive. The nearest Russian soldier was not at the Brandenburg Gate but near Brest-Litovsk, on the far side of a strongly anti-Russian Germany and an even more strongly anti-Russian Poland. Mr. Nehru saw a revolutionary Russia absorbed in internal tasks and struggles during its first two decades, and this perhaps influenced him to believe, as he often said, that a revolutionary China was similarly wholly absorbed with its internal problems. But whereas Stalin eliminated the world-revolutionary Trotskyists in Russia, it is their line of thought that has prevailed in China, alongside a veneration of Stalin.

In deciding that India's foreign policy should be one of non-alignment, Mr. Nehru was motivated by larger and impersonal reasons also, especially by that basic factor, national self-interest. In his speeches he refers to this a surprising number of times for one who was reputedly an idealist.[4] For example he once said, 'I do not think it [non-alignment] is purely idealistic; I think it is, if you like, opportunistic in the long run.'[5] Some of his reasons relate exclusively to India. Thus he frequently asserts that India could not be a camp-follower and must 'inevitably' follow an independent policy because of its great past and because it was not 'some odd little nation somewhere in Asia or Europe' but 'potentially a great nation and a big power'—one of the Big Four with America, Russia and China[6]; also because geography had placed it out of the line of fire,[7] and because, internally, non-alignment represented the highest common factor of agreement in Indian thinking on foreign policy.[8]

However, most of the reasons he provides for non-alignment—and they are numerous and convincing—apply equally to any newly-independent country in Asia and Africa. There is, for instance, the argument that the problems of the Cold War, and the 'isms' and ideologies behind it, are all European and remote from Afro-Asia.[9] Present-day blocs can change and dissolve, with allies quickly becoming enemies and vice versa.[10] The new countries have inherited no legacy of hatred towards either side in the Cold War; 'Why should we then start this train of hostility now with any country?'[11] In fact he doubts whether the differences between the great powers and their blocs are really ideological at all, whether they are not just the continuation of old nationalist struggles disguised by the same slogans about 'democracy' that were used in World War I.[12] Attacking the basis of the Cold War with military realism, he points out that there are only two great powers in the world today, and that since neither can destroy the other without destroying itself, they might as well talk to each other instead of trying to force minor allies to join up.[13] He appeals to Asian pride by asserting that Asia is now the equal of Europe and should not slip back into the position of a junior partner.[14] Perhaps his most persuasive argument, and certainly one that has been most frequently accepted and acted on by the Afro-Asians is: 'in accepting economic help, . . . it is not a wise policy to put all our eggs in one basket';[15] diversified help from both sides would obviously be both safe and more substantial.

Mr. Nehru combined the realistic and the practical when he emphasised that Afro-Asia needed a generation of peace to allow its plans of economic development to get under way,[16] and that non-alignment helped forward the great cause of world peace by holding the balance of power between the two sides; this it did by keeping them guessing and by extending the area of a non-military buffer zone[17]—an area which might yet save something from the wreckage of another war.[18] This reasoning not only provides non-alignment with a moral basis against the 'immoral' Cold War, it also enables Afro-Asia to play a distinctive part in great affairs.[19] But lest this ambition should lead to vaingloriousness he utters a warning that, apart from the Big Two, everyone else can have only a modest role[20] and that a non-aligned Third Bloc or Third Force would not only be a contradiction in terms, but not possible, since it has no force.[21] Since there was to be no organised bloc there was, naturally, no question of leaders and followers—certainly not according to Indian thinking, which ought to have been reassuring to smaller South Asian countries.[22]

It is surprising that despite this wealth of argument Mr. Nehru, perhaps out of politeness, perhaps out of policy, did not refer publicly to one of the most important reasons against complete commitment of Afro-Asia either to America or to Russia. Clearly, because of the interplay of political with economic systems, neither country is wholly attractive nor wholly repellent. In the United States freedom and political democracy are combined with racialism and the economic system of capitalist private enterprise—plus and minus factors. In the Soviet Union a planned economy that has produced impressive results is paid for by totalitarian state control of the individual—plus and minus again. The United States has no imperial past but is the ally of the imperial countries of Europe. Russia, too, has no imperial record in Africa and Asia outside the forgotten areas of Central Asia, but tries to interfere through local Communist parties that are, however, in most Afro-Asian countries too weak to be more than a serious irritant: plus and minus on both sides yet again. With this evenness of balance questions of Communism and anti-Communism are, in Mr. Nehru's words, 'trivial' and 'superficial'.[23]

It is strange and deeply regrettable that with this abundance of real and really valid reasons for the choice of non-alignment as a foreign policy, India has added to this concept various spiritual excrescences. For this unnecessary blurring of ideas originally clear-cut, Mr. Nehru himself is partly responsible, but the real damage has been done by his over-eager acolytes.

For them it was not sufficient that non-alignment was a policy that worked, that it was perhaps correct and even moral: it had to be elevated into a creed that was the embodiment of the Good and the True. It was not merely something contemporary and respectable, it had to be presented as ancient and venerable as well. All these subsequent interpretations have one thing in common: they are the expressions of a regressive and retrogressive Indian atavism. Misguided attempts to drape secular and political non-alignment in the sweeping robes of moralistic religiosity have had only one result: they have befuddled India, confused her friends abroad, and laid her wide open to the attacks of her enemies.

The aberration takes two forms: the first is to allege that non-alignment is non-violent and Gandhian, the other is to claim that it is pacifist and Buddhistic.

Mr. Nehru himself both erects and demolishes the Gandhian thesis. On the non-violent Gandhian impact he has this to say: 'it [non-alignment] is a policy inherent in the past thinking of India, inherent in the whole mental outlook of India, inherent in the conditioning of the Indian mind during our struggle for freedom', and 'basically our outlook is derived from that old outlook which Gandhi gave us and which made us powerfully in favour of peace and peaceful methods'.[24] But he has also said, 'I am not saying that a military approach can be completely given up in this world. I am not speaking like a pacifist';[25] 'we may not, in the world as it is constituted today, even rule out war absolutely';[26] 'I am not a pacifist. Unhappily the world of today finds that it cannot do without force'.[27]

If, as Mr. Nehru asserted, India's non-alignment is a product of the national movement, then it is certainly not intrinsically non-violent, for that movement was not so: the Congress Party made it clear to the Mahatma himself that it was merely using his technique of non-violent non-co-operation as a tactic because it lacked arms. Long before independent India emerged, it was also emphasised that it would not be a non-violent pacifist state.[28] Nor—with the Indian Army, Navy and Air Force—has India been so. Gandhi expounded his vision of free India as a torch-bearer of non-violence because she 'has an unbroken tradition of non-violence from time immemorial . . . her destiny is to deliver the message of non-violence to mankind';[29] but Mr. Nehru, despite his respect for his master, described this interpretation of Indian history as 'far-fetched and many Indian thinkers and historians did not agree with it'; nor did he agree with it himself.[30]

What then is left of the Gandhian imprint on non-alignment? The remaining traces are that it should not be 'a policy based merely on fear and passion',[31] and that it should be in favour of 'a peaceful solution of all international disputes'. In any century but our own harsh one these rules would be a commonplace of international behaviour. In Europe in the seventeenth and eighteenth centuries warfare was a tedious necessity left to the soldiers, while the civilians of the warring countries preserved between themselves the amenities of polite and cultured behaviour. It is a measure of the lowering of the standards of international conduct, rather than the elevation of Gandhian ethics, that the reasonable discussion of international disputes which non-alignment recommends is ascribed, inaccurately, to a latter-day saint. It surely derives as much from Mr. Nehru's aristocratic, non-pacifist loathing of vulgarity as from his upbringing in the tolerant, bi-cultural Hindu-Muslim society of his home state of Uttar Pradesh.

The Buddhist origins of the 'tolerance' and 'gentleness' of non-alignment seem more impressive because they are more ancient, and therefore less well known, but they are insufficiently founded on fact. Here we run into a powerful myth, the myth of the Mystic East and of Spiritual India. In fairness to the East and to India, it must be emphasised that this was the creation of the intellectuals of nineteenth-century Europe who, unsure of their own spiritual moorings, and for the first time in bedazzled contact with Indian religion and philosophy, built up an image of India as a source of spiritual wisdom, ignoring all other aspects of Indian life and thought. To a subjected India, deprived of all other elements of strength and pride, this was a flattering image which she readily accepted and finally believed in. And this etiolated stereotype was hardened by the non-violent tactic used by the national movement. Because this image reflected from the West lingers on in India, since 'it takes a long time for a new state to gain a sense of its own identity',[32] we find Mr. Nehru frequently referring to the Buddhist roots of non-alignment, and Mrs. Pandit writing: 'This particular [Indian] approach to peace is not new to India. It is her traditional outlook both philosophical and historical'—philosophically in Buddha and historically in the Emperor Asoka.[33] Here we must note that while reference is made by Mrs. Pandit, as by Mr. Nehru, to non-alignment being 'inherent in the past thinking of India, inherent in the whole outlook of India', their actual references are made not to the whole mental outlook of India but only to one small portion of its long history, to the period of Buddha and Asoka. There are compelling reasons for this extreme selectivity.

Hindu political thought is brutally, even sickeningly, realistic; it is so immoral as to be amoral, so disillusioned as to be beyond the range of cynicism. For nearly 3,000 years, from 1500 B.C. to A.D. 1300, through the works of a score of writers, and with what one Indian historian calls 'wonderful continuity', Indian political theorists taught that the substance of politics is power, coercion, embodied in kingship, whose sole object and sacred duty is to set up a strong 'collective and totalitarian' state at home, and to aggrandise itself abroad through war, which is an imperative obligation on a king.[34] This end justifies the use of every sort of means: lying, treachery, deception, corruption, torture, poisoning, spying, even the deliberate exploitation of religion (to raise money) and of priests (as spies). There are twenty classes of persons with whom peace should not be made; and neutrality is to be observed only when the outcome of a war is not certain victory. These ideas are commonly associated with the treatise *Arthasastra* of Kautilya, the adviser of the Emperor Chandragupta in the fourth century B.C. But similar ideas had been expounded for a thousand years before him by a long line of authors. The same single-minded devotion to force is to be found in the works of the great lawgivers Manu and Yajnavalkya, in the epics of the *Ramayana* and *Mahabharata*, even in collections of tales such as the *Panchatantra* and the *Hitopadesha*.[35] Kautilya is often compared to Machiavelli: this is unfair to Machiavelli, whose ideas of power politics were inspired by Italian patriotism, whereas the ruthlessness of these Indian thinkers is detached and coldly scientific—their faithful modern disciples are Hitler and Stalin, not Mr. Nehru. Thus the mainstream of Hindu Indian political thought runs completely counter to the moral attributes ascribed to non-alignment.

After the Buddha, Indian political thought was partially 'sicklied o'er with the pale cast' of Buddhist and Jaina theorising, according to which power leads to unhappiness and the duty of asking is to foster virtue. This non-Hindu strain was also expounded in numerous treatises for many centuries,[36] till Hinduism reasserted itself and Buddhism disappeared from India.

But it is not in these ancient and obscure texts that Mr. Nehru finds the links between Buddhism and non-alignment, but in the practice of the Emperor Asoka, who in the third century B.C. renounced war as a means of policy and propounded the Buddhist faith through sermons inscribed on pillars, and in rock-carvings scattered all over India. There are about twenty-five of these edicts in which a somewhat self-righteous ruler inculcates a grim piety. From these twenty-five Mr. Nehru picks out one, the only one of its kind, and quotes it in several of his books. In this precept Asoka says that a person ought not to 'extol one's own sect or disparage another on unsuitable occasions, or at least to do so only mildly on certain occasions. On each occasion we should honour another man's sect, for by doing so one increases the influence of one's own sect and benefits that of the other man'. This qualified recommendation to tolerance, put into contemporary political terms, emerges—because it hints that there is no monopoly of the truth—as a refusal to ally oneself with one bloc or one ideology; in short, as non-alignment.

This is admittedly an extremely slender base on which to build a Buddhistic connection with non-alignment; and it is all the more surprising since, as Mr. Nehru himself says: 'The pessimism of Buddhism did not fit in with my approach to life, nor did the tendency to walk away from life and problems.'[37] The link is so improbable, and so unconvincing on the evidence, as to prompt the suspicion that it was deliberately thought up to serve a political purpose. An Indian biographer of Asoka[38] suggests that the Buddhist Emperor used his religion politically as a force to unify India; other historians believe that the Moghul Emperor Akhbar tried to produce his own syncretic religion for the same purpose. Was a later Indian ruler, Mr. Nehru, trying to do the same, even unwittingly? Was he, by connecting non-alignment with Gandhi and Asoka, trying to anchor his policy in the Indian past, proximate and remote, and to root it in the Indian veneration for these great leaders? Moreover, the Buddhist connection might also make non-alignment more acceptable to India's devoutly Buddhist neighbours, Ceylon and Burma (and even to Indonesia where Islam has been marked by Buddhism), neighbours with

123

whom Mr. Nehru always wanted close relations. Yet by trying in this way to find some roots of non-alignment in Buddhism, Indian theorists are not doing non-alignment any good, for they are limiting its appeal to one cultural religious pattern and to one particular area in Asia.[39]

In passing, one may note that the concept that peaceable, tolerant Buddhism passed this element on to non-alignment is so generally accepted that even someone like Mrs. Pandit felt able to say[40] that Buddhism was responsible for the peace that has generally prevailed among Buddhist countries. This is utterly contrary to the facts because, notwithstanding their Buddhism, the Burmese, the Thais, the Laotians, the Cambodians and the Annamese fought prolonged and bloody wars till European conquest put a stop to them: the Burmese sacking of Ayuthia in 1767 is still a theme in Thai songs and plays.[41]

Buddhism as a religion, if it is one,[42] is no better and no worse than any other. Non-alignment as a policy is no worse and perhaps a little better than other policies for Afro-Asia, because it is practicable and profitable and fits the spirit of the age. The attempt by some people in India to give to it an aura of moral superiority borrowed from Buddhism is neither necessary, nor valid, nor correct. But one more supremely foolish borrowing was to be made.

Besides the many general reasons provided by Mr. Nehru which would commend non-alignment as a foreign policy to the countries of Afro-Asia, each of them had its own special reasons for accepting the policy dictated by separate national interests which can never be identical.

Indonesia, which adopted non-alignment as soon as she became independent, did so, according to former Vice-President Hatta,[43] because, unlike Belgium, she was not on an invasion route; because she needed a diverse market for her varied products, which otherwise would tie her to the economies of a few countries; because the Indonesian people are traditionally friendly to all races, and because a foreign alignment would make the task of internal reconstruction more difficult: this was probably a delicate reference to the existence in Indonesia both of a strong right-wing Muslim party and of a stronger Communist one.

Burma, too, freely chose non-alignment for geographic reasons that are the opposite of Indonesia's. With two great neighbours, non-Communist India and China—Communist from 1949—a middle way was the least controversial position to adopt. Heavily dependent on finding markets for its major crop, rice, Burma, after a world surplus developed in 1953, found her main buyers in the Communist bloc. At the same time she was plagued with local Communist insurgents whom Premier U Nu, with comical forthrightness, described as 'stooges and veritable sons of bitches who sell their national birthright for a mess of pottage'. On the other hand the United States was competing with Burma on the world rice market, and was at least morally responsible for the presence of Kuomintang deserters and freebooters who were harrying eastern Burma in 1953–4. There was equal revulsion against both sides in the Cold War.

If Indonesia and Burma freely chose non-alignment, Laos and Cambodia had non-alignment thrust upon them by the Geneva Agreement of 1954. Like Austria they are wedged in tightly between the blocs and like Austria they were neutralised, at least supposedly so. This is probably why the leaders of these two countries preferred to say that they were neutral rather than neutralist or non-aligned. In 1956 Prince Souvanna Phouma, said 'ours is a position of complete neutrality like Switzerland's. There is no question of neutrality between philosophies but only of neutrality between two military blocs'. Norodom Sihanouk, the Prince-President of Cambodia, was equally specific: 'We are neutral in the same way as Switzerland and Sweden are neutral—not neutralist like Egypt or Indonesia,' and for reasons of security, so as not to 'risk provoking the Chinese and Soviet colossi', and by eliminating 'any pretext for aggression'.[44]

Its geographic position, wedged between China and India likewise pushes Nepal into the non-aligned group. And Afghanistan, perhaps the doyen of the non-aligned, began practising the policy for similar reasons several generations ago.

Ceylon's non-alignment is a by-product of tea and rubber: the first she sells almost exclusively to Western countries, the second, again almost exclusively, to Communist countries. After a large-scale agreement in 1952 for the exchange of her rubber for rice from Communist China (which China bought from Burma), Ceylon had little alternative but to be nominally non-aligned, though her governments till 1956 were openly pro-Western in their sympathies.

The non-alignment of the Arab states is principally the result of anger over the creation of the state of Israel, which was approved by both the United States and the Soviet Union. For Egypt, till 1955, non-alignment was the product of dual revulsions: from the West represented by Britain, because she had troops on Egyptian soil, and from Russia, because she supported the Egyptian case but was

125

governed by atheistic Communism. Even after 1955, when Egypt became dependent on Russia for arms, closer *rapprochement* was impossible because of President Nasser's steadfast rejection of Communism as the solution for Egypt's problems. For little Lebanon, with its population evenly divided between pro-West Christians and anti-West Muslims, the compromise of non-alignment was inevitable; indeed she has to be doubly neutral in Arab affairs between the neutralists and the non-neutralists.

As for the new states of Africa, non-alignment had become so much a cliché of Afro-Asian politics by the time they attained independence that they really had little choice but to swim with the tide, that is, if they were not economically dependent on outside powers, especially on France, as many of them were and are. Non-alignment is an easy policy for Africans to implement, because Africa is geographically far from the crunch-zone of the Cold War, because this policy opens the way to economic aid from both sides, and because it might conceivably help in keeping that continent an atom-free zone.[45] This last argument counts much with those parties in Japan who would like to see her among the non-aligned.[46]

Finally, Yugoslavia found herself non-aligned, because as a Communist heretic she was anathema to the true believers in the Communist camp, and as some kind of a Communist she was unacceptable to the West.

A rapid sweep through the wide gamut of motives of the non-aligned reveals that this policy is a capacious house of many mansions, the central meeting point of a great variety of national interests that reach the same end from exactly opposite directions.

For example, anger with the two blocs brought some countries, such as the Arab states, to non-alignment: the absence of hostility to anyone was the motive of others, such as India. The politico-geographic squeeze of large neighbours forced Nepal, Laos and Cambodia to non-alignment: whereas their position of strategic 'openness' furnished the impulse to Indonesia and India. The proximity of a great power makes non-alignment the path of safety for Afghanistan: while the remoteness of the powers makes this policy possible for Ghana. India's vastness pushes it towards non-alignment: for Lebanon it is its smallness. A free choice of non-alignment was made by most of Afro-Asia; but it was dictated to a few, Cambodia and Laos. Varied markets for its numerous primary products made non-alignment an economic necessity for Indonesia, and because they were tied to limited markets for their few crops it was equally a necessary policy for Burma and Ceylon. Because they did not wholly favour either of the two sides in the Cold War, most of the Afro-Asian countries turned to non-alignment as the third course, but Yugoslavia did so perforce, because neither of the sides wanted her.

A policy that is adopted for such a variety of reasons clearly fills a need and is versatile and adaptable. It is not, as we have seen, in need of moral underpinning. Still less is it in need of a moral super-structure. But that is what India planted on it—a vast, flimsy confection that crumbled at the first shock.

The Afro-Asian movement is curious in that one can pin-point with precision the decisive moments in its development, usually at a social or semi-social function. It began over the teacups in Mrs. Pandit's suite in a San Francisco Hotel in June and July of 1945; and the Afro-Asian group at the United Nations held its first meeting over drinks in Sir B. N. Rau's penthouse living-room in New York on the 5th December 1950. The next stage in Afro-Asian non-alignment, the period of the Five Principles or Panchsheel, began over the coffee after a state dinner in the vast and splendid banqueting hall of the palace of the former viceroys in New Delhi, on 23rd September 1954.

The Five Principles, not yet called Panchsheel, were first listed, rather incongruously, as part of a long, detailed and prosaic Agreement on Trade and Intercourse between India and China relating to Tibet, issued in Peking on the 29th April 1954. For the most part, the document deals with the movement of traders, pilgrims, porters and mule-drivers between India and Tibet; it lists the market-places they may use and the passes in the Himalayas through which they may cross. It is in the section on trade that the two governments state that, to facilitate pilgrimage and travel, they entered on this agreement based on the following principles:

1. Mutual respect for each other's territorial integrity and sovereignty.
2. Mutual non-aggression.
3. Mutual non-interference in each other's affairs.
4. Equality and mutual benefit.
5. Peaceful co-existence.

This utilitarian document was signed by a Chinese Vice-Minister of Foreign Affairs and by the Indian Ambassador to China.[47]

The principles, still not called Panchsheel, were given maximum importance when Mr. Nehru and Mr. Chou En-lai put them forward, for the first time, as a universal panacea for peace a joint statement in from New Delhi, on the 28th June 1954. The two premiers said, 'If these principles are applied not only between various countries but also in international relations generally, they would form a solid foundation for peace and security and the fears and apprehensions that exist today would give place to a feeling of confidence.'

This was the first move in a vast propaganda campaign that was to be mounted in the next five years jointly by the Communists and the non-aligned. For the Communists, and as subsequent events have shown, especially for the Chinese Communists, it was a tactic aimed at relaxing vigilance in the opponent by lulling him into a sense of false security. For the non-aligned it was an attempt to preserve the peace from the loftiest moral motives. It is the moral tinge that is the distinguishing characteristic of the Panchsheel period and that enters when the Five Principles are given that name. This is because the Panchsheel of non-alignment is in the line of descent from two other groups of Five Principles, of which the first was wholly religious and ethical, and the second partly so. The first was the Pansil of Buddha, the first five of his Ten Commandments propounded 2,500 years ago; these are: not to take life, not to steal, to be chaste, not to lie and not to drink intoxicants (among the second five command-ments are prohibitions on dancing and music, flowers and ornaments and the use of wide beds). The second set of Five Principles are the Pantja Sila propounded by Dr. Sukarno in Indonesia on the 1st June 1945. These philosophic bases of the state of Indonesia are: national-ism, humanism, freedom, social justice and faith in God.

In September 1954 the Indonesian Premier, Dr. Ali Sastroamid-jojo, was visiting New Delhi to persuade, or rather to plead with, Mr. Nehru to agree to the holding of an Afro-Asian conference (that which later became the Bandung Conference); in the course of a speech to the Indian Parliament he mentioned Indonesia's Pantja Sila. That same night Mr. Nehru in a speech after dinner given in Dr. Ali's honour said: 'We talk also of another Panchsheel or Five Principles which have recently come to the fore. You may call them Panchsheel also in the same way, which on the face of it, is difficult to imagine how to oppose them or dislike them unless one thinks that behind them is hidden some evil motive'—which was the case. However, it was in this sentence, of doubtful syntax, that Mr. Nehru launched Panchsheel into international affairs.[48]

By the time of the Bandung Conference, eight months later, Panchsheel had been accepted as the regulating basis of relations between India and China, North Vietnam, Yugoslavia and Cambodia, and between Burma and China and Yugoslavia.[49] What did Mr. Nehru, one of its two parents, see in Panchsheel? He admits, perfunctorily, that 'there is nothing new about it. No great truths may be new'; but on many other occasions he not only asserts that they are 'great truths' but that there is something new in them: 'a new application' in 'a particular context'; 'both the countries [India and China] raised a new voice in the world—the Panchsheel', and so on. Clearly he genuinely thought that Panchsheel was an active and practical formula for peace: 'They have not only spread in the world and influenced more and more countries, but they have acquired progressively a greater depth and a greater meaning too.'[50] He even refers to 'the force of a correct policy like Panchsheel' and 'you see the force of our idea: how although it is not acted upon, yet, nobody dare deny it'.[51] And besides being 'new', and 'correct' and forceful, Panchsheel was also of course ancient and Indian: 'it has been our way of life and is as old as our thought and culture,' he said, and then that single, seriously-worded edict of Asoka makes its appearance again.[52] How much of his policy Mr. Nehru came to hang on that one ambiguous carving on the rock! First it was non-alignment, now it was Panchsheel and peaceful co-existence. A final quotation: 'we welcome association and friendship with all and the flow of thought and ideas of all kinds, but we reserve the right to choose our own path. That is the essence of Panchsheel'—which makes it no more than an elaborate re-statement of the essential idea of non-alignment. But it was a re-statement of other ideas, too.

Even an official publication of the Indian Government admits that 'Panchsheel is a re-statement, in more specific terms, of the principles embodied in the United Nations Charter. In point of fact that Charter is more specific. The first of the Principles is contained in Articles 2(1) and 2(4) of the Charter; the second Principle in Articles 1(1), 2(3) and 2(4) and the third Principle, non-interference in internal affairs, stems from Article 2(7). This last is an irony, for 'Two-Seven' is a familiar foe of the Afro-Asians at the United Nations, the first hurdle they invariably had to cross before they could get their anti-colonial items inscribed on the agenda. The fourth Principle is covered by Articles 2(1) and 2(5); and the fifth, co-existence, is amply defined in the words of the Charter Preamble, 'to practise tolerance and live together in peace with one another as good neighbours'.[53] There are derivations too: the second Principle harks back to the Articles for the Pacific Settlement of International Disputes in

Pacts and Panchsheel, 1949 to 1954

The Hague Conventions of 1899 and 1907, and the Paris Pact of 1928: while the fourth Principle on 'mutual benefit' equates with the most-favoured nation clause that usually forms part of trade treaties.[54]

A more serious criticism of Panchsheel is that the third Principle, that of non-interference, can freeze the *status quo*. Mr. Nehru admits as much: 'you will see that the only way to avoid conflicts is to accept things more or less as they are.'[55] This same principle, it has been pointed out by Dr. Hatta of Indonesia, puts the democracies at a disadvantage *vis-à-vis* the Communist states—'democracies cannot interfere in Communist states but the latter can, through local Communist Parties', and he concludes 'this is a risk which a democratic state . . . must be prepared to accept'.[56]

There is above all the question whether Panchsheel, unlike non-alignment, leads to co-existence between good and evil, between aggression and non-aggression. According to some Asian leaders it does not. We have seen Prince Suvanna Phouma of Laos saying that neutrality applies only to blocs, not to their philosophies; Dr. Hatta asserted that there could be no neutrality for any United Nations member; and President Nasser has said, 'We are not neutral morally.'[57] There is also Mr. Nehru's famous statement to a joint session of the United States Congress: 'Where freedom is menaced or justice threatened or where aggression takes place, we cannot and shall not be neutral.'[58] But that was said in 1949, and the later obliquities of Panchsheel soften this resolve considerably.

The final and fundamental question about Panchsheel is this: Why should anything so obviously and repetitiously platitudinous have been promulgated at all? The motive of one of the co-authors is all too clear: for we now know that it was about this time, the middle of 1954, that the Chinese were taking the first decisions to build their military road through Indian territory in Kashmir; Panchsheel provided an effective smoke-screen. But what were the motives of Mr. Nehru? Was the world situation so inflamed that it was in need of a soothing emollient?

It was not so; there were, rather, several hopeful signs. The first of these was Stalin's death in 1953 followed fairly quickly by a relaxation under Malenkov's leadership. Later in 1953 the Korean armistice was finally signed. In 1954 an armistice in Indo-China was achieved. If the fires of war were being extinguished there was less need than before for new all-purpose extinguishers like Panchsheel.

India's situation in the world, too, was not unfavourable. Since

1950 she had signed twelve Peace or Friendship Treaties with a variety of Asian countries from Japan to Turkey.

We can find adequate motive and justification for Panchsheel only in the precise circumstances that gave it birth: that is, in India's relations with China as they affected Tibet. Mr. Nehru himself said that the Treaty on Tibet was 'the result of long correspondence' between India and China, perhaps during all the four years that had elapsed since the Chinese 'liberation' of Tibet. To this he added, curiously, 'Premier Chou En-lai was not personally concerned with this matter, though no doubt he must have been consulted as I was in India.'[59] The phrase could mean that the bargaining was over the trade rights of the merchants and the transit facilities of the pilgrims, rather than over the wording of the Five Principles in the Trade Agreement. Nevertheless it was the Principles that were of importance to him, for by this time he had begun to feel some anxiety over the presence of a strong, unified China along 1,800 miles of frontier. Certain small, preliminary military precautions were ordered along the border. But the idea of war between India and China was utterly abhorrent to him not only because war, any war, was a bad thing but because conflict between the two biggest Asian countries ran counter to his vision of the continent going forward in brotherly co-operation. As far back as 1950 he was writing, 'I am sure that it is of great importance to Asia and to the world that India and China should be friendly.' 'I have the strong feeling that the future of Asia is rather tied up with the relations of India and China. I see that both the United States and the United Kingdom on the one hand and the Soviet Union on the other, for entirely different reasons, are not anxious that India and China should be friendly towards each other.' This led to the directive that India should not 'support them [the Chinese] in everything. But we must not line up against them anyway.'[60]

Panchsheel represented the least objectionable way of 'lining up'. It should, on the one hand, soothe China's fears, allay her chronic suspicions and convince her that in India she had a friend. On the other hand, it might draw China out of her embattled isolation, and by pledging her to non-interference and non-aggression, pin her down to a peaceful policy, and commit her, through her own solemn undertakings, to staying within her own boundaries.

In the event, this moral-diplomatic interdiction failed to work with the Chinese, because from their side, and almost from the beginning, they used Panchsheel simply as a delaying and confusing manœuvre.

Mr. Nehru's limited, tactical deployment of Panchsheel in the defence of India's integrity and security produced the result opposite to that which he expected.

This local failure of Panchsheel inevitably adds an edge to the criticism of Mr. Nehru and of all the other national leaders who attempted to elevate it into a new, effective principle for the achievement of peace on earth. Mr. Nehru made the point, as an argument in its favour, that none could oppose the Five Principles. This is ingenuous when one admits, as one must, that they merely rephrase the bases of ordinary good-neighbourliness between states. One might as well ask how anyone could be for Sin or against Motherhood.

If adults seriously commend the blowing of soap bubbles as a worth-while occupation, one is entitled to doubt their seriousness. The same is true of the leaders of many lands who solemnly commended Panchsheel. For serious men to spend time on political trivialities, which are so because they are platitudinous, betrays an irresponsible levity. That indeed is the most serious criticism that can be brought against Panchsheel—that it raised hopes among the ordinary peace-hungry people of the world, hopes which it could not possibly fulfil. Nowhere was this more tragically exemplified than in Afro-Asia.

As non-alignment at this stage, in 1954 and 1955, begins to emerge from the chrysalis of Afro-Asianism, we can with safety strip from it some of its stifling, moral wrappings. It was, essentially, the product of a variety of realistic general motives and of a realistic variety of national interests. It had, and has, no specific connection with pacifist Buddhism or Gandhianism, nor with Panchsheel and peaceful co-existence. The latter, it should not be forgotten, appeared only eight years after non-alignment had begun to develop as a separate organism within the amorphous mass of Afro-Asianism. Another and perhaps an even tougher growth had begun to develop within the parent body at about the same time.

A variety of reasons as large as that which impelled some Afro-Asian countries towards non-alignment, moved other Asian governments to choose the opposite course—of alignment with one side or the other in the Cold War through military pacts.

Those countries that did so entirely of their own free will, without crushing compulsion from circumstances, are five in number: Iran, Iraq (pre-1958), Pakistan, Thailand and the Philippines. These could have been non-aligned but chose not to be so.

For some of the Asian countries that 'chose' alignment there was really no choice. Once the Communist-led revolution succeeded in China, a military link-up of China with the Communist motherland, Russia, was inevitable, quite apart from any fear of the United States. The same was true of North Korea and North Vietnam.

Similarly the actual physical presence of American forces in Japan and South Korea gave those countries no option but to be in the United States' camp. When India suggested that the United States should permit Japan the appearance of entering freely into military alliance, by signing this document even a few hours after the Peace Treaty that gave Japan independent status, the suggestion was scouted by a distrustful America; and the military agreement was signed while Japan was still an occupied country.

It was history and geo-politics that gave Turkey no choice but the Western alliance. It is true that she was neutral during World War II and for the most part neutral towards the Nazis. But after bravely rejecting a request from Germany at the time of Stalingrad, when German power was at its height, that Turkish ports should refuse refuge to the Russian Black Sea fleet, Turkey was ill-recompensed by Russia. Immediately after the War, Russia revived Tsarist claims, repudiated by Lenin himself, to the territories of Kars and Ardahan, and asked for military bases in Turkey in the area of Istanbul. This monstrous demand, which the Turkish Ambassador rejected without leaving Mr. Molotov's office, revived so vividly the strong Turkish traditional hatred of Russia that Turkey, swallowing its equally strong pride, forced its way into NATO after a long struggle against the open reluctance of the other member states. So much for the Asians aligned willy-nilly.

The official reason given by the Asians who have freely joined with non-Asians in military alliances is that by this means they are defending the 'free world' against the threat of Communist domination. There is here the same degree of smirking hypocrisy as when others say they are non-aligned to save the world from war by enlarging the area of peace. In both cases the real reason is national interest. In Iran, for instance, a feudal monarchy was likely to feel itself threatened by a belligerent Communist Russian neighbour, who had set up separate Communist regimes in Iranian Kurdistan and Azerbaijan in 1946, and who had to be ordered out of Iran by the United Nations in 1947. Iran could conceivably have stood on her own, like monarchist Afghanistan, but she felt cosier under the anti-Communist blanket provided by America.

Monarchist Iraq, before 1958, also claimed to feel threatened by a greedy Russia only a few hundred miles away from her rich oil-fields. Before considering joining the Baghdad Pact in 1954, Iraq went through the motions of seeking military protection from the non-aligned. The Iraqi Premier, Nuri Said, visited Mr. Nehru and said that Iraq would not sign on with the West if India, in case of need, would, as she had done in two World Wars, send troops to defend Iraq, obviously against a Russian attack. Even if the Indian Army could have assumed such a large military responsibility, there was little chance of Mr. Nehru's agreeing to play a protective military role at a time when India was just about to seek protection in Panchsheel. In fact the fears of Russia then professed by Iraq do not seem justified. She may have thought that by pleasing the Western governments she could wean them away from Israel—a forlorn hope. One other possible reason was her expectation that the military aid which would come to her under the alliance would bolster her strength and importance within the Arab world *vis-à-vis* Egypt, now under the dynamic leadership of Colonel Nasser. Certainly Iraq's actual entry into the pact was marked by singular confusion and charges of broken promises from the other Arabs.[61]

Pakistan's reasons for joining both the Baghdad Pact and SEATO are very simple: she wanted arms and political support against India —who, she said, was a threat to her especially because of their dispute over Kashmir. India at the time said that this was Pakistan's reason, and after a while, Pakistani spokesmen, by no means *sotto voce*, said so too;[62] the United States, naturally, had to disclaim any such motive. But it has since become absolutely clear that Pakistan never had any fear of attack from Russia or China, against whom the Baghdad Pact and SEATO were organised. Besides acquiring modern weapons free of charge, it was Pakistan's hope that by giving the Western Powers what they wanted by way of base facilities and political support, she would draw them to her side over Kashmir, particularly in the voting on this question in the Security Council. These hopes were disappointed, perhaps because on account of India's size and growing importance, neither the Western governments separately, nor these alliances collectively, were prepared to antagonise her by giving outright support to Pakistan on the issue of Kashmir.[63]

Thailand's reason for joining SEATO was a direct fear of Communist China. A leftist Thai leader, Pridi Panomyong, had been granted asylum there, and was allowed a certain degree of political activity, directed against the Thai Government; a Thai Autonomous Area had been set up just across the Chinese frontier, and there was a strong Chinese minority within Thailand. Only a genuine apprehension could have pushed Thailand out of the posture of neutrality that she had maintained profitably in two World Wars. Hence the Thai Foreign Minister, Prince Wan, could say, with some justification: 'Thailand has tried many policies in the past, such as those of neutrality and of non-aggression treaties, but found that they did not work, nor can any reason be seen why they should work now.'[64]

The Philippines were also afraid of China but, as with Iraq, one doubts the real strength of these fears, for at no time was there any serious possibility of the Chinese launching an airborne or seaborne landing across hundreds of miles of open sea. The Philippines itself did not take its worries too seriously; it agreed to join SEATO with some hesitation.[65] Perhaps its real reasons were economic: if the United States were pleased by the grant of base facilities, the economic assistance, both governmental and through private enterprise, that the Philippines needed would be more readily forthcoming.

Why, in 1954, when the Baghdad Pact and SEATO were pieced together did the Western Powers want Asian military allies? Why was it not possible for them to leave Asia alone? The purely military reason was the need not for Asian manpower, but for bases on the Asian mainland to surround and contain the Eurasian heartland. Even in purely military terms this reasoning does not carry conviction. For no bases of any very great use or importance were ever established in Iran or Pakistan or Thailand. Those that were set up have not added much, if anything, to the offensive or defensive power of the forces using already established bases in Turkey, Formosa and Japan. The same purpose could have been achieved through bi-lateral treaties between the United States and these countries; they need not have been grouped into alliances. This grouping, because of its convenience for co-ordinated planning, would have been understandable if the alliances had been assigned a vital military role, but they never were; and today CENTO and SEATO are anaemic organisations trying, apologetically, to pretend that their real function is economic uplift. The real reasons for the creation of these pacts, as for the concoction of Panchsheel, were not military or political but moral.

Looking back on all the time and energy wasted by Mr. Dulles on the construction of these two clumsy and valueless alliances, and all

the effort wasted by Mr. Nehru in opposing these brainless, vege-
tarian brontosaurs of international politics, one comes to this conclusion: the natural development of Afro-Asia into a separate Third
Area, exemplifying the Third Alternative of non-alignment in the
Cold War, was deflected and even distorted by these two men—Mr.
Dulles and Mr. Nehru. Both, unfortunately, were moralists, one a
Christian and the other a neo-Buddhist. Carrying their beliefs into
politics, one was convinced that he was preventing war by fighting
the good fight, and the other was equally convinced that he was preventing war by eschewing anything warlike. So, naturally, they dis-
liked each other personally. According to the record, as it has un-
folded so far, Mr. Dulles seems to have been the more correct in his
claims and forecasts.

But basically both were inaccurate in their analyses of world
forces: Mr. Dulles because he was unduly suspicious and Mr. Nehru
because he was unduly trusting. Mr. Dulles failed to recognise that
after Stalin's death the Russia of Malenkov and Khrushchev did not
want open war; and Mr. Nehru did not see that China would risk war
to achieve her objectives. Thus while Mr. Dulles stimulated vigilance
against Russia by quoting China's intransigence, Mr. Nehru preached
understanding of China by quoting Russia's conciliatoriness.

Mr. Dulles was a crusader; Mr. Nehru recognised this and attacked
the crusader approach, repeatedly and sharply,[66] and thus became a
crusader against crusading. Because the policy of these two leaders
was inspired by beliefs, they needed believers who had to be gathered
into the fold of the faithful, brands plucked from the burning, who
were saved not so much from Communist domination or imperialist
subordination but from something much worse—from having wrong
ideas.

After 1954, without Mr. Dulles there would have been no pacts:
without Mr. Nehru there would have been no Panchsheel: without
both, Afro-Asia today would be a reasonably united and coherent
Third Area.

On one very important issue, however, Mr. Nehru was profoundly
right and Mr. Dulles profoundly wrong. This was Mr. Nehru's recognition that the resurgence of Afro-Asia was a major fact in world
history. Russia, after Stalin, saw it. Mr. Dulles did not, for he seems
to have been as contemptuous of independent Asia as was Stalin.

Apart from politics or morals, the timing of the irruption of the
Western Powers into Asia through their offers of pacts was extra-
ordinarily inept. The Western progenitors of Israel offered a Middle

East Defence Organisation to the Arab enemies of Israel in October 1951, at the very time when Egypt, the leading Arab state, was in a crisis of antagonism against Britain. Naturally, it was rejected out of hand. Anglo-Egyptian hostility having been overcome and, by late 1954, Anglo-Egyptian relations having being stabilised on an almost friendly basis, Iraq was rushed or inveigled into the Baghdad Pact that Egypt had already openly opposed. This timing guaranteed Arab nationalist opposition to the pact, and because of that opposition the pact contributed very largely to the destruction of the Iraqi monarchy in 1958; it disrupted the Arab League, and pushed the Arab nationalists into working arrangements with Russia which brought Communist influence into the Arab world: the one thing the pact was meant to prevent. Nor has the pact ever made much sense militarily, since the thin crust of the Northern Tier is fragile without the support of north-south lines of communication that only the Arab governments can, but will not, accord.

The timing of SEATO's formation fully justifies Mr. Nehru's accusation that it was an angry response (by Mr. Dulles) to the Geneva Agreement on Indo-China in 1954, to which the United States refused to be a party because it formalised a Communist advance through the creation of North Vietnam. America's principal allies in the alliance, Britain and Australia, were very dubious about its utility without adequate Asian participation, and had to be pushed into it. And the Asian members had to be cajoled into participation. At the founding conference itself, at Manila, the members were at cross-purposes. The Asian states demanded, but did not obtain, a greater emphasis on economic assistance than on resisting Communist expansion—a matter which did not greatly worry them but which obsessed Mr. Dulles. Because of these cross currents the hard core of the pact could not be included in the main treaty document; consequently, the main participant, the United States, defined its enemy, international Communism, in a separate declaration, and the crucial delimitation of the area of application of the pact was likewise defined in an appended protocol.

The clumsiness of SEATO's formal structure was reflected in its operations. The purpose was to cordon off Communist China and North Vietnam. This could only be done if their southern neighbours, Laos, Cambodia and South Vietnam became pact members. But the three states could not do this because of a private, unwritten bargain between Chou En-lai, Eden and Mendès-France at Geneva, which had neutralised them. So SEATO tried to get round this obstacle by taking them under its protective umbrella willy-nilly; a protection which they rejected because, as Prince Norodom of Cambodia said, 'it can only bring us dishonour'.[67] The result is that SEATO has been unable to come to grips with, or in any way prevent, the slow but steady Communist subversion of the Laotian Government—precisely the sort of situation it was intended to meet.

The confusion of purpose inherent in SEATO, as also in CENTO, the post-1958 version of the Baghdad Pact, is proved by the fact that though their principal proclaimed objective was military containment, in neither is there a central military command on the NATO model, despite pleas for this made by Thailand and Pakistan respectively.

Mr. Nehru, as the foremost spokesman for non-alignment and therefore the leading critic of its converse, alignment through military groupings, confined his attacks on pacts to precisely-defined targets. He condemned pacts in general only in so far as they represent the military approach to political problems, but he did not criticise NATO, or ANZUS or the Arab League Collective Security Pact, as long as these regional arrangements remained confined to their original regions. In particular, he was singularly understanding of NATO's role. In 1952 he said: 'It began—this community of Atlantic nations—as a defence against aggression. Well, no one can object to that',[68] and in 1954 he recalled that it seemed to him 'a justifiable reaction'.[69]

What he, and other Afro-Asian non-aligned leaders, objected to were alliances like CENTO and SEATO that linked countries with the non-Asian great powers, or the extension of NATO from the Atlantic Ocean to cover Goa on the Indian Ocean. Against such military grouping he deployed a varied array of arguments. Making an appeal to Asian pride, he compared the extension of the area of action of these pacts to the old 'spheres of influence', and to the old 'unequal treaties', because the Asian members, with their military weakness, were certainly subordinate to the far stronger Western partners.[70] By enabling Western troops to come back to Asia, they represented a reversal of history.[71] He also used a favourite but curiously tough-minded military argument: since there are only two real military powers in the world today, any talk of filling 'power-vacuums' was nonsense since, in comparison with America and Russia, the whole of the rest of the world was one power-vacuum;[72] the Big Two did not really need weak allies who only added to their responsibilities and liabilities; nor did these allies need the Big Two, for by unnecessarily getting themselves involved in the great powers' disputes they attracted greater dangers, not greater security.[73] The pacts also put too many irresponsible, itchy fingers on the atomic trigger.[74]

Apart from these general considerations a due regard for India's national interest also played a major part in Mr. Nehru's opposition to CENTO and SEATO. He felt that they were directed against India and aimed at encircling her[75] by providing India's antagonist, Pakistan, with arms. On this ground both pacts were equally objectionable, but for another SEATO was more dangerous than CENTO and so was much more the object of India's ire. CENTO was aimed against Russia, who was not a neighbour of India's and with whom by 1951 she was not as yet greatly involved. But SEATO was directed at China, a neighbour whom Mr. Nehru was trying to contain through its commitment to Panchsheel. A direct military confrontation with SEATO might not only deflect China from delicate moral inhibitions; it might, as had happened in Korea, exacerbate her suspicions and cause her to lunge outwards. Accordingly the more China showed signs of coming round to the Panchsheel idea, notably at the Bandung Conference, the more angry became India's denunciations of the alternative military approach to China represented by SEATO.[76]

India was not alone in denouncing these two military groupings. In West Asia Colonel Nasser and the leaders of Syria bitterly denounced the Baghdad Pact. Even so good a friend of the West as Sir John Kotelawala, the Prime Minister of Ceylon, remarked that 'what SEATO failed to take into account is that the defence of Asia must first be an economic defence. The military aspect is secondary'.[77] U Nu in Burma frequently made the same point. And in Cambodia Prince Norodom raised the very practical consideration that if small countries got themselves involved in great power conflicts, these powers at that time of conflict would be too busy fighting each other to worry about protecting their small friends.[78]

It was this process, unnecessary and avoidable, of splitting up Asia into the aligned and the non-aligned, and their subsequent consolidation into two antagonistic camps, that dominated Afro-Asian affairs during the year, from mid-1954 to mid-1955, in which were held the two smaller conferences of Colombo and Bogor and the full-scale Afro-Asian meeting at Bandung. Indeed, this split in Afro-Asia is what these conferences were all about.

NOTES TO CHAPTER VI

1. Nehru: *India's Foreign Policy: Selected Speeches of Jawaharlal Nehru, 1946–1961*, Publications Division, Government of India, New Delhi, 1961, p. 80; also pp. 36, 84.
2. *Op. cit.*, pp. 55, 58.
3. It is typical that Mr. Nehru writing about himself in 1937 should say: 'He is too much an aristocrat for the crudity and vulgarity of fascism': *The Modern Review*, Calcutta, Nov., 1937.
4. Nehru: *India's Foreign Policy*, pp. 24, 33, 61, 77, *et passim*.
5. *Op. cit.*, pp. 31, 50.
6. *Op. cit.*, pp. 18, 36, 47, 83, 143. Also Nehru: *The Discovery of India*, 1956, chap. 9, p. 1, and chaps. 10, 11.
7. *Op. cit.*, p. 73.
8. *Op. cit.*, p. 47.
9. *Op. cit.*, pp. 39, 262–3.
10. *Op. cit.*, p. 104.
11. *Op. cit.*, pp. 23, 45, 82, 149.
12. *Op. cit.*, pp. 53, 145.
13. *Op. cit.*, pp. 66, 71, 75.
14. *Op. cit.*, pp. 22, 151.
15. *Op. cit.*, p. 35.
16. *Op. cit.*, pp. 48, 70.
17. *Op. cit.*, pp. 47, 56, 67, *et passim*.
18. *Op. cit.*, p. 58
19. *Op. cit.*, p. 177.
20. *Op. cit.*, pp. 50, 65.
21. *Op. cit.*, p. 77.
22. *Op. cit.*, pp. 12, 260.
23. *Op. cit.*, pp. 265, 268, 305.
24. *Op. cit.*, pp. 49, 74, 80, 85
25. *Op. cit.*, p. 96.
26. *Op. cit.*, p. 183.
27. *Op. cit.*, p. 185.
28. Nehru: *The Discovery of India*, chap. 9, p. 1.
29. Gandhi: *Young India*, 24th Dec. 1928; also P. F. Power: *Gandhi on World Affairs*, Washington, 1960, chap. 5.
30. Nehru: *The Discovery of India*, chaps. 7, 9.
31. Nehru: *India's Foreign Policy*, p. 74.
32. A. B. Bozeman: 'India's Foreign Policy Today', *World Politics*, New York, Jan. 1958.
33. V. L. Pandit: 'India's Foreign Policy', *Foreign Policy*, New York, Apr. 1956.
34. U. N. Ghoshal: *A History of Indian Political Ideas*, Oxford, 1959, refers generally; but see especially pp. 531, 534.
35. Ghoshal, *op. cit.*; also V. P. Varma: *Studies in Hindu Political Thought and its Metaphysical Foundations*, Delhi, 1954; and S. R. Patel: *Foreign Policy of India*, Bombay, 1962, chap. 1.
36. Ghoshal: *op. cit.*, chaps. 4, 14, 19 and 26 for details.
37. Nehru: *The Discovery of India*, chap. 4, pp. 19–21.
38. Romila Thapar: *Asoka and the Decline of the Mauryas*, Oxford, 1961.
39. An amusing attempt to give non-alignment an Indian philosophical and religious base is 'The Culturological Approach to Non-Align-

ment' by U. R. Ehrenfels in the *Indian Year Book of International Affairs*, Madras, 1955, in which the author, who is a German, manages to connect the policy with India's invention of zero and the concept of a mother goddess.

40. V. L. Pandit: *op. cit.*
41. D. G. E. Hall: *A History of South-East Asia*, London, 1955, chaps. 7, 13, 23, 24; and R. H. Fifield: *The Diplomacy of South-East Asia*, New York, 1958.
42. Buddhism has suffered more than any other religion from later accretions and doctrinal deviations. According to one authority, Mrs. C. F. Rhys Davids in her 'What is the Original Doctrine in Buddhism?', that doctrine was turned inside out to eliminate its specifically religious content. Again, Buddhism is generally associated with vegetarianism, even though its founder died after a meal of roast pork.
43. Mohammed Hatta: *Foreign Affairs*, New York, Apr. 1953.
44. Norodom Sihanouk: 'Cambodia Neutral, the Dictate of Necessity', *Foreign Affairs*, New York, July 1958.
45. Nkrumah: *I Speak of Freedom*, London, 1961, chap. 32.
46. I. I. Morris: 'Japanese Foreign Policy and Neutralism', *Internationa Affairs*, London, Jan. 1960.
47. *Foreign Policy of India: Texts of Documents, 1947–59*, Lok Sabha Secretariat, New Delhi, 1959, pp. 103–9.
48. *Panchsheel: Its Meaning and History*, Lok Sabha Secretariat, New Delhi, 1958, pp. 1–8; also *Panchsheel*, excerpts from Nehru's speeches, Lok Sabha Secretariat, pp. 3–4. It is odd that when asked in 1957 to explain the origin of Panchsheel, Mr. Nehru's memory played him false and he claimed that he first applied the word during his visit to Indonesia for the Bandung Conference, when he had done so eight months earlier. Cf. R. H. Fifield: *The Diplomacy of South-East Asia*, New York, 1958, Appendix B, a letter from Mr. Nehru.
49. *Foreign Policy*, documents, pp. 111, 129, 143, 159.
50. *Panchsheel*, speeches, pp. 6, 7, 20.
51. Nehru: *India's Foreign Policy*, p. 105.
52. *Op. cit.*, p. 101.
53. *Panchsheel*, Publications Division, Government of India, New Delhi, 1957, pp. 9–11.
54. C. J. Chacko: 'Peaceful Co-existence as a Doctrine of Current International Affairs', *Indian Year Book of International Affairs*, Madras, 1955.
55. Nehru: *India's Foreign Policy*, p. 67.
56. M. Hatta: 'Indonesia Between the Power Blocs', *Foreign Affairs*, New York, Apr. 1958.
57. W. Wynn: *Nasser*, Cambridge, Mass., 1959, p. 59.
58. Nehru: *India's Foreign Policy*, p. 591.
59. Fifield: *op. cit.*, Appendix B.
60. Sir B. N. Rau: *Private Papers*.
61. Tom Little: *Egypt*, London, 1958.
62. G. Modelski (ed.): *SEATO: Six Studies*, Melbourne, 1962, pp. 131, 137, 138.
63. *Op. cit.*, pp. 138, 237.
64. To the Manila Conference, Sep. 1954.
65. *SEATO*, p. 130.
66. Nehru: *India's Foreign Policy*, p. 554.
67. On 18th Feb. 1956.

Pacts and Panchsheel, 1949 to 1954

68. Speech to the Lok Sabha, II, ii, col. 1670 (1952).
69. Nehru: *India's Foreign Policy*, p. 90.
70. *Op. cit.*, pp. 66, 89.
71. *Op. cit.*, p. 472.
72. *Op. cit.*, p. 195.
73. *Op. cit.*, p. 98.
74. *Op. cit.*, p. 95.
75. *Op. cit.*, pp. 94, 476.
76. *SEATO: Six Studies*, Part V.
77. Sir J. Kotelawala: *An Asian Prime Minister's Story*, London, 1956, chap. 17.
78. Norodom Sihanouk: *op. cit.*

142

CHAPTER VII

The First Colombo Conference, April 1954

'I made a casual suggestion for convening a conference of Asian prime ministers at an after-dinner speech some five months ago, and it was that suggestion that has now materialised into a meeting of world-wide importance.' The speaker was Sir John Kotelawala, Prime Minister of Ceylon, on the 28th April 1954, the day on which a conference of the Prime Ministers of Burma, India, Indonesia, Pakistan and Ceylon began in Colombo.

Unlikely as it might seem, yet another decisive development in the Afro-Asian movement began with yet another after-dinner speech. This was a decisive development indeed, for from the Colombo Conference directly stemmed the Bandung Conference with all its immense consequences.

When with the passage of time, all this had become clear, Sir John tried to make his initiating idea seem less casual and more planned and portentous. Writing two years later, in his *Autobiography*, he remarks: 'Ideas . . . have the most unlikely origins'; thus 'it has been said that it [the Colombo Conference] all began with my thinking aloud at a social function "let's have an Asian conference".' It was not so, he avers, despite his earlier admission, because the idea of such a conference had been taking shape in his mind for seven years, and he had first stated it in a broadcast talk in Rangoon in 1948. But, he confesses, it was Mr. C. C. Desai, the Indian High Commissioner to Ceylon, 'who was responsible for fixing the right time for me to invite the Asian premiers to get together'. This timing was ' "the stroke of genius" for which I have been given full credit'—and which he does not disclaim.

The time and place of Mr. Desai's fateful suggestion was the annual dinner of the United Nations Association for Ceylon, on or about United Nations Day, 24th October. Looking round at the heads of the diplomatic missions there assembled, Mr. Desai suggested to his host that it would be a good thing if heads of government could similarly meet in annual reunion. Promptly Sir John improved the shining hour, and the suggestion, by proposing an Asian conference; and with this he persisted in the cold light of day.[1]

The gesture was typical of the man, for Sir John Kotelawala was in the best sense of the words 'a simple soul', direct and forthright in his impulses. Perhaps the nearest resemblance to him among living Asian leaders is Tunku Abdul Rahman; both of them are rich, well-born playboys, who went into politics because that was the 'done thing' for rich, well-born young men to do, and were then sobered down into shrewd, thrusting, conscientious leaders. In his politics Sir John was no firebrand, of course—he would hardly have got his knighthood if he had been; but one should not judge him too harshly for this, because Ceylon had barely a minimal nationalist movement. A young compatriot of Sir John's has cruelly, but with cruel accuracy, dubbed Asian leaders of his stamp 'the Brown Sahibs', creatures of a transitional twilit period.[2] So they may be, and in a general election two years later Sir John was bundled out of office; but in his case all, or almost all, is redeemed by a *naïveté* that is honestly innocent. He could not conceal his motives in calling this conference, the first Asian meeting after a lapse of five years. He had just become prime minister and it would be no bad thing for his prestige were he to play host to the leaders of much larger neighbouring countries. When his ideas had been accepted he said in a public speech that this had convinced him that 'we have as important a part as any to play in the conduct of Asian affairs'.[3] From any other leader of so small a state as Ceylon this would have been an absurdity; but what instruments of derision can one use on a man who, writing of his role in calling the conference could say, in all seriousness: 'I felt my hour had come'?

Sir John probably made his first informal soundings with the Premiers of India, Burma and Pakistan in November 1953, and found none of them particularly enthusiastic. In early December he made a tentative suggestion to Mr. Nehru in which, as a bait, he reaffirmed his faith in Ceylon's policy of non-alignment. When even this was received in silence, he put his invitation into writing on the 18th December, suggesting that 'the four Prime Ministers of Burma, India, Pakistan and Ceylon could meet together, say once a year if not more frequently, and discuss matters or exchange views informally and without an agenda';[4] the first meeting might be held in Ceylon or in alphabetical order beginning with Burma.

This tactful offer to Burma was an attempt to remove the main obstacle to U Nu's acceptance—which was his annoyance that Sir

The First Colombo Conference, April 1954

John should have taken this initiative about a conference that U Nu was on the point of calling himself. He was not easily mollified and did not give his acceptance till the last week of February.

Pakistan's reluctance sprang from her fear that she would be put in the dock by the others for opening negotiations with the United States for a military alliance, and thus breaking away from the more or less non-aligned group of South Asian states. At the end of December and again early in January 1955 Ceylon gave Pakistan formal assurances that this subject would not be discussed, and Pakistan then agreed to attend.

Pakistan's policy was the very reason for Mr. Nehru's reluctance, for he wished to confront Pakistan with the disapproval of its neighbours, and feared he might not be given the chance to do so. In his reply to Sir John, in which he accepted, he added that the proposed United States arms aid to Pakistan was 'very disturbing', and was happy to note that 'you [Kotelawala] view this proposal with some concern'. There was something less than concern in Sir John's response to this: he said he wished to play down any mention of American arms aid to Pakistan 'lest Pakistan be frightened by the proposed conference'. Hence in the middle of February Mr. Nehru was advising U Nu not to make too much fuss about this meeting; and as late as the fourth week of March, just a month before the meeting, Mr. Nehru was saying testily that he did not attach much importance to the conference, that he was not at all keen on going, and would do so only because the meeting had already been decided on. We shall find him displaying the same last-minute reluctance before the Belgrade Conference—almost a kind of stage-fright.

Before describing his wider reasons it should be noted that there was one enthusiastic invitee, Indonesia. Mr. Nehru had suggested adding the Indonesians while conceding that 'it is true that the larger the number the vaguer the talk'. Ceylon agreed to the suggestion and Indonesia received and accepted its invitation a week before Burma and Pakistan. Other countries, like Egypt and Afghanistan, enquired why they were not invited, and expressed disappointment when told that this was a meeting of neighbours. Only the original invitees were hesitant.

The general reasons for Mr. Nehru's hesitation sprang from a gloomily realistic assessment of the continental scene: 'As for Asian unity,' he wrote, 'such unity has to be based on some common understanding and common objectives. I see little in common except, perhaps, between India and Burma.' But he was not without hope: 'Of course if there is some common approach we should welcome it.'

It is significant that, in his thinking, Asian conferences were still linked to the possibility of a permanent organisation, and because the conferences had not been able to produce an enduring body they were, perhaps, of doubtful utility. Just before Colombo he surveyed the past record. Ever since the Asian Relations Conference he 'had been trying to build up some kind of formal or informal meeting place for Asian (and African) countries'. The ARC had tried to form a permanent organisation. 'This did not function though we have still got the relics of a branch in Delhi.' In 1948 he met the representatives of the Afro-Asian states at the United Nations General Assembly in Paris, and discussed the question again: 'There was general agreement that some such thing was desirable' but it had to be referred to the governments; 'ultimate result nil'. The 1949 conference on Indonesia, 'which was a success chiefly because it was confined to one subject', discussed the need for frequent meetings and some organisational set-up: 'we circularised the various governments at the time, but the response was lukewarm and the idea was dropped. Result again nil.' Discussions on this topic between him and U Nu and President Sukarno had revealed 'insuperable' difficulties. Hence 'any large-scale conference was likely to bring about more an exhibition of differences of opinion than unanimity'. Who was to be invited? Some countries were now tied to the United States. Others were Communist 'who perhaps may not be invited. Not inviting them of itself has a certain implication'. So, he concluded, one should await the outcome of the Colombo Conference—the first meeting after a five-year gap. It was to bring him no encouragement whatsoever.

A more specific reason for Mr. Nehru's hesitations was that, in the six months between Sir John's first casual approach and the conference itself, the development of international events had produced a direct confrontation between alignment and non-alignment in Asia. On the one hand, Pakistan was moving by no means slowly or steadily into a military alliance with the West, and on the other, the French military collapse in Indo-China had spurred Mr. Dulles into a burst of activity, aimed at the swift creation of SEATO, just before the convening of the conference at Geneva on Korea and Indo-China.

Early in 1953, Turkey suggested that Pakistan and Iran should be brought into a Middle East Defence Organisation for which Mr. Dulles had begun to press, and that would also include America, Britain, France and Turkey. Pakistan was only too agreeable, and the pace of negotiations quickened after April 1953 when Mr. Mohammed Ali, formerly an ambassador to Washington, became Prime Minister. Later in the year Mr. Dulles visited Pakistan, where he denounced non-alignment as 'immoral', and by the end of 1953 negotiations had begun for a Pakistan-United States military aid agreement. This move was a deliberately calculated risk on the part of the United States. Before it was taken, American envoys in South-East Asia met at Nuwara Eliya, in Ceylon, and decided that military aid to Pakistan should be granted despite Indian objections; and that these were to be neutralised by canvassing support in Indonesia, Burma and Ceylon. Ceylon, which was then trying to obtain an American loan, might have been considered an easy target, but the approach to Burma was utterly maladroit. On his way to the Colombo Conference, U Nu revealed that about a year earlier Burma had turned down an American offer of a mutual security arrangement[5]—proposed at a time when Burma had just declined further United States economic assistance, because America was involved, via Formosa, with Kuomintang bandits in eastern Burma. This approach not only displays Mr. Dulles's insensitivity and poor timing, but reveals that he was trying to disrupt the area of non-alignment in South Asia as well as in West Asia.

In Indo-China the desperate plight of the French Army in the battle of Dien Bien Phu, which began in the middle of March, had brought the United States to one of Mr. Dulles's 'brinks'—the threat of intervention with atomic arms. The British Government managed to ward this off but, as a price, had to agree in principle, on 13th April to the creation of a South-East Asian collective defence system.[6]

Thus, quite by accident, the Colombo Conference met in the midst of decisive events. Twenty-four days before it opened Pakistan, on the 2nd April, signed a military agreement with Turkey—its first step towards membership of the Baghdad Pact; the idea of SEATO was promulgated fifteen days earlier; the Geneva Conference began two days before the Colombo meeting; Dien Bien Phu fell five days after it ended; and seventeen days later, on the 19th May, the Pakistan-United States military agreement was signed. These events, significant for the movement towards alignment in Asia, were matched by an event of significance for non-alignment: the day after the conference opened came the announcement of the agreement between India and China on Tibet, which included the first mention of the Five Principles. Mr. Nehru was surely justified in thinking that there was a certain lack of 'common objectives' among those meeting, a defect which had been highlighted by the fact that while India and Burma had refused transit permission for American planes air-lifting French reinforcements to Indo-China, Pakistan and Ceylon had granted permission a few days before the conference began.

This uneasy setting for the Colombo Conference dominated its debates and gave it its short-term importance. Its long-term importance, however, sprang from a different question—one which the conference treated summarily as an unimportant side-issue. This was Indonesia's proposal for a full Afro-Asian conference.

If this difference between short-term and long-term results is a familiar characteristic of the Asian conferences, so was the Western reaction to Colombo. American and British diplomats were busily in contact with the Ceylon Foreign Ministry: the Americans because of their fears that the meeting might lead to an extension of Mr. Nehru's influence, and the British because they were afraid that the Commonwealth idea might be weakened by such a regional gathering.

One aspect of Commonwealth practice did, in fact, have great influence on this meeting, and on all subsequent Asian conferences— namely, the procedure adopted at Commonwealth Prime Ministers' conferences, with which Mr. Nehru was by now familiar. It was he who suggested this procedure, brushing aside Ceylon's suggestion for a formal agenda, and preferring 'informal talks without commitments' on a broad range of subjects. Likewise questions in dispute internally between members were to be eschewed. Finally, decisions reached were to be unanimous. It was these two provisions that produced the unanimity at Bandung, which was so striking that it was hailed as the new, accommodating 'Bandung Spirit'; it would have been more accurate, historically, to refer to it as the old Commonwealth Spirit.

In accordance with the increasing formalisation of the Asian conferences, the meetings in Colombo were held in the small chamber of the Senate and were not open to the public or press, even for the opening and closing sessions. A large public meeting that was to have been addressed jointly by the premiers was cancelled 'as a security measure'.

The Colombo Conference was by far the most quarrelsome of all the Asian conferences. The contentiousness is ascribable to the fact this was the first face-to-face meeting between these leaders just after some of them had taken momentous decisions as to whether their countries should be aligned or non-aligned. Also, although none of the items on the agenda referred directly to any of the participating countries, some of these questions impinged, obliquely but force-fully, on most sensitive areas of national interest. Thus when Mr. Mohammed Ali spoke about Indo-China he was really referring to Kashmir and when Mr. Nehru took a certain stand on inter-national Communism he was, in effect, thinking of his policy towards China.

Perhaps, too, the intimacy of a few leaders meeting round a table may have encouraged them to speak their minds with a frankness that was often bitter; as did also the belief that what they said to each other was in strictest confidence. But as in other 'secret' Asian meetings, all that secrecy amounted to was that for each delegation it was possible, with impunity and without fear of contradiction, to 'leak' partial and partisan versions to the Press. It is amusing and sometimes instructive to compare the differing versions, found in the various national presses, with what actually happened as recounted, impartially, in the official minutes.[7]

If matters had been left to the prime ministers themselves the con-ference would probably never have reached agreement. Reading the minutes of the meetings we find them worrying away at the contro-versial problems, dropping them when they reached deadlock and returning to the charge again and again in later sessions.

Fortunately for the political leaders, trapped in their public atti-tudes, the real work of the conference was done by professional bureaucrats and draftsmen, behind closed doors in the drafting com-mittee to which all the many unresolved problems were referred. Although all five delegations were members, its two outstanding participants were Sir Oliver Goonetilleke of Ceylon and Mr. Krishna Menon of India. Sir Oliver, after a lifetime of service as a bureaucrat, was well fitted to find compromises between extremes; Mr. Krishna Menon, no moderate in his ideas, is a master at finding words with the exact shade of meaning to fit ideas—for while he can, with con-summate artistry, use words to conceal his meaning he is equally adept at making it plain.

The depth of the differences between positions rigidly maintained was shown when, after one particularly stormy session towards the end of the conference, Sir John as chairman had no option but to suggest that the draft communiqué should simply give the consensus of opinion on each subject rather than the individual resolutions, on which it seemed impossible to agree; and the baffled, weary leaders actually adopted this desperate suggestion. This decision meant that on certain subjects at least the conference was prepared to admit failure and accept an agreement to differ. At no subsequent Asian conference did the clash of ideas reach quite this pitch of bitter intensity.

The first shots were fired in the opening speeches. Mr. Nehru welcomed the Geneva Conference, and then said that events which had happened since the invitation 'made this meeting of even greater significance than it might have been'; this he also said about Bandung and Belgrade. He spoke of the Asians' need to extend and consolidate their newly-won freedom by improving living conditions and by preventing any encroachment on this freedom by any external agency. Thanks to non-alignment they had a fresh outlook and were not tied to old hostilities.

Mr. Mohammed Ali, after recalling Pakistan's role at the United Nations in aid of such Muslim countries as Palestine, Libya, Morocco, Tunisia, went on to express his doubts whether any 'association' was possible unless Asians could settle their own problems, such as Kashmir, and that till these were settled it was 'perhaps a little presumptuous for us to preach peace to others'.

After these preliminary thrusts the conference began considering its agenda. Items proposed for inclusion were: the situation in Indo-China, proposed by Ceylon and India; hydrogen bomb tests in Asia, proposed by India and Indonesia; colonialism, proposed by Ceylon, India and Indonesia; racialism, proposed by India; Communism, proposed by Ceylon, supported by Pakistan and Burma; economic co-operation, proposed by Ceylon, Indonesia and Burma; Kashmir proposed by Pakistan; and a future Afro-Asian conference, proposed by Indonesia. India evidently had proposed as an item 'the United States move for organised collective defence against Communist aggression in South-East Asia', but thought better of it and did not press the proposal, perhaps because discussion would inevitably have led to controversy.

Mr. Ali said it would be 'unrealistic' to discuss other conflicts unless first priority were given to problems like Kashmir. Mr. Nehru opposed this on the ground of the precedent of Commonwealth conferences, where internal disputes were never discussed, but said that he was ready to discuss Kashmir if American arms aid to Pakistan were also to be discussed. It was at this stage that Mr. Nehru was supposed to have said that he would 'tear to pieces' Mr. Ali—a remark that produced the explanation, unnecessarily, that the words applied to the arguments and not the person of the Pakistan Premier. With his usual engaging frankness U Nu said that such a discussion would be 'the beginning of the end', and supported India's stand on internal disputes, as did Indonesia. Mr. Ali, having shown that his heart was in the right place on Kashmir, then accepted the majority view.

The most controversial issue in a generally contentious meeting was Indo-China, not merely because of its topicality but because, as with the Delhi Conference on Indonesia, this conference was hoping to influence the actual course of events. This was possible since the British Foreign Secretary, Mr. Anthony Eden, had linked the Colombo meeting with the Geneva Conference—even though India, owing to American pressure, had been deliberately excluded from Geneva and none of the other four participants were represented. Mr. Eden very wisely recognised that any settlement for Indo-China reached at Geneva, as well as the proposed security arrangement for South-East Asia which would guarantee that settlement, would only be effective if Asian states, especially India, were associated with both. Since the Asians would not agree to proposals which accepted any of Mr. Dulles's militant ideas, the British Foreign Secretary utilised the possibility of gaining Asian support as a brake on Mr. Dulles.

Accordingly on the second day of the Colombo Conference, 29th April, Mr. Eden sent a cable to the three Commonwealth prime ministers in Colombo assuring them that the United Kingdom would not wish to be party to any decision taken at Geneva that would conflict with the legitimate aims of the Asian countries. He asked them if they would be prepared to participate in a guarantee (naturally of a military nature) to assure Indo-China's future. To make quite sure that there was no misunderstanding between Colombo and Geneva, a direct wireless link between the two cities was installed, through which Mr. Eden kept the Asian premiers fully informed.[8] Furthermore, against Mr. Dulles's wish, Mr. Eden got the Geneva Conference to give priority to the other item on its agenda, Korea, in order to afford the Colombo powers time to formulate their ideas on Indo-China.[9] Because of this almost direct involvement in a major Cold War issue, the participants at Colombo could not take refuge in platitudes, and so could not easily reach an agreed formula on Indo-China.

At the second session of the conference Mr. Nehru was asked to clarify the six-point proposal about Indo-China which he had put forward in New Delhi on the 24th, obviously designed for the conference. His first two points—that all parties concerned should refrain from belligerent talk, and that there should be a cease-fire to be negotiated by France, the three Indo-China states and the Viet-

minh, excluding the United States and China—required no explanation. On his third point, a promise by France to grant independence
to Indo-China, Mr. Nehru said that the details of the transfer of
sovereignty were for the parties concerned to decide; he did not suggest that France should withdraw immediately, because a vacuum
would be left which some other power might fill (a very worrying
prospect, especially for U Nu). This led to the fourth point, which
covered direct negotiations about the future of Indo-China between
the parties 'immediately and principally concerned', that is, France
and the Indo-Chinese. The fifth point suggested that an undertaking
not to intervene in Indo-China be made by the great powers under
United Nations auspices and put under their supervision. The United
States and China had not denied that they were intervening in Indo-
China; and, he explained, if this was stopped, the problem would be
localised—in short, taken out of the context of the Cold War. His
sixth point, which required that the United Nations be kept informed
and asked to implement a settlement, was designed to allow for the
possibility of impartial supervision.

Dr. Ali Sastroamidjojo, for Indonesia, expressed agreement with
Mr. Nehru's approach, but introduced the irrelevant suggestion that
the cease-fire proposal should be linked with a recommendation that
China be given a seat in the United Nations. If China were given this,
he said, it would put her into an amenable frame of mind.

Mr. Mohammed Ali stated that the war in Indo-China was a war
between colonialism and Communism and that he, like U Nu, did
not want a vacuum to be created there that might be filled by Communist China: if that was likely to happen he would even be opposed
to a withdrawal by France. A choice had to be made between two
evils: colonialism was less dangerous because it was subject to the
pressure of world opinion. He agreed that there should be a cease-
fire, but only as a part of a general settlement; cease-fires by themselves often led to added tension and bitterness. More surprisingly,
he suggested that in order not to compromise Geneva, developments
there ought to be awaited before any proposals were formulated.
Fortunately this plan was rejected after some discussion, on the
ground that ideas voiced at Colombo might actually assist Geneva.
As Dr. Ali said, it was not consistent with the dignity of the Asian
countries to stand idly by, waiting on the Geneva Conference. U Nu
then proposed that any formula which was agreed should be taken
to Geneva by one of the prime ministers in person; this, too, was
rejected as being impracticable and embarrassing.

The First Colombo Conference, April 1954

Battle was joined when Mr. Mohammed Ali, having failed in his attempt to divert the conference from Indo-China altogether, gave his detailed reaction to Mr. Nehru's six points. He agreed to the first point, a cease-fire, but not to the second, which would exclude the United States and Communist China from the group arranging the cease-fire. He accepted the third point, concerning France's grant of independence; but the fourth and fifth points, covering non-intervention, he described as unrealistic and impracticable and likely to be embarrassing: they contained the implication that intervention had taken place. This was the heart of the matter, for the sixth point, which dealt with the role of the United Nations, was consequential.

Mr. Nehru, with U Nu and Dr. Ali agreeing, argued that non-intervention was essential if the cease-fire were to have any meaning. Thus the two opposing positions on non-intervention were defined.

Mr. Mohammed Ali sought to clear up his own position, which was so far undefined. He was not against the principle of non-intervention in Indo-China but only against the inclusion of this particular clause in the communiqué of this particular conference. The details of the transfer of sovereignty ought to be worked out by the Geneva Conference without laying down non-intervention as a condition. By saying this, the Pakistan Prime Minister admitted that he was aware of the impact that Colombo was going to have on Geneva—although he had tried to brush this aside a few moments earlier.

In reply, Mr. Nehru said that both the United States and China had admitted their intervention; any proposal of the conference should make clear in principle its attitude towards that accepted fact.

Three separate discussions on Indo-china at Colombo produced no agreement because of Pakistan's adamant refusal to support a specific request to the United States, United Kingdom, the Soviet Union and China not to intervene, while it accepted the principle of non-intervention. On the other side U Nu was equally determined in his refusal to accept a resolution on Indo-China unless it recommended non-intervention.

In the drafting committee, Sir Oliver Goonetilleke and Mr. Krishna Menon had laboured through the nights of the 29th and 30th April to have some formula ready for the premiers when they reassembled in Kandy on the 1st May. This was to be the last day of conference, make or break. It was natural that differences among the principals should divide the drafting committee also, especially on the question of whether or not the great powers were to give an undertaking not to intervene in Indo-China. On the night of the 30th April the com-

153

mittee also was at deadlock. In desperation, it asked Sir Oliver to try to produce a draft on his own responsibility, though, cravenly, it added 'with the assistance of the drafting committee'. He pulled the rabbit out of the hat—the formula that the success of the cease-fire in Indo-China required that 'outside powers should refrain from adding to the war potential of the belligerents'; this formula even the Pakistan members of the committee accepted.

This suggestion the prime ministers studied as they travelled by train from Colombo through jungle-covered hills to Kandy, a summer resort and the ancient capital of the kings of Ceylon. In its cooler atmosphere they spent the latter part of the morning sightseeing; they visited the famous botanical gardens and the even more famous Temple of the Tooth, one of the most sacred shrines of Buddhism. At 5.15 p.m. they reassembled in the Kings' Pavilion, but the lovely hills and lakes of Kandy had not soothed them.

Resumed discussion about non-intervention in Indo-China provided one more example how, during this conference, agreement was hampered more by narrow considerations of national interest, than by differences of principle. Pakistan this time caused the obstruction; the impact of the Kashmir question on an unconnected issue was thus revealed.

Mr. Mohammed Ali began the proceedings by saying that he could not accept the new Goonetilleke formula about Indo-China: he repudiated his own officials. The necessity for a cease-fire was obvious, he said. Prior conditions need not be laid down for it. A cease-fire had been arranged in Kashmir without asking India and Pakistan to refrain from getting war material from abroad: they ought not to preach what they did not practice. The wording of the draft conflicted with a cardinal principle of Pakistan's foreign policy, he could not therefore agree to it in any circumstances. Because of Pakistan's continued refusal the matter was handed back to the drafters once more. Formula after formula was put forward, some from Sir Oliver, some from Mr. Krishna Menon, nearly a score, in which they 'tried it this way, then that way', as Mr. Menon said.[10]

All were rejected by Mr. Mohammed Ali. But this verbal pounding at last compelled him to give the real reasons for his opposition: because of the stand taken by Pakistan on Kashmir and its acceptance of American military aid, he could not accept the view that such military aid would hamper a settlement in another part of the world. Thus, through Pakistan, the process of alignment impinged directly on the conference's consideration of Indo-China as, through India, non-alignment and the Five Principles were later to do on its discussion of international Communism.

At last came the final breakthrough—by the action of Burma. U Nu said that it was clear that the divergence was fundamental. He, for one, could not agree to any proposal about Indo-China, unless it contained a reference to non-intervention, because 'it is not the Indo-Chinese who are fighting this war—the war is being fought by the French, the United States and China'. So he proposed that the final declaration omit all reference to Indo-China and a separate declaration on Indo-China be issued by the four prime ministers—for even a hesitant and mainly silent Ceylon had said enough to show that it favoured non-intervention. With the support of Indonesia, a fresh draft relating to Indo-China was at once presented, stating that 'the prime ministers also considered a proposal for a non-intervention agreement but were not able to reach unanimity on this point'.

This formula put heavy pressure on Mr. Mohammed Ali, and under it he gave way. The prospect of isolation from his fellow prime ministers moved him so deeply that his face betrayed his emotions. He protested that U Nu's proposal was 'not fair' to him. He pleaded for understanding of his difficulties—that if he entered into any agreement that even remotely compromised his stand on Kashmir, he would be disowned by his colleagues in the Cabinet, by Parliament and by the people. He emphasised the importance of maintaining unanimity on all issues (which was another way of saying that he did not wish to be left alone on the problem of Indo-China) and he appealed for the dropping of the clause about non-intervention; they could say the same thing individually, so long as they did not say it collectively. Suggestions of this kind have made the name 'politician' a term of disrepute.

Though the discussions continued much longer, the heart had gone out of the fight. Agreement was reached on a statement that the success of the direct negotiations would 'be greatly helped by agreement on the part of all countries concerned, particularly China, the United Kingdom, the United States and the Soviet Union, on steps necessary to prevent a recurrence or resumption of hostility'. Observance of these recommendations necessarily entailed the withholding or curtailment of military aid, but this formula was only a recommendation, very different from the 'solemn agreement of non-intervention' which India had wanted. However U Nu was satisfied with the new wording and he took the text to Mr. Mohammed Ali who accepted it, perhaps without realising its full implications, perhaps because he knew that he had gained the substance of his point. Thus was unanimity reached on the most difficult item on the agenda.

The Indonesian Prime Minister made one last attempt to revive his idea of linking the Indo-Chinese cease-fire with Communist China's admission to the United Nations. U Nu, in forthright fashion, asserted that China's intervention in Korea and Indo-China was not due to chagrin over her exclusion from this body, and that she would not be more restrained, if she were admitted; United Nations membership placed no check on Russia's international conduct. In the highly-charged atmosphere of Kandy the Indonesian idea was given short shrift, as none of the four other premiers would accept it. For the sake of unanimity, Dr. Ali said, he would withdraw the proposal, which had been the 'King Charles's head' of the conference.

Of the two controversial problems discussed by the Colombo Conference the more important one was 'international Communism'. Though this topic did not prove as difficult as the other thorny subject, Indo-China, the discussions on it were the more significant for in them were raised the basic issues of the Cold War and of non-alignment.

The issue was raised in the chairman's opening speech itself. Sir John Kotelawala had shown the draft of his opening speech to Mr. Nehru; in it he attacked 'international Communism'. The Indian Premier suggested that this might be replaced with the circumlocution 'threats to democracy, internal or external, and the appeal to or use of violence'. In the speech itself Sir John referred to 'the threat to democratic freedom by expansionist desires and policies of others', and said that this came from 'aggressive Communism and the retention of and attempt to perpetuate colonial rule'.

In closed session, Sir John lost no time in introducing a strongly-worded draft resolution, as might have been expected from one who called himself 'an avowed and inveterate opponent' of Communism.[11] His resolution described international Communism as 'anti-democratic' and 'aggressive'; its attempt 'to extend to our states a political system by revolution or peaceful infiltration constitutes a threat to our political independence'. It then recommended three courses of action: to reaffirm their faith in democracy (this was done); to take all appropriate measures to prevent interference by international Communism; and to exchange information about the measures taken.

Sir John presented this draft with a speech against the menace of the subversive activities of international Communism. He made the

156

accusation that funds and literature were imported. Russian agents made contact with local Communists: even the Russian delegates who had attended a recent meeting of the Economic Commission for Asia and the Far East, held in Ceylon, had tried to meet local Communists. Scholarships were given for studies in Russia. In his view, all these actions constituted subversive interference. As expected Mr. Nehru opposed the resolution. He asked for a precise definition of international Communism, which to him was an ideology, so that all might know exactly what they were condemning. In India the local Communists had raised difficulties, but 'in spite of all his efforts he had failed to detect any direct contacts between local Communists and Russian agents'. The countries of the area 'were aware of the danger of Communism' and 'must decide on the best way of dealing with these dangers'. The British approach to Communism was preferable to the more aggressive American attitude. He then made his main point: if India accepted this resolution, she aligned herself with one bloc participating in the Cold War. This position she wished to avoid; the resolution was therefore unacceptable.

Mr. Mohammed Ali, of course, fully endorsed the resolution. If delegates wished to condemn colonialism, they ought equally to condemn Communism. 'Hands off Asia' should be said to the colonial powers and to Soviet Russia. (Anti-Communists at Colombo always cast Russia, not Communist China, as the villain of the piece.)

Dr. Ali opposed the resolution, because it would align his non-aligned country. They did not have any particular difficulty in dealing with Indonesian Communists, he said; these were allowed to function and seemed to be of the Yugoslav variety—a singularly inaccurate assessment.

Sir John agreed that local Communists could be controlled and were no great danger; the danger lay in international Communism. The conference seemed ready to oppose colonialism which 'really was of no direct concern' to it; its members ought therefore to be ready to oppose the threat of international Communism 'which they all face in varying degrees'.

A reasoned exposition of the non-Communist attitude was given by Mr. Nehru. If any political party in India resorted to violence he would suppress it, but suppression by force often encouraged further violence. Certainly each country must take all possible steps either by law or by more efficient administrative methods to stop Communist intervention or infiltration into its territory, but mere denunciation achieved little. People's minds had to be won away from

Communism. Intellectuals in all countries were attracted by Communist ideology. The challenge of Russian Communism today was the challenge of her economic system. The real test was: which economy—the capitalist or the Communist—pays better dividends to the people. The ultimate issue was a conflict of ideas: 'The idea that will prevail in the end is that which will be more acceptable to humanity,' Mr Nehru concluded; the approach must be by reason and persuasion, not compulsion.

He made no converts; rather the reverse. U Nu entered the debate to urge Asian countries to be outspoken against the danger of Communism, as they had been against colonialism. The Communists, he said, had gone 'too far' and 'it is time the Asians told them to stop interfering in our affairs'.

This speech was the decisive move in the debate, the more so because it came from the Prime Minister of Burma, the only country with which, in Mr. Nehru's view, India had any common objectives, and which had recently rejected all further American aid. At this juncture the division on Indo-China, the other major issue that the conference was discussing concurrently, was three and a half to one and a half, Ceylon being divided in its views; but on international Communism the score was a clear three to two; so although discussion of this second major item went on further, its outcome was certain. This was another one of U Nu's crucial interventions in the Colombo Conference discussions.

After all the arguing back and forth there were on the table three drafts dealing with international Communism: Ceylon's original formula, a lightly summarised version of this, which stood in the names of Ceylon and Pakistan (this was the second time that Ceylon had submitted two entries on the same subject), and an Indian proposal. The latter spoke of 'firm resolve' on the part of all to 'maintain and protect' their 'independence and integrity . . . and democratic institutions, and to safeguard themselves against any and all threats to their integrity or sovereignty and to any intervention or interference, direct or indirect, in their internal affairs or institutions by any authority or agency whatsoever, Communist, anti-Communist or otherwise'. A more concise version of this repetitive and prosy promise appears in the communiqué. In short, India had reached the limit of her concessions, and it was Mr. Nehru's task to convince the others that she would go no further.

With his eyes more on Europe than on Asia, the Premier of Ceylon tried to lay down the precise definition of 'international Communism' for which Mr. Nehru had asked at the previous session. Sir John described it as 'a very extensive secret political organisation operated by the leaders of the Communist Party in Soviet Russia which had enslaved several countries and sought to enslave more'.

To Mr. Nehru not only was this incorrect, but it went beyond the views even of a country like Britain. By accepting the American definition of Communism they would be allying themselves with one side in the Cold War, and would be contravening non-alignment. To his personal knowledge, Communism had changed considerably since Marx and Lenin and 'he had very good reason to believe that the Cominform would cease to exist in the near future' and that the whole Communist approach to the world was changing. As applied to the Soviet Union, this was a wholly accurate prediction, but at that time it was too far ahead of general opinion to gain credence.

At long last, Mr. Nehru gave his real reasons for opposing the resolution; he mentioned that 'India is about to enter into a treaty of great significance to the country with Communist China' (this had happened the day before), and that it would very seriously embarrass him in India's relations with Communist China to associate himself with the charge implied in the statement made by Sir John. All his arguments about combating Communist ideology on the intellectual plane were valid, but beneath them lay this realistic consideration of India's national interest.

In an attempt to break the deadlock, Mr. Nehru suggested that the officials present withdraw, and the five premiers were left alone for just over an hour. Behind closed doors the consequences of joining alliances and of giving up the whole concept of non-alignment were discussed, but without result. It was probably during this private meeting that the incident took place which Sir John Kotelawala described in his autobiography when, according to him, one prime minister banged the table and shouted, 'You are nothing but an American stooge,' to which the other retorted, 'And you are nothing better than a Russian stooge.' Sir John lost his temper and shouted to them to stop bickering and behave themselves. 'I asked them to remember that we were prime ministers'; they 'came to their senses at once' and apologised.[12] There is no reason to doubt that some such incident took place; nor does it require much deductive power to identify the protagonists as Mr. Nehru and Mr. Mohammed Ali. It is sufficient to say that when the full conference was resumed the premiers dropped the Communist item and turned once again to Indo-China.

The First Colombo Conference, April 1954

All the discussions at Colombo on 'international Communism' were unproductive of agreement and were resumed at the final session in the Kings' Pavilion at Kandy: it was 10 p.m. on the final night before the prime ministers reached this most important item. The general trend of their discussion was exactly the same as before. Pakistan, with U Nu agreeing, said that if colonialism was to be condemned the threat of Communist subversion must also be stigmatised. Mr. Mohammed Ali relaxed his position a little, perhaps as a *quid pro quo* for the success he had by then achieved on the topic of Indo-China; he consented to omit from his joint resolution with Ceylon the paragraph on ways and means of resisting Communist interference.

Mr. Nehru defended the phrasing of the Indian proposal. They had to guard against interference from anti-Communist agencies, and he suggested the more compact wording 'any external agencies, Communist, anti-Communist or other'. The words 'international Communism' were not sufficiently precise, he said, and were a mere echo of the American thesis.

Pakistan disagreed, and the wrangle continued till midnight. Then, Sir John writes in his autobiography, 'I retired to bed. This novel act of chairmanship must have dealt the finishing blow to the debate,' for agreement was reached half an hour later. And he adds that 'much of the success of the Asian conference' was due to the fact that he was 'completely innocent of diplomatic guile'.

Whether or not his withdrawal worked the miracle, Mr. Mohammed Ali in the end accepted the Indian wording 'for the sake of unanimity'; protesting to the last that he did not know what 'anti-Communist' interference referred to, till U Nu reminded him of the Kuomintang freebooters in eastern Burma, and their barely concealed connection with the United States Central Intelligence Agency.

On the matter of hydrogen bomb tests, Mr. Nehru explained a four-point proposal he had made a few weeks earlier, calling for a standstill of test explosions, for publicity about production, and for the stoppage of any further development of weapons of mass destruction. Pakistan questioned the advantage of a standstill on test explosions, if research on weapons continued and explosions were set off secretly. Mr. Nehru said that such secrecy was not possible; his proposals were only interim measures, as a prelude to more lasting agreements. There was general agreement and the subject was referred to the drafting committee.

This interchange, though brief, is important. It was the first time

160

that Asian leaders, or any responsible statesmen as a group, opposed atomic weapons. Even at the Belgrade Conference seven years later, few of their Afro-Asian colleagues made so strong a stand, though many hydrogen bombs had by then been exploded; and, ten years later, at the second non-aligned conference in Cairo, there was even greater reluctance to take positive action against nuclear proliferation.

When we reflect how eagerly some small states later competed for United Nations membership, not merely as a guarantee of their independence but as a proof of their existence, it is refreshing to find that at Colombo one of the participants was reluctant to become a member. This was Ceylon, whose admission had been vetoed by Russia. Mr. Nehru proposed that the four other participants should jointly recommend Ceylon's admission. Sir John replied that the matter had been discussed by the Ceylon Cabinet; it preferred Ceylon's request to 'take its normal course'—that is, be further delayed. Admission, it considered, would cause difficulties because of Ceylon's vital rice–rubber trade agreement with Communist China, rubber being one of the strategic materials included in the United Nations' embargo on trade with China. Mr. Nehru said that no absolute ban was enforced, but Ceylon prudently did not wish to take any risks. Ceylon's rice–rubber deal with China was to cast a long, dark shadow over yet another conference held in Colombo, that of 1962.

The discussions on the item labelled 'colonialism and racialism. were, as might have been expected, brief and non-controversial; indeed racialism was not talked about at all. In supplementary remarks introducing an Indian draft of some length, Mr. Nehru noted that in Asia opposition should be expressed both to classical colonialism in North Africa and to white-settler governments in Central and East Africa—an anticipation of 'neo-colonialism'.

The conference considered in a mood of tolerant indifference the Indonesian proposal to hold an Afro-Asian conference. This was the fruit of many months of effort on Indonesia's part; as the effort culminated in the Bandung Conference, it is worth recounting. Whether the idea of holding such a conference in Indonesia was originally an Indonesian idea may be doubted. The first mention of any such meeting is curious. Late in December 1953, on the suggestion of some Asian diplomats in Jakarta, the Ceylon Minister there had discussed with President Sukarno the idea that he, Mr. Nehru and General Neguib, then ruler of Egypt, should summon an all-Asia conference at which an Asian Confederation should be discussed. President

The First Colombo Conference, April 1954

Sukarno replied that he was 'very happy to hear this' and would 'like to have the conference in Indonesia'. There is no indication that Indonesia had already been thinking along these lines. One hears an echo of this hare-brained suggestion in the request, reported to have been made in mid-January 1954, by Dr. Sastroamidjojo to Sir John Kotelawala, that General Neguib should be invited to the Colombo meeting.

Whatever its true origin, by March 1954 Indonesia was actively sponsoring the plan that the next, larger conference should be held on her soil on the 17th August, her Independence Day. Particular pressure was applied to India, and caused India embarrassment; for U Nu had already let it be known that, having been forestalled by Ceylon about the premiers' conference, he would like to play host in Burma to the next meeting. Once again, however, Burma let herself be forestalled; so that, in his opening speech at Colombo, the Indonesian Premier spoke of the next conference as an exclusively Indonesian proposal. He even suggested that the details for it might be worked out at the Colombo Conference itself.

When presenting the idea to the prime ministers, Dr. Ali said that simply to have an Afro-Asian group at the United Nations was not enough: organised contacts were too few and there was no machinery of consultation. He was not suggesting the formation of a bloc, but only occasional meetings for exchange of ideas by a group of nations having common principles.

U Nu agreed in principle but Mr. Nehru foresaw difficulties. If a large conference were summoned, there would be differences of opinion, and it would be difficult to reach agreements. Whom were they to invite, especially from Africa? Arab-Israeli hostility presented yet another problem. Yet he welcomed the idea: earlier attempts to organise an Afro-Asian conference had all been abortive; if they accepted the Indonesian proposal it was essential to ensure that it did not fizzle out too, and considerable preparatory work at the official level would be necessary.

The Pakistani and Ceylon Premiers raised questions about membership; they also enquired whether any soundings had already been made and whether colonial territories in Africa would be invited.

Dr. Ali replied that the first intention was to invite only the members of the Afro-Asian group at the United Nations, certainly not the colonial territories. Most of the Middle East countries had already responded favourably. If the principle were accepted now, the details could be settled later, he said cautiously; Indonesia was ready to undertake the preparatory work.

U Nu preferred the possibility of holding an unofficial meeting, composed of leaders of political parties representing their countries: he probably had in mind something similar to the Asian Socialists' Conference held in Rangoon a year earlier.

This was impracticable, replied Dr. Ali: in his country alone there were over twenty parties and if all were not to be invited who would make the choice? Answering a question asked by the Ceylonese, he suggested that the conference be governmental, and at the highest level.

Mr. Mohammed Ali supported this suggestion, but proposed that they should meet 'as individual governments' rather than collectively as a conference.

Dr. Ali said he would be satisfied with a decision that the conference should be sponsored by Indonesia. This may have been humility; he may have wanted to win kudos solely for Indonesia; perhaps both motives were present.

Mr. Nehru clinched the matter by saying that, despite foreseeable difficulties, he was attracted to this plan: he himself had for some years had such a plan in mind. Indonesia ought to have their moral support; it must be mentioned in the final communiqué. Thus the Colombo Conference, with no controversy and little debate, took the one decision for which it is now remembered.

On the subject of Palestine, Pakistan moved a draft resolution calling down fire and brimstone on Israel: it condemned the establishment of the state as a violation of international law; it condemned Israel's aggressive policy towards its neighbours; it expressed grave concern for the plight of the Arab refugees.

India, Mr. Nehru said, had always had great sympathy for the Arab cause. But she had recognised Israel: it was therefore difficult for him to say that its creation was a violation of international law. The attempts that the United Nations were making to settle this problem would be prejudiced by the Pakistani resolution.

After U Nu had said that the draft ought to be modified (Burma already had close relations with Israel) Mr. Mohammed Ali said he would be satisfied if the conference condemned Israeli aggression in Palestine and expressed sympathy for the victims of the aggression. In their final discussions on Palestine the premiers, after deleting several paragraphs of the Pakistani draft, wondered whether they would be correct in reiterating United Nations resolutions on the resettling of the Palestine refugees in their original homes: they were not sure that United Nations had so decided. Their ignorance that this important decision had in fact been taken is extraordinary. So the recommendation to rehabilitate the refugees was retained, but as if it were an original suggestion. This indicates how seriously the Arabs had failed to enlighten even their friends on their principal problem.

It is instructive to compare with the original Pakistani demands the paragraph on Palestine as accepted in the final communiqué. The two are far removed; their unlikeness is a touchstone for testing the claims made by Pakistan soon after the conference that she had vigorously championed the Arab cause against the active opposition of India.

Thanks to the lateness of the hour the closing speeches at Kandy were mercifully brief. The conference ended at 12.40 a.m. on the 2nd May, at almost exactly the same hour as the final session of the Belgrade Conference, after a session of similar length.

The long and angry debates at the Colombo Conference revealed certain individual attitudes and national policies; but they were very much 'about it and about'. The discussion on international Communism brought no change of alignments in the Cold War; the discussion about non-intervention in Indo-China did not prevent the Indo-Chinese states from asking for intervention later; this possibility had been recognised during the course of the debate.

Mainly because the debates were less about facts than about wording, the length of the discussions was out of all proportion to the results achieved. Pakistan accepted the principle of non-intervention but did not want to say so publicly, and for a long time refused to admit that her prospects in Kashmir and her bid for American military aid might be adversely affected. Mr. Nehru agreed about the danger of local Communists and partially admitted the dangers of 'international Communism'; but he eschewed that particular phrase—a weapon drawn from the verbal armoury of the Cold War—because he was reluctant to admit his unwillingness to criticise China, a partner in international Communism, at a time when he was trying to apply moral rather than military interdictions to her. It is noteworthy that the criticisms of Communism were directed entirely against Soviet Russia. Why, after events in Korea and Indo-China, China should have been exempted is a mystery. This anti-Communist concentration on Europe was apparent also at Bandung, and there it was even less justifiable. Pakistan and Ceylon were perhaps trying to please friends, who evidently felt more alarm about Russia than about China. Here may lie the explanation why Pakistan and Ceylon, which had had no direct experience of Communist intervention, should express alarm, while India and Indonesia, which had had the experience, were not so alarmed.

Each country naturally sought to advance some particular national interest through the conference. Indonesia was interested in the next conference and in China's admission to the United Nations; Burma and India, each for different reasons, were most concerned with Indo-China. Burma's chief concern was that a hurried French exit should not lead to a Chinese entrance, bringing greater Communist pressure to bear on an already troubled area just across her frontiers: she had one Communist neighbour and was not keen on another. India's policy at Colombo was to try and strengthen the hands of Britain and France at Geneva as against the more adventurous United States. An understanding on non-intervention by all the major powers, she felt, might win China's acceptance and so lead to an agreement to neutralise the three Indo-China states; this decision was in fact taken privately between Eden, Mendès-France and Chou En-lai at Geneva. This neutralisation would not only remove the threat of America's atomic intervention but also extend the area of non-alignment.

From the Indian national point of view it would do more: the inclusion of the three Indo-China states in the non-aligned area would help to draw a line east of Laos and Cambodia which marked the frontier between the 'Indian area' and the 'Chinese area' in South-East Asia. This line runs roughly along the Mekong River, which is an historical as also a culturo-gastronomic border between the Indianised eaters of rice with their fingers and the Sinofied eaters of noodles with chopsticks. Mr. Nehru was concerned with drawing this line, because at this time Indo-China's future was being decided, and Colombo was a link in the chain of decision. But having got what she wanted India then lost interest in the area.

Pakistan and Ceylon were, of course, concerned with pleasing, or at least not displeasing, the West; and Pakistan in particular came off well in its exchanges with India. On the crucial question of Indo-China Pakistan preserved her essential position, even if only through pity for Mr. Mohammed Ali; she conceded to India a recommendation that was just strong and clear enough to help Eden and Mendès-France. On the other hand, Pakistan pushed Mr. Nehru into actually naming Communism in a pejorative context, something to which he never agreed again; at Bandung Pakistan and Ceylon tried to repeat this success, but failed.

The First Colombo Conference, April 1954

The key role at this conference was undoubtedly that of U Nu. Since the other four participants were equally divided on the crucial issues of Indo-China and international Communism, he was in a position to swing the balance, and with fine impartiality he did so, on Indo-China siding with India and on international Communism with Pakistan. In short, a good example of non-alignment. He also provided one of the few lighter moments when at Kandy he left the conference room to return with a towel round his head, not as a reflection on the course of the discussions but merely as protection against the draught caused by the ceiling fans.

This was the first Asian conference, but not the last, at which the need to reach unanimous conclusions had a great effect on the discussions. Why were the five prime ministers shy of admitting openly that they could not agree on certain subjects? Apart from Pakistan's fear of isolation, shared in a lesser degree by India, Commonwealth precedent offered strong inducements to agree. All would have been ashamed to admit that a smaller, Asian conference composed mainly of Commonwealth colleagues could not reach the same degree of unity as the larger Commonwealth meetings always contrived to do. Additionally, all were moved by the fear, made real by Mr. Eden's message, that failure at Colombo would increase the chances of failure at Geneva, leading to war between America and China.

Some Indian sources believe that unanimity was reached because Mr. Mohammed Ali did not know exactly what he agreed to on the topic of Indo-China in the last long punishing session in Kandy (there would be nothing remarkable in this, for 'ignorance is bliss' was the sign inscribed over other Asian conference communiqués). But this was probably not so, for on his return to Karachi he refused to discuss the 'Communist' paragraph with the press, and contented himself with saying that he was not completely satisfied with the conference. He clearly knew what he had not obtained at Colombo.

The conference, as we have seen, did not discuss the offer by Mr. Eden that the participants should be associated with the 'guaranteeing' of the Indo-China settlement. Ceylon and Pakistan announced that they could supply no troops for the purpose and India replied that she would be prepared to participate in a guarantee arrangement only if she were invited to do so by both sides. This invitation did not materialise and it was left to SEATO to try to furnish the settlement with some sort of military backing.

This ignoring of the British proposal angered the Press in Britain, which dismissed the final communiqué as a colourless compilation;[13]

criticisms were so sharp that the government felt the need to dissociate itself from them.[14] The American Press was more complimentary, seeing in the conference three favourable signs—a healthy reaction against Communism, the failure of a plan by Mr. Nehru to
found a neutral bloc[15] and proof that 'India doesn't rule Asia'.[16] The
Russians were equally pleased because, according to Moscow radio,[17]
the communiqué was another major blow to Washington politicians
and ran clearly counter to United States diplomacy. The Pakistan
Press reaction was equally simple, and simple-minded: to that
country's largest and most influential paper the conference discussions proved that Mr. Nehru 'has become an agent of Soviet imperialism'.[18]

On the contrary, it was the depth of anti-Communist feeling expressed at Colombo, especially by U Nu, that impressed Mr. Nehru;
he echoed these fears, as genuine and well-founded, in the months to
come. He remarked in a speech to Parliament in September 1954[19]
that national Communist parties being 'intellectually, mentally and
otherwise tied up with other groups in other countries' had 'caused a
good deal of apprehension and disturbance in various countries' such
as Burma and Thailand. It is unlikely that he would have uttered this
judgement publicly before the Colombo Conference.

The conference, as is now known, helped in some measure to bring
about the Geneva Agreement. But its real place in history is as the
originating point for Bandung, a fact which as Sir John Kotelawala
admitted, 'passed almost unnoticed at the time'.[20] History and The
News operate on different wavelengths.

NOTES TO CHAPTER VII

1. Sir John Kotelawala: *An Asian Prime Minister's Story*, London, 1956, chap. 15.
2. Tarzie Vittachi: *The Brown Sahibs*, London, 1962. A slight and amusing study, more penetrating and significant perhaps even for Africa than for Asia.
3. Radio address on 4th Feb. 1954.
4. These and subsequent quotations are from official records obtained from a variety of sources in the countries concerned.
5. *The Hindu*, Madras, 29th Apr. 1954.
6. *SEATO: Six Studies*, Part II; and D. Lancaster: *The Emancipation of French Indo-China*, Oxford, 1961, chaps. 16 and 17.
7. The details of the conference given below are taken from the official minutes prepared by the Ceylonese civil servants who comprised the secretariat of the conference. These minutes were approved by the delegations before being printed and issued, in a limited number, to

the participating, as well as to some other Commonwealth, governments.

8. *The Times*, London, 30th Apr. 1945.
9. Kotelawala: *op. cit.*, chap. 15.
10. In conversation with the author.
11. Kotelawala: *op. cit.*, chap. 15.
12. *Op. cit.*, chap. 15.
13. *The Times*, London, 3rd May 1954.
14. *Manchester Guardian*, 4th May 1954.
15. *Christian Science Monitor*, Boston, 4th and 5th May 1954.
16. *New York Times*, 3rd May 1954.
17. On 6th May 1954.
18. *Dawn*, Karachi, 3rd May 1954.
19. Nehru: *India's Foreign Policy*, p. 93.
20. Kotelawala: *op. cit.*, chap. 20.

CHAPTER VIII

The Bogor Conference, December, 1954

When the five prime ministers next met, at Bogor, on the 28th and 29th December 1954, to arrange the Bandung Conference, they were formally and officially divided into two camps as a result of Pakistan's entry into SEATO in the previous September. The life of the Colombo Powers as a political group had been short and stormy. Even in the months before that act of alignment, between May and September, there had been two moves, one unfriendly, the other awkward, that agitated the Five—a more accurate description now than the Colombo Powers.

In May, soon after the Colombo meeting and almost certainly because of it, the able Foreign Minister of Pakistan, Sir Mohammed Zafrullah Khan, had tried to outmanœuvre India by bringing the other three countries—Ceylon, Burma and Indonesia—into the South-East Asian alliance, which was then in process of formation.[1] The attempt came to nothing.

Early in August Sir John Kotelawala asked for another meeting of the prime ministers, to be held this time in Rangoon. Pakistan and Burma were willing to attend but Mr. Nehru replied that he was too busy to go to Rangoon. Sir John shifted the venue to New Delhi to suit Mr. Nehru's convenience; Mr. Nehru thereupon said that in his view any meeting of the Five at that time might be construed as a re-thinking of views expressed at Colombo, and might lead to mis-understanding.[2] Probably the Ceylon Premier, in asking for this meeting so soon after the Colombo Conference, intended 'to force Mr. Nehru to articulate an alternative security scheme for the region'. He told the Ceylon Parliament in August that Mr. Nehru had given some intimation of an alternative to SEATO, but this Mr. Nehru said was due to a misunderstanding.[3] Mr. Nehru feared, with reason, that another conference would not only widen the existing rifts between the Five; it might also reawaken China's suspicions. Furthermore, if he did not provide an alternative to SEATO (which

169

he could not do) he might supply Ceylon with a reason for joining SEATO, as she was eager to do.

Apart from these practical difficulties, Mr. Nehru might well have argued that there was no need for an alternative security arrangement in South-East Asia after the Geneva Agreement on Indo-China. After a visit to New Delhi, Chou En-lai had agreed to withdraw his earlier demands for a partitioning of Laos and Cambodia, as well as of Vietnam, in return for the understanding that they would be neutralised. Neutralisation was to be effected by giving India the chairmanship and the deciding vote on the three-nation international commissions for supervision and control in the Indo-China states.

At the same time as India was making this concession to China, China was being pinned down to the promises of good behaviour in Panchsheel. As Mr. Nehru told the Lok Sabha in New Delhi: 'It is not a question of believing the other party's word; it is a question of creating conditions where the other party cannot break its word, or if I might say so, where it finds it difficult to break its word.'[4] In the next nine months, which led up to Bandung, Mr. Nehru was trying to 'create conditions where China's verbal guarantees would extend over as wide an area as possible in Asia and would be repeated on the most public platform that could be found'.[5]

At the same time he was making it clear, with a new sense of realism, that there was genuine fear of China in the South-East Asian countries; and, he added, 'I can understand them.'[6] This plain speaking happened just before a visit which he made to China in October; from this he returned much impressed.

During this period General Neguib was replaced by a young Colonel Nasser as the ruler of Egypt, and on the 1st November 1954, the Algerians began their long, desperate struggle for freedom.

Against this background, Indonesia was making steady efforts to get a full Afro-Asian conference going. Having obtained the approval of the Colombo Conference, offhand and lukewarm though this was, Indonesia spent the following three months in taking soundings, as she had been asked to do. The replies she received were sufficiently encouraging to lead her to a formal proposal for such a conference. This she made in an aide-mémoire of 23rd July. This said that 'it would be wise' to invite only 'the countries of the Afro-Asian group at the United Nations with the addition of Ceylon and Jordan'— eighteen countries in all. It reiterated an earlier suggestion that the conference should be held in September or October: this proposal, made in the last week of July, illustrates the lack of practical realism among the Indonesians—a defect that the organisers of the conference were amply to experience later on. The purpose of the conference, the note went on, was to find an answer to the question posed by the Indonesian Premier at Colombo: 'Where do we stand now, we the people of Asia, in a world like ours today?'

Mr. Nehru took almost a month to reply. On the 18th August he wrote to Dr. Ali saying that he welcomed such a conference and hoped it would be held in Indonesia. Since the matter had been discussed only 'rather briefly' at Colombo he invited the Indonesian Premier to Delhi for 'a full and frank' talk about the conference in September and suggested that after it the Five might meet in Indonesia: this was the genesis of the meeting at Bogor. He pointed out that at least six months' preparatory work would be required for the main conference. While committing himself to the idea, Mr. Nehru evidently still had some doubts; these he wanted to clear up personally with Dr. Ali.

Writing of the motives that led him to favour holding the conference Mr. Nehru made it clear that these sprang from his fear of what might result from the 'so-called South-East Asia conference' to be held in Manila. Its results would be 'misconceived' and dangerous. In his usual gloomy, apocalyptic style he also wrote of the 'explosive' situation in the area of the China Seas, Korea and Formosa.

He suggested a broader membership; if confined to the group at the United Nations, Africa would be excluded except for Ethiopia and Egypt, and the Arabs were not much interested in 'Asian problems as a whole'. Tunisia and Morocco ought to be included, being self-governing territories, and also the Gold Coast, Nigeria and the Sudan. Even the preliminary conference should be held later in the year.

Dr. Ali replied that he was glad to receive Mr. Nehru's ideas and his invitation, but that his suggestions about timing were disappointing. He hoped the main conference could be held in February 1955.

The Indonesian leader paid his visit to Delhi, and during it Mr. Nehru renamed the Five Principles 'Panchsheel'. By the 26th September Mr. Nehru's last doubts were resolved, and he and Dr. Ali in a joint statement agreed that an Afro-Asian conference should be held 'at an early date'.

Thereafter Mr. Nehru allowed his mind to range freely over the scope of the conference. At the end of September he remarked that it should not discuss local disputes like Indo-China or Palestine. He was still inhibited by the idea of a permanent organisation, for he wrote that while it was not desirable to have a formal set-up 'some simple machinery for consultation appears desirable,' especially as the group at the United Nations was 'rather vague and fluid'.

Three months later, from a note he sent to the other prime ministers just before the Bogor meeting, we learn that his ideas on the Afro-Asian conference had become clear and precise; and these ideas determined its final shape. He suggested that about thirty countries should be invited; and since he wanted the meeting to be 'business-like and effective', not 'vague and amorphous', it should be at the level of prime ministers or foreign ministers. 'The whole object should be to create an atmosphere of co-operation and to put Asia and Africa more in the world picture' since 'the old balances no longer hold good'. Therefore controversial items must be excluded and only broad issues placed on the agenda; among these he included 'good neighbourliness and the Five Principles'; one can only wonder whether this was meant seriously. Reverting to detail in a way that was typical of his practical mind, he proposed an international secretariat to arrange the conference and a sharing of its expenses among the sponsors.

When he came to membership of the conference he applied the surgeon's knife: 'I would not invite the Soviet Asian Republics. We should consider the Soviet Union as a unit. It can hardly be described as an Asian power,' which both is and is not true. Russia, of course, is not an Asian country, but she is an Asian power today in the way in which Britain, France and Holland were Asian powers twenty years ago. Yet his remark is far removed from the romantic enthusiasm of 1946. Mr. Nehru went on: 'In the final analysis I think it is better not to include Israel, if that is likely to lead to the Arab countries keeping away.' 'It is out of the question for us to leave out China' since she was the biggest Asian country, and the Asians had been recommending her membership of the United Nations. The representatives of one bloc were to be invited; if China were not asked only one bloc would be represented. He excluded all the four Indo-China states. The accusations of erecting racial or colour bars would be met if the Central African Federation were to be invited. In short, 'we must invite every independent country in these areas, subject to some minor variations'.

A vision of a grand assemblage of the two continents rather than of an amplified Afro-Asian group meeting was carried by Mr. Nehru to Bogor.

The Bogor Conference was a brisk and business-like meeting: the details of the Bandung Conference were worked out in two sessions. The political differences of the Five were indicated, and were maintained but not pressed in debate; controversy was reserved for the main conference. This was only the precursor, setting the stage.[7]

Thus Sir John Kotelawala and Mr. Mohammed Ali made points that are significant in their presage of the great debates at Bandung.[8] The Ceylon Prime Minister expressed strong doubts whether 'the aims and objectives of Communism have undergone any radical change' in the context of 'the role of China in the world of the future'. He meant that he doubted whether the restraints of Panchsheel were going to work in China's case. 'If China wants to be friendly,' he went on, it was up to her 'to demonstrate that her intentions are genuine'. And the Pakistani Prime Minister asserted that there should be no Afro-Asian colonialism, echoing the 1947 conference, this time more out of spite than from fear.

In closed session and after only a brief discussion on the purpose of the conference, a four-point statement of objectives put forward by Mr. Nehru was accepted.[9]

On the sponsorship of the conference, Pakistan proposed that it be collective under the aegis of Indonesia, but with some assistance from the others. Mr. Nehru said that this placed an unfair burden upon Indonesia. He suggested a joint secretariat from all five countries to prepare and run the conference, which was accepted. U Nu wanted its expenses also to be shared. In the end it was agreed that Indonesia would sponsor and stage the conference at the request of the Five.

There was agreement about an Indonesian suggestion that the conference should be held in the last week of April for approximately ten days; by now Indonesia knew that the meeting could not be rushed. There was also quick agreement on the proposal from India that delegations should be on a ministerial level, wherever possible prime ministers or foreign ministers.

India suggested that the agenda should be drawn up by the conference itself but Dr. Ali, unaccustomed to the convention of Commonwealth conferences, proposed, as he had done at Colombo, that the agenda be fixed beforehand and be sent out with the invitations. Burma disagreed with this procedure lest it give the impression that they were imposing their ideas on their invitees. In any case, Mr. Nehru observed, an agenda made now would be out of date in three or four months. So it was agreed that the conference should frame its own agenda.

On the most difficult issue of membership, Dr. Ali felt that certain principles should govern invitations, but he made no proposal, asking only whether observers should also be invited. Mr. Nehru opposed this as being discriminatory against those invited as full members. Despite a further Indian objection U Nu repeated the point he had made at Colombo, that nationalist parties should be represented since anti-colonialism would be discussed. What, Mr. Nehru asked, if Mau Mau wanted to be heard or the Communist Party of Malaya or any banned party? They could be admitted as visitors, said Dr. Ali. Mr. Nehru said that they could, of course, come, but he was against inviting them. Indonesia, however, insisted that nationalist representatives should be heard; it was so decided. But at the conference itself no such representative was given a hearing.

Mr. Nehru put forward a principle for membership that was agreed: those countries of Africa and Asia which have independent governments, to be considered country by country, plus some borderline cases.

When this detailed consideration was taken up the five sponsoring countries and the fourteen Afro-Asian members of the United Nations were immediately accepted. There was ready agreement on inviting Nepal, Turkey, Japan and the four Indo-China states; as also on the borderline cases of Sudan and the Gold Coast, proposed by India. There was, however, some resistance, from Ceylon and Pakistan, to the further Indian suggestion that the Central African Federation should be invited to show that the conference had no racial bias. Eventually Mr. Nehru's arguments that such an invitation would be an encouragement to both Africans and liberal whites, and that if it was not accepted the European rulers of the Federation would stand revealed as racialists, were accepted as valid.

There was debate on invitations to only two countries, Israel and China. On Israel, an important development had taken place before the conference. Mr. Nehru, flying to Bogor in the Dakota he affectionately referred to as 'my bus', had picked up U Nu at Rangoon. During the flight the two leaders discussed the conference and, inevitably, the question of inviting Israel. By 1954 Israel, being a socialist state like Burma, was firmly entrenched in that country. So close were the links that U Nu told Mr. Nehru that if Israel were not asked, Burma might not attend. Mr. Nehru agreed that Israel ought perhaps to be invited, but pointed out that if she were present the Arab states would stay away, which would mean that almost the whole of West Asia would be absent. The conference would therefore be so unbalanced that India would have to reconsider whether her own attendance would be worth while. The subject was dropped after this display of pressure and counter-pressure.

When the conference discussed the invitation to Israel, Burma raised no objection; Indonesia objected and Pakistan renewed the argument advanced by India. Ceylon proposed that the Arabs should be approached and reasoned with, but Indonesia said this was pointless since their view was known and the Arab League had recently issued a warning on this very point. After Pakistan had pointed out that the Arabs were still legally at war with Israel, India said that though the invitation might be justified it would be unwise to flout the wishes of the Arab countries. Burma fell in with this view and it was finally decided not to invite Israel.

A tentative proposal that Formosa, as well as Communist China, be invited prompted U Nu to threaten to withdraw as co-sponsor if this were carried. The Burmese leader was, at this conference, in a mood to walk out on any pretext.

Speaking on Communist China, Mr. Mohammed Ali, using the same argument as against Israel, said it was likely that the Arab countries, as well as Thailand and the Philippines, would not participate if China were present, since none of them had recognised it. A main purpose of the conference was to improve economic relations, and this was not possible without diplomatic relations. Would it be wise, he asked, to sacrifice ten countries to win one? This invitation also might jeopardise the success of the conference. U Nu countered with the telling point that if the conference would be a failure without the Arabs, it would equally be so without China. Mr. Nehru said that in Japan, and even America, there was a tendency towards closer economic ties with China even though political links were lacking. At the Colombo Conference, China had been recommended for membership of the United Nations. If they did not invite her they would virtually be reversing that decision. In view of the general background of the Geneva and Colombo conferences, and since the four Indo-China states were being asked, China must be invited also. Pakistan conceded that Indonesia might be asked to approach the Arabs once again. If it was certain that some Arab countries would not attend, China ought not to be invited. If there was no risk of jeopardising the conference, Indonesia could decide to invite China. Dr. Ali said it would be difficult for him to decide at what point the conference was being jeopardised, and Mr. Nehru argued that other countries might stay away if China were not invited.

Dr. Ali now said that no one present was actually against inviting

China, but it was a question of expediency; did all agree that on principle China ought to be invited? Mr. Mohammed Ali said that in principle he agreed but for reasons of expediency was opposed. At this point U Nu said that Burma would not attend if China were not invited. Mr. Mohammed Ali immediately withdrew his objection, because if Burma and China were absent, the whole picture would be altered; but he sounded a warning about possible abstentions. So it was decided to invite China; Indonesia, along with Pakistan, was asked to explain the matter to the Arabs.[10] It was mainly in the context of the invitation to China that the conference decided to allay the fears of those who would be participating at Bandung with governments that they did not recognise, by inserting in the final communiqué a note explaining that sitting at the same table would not involve, or even imply, a change or view about the status of any fellow member.

This decision to invite China was the most important one taken at Bogor. In the discussion, anti-Communist Ceylon took no part, and Pakistan's objections were based on the alleged objections of other countries. Was Mr. Mohammed Ali using the Arabs as a stalking horse for some sniping of his own? Yes and no; in the end none of the Arab governments raised any objection to China's presence, but Dr. Fawzi, the Egyptian Foreign Minister, had earlier expressed some reservations about it. When Sir John Kotelawala was asked why he had agreed to the invitation to China, he replied: 'The answer is simple. Asia is one and indivisible.' This, coming from him, was almost too good to be true.[11]

Indonesia next asked whether Outer Mongolia was to be invited. When Mr. Mohammed Ali said that it was part of China, Mr. Nehru reminded him that he was thinking of Inner Mongolia, and Dr. Ali observed that Outer Mongolia had applied for United Nations membership. Nevertheless it was decided that neither Outer Mongolia nor North nor South Korea should be asked. The final list now contained thirty approved invitees, compared with an original eighteen. When Mr. Nehru was asked why the two parts of a partitioned Vietnam had been invited, but not those of a partitioned Korea, he admitted that the two cases had much in common; but while the Five had a feeling of special responsibility for Indo-China, because of the Colombo proposals and the Geneva Agreement, they had no such personal sense of responsibility for Korea.[12] This is factually correct but morally unconvincing. The real reason was that whereas Korea had been divided by the two principal protagonists in the Cold War, the Five still hoped to keep one part of Vietnam out of that contest. Since the other four had accepted Mr. Nehru's exclusion of the Soviet Central Asian Republics, as being part of European Russia, in a note circulated before Bogor, the conference did not discuss the issue. The Russians did not take this airy dismissal lying down. A few weeks later Mr. Molotov, speaking of Bandung, reminded an Indian visitor that there were Asian states in the Soviet Union, and that these attached great importance to the conference; the Soviet Government likewise welcomed it. Naturally no invitation was asked for openly, but a question mark was left suspended in mid-air.

One question which the decision about membership raised was why Australia should be excluded: the possibility of inviting her does not even seem to have been discussed at Bogor. Bandung was to be the first large Afro-Asian meeting after the New Delhi Conference of January 1949. In this Australia had taken a leading part; and it was being held in Indonesia, on whose behalf Australia had done a great deal. The reasons for her exclusion are evasive and unsatisfying. Dr. Ali's reply was 'because Australia is a separate continent', and any request for admission from Australia depended on the decision of the five prime ministers. The Indian Government said that it would have welcomed the inclusion of Australia and New Zealand; it would support any such suggestion if in the future the 'limits of the area' were reconsidered; any such suggestion must be made to Indonesia. This shelving of the responsibility, indicating embarrassment, discloses the real reason why, in the first place, the 'limits of the area' were not extended to include Australia, as had been done at New Delhi. The Bandung Conference could not avoid criteria of race and colour. This comment is not invalidated by the invitation to the Central African Federation: to ask the white rulers of black men from the middle of a black continent is quite different from asking the white rulers of white men from a white continent. But the embarrassment shows that the sponsors were uncomfortable about this basis of their meeting, and they did not allow the two factors to influence the actual deliberations.

A general discussion of the world situation next occupied the prime ministers; it consisted almost entirely of a long disquisition from Mr. Nehru. The most interesting part of Mr. Nehru's survey covered his impressions of China after his recent visit there. This exposition was of singular importance for it not only revealed the basic approach behind India's policy towards China but also Mr.

Nehru's forecast of China's policy towards the world. In particular, it was this assessment that governed his conduct towards Chou En-lai at the Bandung Conference. China, he said, was anxious to avoid war, even any possibility of conflict. She urgently desired peace because she was passionately concerned with the problem of economic improvement. She wished to be left in peace and to develop normal relations with other countries. No attack would come from China. But she was afraid that neighbouring countries could be used to attack her, and it was important for her to know the intentions of neighbouring countries; for this reason the Geneva Agreement was important, in particular the clause proving that in Indo-China, no outside interference would be allowed.

Referring to the Five Principles, he remarked that they had a few days before been endorsed by a European leader, Tito; and he would like the Afro-Asian conference to consider them, because the South-East Asian countries were also concerned with problems of aggression and interference.

He conceded that the Communist parties in South-East Asia were aided at least morally by outside parties. He did not think they were receiving direct support from China, nor was the Soviet Union encouraging local parties; rather was she discouraging them, as she also wanted peace.

China had been thrown into Russia's arms by the Korean war and by the United Nations embargo. But it was his opinion, from what he had seen in China, that the Chinese people remained essentially unaltered. The Chinese, having discovered rich mineral resources in Sinkiang, now intended to make that region a highly developed industrial area. For China, economic development came first; political problems were a minor issue. The whole face of Asia had changed; the continent must try to achieve its proper place in world affairs, he concluded.

In the meantime those labourers in the vineyard, the drafters, had been working over the communiqué, the final version of which was the work of Mr. Krishna Menon. When it came up for consideration, Mr. Nehru said that the full conference should be styled 'Asian-African' because the Five who initiated it were Asian and because the abbreviation 'Afro-' might cause resentment in Africa as the word 'Asiatic' did in Asia. 'Asian-African' became Bandung's official epithet, but before long common usage reverted to the more euphonic 'Afro-Asian'.

Mr. Mohammed Ali wanted a reference to international Communism, but Indonesia objected since the conference had not discussed the topic.

The Pakistan Premier promptly used the same argument to obtain the deletion of three paragraphs referring to the Five Principles. All were mentioned in the United Nations Charter, he said, and all the participants were United Nations members. If these were specifically mentioned, a reference to the collective security measures, also mentioned in the Charter, should likewise be made.

The paragraphs were, in any case, so arrogantly worded that they would never have found general acceptance: countries, the draft said, 'must and can live and progress only by the recognition of these principles and their determination to respect them and live peacefully'; they are 'capable of wider application and their acceptance would help to lower present world tensions'. There is here that same moral, crusading tone for which Mr. Dulles was well known.

The Press in two of the participating countries, Burma and Indonesia, was not unduly enthusiastic about the results of Bogor. In Burma, the exclusion of Israel was unanimously condemned; principle had been sacrificed to expediency, newspapers claimed, and the conference had let itself be blackmailed by the Muslim bloc led by Pakistan.

In Indonesia, the many opposition newspapers criticised the Government for wasting time on such matters as Afro-Asian conferences. The Bandung Conference was very much an issue in Indonesian internal politics. Much of the Indonesian Government's inordinate keenness to hold it must be ascribed to its desire to gain prestige for the governing Nationalist Party of President Sukarno and Dr. Ali, just before Indonesia's first general election (this was held a few months after Bandung and its date was announced on the eve of the conference). The opposition parties were wholly excluded from the arrangements for the conference, and they in turn boycotted it.

Mr. Nehru's reaction to this Bogor-Bandung phase was typical of his response to subsequent Afro-Asian conferences—a reaction that did not endear him to his fellow sponsors. It consisted of Indian reluctance at the outset, when with great coyness India seemed to be playing 'hard-to-get', followed by an acceptance and an Indian assumption of leadership within the conference.

Thus, in the preparations for Bandung, Dr. Ali had to go to Delhi to get Mr. Nehru's final approval; after this the latter's ideas shaped Bandung. Its purposes, number of invitees, level of representation, timing, agenda (or lack of it), and its international secretariat were

179

all determined by his directives of five months earlier. The Indonesians, lacking ideas of their own, accepted Mr. Nehru's, but they did not like the Indian swaddling bands that enveloped their baby.

Some of India's suggestions, such as the exclusion of observers and of nationalist representatives, already bear that air of solid caution which later led to accusations made by the young nationalists of the Arab World and Africa that she had become old and effete and 'stuffy'.

The ideas about Communist China expressed by Mr. Nehru at Bogor leave, in retrospect, a taste of bitter irony. There were in his assessment of that country two fundamental flaws. He thought China would be like Soviet Russia in the past, in its first generation, absorbed by internal problems and, unlike Soviet Russia at a later date, not wholly immersed in the bitterness of the Cold War. The first mistake was perhaps due to the leftist thinking of the 1920's and 1930's that had so greatly influenced him and that led him to give the Communists the benefit of the doubt; as to the second, it was his Asian feeling that led him mistakenly to believe that ancient, supple China would not take on the rigidities of European Russia. But, as we now know, China was interested not merely in internal development; and she has proved more rigidly dogmatic than Russia.

It is particularly ironic that the Chinese must have told Mr. Nehru of their industrial development of Sinkiang, for though he mentioned this, he had not personally seen that area during his visit. For the sake of an easy link with Sinkiang over the Tibetan plateau, rather than across the Gobi Desert, China secretly built a road across Indian territory in Ladakh, and this became the prime cause of their later dispute. The Chinese must have been planning the construction of the road at about the time Mr. Nehru was in China. Did his Chinese interlocutors smile inwardly as they gave him information about Sinkiang?

All this lay in the womb of time. After Bogor the whole horizon was filled with the sunlit heights of Bandung.

NOTES TO CHAPTER VIII

1. *New York Times*, 28th May 1954.
2. *The Hindu*, Madras, 10th, 11th, 13th Aug. 1954.
3. *The Times of India*, Delhi, 4th and 27th Aug. 1954. Also *SEATO: Six Studies*, Part V, for an excellent analysis of this period.
4. Lok Sabha Debates, VII, ii, cols. 3692–2 (29th Sept. 1954).
5. *SEATO: Six Studies, ibid.*

The Bogor Conference, December 1954

6. Nehru: *India's Foreign Policy*, pp. 88, 92.
7. Speeches given in the *Bogor Conference* pamphlet published by the Ministry of Information of Indonesia, 1955.
8. Information on the closed sessions was obtained from a variety of official sources who wish to remain anonymous.
9. See paragraph 4 of the Bogor communiqué, Appendix A.3.
10. Paragraph 9 of the Bogor communiqué.
11. Kotelawala: *op. cit.*, chap. 19.
12. *The Hindu*, Madras, 2nd Jan. 1955.

CHAPTER IX

High Noon at Bandung, April–May 1955

Two conferences were held at Bandung in April 1955. One was the real conference, about which not very much is known, about which people care even less, and which has faded away like a bad dream. The other was a quite different conference, a crystallisation of what people wanted to believe had happened which, as a myth, took on reality in the Bandung Principles and, later, in the Bandung Spirit. The real conference aroused interest mainly because it contributed towards the solution of a crisis then much in the news but which history scarcely troubles to record.

Though only three and a half months separated Bogor from Bandung, this period included two military incidents, one off the eastern shores of Asia, which was immediately dangerous, the other on its western coastline which had immense long-term significance.

At about the time of the signing of the SEATO Pact in Manila in September 1954, the Chinese Communists had resumed the shelling of the two islands of Quemoy and Matsu, which lie a few miles from their coast but which are garrisoned by troops of the Formosan regime. Responding to this military action the United States extended its system of military pacts in the area by concluding a Mutual Security Treaty with Formosa on the 2nd December; but in return the United States obtained from General Chiang Kai-shek a formal undertaking not to attack the mainland without prior consultation with the United States. The Chinese ripostes to these moves came on the 18th January 1955, when Chinese forces attacked and captured some small islets near Matsu and bombed others from the air. The United States suggested United Nations intervention; Peking, not being represented in that body, naturally refused. On the 24th January President Eisenhower asked Congress for authority to use the American armed forces to defend Formosa and the Pescadores Islands. In this dangerous situation the British Government made clear that it was in no way committed to defend the off-shore islands, and the Security Council debated the crisis to no avail, because Peking declined an invitation to take part in the discussion.

While the crisis was unfolding Indonesia tried, without success, to call an emergency meeting of the Five to discuss it. A more serious suggestion for Asian mediation came from Russia, at the end of January, suggesting that the matter be handled by the Five along with the United States, the United Kingdom, Russia and China, the initiative in calling such a conference being left to the United Kingdom, Russia and India. This proposal came to naught because the Security Council was discussing the question at that time, and also because the Russians had left both Formosa and United Nations out of their plan. But it indicates how quickly Russian diplomacy played up to and sought to use this new Asian grouping, for which Mr. Dulles had only ill-concealed contempt. In the weeks to come, the situation in the Formosa Strait remained quiet but tense.

In Western Asia a military pact was signed in Baghdad on the 24th February 1955 between Iraq and Turkey. This pact immediately aroused the bitter opposition of Colonel Nasser and of the nationalists in the other Arab countries, not least in Iraq itself. Four days later, on the 28th February, the Israeli Army made a raid in force on the town of Gaza, in which thirty-eight Egyptians and eight Israelis were killed. Though small in scale, this action was one of the turning-points in recent West Asian history. Under strong pressure from his ill-equipped army Colonel Nasser went shopping for arms. When the West refused to sell him these in any quantity he turned to Russia, and in September a massive arms deal was concluded, ostensibly with Czechoslovakia. This, in turn, led to the withdrawal of American financial aid for the Aswan High Dam project, and that brought the nationalisation by Egypt of the Suez Canal and, ultimately, the tripartite aggression against Egypt in October 1956.

In the early months of 1955 Colonel Nasser was turning not only towards the Communists but also towards India and non-alignment. He saw a parallel between India's hostility towards SEATO and his own objections to what he called the 'crazy' Baghdad Pact aimed at isolating and disrupting the Arab League. A friendly communiqué was issued after a visit paid to Cairo by Mr. Nehru in February, and an Indo-Egyptian Friendship Treaty followed in April, just before the issue of the Five Principles, which figured prominently in similar agreements concluded by India with several other countries at this time. Colonel Nasser, with typical caution, was feeling his way in the direction of this new policy.

High Noon at Bandung, April–May 1955

In Russia, too, the pre-Bandung period witnessed an event of great importance for Asia. On the 8th February 1955, the day on which Malenkov was ousted, Mr. Molotov announced that the Soviet Government accepted the Five Principles, on which, according to him, Soviet foreign policy had always been based. He asked other governments why the Principles could not become the common platform for the maintenance of world peace. The banns of marriage with doctrinaire Communism were thus formally published.

China's favourable reaction to the Bandung idea had come even more promptly. Within a few days of the Bogor communiqué the Chinese Press was describing it as a major step by the Afro-Asian nations towards peace, while the American warmongers were trying to prevent the holding of the conference. In welcoming it, Peking uttered the warning that the conference 'should not be an exclusive regional bloc'—an understandable reservation since China was a member of another bloc. By March, indications from Peking[1] were that the Chinese believed that, in a composite gathering like Bandung, it was better only to discuss subjects of common concern; this shows that Chou En-lai's conciliatory policy at Bandung was thought out well in advance. Early in April the Dutch Embassy in Peking reported that China would be moderate and helpful at the conference;[1] its prediction was correct.

All this friendliness strongly contrasted with the reaction of sour distrust exhibited by the United States; this accurately reflected the mental attitude of Mr. Dulles. 'An ambiguous document' is his description of the Bogor communiqué; and some time later, when asked about Bandung, he replied that he had heard something about a 'so-called' Afro-Asian conference. For him Bandung was doubly dangerous: not only could it cause some of the faithful to stray from the fold into the wider, tempting pastures of non-alignment, but there was the risk of contamination from direct contact with one of the enemy, China, who might thus be able to break through the *cordon sanitaire* that had been drawn round her. From the reactions of America's Asian allies and client-states to the invitations, it is possible to plot accurately the change in the attitude of the State Department.

Early in January the Philippine Vice-President and Foreign Minister said that their country could not attend; it was 'unthinkable' that they should deal with Peking. The Japanese Foreign Minister wistfully remarked that Japan would like to attend but that the United States was cool to the idea. Thailand's initial reaction was that she might, at most, send an observer. Even late in January the King of Cambodia confessed that there was strong American pressure against acceptance, coupled with the threat that American economic aid to Cambodia might be cut off. Similar pressure was exerted on some of the Arab countries.

The first crack in this hostile front came in Thailand where (as in the case of the New Delhi Conference of 1949), the Government accepted its invitation, on the 2nd February, after controversy in government circles. The real change in the American attitude came as late as the middle of March. On the 23rd February Turkey said she would not attend because of the presence of China, but she accepted on the 8th March; Iran did so on the 11th March, the Philippines on the 16th March and Lebanon on the 17th March. The reason behind this change was purely tactical: as an American newspaper noted, if all the invitees accepted 'America's friends will out-number her enemies and they will defend the United States when necessary'.[2]

The attitude of the British Government certainly contributed to this change in the American approach. Generally alarmed at Mr. Dulles's brinkmanship, it had parted company with its ally over Indo-China and the issue of the off-shore islands. It had worked closely with the Colombo Conference, with beneficial results, and it did not believe that 'neutralism is immoral'. Three of the five sponsors of Bandung were Commonwealth countries; it had itself recognised Communist China. In consequence, those countries that were under British influence were more prompt with their acceptances—Iraq on the 15th February and Jordan on the 1st March. There had been earlier British doubts on the wisdom of acceptance, and a majority of the British diplomatic missions in the area who were consulted had advised against participation; however, the opinion of those in favour had been powerfully reinforced by the affirmative view of Mr. Malcolm Macdonald, the Commissioner General for South-East Asia in Singapore, and that opinion had ultimately prevailed. After this, Britain's friends were supplied with 'full documentation'.[3]

These facts illuminate a report from Ankara[4] that it was on the entreaty of her allies—the United Kingdom, France, Pakistan and others—that Turkey accepted this invitation, 'giving the West a most effective spokesman'. Pakistan also circulated an aide-mémoire to several countries urging attendance.

By late March a secret committee set up in the State Department was able to produce the following remarkably accurate forecast of Bandung: China would be moderate, in order to raise her prestige and show herself diplomatically acceptable; because of the diversity of the membership, conference resolutions were likely to stick to general principles; for the same reason the conference was not expected to result in any kind of regional alliance, but it was expected to make plans for further meetings to advance the principles it adopted; Chou En-lai would be cautious and reasonable, and there would be a struggle for leadership between him and Mr. Nehru, who was expected to give the meeting a non-racial lead. The conference would endorse the Five Principles. The United States had urged its friends to take a positive and constructive attitude at the conference but to be prepared to resist proposals that were merely anti-American. These 'friends' were listed as the Philippines, Japan, South Vietnam, Laos, Thailand, Turkey, Pakistan, Ethiopia, Libya and the Central African Federation.

The best comment on the Western reaction came from that good friend of the West, General Romulo of the Philippines: 'That the West was generally apprehensive about Bandung betrays an uneasy conscience, a sense of guilt.'[5]

Reaction to Bandung from other quarters varied greatly, from the warm welcome of the Yugoslav Press to a warning from an Australian cabinet minister that if Australia were not invited and Mr. Menzies were not there, then Chou En-lai would have his own way. A more sophisticated response came from Mr. Casey, the Australian Foreign Minister, that Chou En-lai's attendance opened up an area of discussion that could be useful.

As in 1949 the United Nations, or its Secretariat, echoed Western suspicions of the Asian gathering. There was a feeling in New York that the meeting implied criticism of the United Nations unsatisfactory handling of anti-colonial issues brought forward by the group.[6] Asia may have thought this in 1949 but there is no evidence of any such opinion in 1955. Senior officials in the Secretariat thought that United Nations ought to have been invited to send an observer. Perhaps as a follow-up of this notion, Indonesia suggested tentatively that Mr. Hammarskjöld might be asked, but the suggestion was firmly negatived by India. It would have been embarrassing for everyone concerned if, at Bandung, Mr. Hammarskjöld had been invited to the private sessions, and equally embarrassing if he had been left out.

Although, as we have seen, some pro-Western governments took nearly nine weeks to reply to the invitation, all the invitees eventually answered except for the settler Government of the Central African

Federation which, perhaps rightly, felt that there was no place for it in such a gathering. Thirteen of the delegations were led by prime ministers and seven by foreign ministers; there were one ex-king, from Cambodia, three princes—from Saudi Arabia, Yemen and Thailand—and one Grand Mufti. Though the conference was styled Asian-African only four of the twenty-nine countries present were really African—Ethiopia, the Gold Coast, Liberia and the Sudan— though perhaps the latter is more correctly included with Egypt and Libya among the Arab states.

In his opening speech the Ethiopian representative stated: 'We represent, so to say, more than half the peoples of the earth'—56 per cent or 1,400,000,000 producing 15 per cent of the world's income. In a second sense the conference represented only half, or perhaps less, of the people in the world for there was no woman among the 340 delegates. It is a measure not only of the world interest aroused by the meeting, but of the greater importance given to Image than to Fact, that newsmen should have outnumbered delegates by two to one; 655 newsmen despatched 280,000 words a day on happenings in Bandung.

In the end Mr. Nehru was successful in keeping the conference purely official, for on the 21st March the secretariat announced its decision that observer status would not be granted to representatives of nationalist movements. Nevertheless many of them were present in Bandung and were at least provided with accommodation. They included members of the African and the Indian National Congresses from South Africa; of nationalist parties from Malaya and Sarawak; Archbishop Makarios of Cyprus; a strong group of Arab nationalist leaders, including the Mufti of Jerusalem, who was made a member of the Yemen delegation; and representatives from Tunisia, Morocco and Algeria, who attended the debates on North Africa as part of the Iraqi delegation. Perhaps the oddest of these non-official partici- pants was the American Negro Congressman Adam Clayton Powell: it was never clear what he was aiming at, apart from publicity, and he had an embarrassing habit of distributing cigars to all and sundry, with or without provocation. The most embarrassing figure of all was a spokesman for the freedom movement in Turkestan, in Soviet Central Asia; him the secretariat requested to maintain a discreet silence. Two well-known Australian scholars, J. W. Burton and C. P. Fitzgerald, also attended unofficially and expressed the view that 'Australia should have been invited to this conference and should have accepted; and should on all future occasions be invited and attend'. The secretariat took a bold step when it conferred a flag on the Sudan, which did not as yet possess one of its own. It considered using the United Nations flag with 'Sudan' across it, or a red flag with the word in white, and finally chose a white flag with the word in red as being more innocuous.

The international secretariat which arranged the conference had two principal difficulties to overcome—its being held in Bandung, and the cheerful insouciance of their Indonesian colleagues. Bandung is a pleasantly cool hill resort set beneath one of Java's semi-somnolent volcanoes, with a cosy, cheerful charm of its own. It is not a large town, and to squeeze a large and high-powered international conference into its limited accommodation was a genuine problem, solved only by obliging most of the delegates and all the pressmen to share rooms. Telegraph and telephone communications into and out of it had to be expanded many times over. All the important sections of the Secretariat were headed by officials lent by other countries, and fortunately the mechanics—typing, interpreting and so on, were also handled by foreign staff; for not only did the Indonesians lack experience of conference work; they assumed that if a decision were taken that something should be done, that meant, automatically, that it had come about; an immense willingness was present, but not always drive or attention to detail. This defect greatly worried Mr. Nehru, and one of his directives the author cannot forbear to quote at the risk of infringing the Official Secrets Act. Mr. Nehru wrote: 'Above all one fact should be remembered, and this is usually forgotten in Indonesia. This fact is an adequate provision of bathrooms and lavatories. People can do without drawing-rooms but they cannot do without bathrooms and lavatories. I am writing about what might be considered trivial matters. But these trivial matters upset people and frayed tempers are not good when we consider important problems.'[7] In one respect the Hospitality Committee took its name almost too seriously when, as revealed in the Indonesian Press, it made very efficient and discreet arrangements for the provision of feminine company.

The siting of the conference at Bandung also raised a security problem because the armed rebels of the Dar-ul-Islam movement were active in the area. The crack division of the Indonesian Army moved in on Bandung and established three concentric circles of security around and in the town, the last ringing the area of the conference building and the main hotels; to get through it several passes had to be produced. The Government later claimed to have frustrated a rebel plot to kidnap some of the delegates.

During the last month of the conference political pressure of varied kinds and degrees was applied especially to the sponsors, and especially from anti-Communist and Western sources. From Istanbul came a letter from the National Centre for the Liberation of Eastern Turkestan (Sinkiang), stating that since this area was under Chinese domination it fell within the purview of the conference; it therefore requested that China be excluded as an imperialist power. Her Majesty's Government hoped that Colonel Nasser would be advised to be sensible about Palestine, where boundary rectifications favourable to the Arabs were offered as a bait. Australia urged moderation about West Irian, and Holland asked that there be no discussion of it unless British Borneo and Australian New Guinea were also discussed; there may be honour among thieves, but there is little between imperialists. Even Mr. Hammarskjöld, speaking out of turn, 'was sure' that the conference would not become a negative, anti-Western meeting—a most revealing association of ideas. Finally the International Red Cross from Geneva requested that its humane and peaceful role might be emphasised at Bandung; unfortunately it was not. By the middle of April the name of the Javanese town had gone round the world and had become the focus of world attention.

The Communists, far more sensitive than the West to the strength of the popular ground-swell beneath Afro-Asianism, very quickly decided to ride with it. This they did through the self-styled Afro-Asian Solidarity Movement, a parody of the real thing, which will be examined later. For the moment we need only note that the first conference of this movement was held in New Delhi on the 6th April with 188 delegates attending from thirteen countries, including Russia and China. This move was clearly an attempt to steal some of Bandung's thunder, and Dr. Ali was justifiably displeased, the more so because it was being held in one of the sponsoring countries. The Government of India was equally displeased, dissociated itself from the meeting and tried, without success, to get it postponed till after Bandung. The Communist bias of the solidarity conference became sufficiently apparent to prompt an Indian cabinet minister to walk out of its meetings. Nevertheless the conference proceeded to give its full support to Bandung, to Panchsheel and to 'the enlarging of the peace area'.

An even more sinister act of direct sabotage was committed by the anti-Communists at this time. The Chinese Government had chartered a plane of Air India to fly members of its delegation from Hong

Kong to Jakarta. The Chinese gave the British authorities a warning about possible sabotage and, allegedly, special precautionary measures were taken at Hong Kong. This request started rumours that Chou En-lai himself might be in the Chinese party. As the plane approached the coast of Indonesian Borneo, on the 11th April, an explosion took place aboard; thanks only to the courage of the captain and his crew was the plane brought in for a crash-landing in shallow water. This prompt act did not save the lives of any of the passengers, but it enabled two of the crew to escape to tell the tale, and facilitated the lifting of the wreckage, amongst which pieces of an infernal machine were discovered. A committee of enquiry later established that because of the Easter week-end, during which Hong Kong's officials scattered to the beaches, extra precautions had not been taken there. And though, weeks after the crash, the committee gave the police the name of the suspected saboteur, a well-known Kuomintang agent who was still in Hong Kong, he was able to get away to Formosa. Such gross and protracted negligence is tantamount to connivance.

After this, of course, Chou En-lai's movements were kept secret. He was expected in Rangoon, but flew in without advance notice in the middle of the night, bringing with him drums of petrol to refuel his plane, and he left equally unexpectedly and again at night. At Bandung the Chinese Embassy, not the secretariat, chose the house he lived in and paid for it themselves. These events injected an element of gang-warfare brutality into the brotherliness prevailing at Bandung.

Otherwise all was brotherhood. Colonel Nasser, making his first visit outside the Arab world, was given a warm official and public reception in New Delhi, which he visited *en route*. Then, joined by Premier Naim of Afghanistan he, with Mr. Nehru, flew to Rangoon for a brief visit, where the premiers enjoyed themselves ducking each other for the Burmese Water Festival. Giving an unusual show of courtesy Chou En-lai, who had arrived a little earlier, came to the airport to greet the three prime ministers. This was his first meeting with the Egyptian leader; he shook hands with him with especial warmth and invited him, on the spot, to visit China. The next day the Chinese Premier met Colonel Nasser twice, alone and with Mr. Nehru, but won from him no support for China's admission to the United Nations, or even recognition. China, however, offered to buy Egyptian cotton, and this alone, was immensely encouraging news for Egypt. This was only the first step in a deliberate effort made by

China at Bandung to please and befriend the Arab governments, with whom she had till then had very little contact.

Other delegates, too, were on their way, dropping statements to the press at each airport. The most honest of these, by the Prime Minister of Yemen, Prince Sword-of-Islam al-Hassan, cannot go unrecorded, for at Calcutta he declared: 'We have not heard of Panchsheel. We have never heard of China's entry into the United Nations.'[8]

At this point, on the threshold of the conference, it would be appropriate to estimate what the various participants hoped to gain by embarking on it. For the group of the committed—Turkey, Iraq, Iran, Pakistan, Thailand and the Philippines—Bandung was an opportunity to defend their choice of alignment with the West, and to draw the attention of the non-aligned to the dangers of Communism. In addition Pakistan was doubtless hoping to make capital out of advocacy of Arab causes, which she did after, though not at, Colombo and Bogor. For China, the meeting offered a splendid chance to break through the isolation that America had tried to impose on her, to make new friends and to show them and the world that she was not a crimson monster; and, of course, in the process to get in a few hard blows at the United States. The Arabs, having at last to some extent learnt the lesson of the importance of publicity, were hoping to gain support for their campaigns against Israel, Britain and France. For Laos and Cambodia participation was a guarantee of their independence, and for the Sudan and the Gold Coast it was the first evidence thereof. Japan was looking for assurances that Asia had forgiven her wartime activities and was prepared to do business with her. India's, and to some extent Burma's, motives were perhaps the most complex. They wanted to show China that she could have friends in Asia, and by so doing to draw her away from her connection with Soviet Russia, through whom she was linked to the antagonisms of the Cold War. They also hoped to apply a moral interdiction to China's possible expansionism by persuading her to accept, as publicly and as widely as possible, the promises of good behaviour contained in Panchsheel.

But, at least for India and Mr. Nehru, Bandung meant more than these considerations of practical policy. He went to Bandung with the desire to assert Panchsheel as a general principle of international conduct, as the only possible basis of world peace. It will be recalled that these dogmatic claims had been made for the Five Principles in the paragraphs that Pakistan had ousted from the Bogor communiqué. Nothing daunted Mr. Nehru, in a speech to Parliament on

the 31st March, said that Panchsheel was a 'challenge by Asia to the
rest of the world' and each country would have to give a direct answer. 'I hope the question will be posed at the Afro-Asian conference
in all its straightness and that each country will be asked to say
whether it stands for non-aggression and non-interference or not.'
Here is black-or-white crusading zeal in the best Dullesian manner:
either one accepts Panchsheel or one supports aggression. And his
confidence was based on a claim that has a Marxian ring: 'We are
marching in step with history and so success must come to us,' he
said, a few days before the conference. He had little other cause for
confidence since he himself had noted that 'we shall have a very mixed
lot of people at the conference'; of its twenty-nine participants only
eight had accepted Panchsheel.

'Mixed lot' or not, there was one motive common to all the invitees—a desire to preserve the peace, especially in the area where it
was most immediately threatened, the Formosa Strait. In his usual
gloom-and-doom fashion Mr. Nehru had given the opinion: 'I cannot rule out now, as I did previously, the possibility of a major war.'
Consequently most of the publicity at the time centred on the developments at the conference that affected the crisis in the Strait.

At Bandung itself the first ranging shots were being fired. One of
the earliest arrivals there was General Romulo; he openly called on
the non-Communist delegations to prevent the conference becoming
'anti-democratic' as he put it; and with this slogan he busied himself
among the pro-West delegations, trying to work out a joint stand on
controversial issues. In this, as we shall see, he certainly succeeded.
Ceylon, in the meantime, had put forward a working paper which
was a sustained onslaught on Communism: 'Communist protesta-
tions of sincerity are received with suspicion and even doubt,' peaceful co-existence is 'a slogan behind which the consolidation of existing
Communist regimes can proceed', and while 'there is no question of
aggression or subversion from that quarter' (the West) Asian countries had experience of this from the Communist side; after much
more in this vein, China was informed that she was 'in the best position to take the initiative in creating conditions favourable to an
international accord'.

The anti-Communists had seized the initiative at Bandung; the
Communists held it on the world scene. While messages of goodwill
came to the conference from Marshal Voroshilov and the presidiums
of five Soviet Central Asian Republics the United States Government
had not yet emerged from its sulks. As Congressman Powell put it,

President Eisenhower had 'stupidly' rejected his suggestion to send greetings; he had a telegram from the State Department to prove it, which stated that the Department doubted whether the relationship of the United States to the conference 'would warrant a message'. Could the Congressman's cigars have been meant as an apology for his President's stupidity? The SEATO Council, however, meeting in Bangkok, tried to be friendly and sent its 'cordial greetings' to the 'other free countries' at the conference.

On his arrival at Bandung airport, Mr. Nehru started enunciating his ideas about the conference without delay. It ought, he said, to discuss only broad issues, which ruled out Formosa and SEATO, and it ought not to decide anything by vote.[9]

These suggestions were willingly agreed at the informal meeting of heads of delegations, held at the residence of the Indonesian Prime Minister on the afternoon before the conference began. According to one account, it was readily agreed that there should be no question of majority or minority votes, but that the consensus of opinion should form the basis of the conference decisions, to be embodied in a final communiqué. The conference thus accepted the procedure established at Colombo, based on the precedent of the Common-wealth Prime Ministers' Conference; by doing this it bound itself to unanimity. Compulsion to agree was part of the conference's procedural machinery, and not an emanation of some non-material 'Spirit'.

There was quick agreement also on an agenda of seven items: economic co-operation, to be discussed by an economic committee, to which was also allotted the item on the peaceful uses of nuclear energy; cultural co-operation was allotted to the cultural committee, and the political committee was given problems of dependent peoples, Human Rights and Self-determination, the Promotion of World Peace and Co-operation and two smaller items—Weapons of mass destruction and Universality of United Nations membership.

Only grudging agreement was given to another of Mr. Nehru's suggestions: that even the twenty-minute opening speech allotted to each head of delegation should not be delivered but only circulated in printed text. The argument in favour of this procedure was that it would save a full two days of the conference's time; but doubtless Mr. Nehru also wanted to avoid the public adoption of hostile attitudes at the outset which might vitiate the conference atmosphere, and make later compromise difficult.

Since there were only twenty-two of the twenty-nine delegations present at this first meeting, these were not, as yet, conference decisions. In particular, one of the sponsors, Pakistan, was absent, its delegation arriving later in the evening. When the five sponsoring prime ministers met that night, Mr. Mohammed Ali angrily rejected the agreements on speeches and on the recording of decisions, and insisted that they be discussed afresh by the full conference the following morning.

At this meeting Pakistan succeeded in loosening the procedure on decisions by the addition of a directive stating that if no consensus of opinion could be found on a particular subject no decision would be recorded: all decisions would still be unanimous but a single dissenter could impose a veto on a decision being reached. On the question of making opening speeches several delegates bolted their agreement of the previous day. They were led by Turkey and by the acting Secretary of State of Liberia, Mr. Dukuly, who said, feelingly, We have come here to be heard.' The speeches consumed too much time; while some were interesting none were important, except that of China; and they were liable to stir up the dust of controversy. Nevertheless Mr. Nehru was unkind in suggesting a self-denying ordinance. His speeches, in India or outside, were reported round the world, but for many, or most, of the other delegates this would be the first, and perhaps the last, time they would draw the spotlight of world attention. To expect them to forgo this publicity was asking too much. In the end, nineteen of them delivered speeches and seven circulated copies. Only India and Burma and Saudi Arabia maintained silence.

The army's security precautions were pushed aside on the opening morning by large and enthusiastic crowds which lined the pavements to cheer the delegates as they walked from their hotels to the Freedom Hall nearby. Chou En-lai was one of the few who drove up and though he, with Colonel Nasser, attracted the most applause his manner was stiff and nervous, reflecting his delegation's fear for his safety.

The opening speeches[10] had certain themes in common, of which colonial experience and the pleasure and importance of meeting together were the most frequently mentioned. On the latter theme, several speakers made the mistake of describing the conference as the first of its kind, and on the former there was a surprising absence of bitterness, though a determination to prevent a return of colonialism was often expressed. It was encouraging that the principle of support for the United Nations was scarcely less often mentioned; the new, small countries showed that they had already realised that the world organisation was for them not only a forum but a bulwark. The need for economic development in Afro-Asia was, naturally, another very popular topic. A few speakers referred to the danger of nuclear war. A few continued to reassure the West that neither a racial nor a religious nor a political bloc was in process of formation. Having had a long caucus meeting the previous day, all Arab speakers were repetitively insistent about Palestine and North Africa.

Among the more interesting individual ideas presented were the assertions by President Sukarno that this was 'the first inter-continental conference of coloured peoples in the history of mankind' and that 'colonialism is not yet dead'; this he was still claiming at Belgrade, six years later. He was on surer ground when he argued that though the Afro-Asians had the colonial experience, religions, cultures and economic problems in common 'yet we know so little of each other'!

As Mr. Nehru had feared, speakers took up positions for the subsequent struggles between the aligned and non-aligned, and he sat through the speeches with ill-concealed irritation. All those who had already subscribed to the Five Principles referred to them—Cambodia, Laos, North Vietnam and Indonesia (which only mentioned the first four, omitting peaceful co-existence), and China and Nepal, the two latter recommending wider acceptance.

The aligned countries displayed so much agreement on targets, and even in the phraseology they used, that it was plain that, through close prior consultation, co-ordination of strategy had been achieved. Iran spoke of 'subversion' and of 'ideological interference'; Iraq referred to 'Communist subversion' as a 'deadlier colonialism' and called for 'ideological disarmament'; for Pakistan 'ideological domination' was 'a new and more insidious form of imperialism', and for the Philippines there was danger of 'a new super-barbarism, a new super-imperialism'. But when the representative of Libya mentioned the threat of 'external ideological interference' and of 'intellectual slavery', it imposed a great strain on one's credulity to believe that this alarm was spontaneous, for rudimentary Libya had no direct experience of these new and sophisticated horrors; in this case the tutoring was too well done.

One strange absentee from this anti-Communist chorus was Sir John Kotelawala, despite Ceylon's anti-Communist working paper. He was doubtless reserving his fire. The new suggestion in his opening speech was that the Afro-Asians should officially offer themselves as mediators in the Cold War.

In all this anti-Communist clamour, only one speaker gave a clear and specific example of Communist intervention; this was, moreover, the only specific accusation levelled at Communist China throughout the entire conference. Perhaps out of politeness to China, sitting across the table, all the anti-Communist speakers, from the start maintained a careful distinction between international Communism and Communist China—a distinction some of them denounced when it was made by Mr. Nehru. It was the immensely skilled and experienced Foreign Minister of Thailand, Prince Wan Waithayakon, who accused China of helping the dissident leftist Thai leader, Pridi Panamyong, to train agents for 'infiltration and subversion' in Yunnan, across the Thai border. Prince Wan's speech was also notable for a Buddhist counter-attack on the alleged connection between Buddhism and non-alignment. He quoted the Buddha, telling a general that his teaching was not that 'those who go to war in a righteous cause, after having exhausted all meant to preserve the peace, are blameworthy. He must be blamed who is the cause of war'.

From the start the link—almost the mediator—between the two camps, proved to be Chou En-lai, especially in the second of his two speeches at the opening session. The first, which was only distributed as a text, was for the most part a Cold War polemic in which he referred to tension in the Formosa area, the setting up of more bases, and preparations for war. Developing the new Chinese interest in Arab problems he mentioned Tunisia, Morocco, Algeria, Palestine and the Suez Canal Zone, and also West Irian and Goa. Even in this speech there were conciliatory gestures: he said that the sovereignty and integrity of all states should be respected, and he offered to extend the guarantees of good behaviour contained in the Five Principles to Thailand, the Philippines and other neighbouring countries.

He amplified these points in supplementary remarks made in direct reply to criticisms of Communism. (It came as a surprise to many to discover that the Chinese Premier spoke in a high falsetto.) He admitted differences in ideology and social systems between the less-numerous Communist countries and the more-numerous nationalist states; but he claimed that the Five Principles could be the basis of friendly relations between the two groupings. On the question of subversive activities he quoted the Golden Rule: China was against outside interference in her own affairs, so how could she wish to interfere in those of other nations? There was no threat to Thailand from the Thai Autonomous Area in Yunnan, nor from the Chinese community in Thailand. The problem was not Chinese subversive activi-

196

ties, but the bases being built round China to direct subversive activi-ties against her. He invited anyone who so desired to come to China 'to take a look' for there was 'no bamboo curtain' around his country. He hoped the conference would extend the area of peace.

From the opening speeches it was evident that the Bandung Con-ference would witness a clash between the aligned and the non-aligned, and that China had cast herself in a conciliatory role.

The Political Committee,[11] composed of the leaders of the delega-tions, began its work on the 20th April with a most confused debate. The confusion was mostly due to the chairman, the Indonesian Prime Minister, Dr. Ali Sastroamidjojo, whose inept handling of the discussion afflicted the committee for the next four days. It was partly due also to the seating arrangements: the delegates sat in two long shallow brackets ()—with the chairman in the centre of them: the delegations at the end of these arcs had so much difficulty in catching the chairman's eye that at one point a device of movable mirrors was suggested, that would focus on a speaker when he pulled a string.

The aligned delegations scored a quick, early success Dr. Ali sug-gested that the *rapporteur* should be one of the secretaries-general, an Indian; Pakistan proposed Prince Wan and Chou En-lai suggested Mr. Nehru, who promptly withdrew in the Prince's favour. China asked for the decision on this appointment to be deferred; Mr. Nehru then suggested a brief adjournment during which he explained to the Chinese Premier that the *rapporteur* had to be an entirely neutral functionary of the committee; Prince Wan proved to be admirably impartial. This little incident revealed Chou-En-lai's lack of know-ledge of conference procedure, from which Mr. Nehru also was not immune: General Romulo later boasted that this deficiency put them at a disadvantage with the more experienced defenders of the West, who 'outmanœuvred' them[12].

The rest of the morning session passed in a futile discussion whether, when recommending the observation of Human Rights, the conference should or should not refer to the United Nations Declara-tion on these Rights. The substantial point at issue was, as Mr. Nehru pointed out, that some of the participants, notably China, were not members of the United Nations and were reluctant to subscribe to its decisions taken in their absence; in fact, most of the time was taken up with delegates arguing with the chairman on what was being argued about. The discussion revealed one fact: namely, that one point in the brief of the pro-Western countries was 'no competition with the United Nations', and this the Lebanese delegate, Dr. Charles Malek, went so far as to describe as an issue 'which might turn out to be the most important item of the conference'. These fears, which were voiced directly by Western sources earlier, were quite outdated. The final division of opinion on the reference to the United Nations Declaration was basically between the aligned and the non-aligned: in favour of such a reference were Pakistan, Iran, Iraq, Turkey, Thailand, Japan, Ceylon and South Vietnam; against were India, Indonesia, China and North Vietnam.

On a proposal from Jordan a sub-committee to draft a formula was constituted, of Lebanon, Thailand, Pakistan, China and India; this selection was three to two against the non-aligned group. This tilting of the balance against the non-aligned continued in several subsequent drafting committees, in which the real work of the conference was done; thus the procedural weapon remained firmly in the hands of the aligned, who had seized it in the first moments of the committee meeting.

At 11.50 a.m. the full committee adjourned 'for fifteen minutes' to give this drafting committee time to work out a form of words, and reassembled at 12.35 p.m. only to announce that its second session would begin at 3.30 p.m. This actually began at 4.20 p.m. This expenditure of time was of more than chronological importance. The conference was committed to a final session on the 24th April. As that date approached, the pressure to reach agreement, which would permit its termination, correspondingly increased. The calendar and the clock were major factors in the creation of the brotherly 'Bandung Spirit'.

On resumption, a draft was read out and accepted. This took note not only of the Universal Declaration of Human Rights but of the United Nations Charter, even though Lebanon and Iran had said that the Charter, which has no particular relevance to Human Rights, need not be mentioned.[13] By accepting, without demur, this double reference to the United Nations Chou En-lai disarmed criticism from the aligned representatives; he also dropped the hint, which was not heeded, that he did not need India's advocacy.

Unwanted advocacy was far more evident in the discussion on the Palestine question that followed. Two resolutions were tabled, one from Afghanistan and a stronger one from Pakistan, both supported in vigorous speeches; Iran made an even stronger and longer speech on the subject. Despite appeals from Dr. Ali that delegates should remember that only two and a half days were left to cover a lot of ground, two of the Arab representatives, Syria and Iraq, indulged in that favourite Arab tactic, the conversion of the converted. Other Arabs were notably silent; Saudi Arabia and Yemen did not speak at all, and the leading Arab representative, Colonel Nasser, spoke precisely two sentences on this principal Arab problem, simply expressing his preference for the milder Afghan proposal.

Mr. Nehru, while expressing full sympathy for the Arabs, tried to raise their sights by asking the questions: What were the international forces behind Zionism, and what could they do about getting the United Nations resolutions on Palestine implemented? U Nu replied that since America, Britain and Russia remained silent on non-implementation of these resolutions, there was not much that the Afro-Asians could do. Admitting that Burma had 'many economic cultural and political ties with the Jews' he requested the conference not to 'force' Burma 'to do what is really beyond our capacity'. He proposed a compromise resolution which called for 'direct negotiations'. In the absence of agreement, and, once again on the suggestion of Jordan, a drafting committee was formed, consisting of Afghanistan, Burma, China, Pakistan, the Philippines and Syria.

On the morning of the 21st April, this group produced the draft on the Palestine issue that forms part of the final communiqué; in this the only change from the original Afghan proposal is the final sentence referring to the implementation of United Nations resolutions. To this China wished to add the words 'under the conditions of excluding intervention by outside forces', such intervention being the root cause of the trouble over Formosa as over Palestine; 'we are suffering from the same cause as the Arab countries,' said Chou En-lai, building another Sino-Arab link. Having made his point he did not press for its acceptance. Burma suggested two changes to give priority to peaceful negotiations over the implementation of United Nations resolutions, that would certainly have been more acceptable to the Israelis; but having made her point, she too did not press for acceptance.

The champions of the Arabs garnered the harvest in a speech from the Syrian representative, Mr. Shukeiry—himself a Palestinian—whose ability is too often overlaid with demagoguery, and Afghanistan, Iran, Pakistan, China, all received their share of fulsome thanks; so did Mr. Nehru, because he had described Zionism as 'an aggressive movement'. This amounted to the healing of a minor breach between the Indian and Arab delegations, for on the previous evening

199

the Arabs had been much upset by Mr. Nehru's speech, owing, as the Arab League Secretary-General later admitted, to an Arab 'mis-understanding'.[14] Concentrating on Palestine as their local problem the Arabs could not appreciate Mr. Nehru's world view; but eighteen months later they saw the importance of his question 'what is behind Zionism?' when the answer to it was given in the Anglo-French collusion with Israel in the attack on Egypt.

The Indo-Arab friction over Palestine was enormously important, from the Indian point of view, because it brought to light two contra-dictory attitudes on the settlement of international disputes. Mr. Nehru, in his best Gandhian vein, had said to the Arabs, 'Whether you are enemies or not or whether you have fought a war, there must be negotiations . . . there is always some kind of a settlement . . . you cannot end any controversy without some kind of talks or negotia-tions.' This is a false set of alternatives, because fifteen years of Arab practice has shown that there can be a state of no war, no peace, no negotiation. India had not yet learnt this lesson in 1962 when she had to grapple with the consequences of the Chinese attack. It is amusing that the Syrian delegate, perhaps embarrassed by Indian reasonable-ness, felt constrained to blame the Israelis for not wanting to talk—an entirely false complaint, since Israel, the successful spoliator, is only too ready for talks with the Arab governments.

Colonel Nasser, who had fought and been wounded in Palestine, had showed in his brief intervention what he thought of this discus-sion; and on his way home he remarked: 'It is just a resolution. However, it has some moral value.'[15] The Arabs, in truth, had no very great cause for congratulation, because, of the non-Muslim states, only India and China spoke in their support.

On the next item, racial discrimination, the chairman said that he anticipated no difference of opinion, and straightway referred it to a drafting committee of Thailand, India, Pakistan, the Philippines and Jordan; Iran suggested adding Lebanon. This meant that no delegate from Africa, the continent of racialism, was included till India pro-posed Ethiopia, Liberia was then constrained to ask for inclusion. This was symptomatic of the very minor role Africa played, or was permitted to play, at Bandung.

On the general question of self-determination, the committee accepted a Chinese draft after a brief discussion. In this there was a reference to a specific United Nations resolution, 637 (viii), which showed that the Chinese argument that China was ignorant of what the United Nations had done in her absence was wearing very thin.

The Afghan delegation broadened this to make it a reference to all United Nations resolutions on the subject; on this the too-helpful Mr. Nehru commented: 'For my part I do not know what all these resolutions are. The delegate of China is totally ignorant of them. It is not quite right to ask him to accept something about which he is not clear'; and this despite the fact that China had already accepted the Afghan amendment.

The debate, a prolonged one, on West Irian did not concern West Irian at all, but the issue of whether the Bandung Conference was competing with the United Nations. The Indonesian delegate opened with a speech of quite unnecessary length, unnecessary because these were not public declarations to an applauding audience but statements in secret session to heads of government who were supposed to be acquainted with the main facts of each case. Then followed a Syrian intervention, in the course of which Mr. Shukeiry introduced a draft resolution which expressed its 'regrets that the General Assembly of the United Nations has failed to assist the parties in reaching a peaceful settlement of the problem'. The Turkish Deputy Prime Minister, Mr. Zorlu, led an attack on this last sentence, predicting dire consequences for the United Nations if it were passed. The familiar line-up of delegations followed. Behind Turkey were Pakistan, Iran, Iraq, Ceylon and Lebanon and on the other side, with Syria and Indonesia, were India and China. The minor variations in alignments were that Burma supported Turkey and Liberia backed Syria. Facing more numerous and clamant opponents, the non-aligned gave ground, and were prepared to drop the words 'regrets' and 'failed' for a simple reference to the United Nations 'inability'. But the aligned delegations, especially Turkey, were adamant, and there followed sharp exchanges between Turkey and Syria, during which Mr. Nehru got in a shrewd debating thrust when he said that the condemnation was not of the United Nations as such, but of 'those who voted against this [West Irian] resolution in the United Nations . . . principally the Great Powers—the United Kingdom, France and the United States', and that he was 'a little surprised at this tenderness' towards them. Pakistan took this point and replied: 'Our intention is not in any way to shield the Big Powers'. At the approach of the luncheon interval Dr. Ali took the usual way out, and appointed a drafting committee of Syria, Indonesia, China, Turkey, Lebanon, Thailand, Iraq, and Burma; this divided three to five against Syria and against the non-aligned. When Mr. Shukeiry asked for more representation from those who supported the Syrian position, Turkey consolidated her victory by getting Iran added to the group, which then became three to six against Syria. Thus constituted, the committee naturally produced an anodyne resolution which merely expressed 'the earnest hope' that the United Nations would 'assist' towards a peaceful solution of the West Irian problem, the wording suggested earlier by Iraq.

It was a taciturn Colonel Nasser—he had spoken three sentences on West Irian—who opened the discussion on North Africa in a speech that lasted less than five minutes, including the presentation of a resolution. He was followed at greater length by Iraq and by Mr. Mohammed Ali for Pakistan, who spoke for three times as long as the Egyptian leader. He concluded by stating that because the Egyptian resolution was 'not comprehensive enough' he would put forward a much more strongly-worded draft. Since it is not possible to believe that Pakistan cared three times as much as Egypt for North Africa, or was doing three times as much to help, this was just another example of Pakistan playing to the Arab gallery. Bandung and other Afro-Asian conferences offer several examples of this political scavenging with one country fattening its prestige on the tragedy of another. Mr. Nehru promptly decried this use of 'agitational language—we "demand" this, we "order" that'; 'these words are normally used when there is not strength behind them', was his accurate analysis. A long series of speakers expressed warm support for the North African cause and declared the Egyptian resolution to be adequate. Having tried to be more Arab than the Arabs, Pakistan ended by withdrawing her resolution. Indonesia, characteristically, suggested a Good Offices Committee to mediate between France and North Africa, to consist of the Five sponsors, two Arab states and the Philippines, but fortunately this was not made a formal proposal.

In the middle of another debate, on 'colonialism, old and new', and after a long, confused procedural discussion, the committee —almost as an interlude—passed its resolution on racialism and in lieu of speeches adopted the Indian working paper on the subject as a conference document—offhand treatment for this very important Afro-Asian question.

It was in this debate on colonialism that the conference grappled with its real task and its real purpose—the justifying by the aligned and the non-aligned of the differing foreign policies adopted by them. The discussion on colonialism was the first half of this justification; in this the aligned, who took the initiative in raising the matter, tried to show the Afro-Asians the new danger with which they were confronted; the debate on pacts that followed explained what practical steps the aligned had taken to meet that danger. The non-aligned, in reply, were concerned with explaining that there was no such danger and so no need for that type of protection through pacts. It is ironic that a solid basis for this debate, the definition of the new danger, was never really laid. This was because, in the course of discussion, both sides became passionately involved in a matter that was of no real concern to an Afro-Asian conference.

Sir John Kotelawala led this famous debate away at a tangent in a speech of which the key paragraph is: 'There is another form of colonialism, however, about which many of us represented here are perhaps less clear in our minds and to which some of us would perhaps not agree to apply the term colonialism at all. Think, for example, of those satellite states under Communist domination in Central and Eastern Europe—of Hungary, Rumania, Bulgaria, Albania, Czechoslovakia, Latvia, Lithuania, Estonia and Poland. Are these not colonies as much as any of the colonial territories in Africa or Asia? And if we are united in our opposition to colonialism should it not be our duty openly to declare our opposition to Soviet colonialism as much as to Western imperialism?'

(This was not the only point made by Sir John: he proposed 'that every colony in the Afro-Asian region should be given its autonomy within the next decade'; that countries with no colonial record should have an international trusteeship over such territories to guide them towards democracy; and that a collective guarantee for their defence be provided for at least twenty-five years. He also asked that no Afro-Asian state should harbour any territorial ambitions towards its neighbours.)

This sudden onslaught on Soviet Russia set the cat among the pigeons and shattered the atmosphere of conciliation that had begun to prevail in the committee room. A very disturbed Mr. Nehru tried to get Sir John to give a precise definition of the new subject he had raised, which seemed outside an already heavily-loaded agenda: 'The Prime Minister of Ceylon referred to Eastern Europe. Let him put down precisely what he is going to discuss and not talk about the sun and moon,' was his irritated comment. Lebanon came to Ceylon's aid by proposing the title 'Colonialism, Old and New'.

As soon as Sir John had finished, Chou En-lai reserved his right to reply the following day. And when the meeting adjourned there was a spirited exchange of remarks between them in the committee room. The Chinese Premier asked Sir John if he wanted to break up the conference; Sir John replied that if Chou En-lai had not responded so agitatedly (in fact he had not) nothing further would have followed from his speech. It might be inferred that Sir John did not expect or want a follow-up. Mr. Nehru joined them and asked Sir John why he raised this question: 'Why did you not show me your speech before you made it?' he queried. 'Do you show me yours before you make them?' Sir John retorted.[16] One must remember that at the Colombo Conference Sir John had in fact shown Mr. Nehru the text of his speech beforehand and had incorporated some of the latter's suggestions. Owing to the Ceylonese intervention, which ought not to have been unexpected,[17] the atmosphere of the conference on the night of the 21st was one of crisis.

This crisis nearly blew over at the beginning of the next session on the morning of the 22nd April. U Nu made a direct, personal appeal for harmony and restraint, saying that if the theme of 'new colonialism' was revived 'this conference is doomed'. Sir John replied, with an air of surprised and injured innocence, that he was not proposing to table a resolution on the subject he had raised; that he had had 'no intention of discussing ideologies' but merely the degrees of independence prevailing in various countries; and he ended by appealing to other delegates 'not to make use of it to fight against ideologies'. Chou En-lai replied in kind, saying that he sought no quarrel, though he could not accept the application of the words 'new colonialism' to the Soviet system.

If Sir John's cracker ultimately fizzled out like a damp squib, it was because he had heeded appeals, made during the previous night, by Mr. Nehru and others that he should not formalise his ideas in the form of a resolution. That he heeded the advice shows his moderation; but a feeling of relief on his part can also be detected, for he took no further part in this debate or, indeed, in any other discussion at the conference.

Sir John, however, wittingly or unwittingly, had opened Pandora's box. Pakistan insisted on elaborating his ideas in a speech which, as these extracts show, had a curious approach: 'It would be wrong on our part to ignore or make no mention of another form of imperialism, Soviet imperialism,' Mr. Mohammed Ali said. But he then continued: 'We have the greatest respect and esteem for the great nation of China. . . . China is by no means an imperialist nation and she has no satellites. . . . We have the friendliest relations with China. China is certainly not imperialistic, she has not brought any other countries under her heel. Therefore it [Ceylon's criticism] was not directed against an invitee, a fellow-delegate, who, we appreciate very much, has shown a great deal of conciliation. . . . It has no reference to China but only to Soviet imperialism which has brought many people under its iron heel.'

Brushing aside an appeal and a warning from Syria that if Soviet imperialism were to be considered, so ought American imperialism; the attack was pressed home by Iraq, Turkey and Iran, using the same verbal ammunition: 'subjugation', 'subversion', 'infiltration'. Their main argument was that in fairness to France and the Netherlands, who had already been condemned, Russia must be condemned too.

Mr. Nehru made one last unavailing effort to stave off a division, in a speech of some length that embraced a variety of arguments. The Eastern European states, he said, could not be described as colonies for they were sovereign national states, recognised not only by the Afro-Asians but by the Western Powers and, some of them, by the United Nations of which they were members: what was happening in East Europe 'is an objectionable thing' but 'is not colonialism'. He, and he alone, raised the question of 'the Central Asian territories', and because he did not know whether 'these people are being subjugated' he suggested 'we should have a commission of enquiry to find out what the people want'. Turning to the general characteristics of Communism he said, 'I am not an admirer of the Soviets. I dislike many of the things they have done, as I dislike many of the things the Western Powers have done.' He then asked how many independent countries were really independent enough to stand up to pressure. Finally, in familiar vein, he alleged 'we are on the verge of war'; therefore a united conference should throw its 'whole weight in a friendly manner in favour of peace'.

After this the splitting-up process continued: South Vietnam spoke on the side of the aligned, and North Vietnam with the non-aligned. Japan, in a brief carefully-worded speech, supported Turkey 'if' there was a Communist danger. Lebanon then explained the resolution that Turkey had prepared overnight of which the operative part was a condemnation of 'eleven types of colonialism'. This was proposed jointly by the hard core of the aligned—Turkey, Iran, Iraq, Lebanon, Pakistan, and the Philippines, joined by the Sudan and Liberia.

India and Egypt had also tabled a draft which called for the 'liberation of independent peoples and the end of colonial rule. The reaction of peoples to alien domination constitutes a denial of fundamental human rights.' This formulation ought to have satisfied the aligned, for it gave them more than they ultimately obtained from the conference. But by now the struggle was not for arguments but for certain evocative 'trigger' words; appropriately, it was on this verbalistic battle-ground that the aligned were utterly outmanœuvred.

In the meantime an undignified scramble was in progress to get supporters on to the key drafting committee on colonialism. Dr. Ali first proposed: China, Turkey, Ceylon, Pakistan, India, Syria, the Philippines, Burma and Liberia, with Thailand as *rapporteur*: four to five against the non-aligned. This majority was too narrow for the aligned delegations so, with machine-gun rapidity, the Philippines added Lebanon, and Pakistan added Iraq and Iran; Syria then proposed Egypt, Pakistan the Sudan, China suggested North Vietnam, and Turkey added South Vietnam—or sixteen in all, more than half the conference membership. At this point in the childish proceedings the chairman, with a rare show of firmness, announced that he proposed to limit the number to thirteen. He then nominated China, Turkey, Ceylon, Pakistan, India, Syria, the Philippines, Burma, Iran, Iraq, Indonesia, Egypt, North Vietnam and Lebanon—seven to six in favour of the non-aligned. When South Vietnam asked to be added, Iran suggested that both the Vietnams be dropped; this would have made it six to six. The chairman then contracted the number further to eight members, four with draft resolutions and four without: China, Turkey, Ceylon, Pakistan, India, Syria ('who has more or less'—as Dr. Ali said), the Philippines and Burma: three to five against the non-aligned. By this time everyone, except the chairman, knew what this game of musical chairs was about: 'We are gradually turning this committee into a replica of the American Constitution which has checks and balances and prevents all growth,' Mr. Nehru remarked sardonically. With a burst of courage the chairman then added himself and Lebanon, making the final count five to five on this crucial drafting committee. Just before the end, Chou En-lai said that he intended to make his reply to speeches made in the committee during the discussions in the drafting committee, where they were effectively buried in secrecy. Not even he knew the power of the procedural weapon.

To an Asian there is a flaw, something off-key—in this debate on colonialism, which never came to grips with what is a very real Asian problem. Here were the representatives of Asia, and a few from Africa, sitting together around a table in a committee room in a hill town on the island of Java in the Sunda Sea; and in a debate on colonialism, the one political fact they all had experienced in common, they talked about Estonia, Latvia and Lithuania on the Baltic.

If the issue was international Communism, why did they not refer to China and North Vietnam, loyal members of that family, who were there to be tackled face to face? Why, instead, did Mr. Mohammed Ali fall all over himself to exculpate Communist China and to exclude it from his anti-Communist diatribes by confining them to Soviet imperialism? Was this due to mere politeness to a guest, or did Mr. Mohammed Ali agree with Mr. Nehru's assessment at that time, that China was Asian first and Communist later?

And if Soviet imperialism was the prime target, why were the former Baltic republics picked out, and not the Soviet republics of Central Asia? There was no excuse for this tender refusal to deal with Soviet imperialism in its Asian setting. The Turkestan Liberation Committee had contacted the conference members, the people concerned were Turkic by race, yet Turkey did not speak up for them. The Iraqi representative referred briefly to Russia's colonial subjects in his opening speech, but did not do so again. It was, as we have seen, Mr. Nehru who referred to them, and who even suggested a committee of enquiry into their condition, yet no anti-Communist picked up and developed this idea. There was, above all, the unanswerable argument that the Soviet Central Asian republics were not present at Bandung, though they had been present at the first Asian conference at New Delhi. They were absent because the sponsors agreed with Mr. Nehru that as parts of the Soviet Union, they were not independent and not Asian: but they are Asian and they ought to be independent.

Faced with these unanswered questions, we can only conclude that the anti-Communists at Bandung were either very ignorant, very unimaginative and quite unresponsive to the Asian atmosphere of the conference; or they were working from a rigid brief drawn up by Europeans about Europe, and when their tutors were not at their elbow they did not feel free enough, or brave enough, to adapt themselves to the shifting currents of a debate. They talked a great deal about 'ideological domination' but their Eurocentric arguments in this deflected debate were themselves excellent examples of mental tutelage.

The second, practical section of the great debate between the aligned and the non-aligned began in the afternoon session of the 22nd April; in it the value and usefulness of pacts and Panchsheel as policies were estimated and contrasted. U Nu opened the discussion by commending the Five Principles, while suggesting that in addition to them the task of dealing with external aggression was the responsibility of the United Nations—even though this organisation had one yardstick for aggression in Korea and another for that committed by the Kuomintang troops in eastern Burma. Subversion, he said, had to be fought by eliminating corruption and promoting education and land reform. (Subsequently U Nu was twice removed from power by the Army because of the corruption in his government.) He concluded by introducing a resolution calling for respect for territorial integrity and non-interference. The Liberian delegate first entered a protest against the exclusion of any African representative from the drafting committee on colonialism, since the Africans were present at Bandung 'not merely as spectators', and then tabled a draft which, in general terms, called for peaceable behaviour. Prince Norodom of Cambodia was more specific. At that time his country was under pressure from the Communists rather than from SEATO. Hence in his opinion 'the problem of co-existence' was 'in the hands of the Communist countries whose policy, chiefly towards countries in favour of co-existence, will be capable of reassuring the rest of the world of their peaceful intention.' His resolution, in effect, asked for a 'hands-off' policy towards Cambodia. A contrite Japan then presented a peace plan based on a renunciation of force and co-operation in the economic, social and cultural fields. Presenting its ideas on the question the Indonesian delegation as in its opening speech referred only to the Four Principles of co-existence but not to peaceful co-existence as such, that estate being considered the end-product and not a principle by itself.

For Pakistan Mr. Mohammed Ali reiterated the Seven Principles he had proffered to the opening session. Three of these—respect for sovereignty, non-interference and non-aggression—were to be found in the Five Principles, to which he added the equality of all nations, the right to self-defence—singly or collectively—the right to self-determination, and the peaceful settlement of international disputes. Nepal contented itself with asking for an acceptance of the Five Principles. The Iraqi delegate, in a preliminary intervention, asked for ideological disarmament by the Communists, in the form of a cessation of propaganda, infiltration and subversion: for him the United Nations Charter was better than any set of principles. In his longest speech to the conference, Colonel Nasser emphasised that co-existence was principally the responsibility of the great powers, who ought not to interfere with the smaller states or try to use them as tools. The Seven Principles that he then proposed included disarmament, the ending of power politics and of colonialism, non-interference, and the right of every country to choose its own political and economic system.

It was Mr. Zorlu of Turkey who made the most thorough-going defence of alignment; since he drew on Turkey's unfortunate experience with Russia it was, within these limits, convincing. But he naturally elevated this individual example into the general principle that there was no safety for any state except through pacts of collective security, which all, of course, were defensive.

Mr. Nehru now made the most impassioned of all his interventions, putting forth a broad defence of non-alignment. His speech had three themes: the first, which strictly speaking was irrelevant, that he and India could and would stand alone because it was derogatory to his and her dignity to tag on to any master; the second, that Afro-Asia as a whole would be demeaning itself if it did this; and, thirdly, that they would be serving the cause of peace, which was in peril, if they formed a separate uncommitted area. His words had a great impact on the conference, and a few quotations would be valuable. 'I belong to neither bloc and I propose to belong to neither whatever happens in the world. . . . I am afraid of nobody. I suffer from no fear complex. My country suffers from no fear complex. We rely on nobody except on the friendship of others, we rely on ourselves and none other. . . . Even a single country can make a difference when the scales are evenly balanced. . . . If I join any of these big groups I lose my identity, I have no views left. . . . If all the world were to be divided up between these two blocs what would be the result? The inevitable result would be war. . . . It is an intolerable thought to me that the great countries of Asia and Africa should come out of bondage into freedom only to degrade and humiliate themselves in this way. . . . Every pact has brought insecurity and not security to the countries which have entered into them . . . the so-called Five Principles . . . is not a magic formula. . . . It is something which meets the needs of the day. . . . Unless one thinks that there is no alternative to this except war, and to be prepared for war, this resolution [U Nu's] has to be accepted'—the familiar, false, intolerant dichotomy: either one accepted Panchsheel or one was a warmonger.

(It was during his speech that Mr. Nehru once banged the table, and he was talking about India's policy at the time. He never did so at any other time during the conference, reports to the contrary notwithstanding.)

Mr. Shukeiry of Syria crossed Mr. Nehru's 't's' and dotted his 'i's'.

High Noon at Bandung, April–May 1955

In a speech free, for once, of demagogy, he filled in the details of the idea first propounded by Mr. Thivy eight years before at Delhi, and explained how Afro-Asia could apply military interdiction on the great powers: 'We are the two greatest continents on earth. We have the greatest pool of manpower, the greatest pool of all, materials. We have the greatest pool of fuel. We have every strategic military base and area. If we are determined, all of us, with our collective will, no strategic war will take place—if we do not participate in any sense.'

After further interventions from Iran and from Turkey, protesting that she did not merely mean to be negative, the conference adjourned for the second day in a continuing atmosphere of discord.

The main reply to Mr. Nehru came, on the morning of the 23rd April, in three speeches—from Mr. Jamali of Iraq, Dr. Charles Malek of Lebanon and General Romulo of the Philippines. They might as well have been a single speech, for the main point they made was identical: India is big, so big that she can stand alone and be non-aligned; but we are small, we are threatened, or at least feel threatened, so we can find safety only in alliance with the big and strong. It was a clever argument, aimed not so much against non-alignment as against India, and having himself introduced the irrelevant issue of India's determination to stand alone Mr. Nehru had no real answer to this pathetic approach.

The speeches all began, in slightly sinister fashion, with fulsome praise for the great leader Mr. Nehru. Amplifying the request made to Mr. Nehru in the previous year by the Iraqi Premier Nuri Said, Mr. Jamali asked the Indian Premier: 'Are you ready to bring us together—the weak and small nations—and form another bloc, so that we carry on our work uninterruptedly and also have protection? But by not doing that you leave us alone in small entities, cut to pieces and our existence threatened every moment.' Dr. Malek, as passionately committed to the Cold War as Mr. Dulles, was so anxious to controvert Mr. Nehru that he was driven into arguing that nuclear bombs were not really dangerous for humanity, and that the words 'peaceful co-existence' should not be used because Stalin first used them in 1926. After a thrust at India for maintaining her defences against Pakistan, and a lengthy explanation of the SEATO Charter, General Romulo gave his case away: 'It was made out that it was humiliating for us to join a regional group. As a matter of fact, we would not like to do so but we have to defend ourselves.'

The lines of division having been clearly drawn between the aligned and the non-aligned, Chou En-lai, with an urbane sweep of

210

his hand, blurred them into something almost attractive. In his speech he had something to offer everybody. If some of the delegates, from the aligned countries, found the words 'peaceful co-existence' objectionable, then 'live together in peace', from the United Nations Charter, would do. China, like the non-aligned countries, was opposed to pacts (no mention was made, of course, of the Sino-Soviet military alliance of 1950). He complimented Mr. Mohammed Ali for telling him that Pakistan 'was not against China', had no fear of her and would not join America in 'aggressive action' under SEATO. He was even more frank about the Communist danger from China than were the anti-Communists: 'The Delegates here have been quite courteous. They have only mentioned the Soviet Union without referring to China; but China is also a country which is governed by a Communist Party. So we feel we are also involved in it by implication.' He then proceeded 'to reformulate' the Five Principles 'to make them agreeable to all the delegates' and they re-emerged as Seven, the third such set. The first principle was respect for territorial integrity: 'We are ready to restrain our Government and people from crossing even one step across our border. If such thing should happen, we would like to admit our mistake . . . we shall use only peaceful means.' Under the Second Principle, non-aggression, he invited Prince Wan to visit Yunnan and General Romulo to tour the Chinese coast to see for themselves that China was making no warlike preparations against their countries. As an example of the Third Principle, non-intervention, he gave pledges to Cambodia and Laos. The Fourth Principle was racial equality, of which China had never been guilty, and for the Fifth, the equality of nations, he invited complaints: 'I will be glad to accept criticism and rectify mistakes.' To exemplify the Sixth Principle, of respect for the right of people to choose their own political and economic systems, he forthwith granted recognition to the current Japanese Government. The last Principle was abstention from doing damage to each other.

On the basis of this display of sweetness and light, Chou En-lai was mediating between Mr. Nehru and the aligned, rather than Mr. Nehru performing that service for the Chinese Premier. Mr. Nehru spoke again; he made interesting points, but his speech was an anticlimax, for with Chou En-lai's urbane intervention the tussle of words between the aligned and the non-aligned was over. Among Mr. Nehru's points were: 'I regret I am no pacifist . . . I do not believe in weakness but in the strength of the people. Weakness creates a vacuum that power fills in . . . I am no believer in the Communist theory . . . basically I think it is out of date today . . . weakness is the greatest crime that a country or a people could have . . . passive resistance, which means that a people of a country are not a live people . . . I have never said that we should form ourselves into a bloc . . . we have to think very seriously before we form ourselves into a common bloc. By all means, if you all think in terms of forming a bloc of small nations, you do so, but there are grave dangers involved in it as I feel that we are in a stage where we cannot help ourselves effectively . . . any organisation like the Cominform cannot in the nature of things fit in with peaceful co-existence.'

In this speech Mr. Nehru gave much ground and registered a notable toughening in his attitude towards non-violence and towards Communist activities, but he did not directly answer Mr. Jamali's question.

A drafting committee on co-existence was now formed through direct nomination by the chairman. It consisted of Cambodia, Ceylon, Burma, China, India, Egypt, Japan, Lebanon, Liberia, Pakistan, the Philippines and Turkey, with Colonel Nasser as chairman. The division here was seven to five against the non-aligned and perhaps even eight to four, if it be accepted that at this time Cambodia was more with the aligned than the reverse. This group went into session forthwith.

The political committee, without much discussion, then accepted a draft recommending eight Afro-Asian states for United Nations membership.

The debate on Indo-China produced a long and acrimonious exchange involving North and South Vietnam, and at the end of it the latter was compelled to apologise for impugning the impartiality of India; the committee then found itself unable even to express the hope that the Geneva Agreement on Indo-China would be fully implemented.

Support of Yemen's claim to Aden was automatically given. And without much discussion the reports of the Economical and Cultural Committees were approved.

When the political committee reassembled on the morning of the last day of the conference, it was merely marking time while awaiting the draft resolutions from the committees on colonialism and co-existence; but it had time and energy for just one more wrangle. At Bandung three subjects that later were greatly to concern the Afro-Asians—racialism, admission of new members to the United Nations, and disarmament—were dealt with in a manner so summary as almost to show indifference. Perhaps because general agreement about them was taken for granted, they were sent to drafting committees directly, without any speeches made in full committee. We have seen that the resolutions on racialism and United Nations membership presented no difficulty, either in sub-committee or full committee. However, in the sub-committee on disarmament, on which among others were represented Turkey, Pakistan, India and China, there was a hard discussion spread over seven and a half hours: so hard, indeed, that at one point India threatened to withdraw. The resolution, as incorporated in the final communiqué, seems innocuous enough. But the non-aligned countries did not wish disarmament affecting conventional weapons to be linked with the prohibition of nuclear arms; they especially wished nuclear tests to be regarded as something apart, which could be stopped without reference to general disarmament. The aligned countries were opposed to both these aims, reflecting the current Western view that the West would be at a military disadvantage if its nuclear deterrent alone were prohibited. Thanks to the stubbornness of Turkey, the Western position was fully expressed in the draft: conventional disarmament and nuclear prohibition are linked, and on nuclear testing a mere appeal is made 'to all the powers concerned to reach agreement to suspend experiments'. This is much weaker than the recommendation of the Colombo and Bogor communiqués, in which suspension was requested without reference to prior agreement on anything else. The reason for this retreat from the previous non-aligned position is perhaps to be found in these words from Mr. Nehru during this debate: 'I will confess that I feel worn out'—possible further evidence of the influence of physiology on politics.

One important point, however, emerged from this tussle. The draft, in somewhat clumsy language, mentioned the need 'to save mankind and civilisation from the fear and prospect of total and wholesale destruction.' The Chinese delegation wanted the whole of this sentence to be removed because, in its own words, 'we believe that what will be destroyed is not the whole of mankind but those who want to start an atomic war'—the unscientific theory of selective survival which it is still debating with Russia. China subsequently asked that only the words 'total' and 'wholesale' be deleted. To this Mr. Nehru refused to agree; while accepting the omission of 'total' he said that the sentence, which was 'scientifically' 'accurate', should stand; and this the Chinese accepted.

The final open session was fixed for 11 a.m. But despite two impatient adjournments by the full committee, the two key resolutions were not ready for it that morning. Only after lunch was agreement on them reached, and they were presented in committee at about 3 p.m.

The really decisive struggles at Bandung took place in these two drafting sub-committees. That on colonialism, it will be recalled, was established on the morning of the 21st April with ten nations as members, divided equally between the aligned and the non-aligned. After two and a half days of discussion the members were still at deadlock about how to describe colonialism, the aligned countries pressing for 'colonialism old and new' or 'colonialism in all its forms'. At any other time 'colonialism in all its forms' might have been acceptable to India, even to China; but, in the context of the attacks on Soviet imperialism China, as an ally of Russia, could not accept it, and India, as Mr. Nehru made plain, considered that the whole item was an intrusion upon the agreed agenda, and simply a Cold War manœuvre. The representatives in these two groups were sometimes the chief delegates—for instance, those of China, Lebanon, Pakistan, and Turkey—and sometimes alternates, such as Mr. Kishna Menon for India. The attitudes of the two camps were so irreconcilable that, after one nine-hour session, the group produced a draft which left blank spaces for the names of delegations that agreed or disagreed with the view that the old colonialism and the new were equally bad: in short, the draft was an agreement to differ, publicly. But since the conference was pledged to unanimity this was unacceptable, and fruitless argument continued till the morning of the 24th. At this juncture was felt the effect of the alteration to the rules of procedure obtained by Pakistan on the opening day. It had originally been accepted that conference resolutions on all items on the agenda must be agreed—a total obligation to unanimity. After the change, it was accepted that there should be resolutions only on items on which there was agreement. This change made it possible for a single dissentient to apply a veto; this veto Turkey and Pakistan applied now. And since these discussions, as everyone knew, were about the key issues, the action these two delegations took constituted a grave threat to the success of the conference as a whole.

In the meantime the twelve-nation sub-committee on co-existence, established on the morning of the 23rd April under President Nasser's chairmanship, had reached agreement in less than twenty-four hours. The non-aligned were in a minority in this group, but President

Nasser got his way by using the same tactics as Turkey—namely, insistent repetition of what he wanted. His object was to establish the formula found in point 6 (a) and (b) of the Conference Declaration on the Promotion of World Peace. He was prepared to give the other side whatever they wanted; and so the right of self-defence, singly and collectively, was accepted as point 5, but only on condition that his formula on pacts was also accepted. When he showed no sign of giving ground, he finally gained his point. But he gained it at the price of making the communiqué self-contradictory. Principle 5 sanctions collective defence arrangements, while Principle 6a says that these should not 'serve the particular interests of any of the big powers', but that is precisely the purpose of almost all collective defence arrangements. Agreement came not through combining or compromising two conflicting positions but simply by juxtaposing them.

Because of this 'success', the other question, colonialism, was now handed over to Colonel Nasser's committee, and he made it clear that he would not let it adjourn, however long the meeting might last, until agreement was reached. This decision showed great perception, for though this was his first international conference, he had clearly grasped its essential spirit, that Afro-Asia must not publicly disagree.

Towards lunch-time agreement was attained. It might have been due to the approach of the meal; it was certainly due, largely, to clever verbal formulation by Mr. Krishna Menon. Instead of 'colonialism in all its forms' he suggested 'colonialism in all its manifestations', which the committee pondered for some time, like Byzantine theologians estimating the proportion of God and of man in the True Nature of Christ, and finally accepted. An appreciation of the subtleties of English vocabulary is required to see the difference between 'form' and 'manifestation', and it so happened that the leader of the aligned, Mr. Zorlu of Turkey, did not know English. However, Dr. Malek, the Thomist philosopher, should have seen that 'manifestation' suggests a single object viewed under different aspects, not different objects of the same type, which is what the aligned wanted. Mr. Menon knew that he had successfully performed a piece of verbal sleight of hand; for as he came out of the committee room he muttered to a group of Indian correspondents: 'Got them to agree to something they don't understand.' Thus was Afro-Asian unanimity preserved at Bandung.

The final act of the political committee, before going into the closing plenary session, was to approve a proposal from China that since the conference had 'made considerable achievements', the five sponsors should consider convening another such meeting; Indonesia suggested that this should be 'within the next year'. But it was another six years before some of the Afro-Asians met again.

In his report on the Bandung Conference to the Indian Parliament Mr. Nehru said[18] that 'the most important decision of the conference is the Declaration'. This refers to the last section of the communiqué,[19] which is supposed to present the distillation of the Bandung Spirit. Curiously enough the Declaration, as such, was never discussed either in plenary session or in committee. There is in the verbatim record no mention of any decision that there should be this special proclamation, so it was probably agreed by the principal delegates in informal discussion. The Declaration is partly a repetition of other parts of the communiqué, as in the sections on atomic war and self-determination, and partly a summation of the debate on co-existence, during which peace plans had been presented by Burma, Liberia, Pakistan, Egypt, Cambodia, Japan and China. These were condensed into ten points which form the Bandung Principles. Of these the world was to hear a great deal in the next few years.

Subsequently Mr. Mohammed Ali claimed[20] that these Ten Principles contained more of his Seven than of Mr. Nehru's Five, and the Japanese asserted that the whole was their idea.[21] In fact, they are taken from the proposals of several delegations. Four of the Five Principles are included, co-existence being omitted; the Liberian suggestion for peaceful settlements through the United Nations finds a place; the wording of the non-aggression clause owes much to the Japanese plan; two of the Egyptian principles are included, in Principle 6a and 6b, and a third in the clause on respect for international obligations; and two also of Pakistan's—collective defence and the use of negotiation, conciliation and arbitration; while two of Chou En-lai's principles—racial equality and national equality—are combined in a single principle. It was indeed, a fair summing-up.

The only question that occasioned any lengthy debate in the economic committee was the proposal for a continuing body to implement its decisions; but the majority of the participants, both aligned and non-aligned, were not in favour of more than a consultative committee and liaison officers; only the latter suggestion was mentioned in the communiqué. The American embargo on trade with China was condemned, even by allies such as Turkey, Thailand, the Philippines, but it was presumably considered too political a subject for inclusion in a resolution on economic matters.

The cultural committtee discussed the most resounding banalities; the one noteworthy aspect of its meeting was that nevertheless it conducted a scramble between the aligned and non-aligned delegations for representation on the drafting committee, just as in the political committee. There was much talk on the dangers of cultural infiltration and subversion, and it was suggested that genuine cultural exchanges and co-operation could only take place between similar political systems, but of this there was no mention in the report. The quality of the committee's work is indicated by the sentence with which its Indonesian chairman concluded its proceedings: 'We are now about to enter the gate that leads us to the Rebirth, Revival and Renaissance of the Coloured Nations.'

China, in its conciliatory role, accepted two assertions that Communists usually contest. In the economic report, it let pass the statement that foreign aid to Afro-Asia (almost exclusively from the West at this time) had made 'a valuable contribution', and in the cultural report the statement that 'the cultures of Asia and Africa are based on spiritual and universal foundations'.

Further instances of reasonableness on China's part, occurring outside the conference meetings, added much to the atmosphere of enthusiasm that prevailed at the closing session. The principal issue in these agreements was the tension in the Formosa Strait between China and America. It was this matter, quite forgotten now, that made headlines round the world at the time of the conference and constituted its short-term importance.

The way to political agreement was smoothed by social meetings between Chou En-lai and South-East Asian leaders, arranged by Mr. Nehru. As General Romulo put it, rather ungraciously, Mr. Nehru played 'mother hen' to the Chinese leader, introducing him 'to polite society'.[22] The first such gathering was a dinner that Mr. Nehru gave Chou En-lai, Prince Wan and General Romulo on the 21st April. At this meeting the two latter put some searching questions to Chou En-lai. When he was asked by them if he wanted to communise Tibet, he laughed and said Tibet was very far from Communism. It would not be possible to establish a Communist regime there; nor was that China's intention. China had no wish to interfere with Tibet's customs or way of life. The Chinese had gone to Tibet because it was an integral part of China (though it was treated now as an autonomous region) and because of imperialist intrigues. What these could conceivably have been in 1950 it is difficult to see.

Similarly, Chou En-lai said, China was prepared to grant autonomy to Formosa and to grant Generalissimo Chiang Kai-shek an honourable position. When asked if he were prepared to renounce force as a means of settling the Formosa question, he replied that America and Formosa were using force against China all the time; he could not give a one-sided assurance.

That same day, at a press conference, Sir John Kotelawala had thrown out an interesting proposal. His theme was 'Formosa for the Formosans'. Accordingly he called for the evacuation of Quemoy and Matsu, the withdrawal of the United States Seventh Fleet from the Strait, a truce in the Strait, a five-year trusteeship for Formosa under Asian governments or the United Nations, and a plebiscite after five years in which the Formosans should choose between Chinese citizenship and independence.

Thereafter he tried hard, but unsuccessfully, to get Chou En-lai to a social gathering with the five sponsors. The meeting between Chou En-lai, the Five, Thailand and the Philippines, finally took place at the home of the Indonesian Premier over lunch on the 23rd April. From this meeting emerged a statement by Chou En-lai: 'The Chinese people are friendly to the American people. They do not want a war with the United States. The Chinese Government is willing to sit down and enter into negotiations with the United States Government to discuss the question of relaxing tension in the Far East, especially in the Formosa area.'

These words struck the conference like a bombshell, thrusting aside every other issue. Bandung saw itself as a possible bridge to peace between China and America. But not for long. The American reply, made the next day, said that Formosa must participate in any discussions, and that China must first give proof of her good intentions by observing a cease-fire in the area, by releasing the American pilots, and by accepting the Security Council invitation to participate in its debate on Formosa (Formosa subsequently said it would not participate in such discussions). Mr. Dulles himself said that perhaps China was 'playing a propaganda game'.

Even America's friends at Bandung were dismayed at this unyielding attitude. Mr. Mohammed Ali had described the Chinese offer as 'a great move'. Sir John said it was reasonable and sincere, and that America had brushed it aside 'without thinking'. General Romulo reported that Washington's reaction gave most people the impression that America was spoiling for a fight. In London a British spokesman said the Chinese offer had 'created a new situation'. Thus by saying no more than that China was ready to talk,

High Noon at Bandung, April–May 1955

Chou En-lai had alienated America from her friends and allies and made the United States appear churlish and intransigent.

Mr. Nehru had hoped to bring all four Indo-China states together in a meeting with Chou En-lai, but South Vietnam refused all his invitations to meals or discussions. Nevertheless China and North Vietnam met with and gave verbal assurances of non-interference to Cambodia and Laos, while North Vietnam in a written undertaking, dissociated itself from the internal dissensions between the Laotian Government and the Communists and both Governments subscribed to Panchsheel. An agreement between China and Indonesia on the vexed question of the dual nationality of Chinese residents in Indonesia was also known to be imminent.

With all this flow of reasonableness there was naturally much enthusiasm at the closing session. A three-hour delay caused by final difficulties with the resolutions only heightened the anticipation and excitement, and the relief when agreement was announced was correspondingly greater. Conferences tend to create their own atmosphere; but of all the Afro-Asian gatherings only the first conference in New Delhi generated a feeling of hope as strong as that at Bandung's last session—a feeling so strong that it lingered on, deceptively, for years.

Chou En-lai himself introduced an element of realistic deflation when in his closing speech he repeated his offer of talks with America on Formosa. This time he added: 'However, this should not in the slightest degree affect the just demand of the Chinese people to exercise their sovereign rights in liberating Taiwan.' This qualification left little to be discussed.

In its closing speech the Indonesia delegation said that the *raison d'être* of the conference was to pass the resolution on colonialism. For the Japanese, Bandung represented 'the dawn of the Afro-Asian renaissance'.

Mr. Nehru did not say anything strikingly new in his closing speech. More important to him than the communiqué was the simple fact that they had met at all. Urging the Afro-Asians not to be yes-men any longer, he asked: 'Are we copies of Europeans or Americans or Russians?' He referred 'to the infinite tragedy of Africa', greater than anything Asia had to bear; 'it is up to Asia to help Africa . . . for we are sister continents'.

U Nu, in slightly gloomy vein, said that they had reached no earth-shaking decisions, and that in any case they were in no position to exercise much influence on the course of world events.

219

But a truer reflection of the atmosphere in the hall was given in the last words of the Syrian delegate: 'We declare to the world that we continue to meet . . . until we see every degree of colonialism and imperialism washed and destroyed down for ever and ever. Amen.'

On the morning following the conference Mr. Nehru talked to the Indian correspondents covering the meeting; to their stunned, silent surprise, he told them that he thought it had been 'a very good conference'. What is more, he seems really to have thought so. He was too intellectually honest not to admit that the final communiqué was a lucky dip, with prizes for everyone who put his hand in, but he still felt that Bandung was part of 'an historic process' which would have a great 'psychological impact'—and on this point at least he was right.

U Nu, as his closing speech showed, was not under any illusions. On the day that the conference ended, he had decided that if another such conference was held Burma would not attend, because this conference had only brought out differences of opinion; even the resolutions passed reflected them. What was the good of repeating platitudes?

Comparing these different reactions from two of the sponsors one can only conclude that Mr. Nehru with his natural buoyancy set his hopes too high.

In other directions the euphoria continued. The Chinese-Indonesian agreement on nationality was signed in the restaurant of Jakarta airport, so that the departing leaders could attend the function; to his surprise, Mr. Nehru was there informed by Chou En-lai that Mr. Krishna Menon had been invited to Peking to continue negotiations for the release of the American pilots; delegates from West Asia visited China and Japan; and tributes to Chou En-lai's reasonableness came from Mr. Mohammed Ali, General Romulo, Sir John Kotelawala and President Nasser: 'not an aggressive Communist,' was the verdict of the Egyptian leader.

Looking back on Chou En-lai's performance at Bandung, we may freely grant that it was a masterly performance, but only a performance. He was lying to the top of his bent, especially to India, but also to Laos and personally to Prince Wan and General Romulo on Tibet. His conduct raises the whole question of how democratic leaders are to negotiate with totalitarians, especially when, at first hand, they are as charming and convincing as Chou En-lai.

There were a few sour notes even in the immediate aftermath. The Indonesian Press, especially the pro-Government papers, delivered personal attacks on Mr. Nehru in which were reflected the hurt pride of Dr. Ali at the fact that Mr. Nehru frequently, and perhaps not too tactfully, set right his bumbling chairmanship of the political committee. Yet this was a warning for the future which was not heeded.

Numerical counting of the aligned versus the non-aligned began soon after. Turkey claimed that the aligned had been in the majority —fifteen to fourteen. The Secretary-General of the Arab League put twelve delegations into the Western camp, while General Romulo claimed eleven.[23] For some countries there were marginal benefits from Bandung too. According to General Romulo, the West backed the Philippines for a seat in the Security Council because of its stand at Bandung.[24] And Sir John received many letters, even from East and Central Europe, congratulating him on his speech,[25] but they did not prevent his being swept out of office by his own people the next year.

The Indonesian Government party, perhaps partly because of Bandung, won its General Election. This may be one reason why, as early as August,[26] Indonesia was pressing for a second Bandung—something that has become a conditioned reflex of the Indonesian Foreign Ministry: no sooner is there a crisis than its call for a second Bandung goes forth.

The Bandung Spirit did not travel very well when carried home to some countries. Despite the recognition in Thailand that Prince Wan had done an excellent piece of work as *rapporteur* it was felt he had gone too far in accepting Chou En-lai's assurances. The Formosan representative in Thailand lodged a protest, and there was, accordingly, no move to despatch the mission of enquiry to Yunnan across the border: this would have been perilously near to granting recognition to Peking.

One achievement of Bandung was gained through inaction: decent burial was given to the persistent idea of a permanent Asian organisation. On his arrival at Bandung Mr. Nehru discountenanced the idea of another international body: 'There are quite enough around already,' he said briskly. There was no mention of it during the conference, except vaguely in the economic committee; and when reporting to Parliament, Mr. Nehru said the conference 'wisely avoided any provision for setting up additional machinery of international co-operation'. Thus the ghost that he himself had summoned up in 1947, and to which he had tried so hard to give a local habitation and a name, was finally laid to rest, mostly by his own words, in 1955.

It was not possible, in the nature of things, for debate on the conference to be long delayed: what did the final communiqué really mean, apart from meaning all things to all men? For General Romulo it was 'a great victory' because there was no mention in it of co-existence or the Five Principles. Mr. Mohammed Ali and Sir John Kotelawala felt that military alliances had been approved,[27] while Colonel Nasser insisted that it gave no approval to such pacts as SEATO and NATO.[28]

From the long analysis of the communiqué that Chou En-lai gave to the Standing Committee of the National People's Congress in Peking on the 13th May, it is clear that he had to do some explaining when he got home. Evidently worried by the interpretations put out by the aligned leaders, Chou En-lai asserted: 'The phrase "colonialism in all its manifestations" denotes colonialism in its political, military, economic, cultural and social manifestations and there cannot possibly be any other interpretation'; and on the 6th Bandung Principle he said: 'It cannot be used to defend the many aggressive military blocs. On the contrary it is firmly opposed to the formation of these blocs,' though the members of the blocs thought the opposite.

Mr. Nehru was uneasily aware of these diverse interpretations. The Declaration, he said, did not amount to 'a surrender of moral principles', if there was 'a watering down' 'that surely is always the case with a compromise resolution'. But the Declaration was not a compromise, a dilution; instead, on one issue, it was a deception and, on another, a juxtaposition of opposites.

One way in which Bandung was truly useful was the fostering of new friendships, of which the most important were the links between China and the Arabs. It has been said that supply of Russian arms for Egypt was arranged through Chou En-lai at Bandung; but this is doubtful, because the Syrians, who received arms from East Europe before Egypt, had already opened negotiations through Mr. Kyshyinsky at the United Nations.

As for Bandung's practical results, the undertaking to Laos was not kept for the Communists there, backed by North Vietnam and China, resumed their political attrition soon after; and the promise given by China to Ceylon, that local Communists would not be given aid or encouragement, has likewise not been observed, in Ceylon or anywhere else in Afro-Asia. The increase in cultural and economic relations that the communiqué recommended has not happened.

The conference did succeed in relaxing tension in the Formosa Strait, for the off-shore islands were not heavily bombarded again till August 1958. Even the sceptical Mr. Dulles agreed that of the forces that brought this about 'one of the most important' was 'the Bandung Conference, where Asian nations made it clear that they did not feel that the Formosa issue should be resolved by a resort to war by one side or the other'.[29]

Bandung's other practical political consequences were, if anything, negative. The acrimonious debates and the firm positions adopted disrupted the Five for good, and never again did they meet as a separate group. It did not have quite so deleterious an effect on the Arab states, because the Arab League, and the existence of Israel, both constituted bonds, but it did divide that body into two camps, Egypt, Syria, Saudi Arabia and Yemen being in one, and Iraq and Lebanon in the other—Jordan and Sudan, at this time, being in the middle.

Above all, by emphasising the differing positions of the aligned and the non-aligned, the Asian-African conference at Bandung put an end to the concept of Afro-Asia. Despite Indonesian insistence, ten years have elapsed without another Afro-Asian conference, and it is most unlikely that there will ever be one. With two exceptions, the participants at Belgrade were all from Africa and Asia, and it was thus a conference of Afro-Asians; but they met on a new basis, wholly different from the simple continental principle that produced Bandung.

Two groups of countries did not make much of an impression at Bandung—the Africans and the Arabs. There were only three really African countries present, Ethiopia, Liberia and the Gold Coast; the last was not yet fully independent. The first two were rather silent and hence were overlooked—a slight at which Liberia was moved to protest. The Arab states were nine in number but apart from Syria and Iraq the other seven said little, notably Egypt. But this was compensated by the decisive contribution made by Colonel Nasser in the drafting committees. If U Nu 'made' the Colombo Conference, Colonel Nasser was the hero of Bandung, with able technical assistance from Mr. Krishna Menon.

In retrospect it was perhaps better for everybody that Australia and New Zealand did not attend. They would have been in the aligned group and it would have embarrassed these Asians to carry this burden of white men.

Everyone outside Afro-Asia thought that Bandung was a Good Thing. President Tito professed himself 'pleasantly surprised'. The British Prime Minister and Foreign Minister welcomed its decisions, and America was relieved. Mr. Dulles himself went further than this: he thanked the Indonesian Ambassador in Washington for the communiqué and said he agreed with it, except for the section on Palestine.

The Russians, of course, gave it their complete approval, but they neither forgot nor accepted their exclusion from the conference. After a visit to Russia in November 1955, U Nu reported that President Bulganin suggested that the Central Asian Republics should join the Bandung group and U Nu agreed that they should do so.[30] It is impossible to say whether this was an expression of Burmese gratitude for a large Russian purchase of Burmese rice, or an example of the strong Burmese sense of humour (for U Nu knew that no such conference would be held).

Marshal Bulganin actually suggested that the Central Asian Republics participate in the next Afro-Asian conference, which was supposedly to be held in Cairo in March 1956. But in December 1955 Mr. Nehru told Sir John Kotelawala that it would be inopportune to hold this meeting because of the unsettled Middle East situation— one of the many Indian deferments which have continued to the present.

It is not easy to see Bandung in perspective because its long-term results flowed from the Bandung Illusion rather than from the Real Bandung. But of the reality it can at least be said that it led to no increase in racial feeling,[31] even while strengthening anti-colonial sentiment. Looking back on Bandung from a little distance Mr. Nehru emphasised this point: 'The common factor was rather against Western domination. Everybody agreed about that. The other common factor was a desire for social progress. Again everybody agreed about that.'[32] It was in his immediate reaction that Mr. Nehru saw the conference as part of history. Speaking to Parliament six days later, he said: 'Bandung proclaimed the political emergence in world affairs of over half the world's populations. . . . It would be a misreading of history to regard Bandung as though it was an isolated occurrence and not part of a great movement of human history.'[33]

At Bandung the Afro-Asians, as free and independent states, had a chance to look at themselves. They looked around the table and saw that they were many, and this gave them added confidence and hope. But that can only be done once if it is to have any effect, and this is why Bandung's greatest significance is to be found in the fact that it was held at all.

This chapter has dealt with the Real Bandung, not with the other,

224

different conference that had such lasting effects. Perhaps the best last word on the Real Bandung is a realistic note of appreciation from Mr. Nehru: 'The seats were comfortable.'

NOTES TO CHAPTER IX

1. Official sources supplied by those who wish to remain anonymous.
2. *New York Herald-Tribune*, 20th Mar. 1955.
3. Information supplied by a British Ambassador who was involved in these proceedings.
4. *New York Times*, 8th Mar. 1955.
5. C. Romulo: *The Meaning of Bandung*, The University of North Carolina Press, 1956.
6. *The Hindu*, Madras, 10th Apr. 1955.
7. The physiological impact on politics has not received the attention it deserves. It is the author's observation, during the United Nations General Assemblies, that more agreements are reached between 1 and 1.30 p.m., just before the luncheon-break, and between 5.30 and 6 p.m. than at any other time of day. With apologies to Milton and A. E. Housman:

> For stomachs do more than brains ever can
> To justify man's ways to man.

8. *The Hindu*, Madras, 17th Apr. 1955.
9. G. McT. Kahin: *The Asian-African Conference* (Cornell, 1956), is a good, brief study of the conference. It was written immediately after it and is not, and would not claim to be, anything more than an initial survey.
10. *Asia-Africa Speaks from Bandung*, issued by the Indonesian Ministry of Foreign Affairs, Jakarta, gives the texts of opening and closing speeches. The Indonesian Ministry of Information has produced a similar volume. A new edition of these volumes is called for because they are easy to come by now, not even in Jakarta.
11. References to, and quotations from, the Political Committee are taken from the verbatim text of its discussions, prepared by the Conference Secretariat.
12. C. Romulo: *op. cit.*, p. 13.
13. For the text see Appendix A.4.
14. A. K. Hassouna: *Report on the Bandung Conference*.
15. *The Hindu*, Madras, 28th Apr. 1955.
16. Kotelawala: *An Asian Prime Minister's Story*, chap. 20.
17. General Romulo reveals that Sir John's speech was not an impromptu effort but had been written in Colombo. Romulo, *op. cit.*, p. 10.
18. Nehru: *India's Foreign Policy*, p. 276.
19. See Appendix A.4.
20. *Dawn* (newspaper), Karachi, 20th Apr. 1955.
21. Japanese Government White Paper presented to the Diet on 7th July 1955.
22. Romulo: *op. cit.*, p. 10.
23. Romulo: *op. cit.*, p. 4. The Turkish list of fifteen pro-Westerners included Turkey, Pakistan, Iraq, the Philippines, Japan, South Vietnam, Ceylon, Iran, Iraq, Lebanon, Libya, Jordan, Liberia, the Gold Coast,

Sudan and Thailand. General Romulo added Ethiopia but omitted
Jordan, the Gold Coast, Sudan, Japan and South Vietnam.

24. Romulo: *op. cit.*, p. 37.
25. Kotelawala: *op. cit.*, Epilogue.
26. Roeslan Abdulgani: 'The Afro-Asian Conference in Retrospect',
    Foreign Affairs Report, Indian Council of World Affairs, New Delhi,
    Aug. 1955.
27. *The Hindu*, Madras, 27th and 28th May 1955, and *Ceylon Daily News*,
    27th May 1955.
28. *The Hindu*, Madras, 28th May 1955.
29. *The Hindu*, Madras, 8th *June* 1955.
30. R. H. Fifield: *The Diplomacy of Southeast Asia*, New York, 1958,
    chap. 6.
31. The American Negro novelist Richard Wright who attended the
    conference found this quite perplexing: *The Colour Curtain*, London,
    1956.
32. T. Mende: *Conversations with Nehru*, London, 1956.
33. Nehru: *India's Foreign Policy*, pp. 279–80.

CHAPTER X

The Waxing and Waning of the Bandung Myth, 1955 to 1960

In a conversation with the author in January 1963, Mr. Nehru said that as the colonial experience of the Afro-Asian countries receded into the past, they had to find a new basis for their relations with each other. They had tried to do this through non-alignment. In addition they needed to do this increasingly through co-operation in economic development. That, in his opinion, would be more difficult, and it lay some way in the future.

In the six years that divided the Bandung Conference from that at Belgrade, non-alignment became a sole basis for Afro-Asianism. There were, at most, twelve non-aligned states at Bandung, but twenty-five Afro-Asians, claiming to be non-aligned, attended Belgrade. The expansion was phenomenally swift for a brand of foreign policy that was only eight years old in 1955.

The spreading of the Bandung Myth was partly responsible for this development. The hard core of the Myth remained the Five Principles of Panchsheel, around which was wrapped the softer coating of the Bandung Principles.

Even before Bandung the Five Principles had begun to find acceptance in the world; nine countries had formally accepted them and they had been commended by Mr. Anthony Eden, speaking for Britain, and Mr. Molotov for Russia. Panchsheel reached its apotheosis in the resolution of the 14th December 1957 in which, without a dissentient vote, the United Nations General Assembly accepted the first four Principles as providing the basis for 'peaceful and neighbourly relations among states'.

Before that climax was reached, sixteen governments signed declarations incorporating Panchsheel.[1] The Principles were referred to appreciatively by such diverse personalities as King Saud and the Emperor Haile Selassie on the one hand, and, on the other, by Mr. Hammarskjöld, Lord Home (now Sir Alec Douglas-Home) and Mr. Casey, then Australian Foreign Minister.[2]

The Waxing and Waning of the Bandung Myth

At a time when these political beatitudes were gaining such wide acceptance, it was unfair and inaccurate for Mr. Nehru to claim, as he often did, that all the participants at Bandung had approved them. The 5th Principle, specifically mentioning co-existence, was not incorporated in the Bandung Declaration, and even representatives of Indonesia omitted it in their speeches. Yet this 5th Principle was the summation of Panchsheel and the most difficult clause for others to accept.

Thus when Panchsheel made its first breakthrough into Latin America, in a joint statement by Chile and India, on the 16th April 1957, the final principle mentioned was not peaceful co-existence, but a pious hope that 'international problems should be solved by peaceful means'.

Even close friends of India found it impossible to accept 'peaceful co-existence' publicly and officially. Afghanistan, although a joint signatory of many declarations with India, never subscribed to it, nor did any of the Arab states, not even Egypt. Afghanistan's reason probably was her dispute with Pakistan; for the Arabs, the reason was their adjourned war with Israel, which for them was non-existent.

The Bandung Spirit, being less controversial, spread even farther afield and was applied to an infinite variety of events. Iran's adherence to the Baghdad Pact in September 1955 took place under its banner, as did a coalition of political parties in Syria in 1957. The nationalisation of the Suez Canal by President Nasser in 1956 was proclaimed by him in the name of Bandung,[3] and the first Conference of Independent African States at Accra in April 1958 solemnly restated the Principles.

The interminable incantatory references to the Spirit and the Principles create the impression that a large part of mankind was seized by one of those mass hysterias that swept over Europe in the Dark Ages. The fever began to subside in 1959 when Panchsheel dropped out of pronouncements, even those made by the Indian Government, and by 1960 all that remained were brief generalised references to the continuing fact of non-alignment, with some flowery allusions to peaceful co-existence. The hard realities of the world could not be ignored any longer.

Some governments used this five-year display of international emotion with cold calculation; for others it was something to be accepted reluctantly as a necessity, for some it was a cheerful, irresponsible game, and for a very few it was, unfortunately, a really serious and important matter. Among these was India.

228

The Waxing and Waning of the Bandung Myth

The Bandung Spirit was not, of course, entirely unproductive of practical results. China's release of the American pilots can be attributed to it; also, perhaps, the 'package deal' by which five of the seven states recommended at Bandung were granted United Nations membership at the end of 1955. China was probably the principal beneficiary; in 1956 several of the Arab states, including Egypt, recognised her, and in the same year the number of Afro-Asian delegations at the United Nations supporting her candidature sharply increased from two in 1954 to ten. To the Afro-Asians this was no more than a return for friendship shown by China, but it was indicative of the trend that gave this period its special savour.

In the Cold War, the non-aligned states of Afro-Asia were like dwellers on an island in the middle of a divided stream, trying to build a bridge to both shores. Quite suddenly the inhabitants of the eastern bank, hitherto unfriendly, change their attitude completely and take the initiative in building their half of the bridge to midstream. It is understandable that the island dwellers view the aloof inhabitants of the western shore with irritated impatience, for if only they, too, would co-operate, the beautiful bridge would be complete.

The Bandung Principles, or Panchsheel, propounded from Cairo or New Delhi or Jakarta were one thing. When they were proclaimed by Mr. Khrushchev from Moscow or by Chairman Mao from Peking, and by the Communist Party in every country in the world, they became something quite different; a change in quantity produced a difference in quality. The new association meant that the non-aligned Afro-Asians were no longer merely honest brokers; they had become partners, perhaps junior partners, but still partners, of one of the two big concerns in world affairs. Panchsheel became not just a strange-sounding word but a slogan to conjure with, literally, 'from China to Peru'.

The friendliness of the Soviet Union and the rest of the Communist world towards Afro-Asia after Stalin's death was a total reversal of his policy, but it was the new Malenkov-Khrushchev line rather than Stalin's that was in accord with the traditional Communist assessment of the importance of these two continents. In accordance with the dictum of Lenin that 'the road to Paris leads through Peking and Calcutta', the Russian revolutionary regime had, soon after attaining power, turned its attention to Asia; a Congress of Eastern Peoples was held at Baku in 1920. This interest was maintained through the 1920's, and evidence of it was the Communist-

The Waxing and Waning of the Bandung Myth

inspired Congress of Oppressed Peoples at Brussels in 1927. But in
the 1930's, with the rise of the Fascist threat in Europe, Russia gave
only minimal attention to happenings in Asia, apart from their value
as propaganda. Stalin was probably also affected by the suppression
of the Chinese Communists by the nationalists in 1927; this may well
have predisposed him to suspect Asian nationalism.

It was not only with suspicion but with contempt and hostility that
Russia reacted to the emergence of the new Asian states. Mr. Nehru
may have held out India's hand in friendship equally to America and
Russia in his very first foreign policy speech, but a dusty answer was
returned by Moscow. In a splendid display of dialectical demono-
logy, the Russians simply said that black was white. In the classic
Soviet Encyclopaedia, Mahatma Gandhi was described as an agent
and accomplice of imperialism. A publication of the Soviet Union's
Academy of Sciences in 1949 described the independence of India
and Pakistan as proof that the 'national bourgeoisies had openly
gone over to the camp of imperialism'. In 1951 there was a reference
to 'the so-called independence of Burma', and in 1953 to Indonesia's
'fictional independence'. The Delhi Conference on Indonesia in 1949
was, for the Russians, a disguised attempt to preserve Dutch rule in
Indonesia; India had sided with the aggressor in Korea; and its
routine friendship treaties with countries in West Asia were really
a cloak enabling Britain to use India as a pretext for keeping her
troops in the area. The coup that overthrew King Farouk in Egypt
was the work of 'a Fascist military dictatorship'. China joined in this
lunatic chorus, and for Peking radio Mr. Nehru at this time was 'a
running-dog of imperialism'.

It was not enough for international Communism to hurl harsh
words at the new Asian governments. As we have seen, after the Calcutta Conference of 1948, it tried forcibly to overthrow them by
promoting armed uprisings in India, Burma, Malaya, Indonesia and
the Philippines.

The Chinese were the first to show some recognition that the
Asians are better than crypto-colonialists. India's efforts in Korea in
1951–2 were treated with a measure of respect. And in October 1952
at 'the Asia and Pacific Area Peace Conference' in Peking, there was,
for the first time, no mention of the need for an armed struggle in
Asia. A Russian speaker at this meeting even said that 'each people
. . . should have freedom to choose their own way of life . . . and
political system and their own ideology'. This is one piece of evidence
that even Stalin, in the last year of his life, was beginning to change

his ideas about Asia. In January 1952 Russia broke a long silence on the Kashmir question, and supported India in the Security Council, and in April Stalin granted his first interview to the Indian Ambassador, Dr. Radhakrishnan, just before the latter's departure from Moscow. In the course of talk, incidentally, the Russian ruler revealed that he thought Ceylon was a part of India, even though his representative had vetoed Ceylon's admission to the United Nations. An even clearer indication of change came in January 1953, two months before Stalin's death, when the official Cominform journal mentioned India, Burma, the Philippines, Indonesia, Tunisia, Morocco, Algeria, Iran, Iraq and Egypt as areas of 'progress' in the conflict between freedom and imperialism. Nevertheless, throughout 1952 and early in 1953 Moscow Radio was still attacking the new Asian states.

The real change came after Stalin's death in March 1953. A Russian initiative led to the signing of the Korean armistice in July, and in August 1953, Malenkov, in a speech to the Supreme Soviet, made what was the earliest favourable official reference to the governments of India and of South-East and West Asia. The Five Principles were agreed between India and China in April 1954, and were accepted as the basis of Russian foreign policy in a speech by Mr. Molotov in February 1955. From that time onwards, the Communist world was in official partnership with the non-aligned. In May 1955, the month after Bandung, it was announced that the Communist Party in Indonesia was supporting that government's foreign policy. The Indian Communist Party gave its backing to Mr. Nehru's foreign policy in August 1955.

In November 1954 Russia opened negotiations with India for the construction of a steel plant, and in September 1955 she concluded the arms agreement with Egypt.

The year 1955 also saw the first exchange of visits between Asian and Russian leaders. Mr. Nehru was in Russia in June, when he was accorded honours hitherto granted to no other foreign visitor, including the privilege of addressing a public meeting of 80,000 people; and in the winter Bulganin and Khrushchev were given an enthusiastic reception in India, Burma and Afghanistan.

This process of making new friends in Asia culminated in Mr. Khrushchev's famous speech to the Twentieth Congress of the Soviet Communist Party in 1956, in which, along with a denunciation and repudiation of Stalinism, he uttered warm praise for the new nations. This necessitated rewriting the Soviet history of recent Asian happenings. Thus the Soviet Orientalists at their conference in 1956 decided that Mahatma Gandhi was 'an ardent patriot', and that 'the national bourgeoisie in such countries as India, Burma and others is still progressive'.[4]

For every act of Communist policy there must be a justificatory dogma. This abrupt return to the Leninist assessment of Asia is, in the language of current orthodoxy, explained thus: 'The various types of contradictions in the contemporary world are concentrated in the vast areas of Asia, Africa and Latin America; these are the most vulnerable areas under imperialist rule, and the storm centres of world revolution, dealing direct blows at imperialism. Therefore the anti-imperialist revolutionary struggles of the people of Asia, Africa and Latin America are definitely not a matter of regional significance but one of overall importance for the cause of proletarian world revolution.'[5] In short, the tree of Euro-American imperialism must be cut down at its Afro-Asian roots.

Tactically, the Communist approach to Afro-Asia is a choice of the lesser of the sorts. If the Afro-Asians cannot be made into Soviet satellites, they must not become satellites in Western-led military groupings; and in Asia this means that they must not provide bases for possible use against Russia and China. If the Afro-Asians cannot be allies, they must, at least, be as friendly to the East as to the West. The approach was made on two levels: correct, respectable relations between government and government were maintained on the one, and on the other the unofficial, noisy, propagandist activities of the Afro-Asian Solidarity Movement were carried on, in which both Russia and China took a leading part.

There are many strands in Communist policy towards Afro-Asia: there are personal contacts, exchanges of visits of every sort and at every level, from presidents and field-marshals to jugglers and weight-lifters. There is also support given to Afro-Asian opposition to Western imperialism itself, or to its friends in the area; so Indonesia is backed against Holland, India against Pakistan over Kashmir, Egypt against the tripartite aggression in 1956 (with the threat of rockets and a belated offer of 'volunteers'), the North African territories against France, and all the Arab states against Israel. And when the actual physical control of the old colonial system is removed, the Communists are ready to back the Afro-Asians against the new shadowy danger of 'neo-colonialism'—an especially fruitful area of co-operation in Africa. Economic assistance is as varied as it is generous: a radio station for Cambodia, a sports stadium for Burma, a steel plant in India, the Aswan High Dam in Egypt, a port for Yemen and a hospital in Ethiopia—these are only a few items in a long list of projects that are accompanied by a marked increase in trade.

Above all in the years immediately following Bandung the Communists displayed sympathetic understanding of the desire of the non-aligned Afro-Asians to keep out of blocs. They refrained, at least publicly, from censoring the position of non-alignment between their bloc and that of the West, gave Panchsheel full official endorsement, and earnestly expressed their faith in peaceful co-existence.

But were the Communists and the non-aligned talking about the same policy when they spoke of 'peaceful co-existence'? The answer is 'no'. 'What is this co-existence?' Mr. Nehru once asked:[6] he supplied the answer that it was 'a mental or spiritual attitude that synthesises differences and contradictions, that tries to understand and accommodate different religions and ideologies . . . and refuses to think in terms of conflict or military solutions'.

From the first appearances of co-existence in Soviet political thought, no one attempted to conceal the fact that it was not an eternal principle emerging from 'a mental or spiritual attitude', but a temporary policy suited to a certain state of political affairs. 'The current streak of peaceful co-existence' had been produced by 'a certain temporary balance of forces', as Stalin said in 1952. In the late 1950's another balance of forces, infinitely more terrible, was struck between the Great Powers, so peaceful co-existence was once more necessary. But even when driven by mutual terror, the Soviet ideologues, under pressure, it is true, would never say that peaceful co-existence was meant 'to accommodate different . . . ideologies'. Governments may co-exist with governments, but not ideologies, not classes, and not the colonisers and the oppressed.

Further, though Communist co-existence accepted non-aligned neutralism, so affording proof of its willingness to co-exist, it could not and did not approve of it in the slightest. A review of a book on co-existence published in Moscow in 1957 by the Soviet Academy of Sciences denied the statement that a policy of neutrality is in all circumstances a form of peaceful co-existence. This Soviet reviewer contended that when the Imre Nagy Government proclaimed a 'neutrality' policy for Hungary after the 1956 revolution, its act was indirect 'connivance with the imperialist war-makers'. Nor, when a country adopts neutrality, is the zone of peace necessarily extended; nor was it possible by a policy of neutrality to establish a 'single collective security system capable of ensuring lasting peace'; rather, 'a collective security system presupposes not the collective neutrality of the member states but their determination and readiness to rebuff any aggression by joint effort'. The Chinese have been more frank in their attitude towards non-aligned neutralism: 'Neutrality is merely a camouflage; a third road does not exist,' wrote Mao Tse-tung in 1948; and they have never wavered in that belief; 'peaceful co-existence or stalemated co-existence is a transitional form. So is peaceful neutralism', as one of their recent statements puts it. Thus the non-aligned and the Communists were not talking about the same policy when they used the words 'peaceful co-existence'; 'competitive co-existence' would be a more accurate description of what the Communists had in mind.[7]

But there was just enough in common between the two concepts for the non-aligned and the Communists to think that they meant the same thing; and for a variety of political reasons this is what both wanted to believe.

Students of Afro-Asia and connoisseurs of the incongruous (and not enough of the first can be counted among the second) noted with a lift of heart that something had been added to their field of enquiry and enjoyment when, in the press pictures of meetings of the non-aligned leaders after Bandung, a solitary white face appeared in the row of brown and black. This was the square, strong-featured, beetle-browed countenance of Josip Broz Tito, President of Yugoslavia, a medium-sized medium-poor country from the bottom right-hand corner of Europe. This incongruous presence was a source of immense satisfaction and encouragement to the Afro-Asian non-aligned, for it could mean that the counter-attack on Europe, that Europe had so foolishly feared earlier on, was now, perhaps, actually developing. Their hopes were false; for, in truth, Yugoslavia needed Afro-Asia far more than Afro-Asia needed Yugoslavia. This improbable Balkan link with Afro-Asia, too good to last, demands an enquiry into when, why, how it came about.

Yugoslavia's non-alignment dates, of course, from 1948 when she parted company with the Cominform. Yet few people would be prepared to grant that she is among the oldest members of the non-aligned club for until she linked up with Afro-Asia, she appears not so much to have chosen non-alignment, as to have been isolated through rejection by both sides in the Cold War—by the West because she was Communist, and by the East because she was not. Sensing this loneliness, various Yugoslav theoreticians began travelling through the non-aligned countries of South Asia in 1950–1 and found links of kinship with Burma, because of her socialism, and with India, because of her well-thought-out approach to non-alignment.

The socialist connection brought the first results. When the First Asian Socialist Conference was held in Rangoon in January 1953, fraternal delegates were present from Yugoslavia's League of Communists. The importance Yugoslavia attached to this meeting was shown when she sent as her chief delegates Milovan Djilas and her Deputy Foreign Minister, Bebler. This conference discussed, but did not decide in favour of, non-alignment, and it was two years before the association with India on the basis of that concept was officially ratified.

This ratification came during the course of a journey to India and Burma made by President Tito in the winter of 1954, just before the Colombo Conference. India at first was not disposed to take the Yugoslav leader too seriously; his fondness for heavily-braided sky-blue uniforms did not appeal to the solemn Indian cast of mind, and India's first ambassador to Yugoslavia had only been appointed that year. However, a careful reading of President Tito's speeches showed that his ideas were in accord not only with non-alignment, but even with Panchsheel, so that he was not merely the first European head of state to visit India; he also became the first European leader to endorse the Five Principles.

Several considerations, stemming from Yugoslavia's national interests, prompted her to seek association with Afro-Asia. Her isolation had been particularly emphasised during 1953 when the West had backed Italy in its dispute with Yugoslavia over Trieste. No longer a member of the close-knit Communist family, Yugoslavia was anxious to find another group to join. And if she became an influential member of a new group, she would gain new standing in Russia's eyes. This came to pass, for late in 1961 Mr. Gromyko described Yugoslavia as a bridge to the Afro-Asian world.

There are again many explanations why Yugoslavia managed to make herself acceptable to far-distant Afro-Asians with whom, at first glance, she might seem to have little in common. Her adoption of non-alignment, even if made of necessity and not from choice, was one link. Perhaps a more substantial bond was her socialist approach, because by this time most Afro-Asian countries, and not Burma alone, were at least saying they were socialist. As an underdeveloped, primarily agricultural country, Yugoslavia's economic problems

235

were not very different from those of the Afro-Asians. Yugoslavia was also able to identify herself, with special sympathy, with the national liberation movements of Afro-Asia, because she had waged just such a struggle against a foreign master during World War II; and since many Yugoslav diplomats had taken part in that heroic effort, they were able to make a particularly strong impression on the recently liberated Afro-Asians. In Afro-Asia, too, Yugoslavia found a market for her high-priced, low-quality capital goods, and an area into which she could escape from the pressures of the Common Market and the COMECON.

It may have been India that suggested to Yugoslavia the idea that she might have a political and ideological influence on Afro-Asia. This hint is discernible in Mr Nehru's frequent public avowals that he especially valued Yugoslavia's analysis of development in Eastern Europe: 'Yugoslavia is a country with which we exchange our appraisal of the world situation more frequently than with any other country.'[8] If they could impress India, the Yugoslavs must have reasoned, how much stronger could be their impact on smaller, newer countries. Ideas and advice have become one of Yugoslavia's principal exports to Afro-Asia; ideas on political structure, party organisation, on decentralisation, and workers' control of industry. And the ideas were not only novel, they came from 'safe' Communists without a great power behind them, and from 'nice' Communists too, much more relaxed and human than their Russian counterparts.

As Communists in theory, if not in practice, the Yugoslavs share the orthodox Communist dogma on the importance of Afro-Asia for the future. They are convinced that these two continents, and Latin America, will ultimately become Communist and will then dominate the world. By getting in quickly, on the ground floor, the Yugoslavs hope to gain sufficient influence to ensure that Afro-Asian-Latin Communism will be of the Yugoslav rather than the Russian, or Chinese, variety.

In non-political terms Yugoslavia's problems seems to be similar to those of Syria: a country with a big soul confined in a small body, restlessly searching for a larger entity in which to spread. She thought she had found this entity in Afro-Asia. By the time of the Belgrade Conference, 600 Afro-Asian students had been granted scholarships to Yugoslavia, 100 experts had been sent abroad to give technical assistance, and credits to the value of $200 million had been granted to about twenty Afro-Asian countries.

Yugoslavia's idea of co-existence is nearer to the Russian than to the Afro-Asian, or at least the Indian, concept. 'It is not pacifism,' according to a Yugoslav authority,[9] nor is it 'a policy of defence of the *status quo* in international relations and even less in internal social relations'.[10]

But whether or not President Tito and his Afro-Asian interlocutors were talking about the same concept, he talked to them a great deal. His long winter cruises to warmer climates became a familiar feature of the Afro-Asian scene. After India and Burma in 1955 came a visit to Egypt and Ethiopia in 1956, and in 1958 a longer trip to Indonesia, Burma, India, Ceylon, Ethiopia, the Sudan and the United Arab Republic. After 1960 it was the turn of the new African states. In one period of fifteen months, President Tito was host in Belgrade to Haile Selassie, Prince Norodom, Presidents Sukarno, Nasser and Abboud of the Sudan, King Zahir Shah of Afghanistan and Presidents Ayub Khan and Sékou Touré. There was, therefore, nothing strange about a proposal that the next big gathering of the Afro-Asians should take place in Europe at Belgrade.

The climactic event in the Panchsheel period of the non-alignment phase of the Afro-Asian movement was undoubtedly when the United Nations on the 14th December 1957 accepted a resolution on 'peaceful and neighbourly relations among states' sponsored by India, Sweden and Yugoslavia.[11] The vote was seventy-seven for, none against, with one abstention—Formosa; and it was taken after a debate in six sessions spread over three days in which thirty-nine speakers in all took part, including sixteen Afro-Asians. Clearly the United Nations thought that this was a matter of importance. But was it? A reading of the text of the resolution shows the world body putting itself on record as being in favour of international virtue and against international sin. And one is confirmed in this assessment when one recalls that it was passed a mere fourteen months after Suez and Budapest, and even more so when one reads the text of the speeches in the debate.

The three-nation draft was a replacement of a Soviet proposal entitled 'Declaration concerning the peaceful co-existence of states'; it may have been prompted by bitter comments from Mr. Nehru about the Five Principles being 'words without meaning' to some countries, 'who claim the right of deciding problems by superior might'.[12] Russia, to show that she still believed in the Five Principles, incorporated them in full in her draft. It was presented with the usual covering letter; this, after mentioning Bandung, condemned 'negotiation from strength' and the attempts by some states to impose their will on Africa and the Near East by military means. Anything less co-existential could hardly be imagined. In the debate U Thant, then a delegate for Burma, said this wording had implications for the Cold War, and Laos took it as proof that the resolution was 'a political manœuvre'. However, the opening speech of the Russian delegate was conciliatory, referring to the wartime alliance of America and Russia and calling for a non-aggression pact between NATO and the countries of the Warsaw Pact.

By this time the three neutralists had already introduced their proposal, which the American representative welcomed as free from 'trick phrases'. He then mentioned Communist expansionism in Tibet, Korea, the Baltic states and Hungary. Calling for deeds not words, he concluded that 'there could be no compromise with a regime of terror'. This tough speech set the tone for those that followed.

Saudi Arabia claimed that co-existence was 'deeply rooted in Arab thinking, traditions and culture', but that it must be based on lawful events. 'Only a legitimate situation could co-exist with other situations.' Hence Zionism 'should not be permitted to exist'. There could be no co-existence between Algeria and France, nor with Britain which was occupying areas of Arabia. States such as Israel, established on the remains of another state, were outside the law and therefore outside co-existence.

Formosa fully agreed with this reasoning, and, after a long recital of Soviet misdeeds, said that the three-nation resolution would raise 'false hopes'.

Sweden admitted that an alternative resolution had been introduced because of the difficulty of defining the 5th Principle—peaceful co-existence itself. Mr. Krishna Menon described the relations between India and China as a notable example of co-existence, but said that though the word did not actually occur in the resolution its intention went further than mere co-existence.

The British delegate stated that it was impossible to accept Russian motives at their face value, and the Philippines' representative described co-existence as another form of the Cold War. Spain recalled Soviet actions in the Baltic states, Poland and Finland, and the Ukrainian delegate retorted by referring Western 'hypocrites and slanderers' to what was going on in Kenya and Cyprus. Russia concluded by accusing America of promoting subversion through reactionary regimes, as during the 'Hungarian *putsch*'; and Hitler's regime, the Soviet delegate recalled, had been based on gold from

American banks. Mr. Krishna Menon had the last word; the differences apparent in the debate he said, had themselves made the resolution more necessary.

It was adopted without dissent. What was reality and what illusion in this strange business? Had the final peaceful wording of the resolution any real substance, or did the heart of the matter lie in the bitter speeches made before its acceptance? That acceptance, possibly, was based on the desire of many delegates to humour the Afro-Asians, and on the harmless platitudes of the wording. Even Mr. Nehru could not make up his mind: 'This may mean a little but it means a lot too.'[13] If—an unlikely event—the whole world accepted Panchsheel, his ambiguous summing-up might prove appropriate.

Not for another three years did the anti-colonial aspect of Afro-Asianism gain the same universal acceptance. Another United Nations resolution, passed on the 12th October 1960, brought this about.[14] But this event, rather than being a climax, was for two reasons anti-climactic in effect. Firstly, by that date the main battles against colonialism had been fought and won; between 1955 and 1960 six more Afro-Asian countries had become independent, and in 1960 seventeen African states gained independence. Secondly, the actual passing of the resolution in the United Nations was marked by a total lack of dignity. It was ultimately passed by general acclamation, but only after a violent exchange of shouted insults, culminating when Mr. Khrushchev banged on the table with his shoe: a vulgar conclusion to Afro-Asia's long struggle for freedom. The wording of the operative clause of the resolution, proclaiming 'the necessity of bringing to a speedy and unconditional end colonialism in all its forms and manifestations', is interesting for its use of both 'form' and 'manifestations'. Nobody was taking any chances this time.

Today, the non-aligned Afro-Asians are simply another group of states, less united than most; and their disunity is primarily due to their failure to act as a moral force. In the words of the poet George Meredith: 'In tragic life, God wot, No villain need be! Passions spin the plot. We are betrayed by what is false within.' But the inner falsity of the Afro-Asians did not even spring from passions, but from calculation. The moral yardstick would not be applied to them if they did not themselves claim to be of high moral standing. They all made this claim, expecially, of course, the progenitor, Mr. Nehru. For him, non-alignment, as we have seen, was the product of Buddhism and Gandhism and Indian culture. Nor was he the only one to make such

239

a claim. The Saudi Arabian delegate, in the debate on co-existence, found it rooted in Arab thought and tradition and culture.

By the high standards which the Afro-Asians set for themselves, their first great failure was in the debates on Hungary in the United Nations in November 1956. On that occasion, they gave a perfect example of a double moral standard of judgement, voicing strong condemnation of the tripartite aggression on Egypt, which happened at the same moment, but taking refuge in mealy-mouthed evasions when mentioning the Russian aggression on Hungary. But it must be said here that those who most angrily denounce the Afro-Asians' double standards are themselves guilty of the same political sin. If there was anything more sickening than Afro-Asian timidity on Hungary, it was the spectacle of British and French delegates simulating (one hopes) moral indignation over Hungary at the very moment when their forces were killing Egyptians. Even America's hands are not clean. She was quick to denounce aggression in Korea and Hungary and, at this time, in Egypt, but she has been much less prompt, and sometimes silent, on other occasions—in Palestine, in North Africa and in Burma. Countries whose voting records in the United Nations permit them to throw stones can be counted on the fingers of one hand.

The strong Afro-Asian reaction against the three-nation assault on Egypt, especially the participation of Britain and France, is entirely understandable. Here was a classic example of large European Powers without a shadow of justification, and on the flimsiest of pretexts, seizing a chance to invade and destroy a nationalist government. Their act jabbed at the rawest and most sensitive nerve of Afro-Asia, and produced a strong spasm of hatred and fear. How could Afro-Asians be expected to show, simultaneously, the same degree of feeling for events in another continent? It is in the degree of discrimination in their reaction that the moral lapse occurs. Mr. Nehru, the most conspicuous of those who lapsed, summed up the double-standard approach in two sentences: 'Some attempt has been made' he protested 'to minimise this utterly unprovoked and brutal attack on Egypt. Attention has been diverted to the grave and distressing occurrences in Hungary'. There is a noticeable discrimination here between 'utterly unprovoked and brutal attack' and 'grave and distressing occurrences'.

The Hungarian crisis had been brewing since the 23rd October 1956. On the 30th October the Soviet Union announced the withdrawal of its troops. On the 1st November Imre Nagy repudiated the

Warsaw Pact and declared Hungary's neutrality, thus making it the second European country to adhere to non-alignment. As we now know, strong Chinese pressure was one of the reasons why, on the 2nd November, the Russian troops moved back and went into action against the freedom fighters.

The first United Nations resolution on Hungary was moved on the 4th November by the United States. This resolution called on Russia to desist from armed attack on the people of Hungary, to withdraw her forces, and to permit United Nations observers to function in Hungary. Seven Afro-Asians voted in its favour, but six of these were allies of the West and can be discounted; the exception was Cambodia. Thirteen Afro-Asians, all non-aligned, abstained. They were Afghanistan, Burma, Ceylon, Egypt, India, Indonesia, Iraq, Jordan, Lebanon, Nepal, Saudi Arabia, Syria and Yemen.

On the 9th November Italy, Cuba, Iceland, Pakistan and Peru tabled a resolution calling on Russia to withdraw her forces, suggesting that free elections should be held under United Nations auspices and that the Secretary-General should continue an investigation of the affair. One Afro-Asian non-aligned country voted in favour, Laos this time; Cambodia joined twelve other non-aligned countries in abstaining; India and Yugoslavia joined the Communist states and voted against.

On the 21st November, largely because of indignation expressed in their own countries, India, Indonesia and Ceylon introduced a resolution urging the Hungarian Government to accede to the request made by the Secretary-General to permit observers to function in Hungary, as called for in the resolutions of the 4th November. Even on this Afro-Asian resolution, Egypt, Ethiopia, Jordan, Saudi Arabia, Syria, Yemen and Yugoslavia abstained.

In the second round of the Hungarian debate a twenty-nation resolution of the 12th December called on Russia to withdraw her troops immediately, under United Nations observation. By this time there had been a stirring of the Afro-Asian conscience and so we find Laos, Nepal, Burma, Ceylon, Tunisia (which had since become a member) supporting this course and eleven Afro-Asians abstaining. Nine months later, in September 1957, a thirty-seven nation resolution won support from seven non-aligned nations—Laos, Morocco, Sudan, Tunisia, Burma, Cambodia and Ghana, with nine non-aligned countries abstaining.

Thus, by and large, a group of five Buddhist countries, after some hesitation, gave a moral judgement, while a group of ten Muslim countries and India refused to do so. This division of opinion, in itself a bad thing for the non-aligned, might seem sufficient to preserve Afro-Asia's reputation. Yet among those who abstained were the principal countries of the area—Indonesia for South-East Asia, Egypt for West Asia, and India for South Asia; India, in particular, failed to save her soul 'before the gun-butt rapped upon the door'.

The reasons given for abstention by some of the non-aligned states make pathetic reading. For instance, Burma, Ceylon, Indonesia, and Nepal all said they had no time to get instructions for the vote on the 4th November. The reason for consistent Arab abstention is quite clear; the Communist states were giving solid support to Egypt against the tripartite aggression, and must not be offended: 'We abstained out of gratitude,' as President Nasser said.[15] When Tunisia or Morocco voted affirmatively, they were being bad Arabs.

The key to India's abstention on Hungary is to be found in Kashmir. All the resolutions she abstained on or voted against provided for United Nations observers or supervised elections or United Nations-supervised troop-withdrawals. If India had accepted any of these proposals a similar demand for United Nations supervision might have been made in respect of Kashmir, and this she would not have been able to accept. It was no accident that Pakistan joined in sponsoring these resolutions. Concern over Kashmir lay behind India's constant reiteration that the United Nations should not, in Mr. Nehru's words, 'reduce Hungary to less than a sovereign state. Any acceptance of intervention of this type, namely, foreign supervised elections, seemed to us to set a bad precedent which might be utilised in future for intervention in other countries'.[16] Mr. Krishna Menon said the same thing over and over again: 'It would be wrong and against the principles of the Charter to ignore the existence of a sovereign state. I do not care how much ridicule one may invite in making such a statement'; and 'the withdrawal of armed forces under United Nations observation would mean the creation of other machinery and reference to other organs of the United Nations and so on'.[17] For 'so on', read 'Kashmir'.

To concern over Kashmir must be added the definitely leftist tendency of Mr. Nehru and the very strong leftist bias of Mr. Krishna Menon who, despite long and frequent speeches on Hungary, contrived to utter not one word of condemnation of Russia, even when expressing sympathy for Hungary. The Communist espousal of non-alignment now brought in a handsome dowry.

The reason for Afghan abstention is obvious: Afghanistan is a neighbour of Russia, not of America. The real mystery is Indonesia's steady abstention, even without the excuse of receiving no instructions. Perhaps her reason was a desire to maintain the solidarity of the Afro-Asian non-aligned areas, in order to achieve that major objective of Indonesian foreign policy, a second Bandung Conference.

On the 2nd November Mr. Nehru informed the Ceylonese Premier, Mr. S. W. R. D. Bandaranaike, that 'no great purpose would be served' by a meeting of the Five Colombo countries to discuss Suez and Hungary. Next day came an announcement that they would meet in New Delhi, and the Indonesian Premier claimed that the meeting was his idea, and that it was preparatory to a second Bandung Conference. Once again a reluctant India had given in at the last minute. The Pakistan Premier refused to attend because a meeting of the premiers of the Baghdad Pact countries was being held at the same time in Teheran; Pakistan, evidently, attached more importance to talking with her current allies than with her one-time friends. The discussions between Mr. Nehru, Dr. Ali Sastroamidjojo, Mr. Bandaranaike and U Ba Swe of Burma on the 12th, 13th and 14th produced a long communiqué which is interesting because of its irrelevance. It spoke strongly and at length about Egypt, and less strongly and briefly about Hungary. It then went on to refer to Algeria and Morocco and, in many hundreds of words, wrung its hands over the blow delivered to Panchsheel by the recent misconduct of the Great Powers. While Rome burned, the non-aligned delivered a lecture on the cause of the conflagration and the theory of fire-fighting.

At the end of the conference, Dr. Ali told the press that the prime ministers had agreed in principle to the holding of a Second Bandung Conference, perhaps in the latter half of the following year; of this there was no mention in the communiqué. He then went on to Pakistan to obtain the endorsement of its prime minister to the Delhi communiqué, but failed in his attempt because Pakistan objected to any reference to Panchsheel. This represented the demise of the group known as the Colombo Powers.

The next failure of the Afro-Asians at the United Nations, which reduced their standing and revealed their limitations, happened at the General Assembly session of 1960. The shooting-down by the Russians of an American spy-plane had disrupted the Paris summit meeting in May. In September, at a great gathering of heads of states and governments for the General Assembly, the non-aligned states tried to push President Eisenhower and Mr. Khrushchev into meeting. A resolution to this effect was tabled in the names of Presidents

The Waxing and Waning of the Bandung Myth

Tito, Nasser, Nkrumah, Sukarno and Mr. Nehru, and the last-named exerted every effort to get it passed. It failed to win adoption by forty-one votes against thirty-seven, less than the required two-thirds majority, with America voting against it, and the Soviet bloc abstaining. The failure was not so much moral as one of tactics, and of a sense of proportion. To many the proposal seemed much ado about nothing, and the over-anxious Afro-Asian matchmakers were taught the lesson that if the Big Two were unwilling, nobody could make them act against their will. Non-aligned nations could always serve passively, as a bridge, but seldom actively, as a clasp; the latter role required patience and discretion rather than dramatic victories at the United Nations.

The large increase in the number of the Afro-Asian members of the United Nations, in 1960 in particular, forced the group to become a more organised body. Numbering by now almost fifty members—nearly half the entire United Nations membership—its meetings could no longer be the casual family gatherings they had been in the early 1950's. They called for a large committee room, and the United Nations Secretariat had to be asked to provide simultaneous translations because of the presence of the French-speaking African members. But this increase in organisation did not bring any greater degree of unity in voting. An analysis of Afro-Asian votes[18] in the Assemblies of 1960 and 1961 shows that even on colonial issues they split into three. On Palestine twenty-five Afro-Asians voted for, eleven against and eleven abstained: on West Irian the respective numbers were twenty-six, fourteen and six; and on the membership of China, nineteen, twelve and fifteen. On Cold War issues the nine Asian states supported America in 19 per cent of the votes cast, and the Soviet Union in 34 per cent; the figures for the twenty-three African states was 30 per cent for the United States and 24 per cent for the Soviet Union. India's individual figures were 10 per cent for the United States and 41 per cent for the Soviet Union. Thus, as before, the group remained a centre for consultation rather than co-ordination.

Only when the Communist side in the Cold War adopted the Bandung Spirit did this achieve world-wide dimensions—through the workings of the powerful Communist propaganda machine. At times it spread through its own modest practical importance. But when, for any reason, the support of the Communists for the Ten Principles because less enthusiastic, there was a corresponding contraction in the applicability and importance of the Bandung Spirit. Events took this shape in the later 1950's and early 1960's.

The Waxing and Waning of the Bandung Myth

Working co-operation was based on the readiness of both parties, the Communists and the non-aligned, to maintain the fiction that co-existence between governments is possible without co-existence between ideologies. In short, Russia's non-aligned friends were expected to accept a situation in which a government can be helped by the Russian Government, while Russia's henchmen in the local Communist Party are doing their best to overthrow it. India and Indonesia accepted the fiction; the Arabs did not. Their interpretation of co-existence was to expect the Russians to live with a situation in which the local government was accepting massive help from Russia, yet was putting equally massive pressure on the local Communists. The Russians have had to tolerate this, but not without protest; they have had several rowdy altercations, especially with the leading Arab country, Egypt.

In 1955 Russia provided Egypt with a large quantity of arms, and in 1956 supported her over Suez and provided wheat and petroleum products; while in 1958 she began seriously to discuss the financing of the High Dam. But early in 1958 Russia had shown displeasure when Syria joined Egypt to save herself from increasing internal Communist influence. From this the Arabs drew the conclusion that the Communists did not want Arab unity if it was brought about by the force of Arab nationalism.

In December 1958 President Nasser, in a slashing attack on Russia, invited Mr. Khrushchev to stop interfering in the internal affairs of the United Arab Republic, and Mr. Khrushchev retorted by describing the President as 'a hot-headed young man'. At the Twenty-first Party Congress in January 1959, there were further open attacks on President Nasser, especially for his continuing suppression of the Egyptian Communists. In March of that year there was yet another direct exchange between Mr. Khrushchev and President Nasser, when the former defended the Communists in Iraq, then very powerful, against attacks from President Nasser, who retorted that 'as we crushed the imperialist agents we will also crush the Communist agents'.

No doubt with such incidents in mind, the World Communist Conference of November 1960 drew a distinction between non-aligned countries that permitted the local Communist Party to function, and those that did not. Among the latter, Egypt and Iraq (now anti-Communist) were condemned. After six years of friendship with the Afro-Asians the Communist movement had discovered, painfully, that there were some non-aligned states that were more, and others that were less, non-aligned than others.

The Waxing and Waning of the Bandung Myth

In the middle of 1961 there was another slanging match between Mr. Khrushchev and Anwar Sadat, one of President Nasser's close associates. Mr. Khrushchev rather crudely reminded the Egyptian how much Russia had done for Egypt, said that Egypt was not socialist though she claimed to be so, and suggested that Communism could not be fought by putting Communists in jail. Mr. Sadat replied that the United Arab Republic, having taken loans from the Soviet Union, regarded her as a banker not a benefactor, that the Marxist analysis of history was wrong, and that the Communists were repeating the mistake of the imperialists in saying there was no third choice outside Capitalism and Communism.

After all this, *Pravda* apologised in an abject editorial. The apology suggests that Russia realises that, for good or ill, she is committed to supporting Egypt, and that perhaps she needs the United Arab Republic more than it needs her. Russia has stood solidly with the Arabs against Israel; but on many other issues her shifts of policy have shown that she very often does not know whom to back in inter-Arab disputes; and whenever she tries to defend or protect the local Communists she angers the Arab nationalists, who have no fear or hesitation in attacking her publicly. It is a sadder and wiser Russia that now supports the Arabs; and she does so as a matter of policy, in her national interest, but without real enthusiam because she has little hope of wielding influence, let alone of capturing power.

The year 1961 was not a good year for Russia in her relations with the Afro-Asians. They rejected Mr. Khruschchev's plan for a 'troika' control of the United Nations. Though this flattered them on the surface, the Afro-Asians recognised it as an attempt to weaken a body to which, almost from the start, they had shown consistent loyalty. They likewise rejected, at the General Assembly that year, Soviet attempts to take the lead on colonialism by means of extreme proposals: thirty-six of the Afro-Asians abstained, and brought about the defeat of a Soviet recommendation that would have proclaimed 1962 to be 'the year of the elimination of colonialism'. Not for the first time, Russia failed in an attempt to be more Afro-Asian than the Afro-Asians. In November 1956, when President Voroshilov had written to Presidents Sukarno and Nasser suggesting another Bandung Conference on the Suez crisis, at the very time when Russian troops were re-entering Hungary, the proposal was rejected as being altogether too blatant a piece of propaganda. It is strange that a proud and independent country like Russia, in her dealings with the much older Afro-Asian countries, often seems unable or unwilling to understand that they cherish similar feelings of pride and independence.

Though the more sensitive Yugoslavs did not meet with the same rebuffs—1961 was the year of Belgrade—their economic connections with Afro-Asia showed little sign of improvement. Eighty per cent of Yugoslavia's export and import trade was still with Europe, and the official figures for 1960 and 1961 showed a net fall both in exports and imports to and from Africa, a reduction in imports from Asia and in exports to South America. This deterioration, coupled with greater understanding shown to her by Russia, reduced Yugoslavia's enthusiasm for finding friends far afield, an enthusiasm that the Belgrade meeting only temporarily revived. Yugoslavia was becoming more at home within her native continent.

Just as Yugoslavia began to find herself less short of friends, so the non-aligned states of Afro-Asia began to find that the Communist bloc was not the only source of sympathy and support. After the death of Mr. Dulles, and even more after the election of Mr. Kennedy, a new understanding of the non-aligned position showed itself in Washington. This new look was effectively expressed by Mr. Dean Rusk, the Secretary of State, when in November 1961 he said of the non-aligned countries: 'They will say things from time to time which will annoy us. They will take points of view in particular questions which differ from ours. . . . But the test is whether they are determined to be independent, whether they are trying to live out their own lives in the way in which their own people would like to have them shape it.'

With the East still friendly, if no longer affectionate, and with the West now friendly and no longer hostile there was no further need for an aggressive, strident assertion of non-alignment. Acceptance by both sides had rendered it a respectable policy, the norm for Afro-Asia, though not the sole panacea for peace that Panchsheel had been claimed to be. The enthusiasm of the Bandung Spirit of 1955 seemed old-fashioned in the early 1960's because by that time non-alignment had made its way in the world, and was no longer in need of supporting myths.

Above all the Bandung Myth faded because two of its main creators, Russia and China, became open enemies and poor examples of peaceful co-existence. Their rivalry was a danger to any unity still left in Afro-Asia; for whereas before 1955 the two sides in the Cold War divided Asians in their search for allies, it was now the turn of the two Communist states to try to push Afro-Asians into

The Waxing and Waning of the Bandung Myth

taking sides and positions of hostility towards each other. This policy for the most part affects the local Communist parties, and almost wrecked the Afro-Asian Solidarity Movement. No one need lament this development. Unfortunately the rivalry also had considerable impact on the governments of countries near to China, whose policy Peking is able increasingly to influence in an anti-Soviet direction. Indonesia, and possibly Burma, are being drawn that way. The process is a continuing one, and the struggle will no doubt be fought out most strenuously among the new states of Africa. It is Afro-Asian misfortune that the Chinese and Russians are agreed at least on one thing—that the future of the world depends on who controls Africa and Asia.

This Communist approach to Afro-Asia, based on the assumption that Afro-Asia is a single unit, is perhaps old-fashioned now, for power-systems are no longer monolithic: polycentrism is the current trend the world over. This tendency is at work among the non-aligned Afro-Asians. The concept of a unified, moralising, crusading Afro-Asia that was the basis of the Bandung Myth was unable to stand the test of time or the pull of conflicting national interests. Nor is the dream of Pan-Africanism any better able to produce a unified independent Africa.

NOTES TO CHAPTER X

1. Burma, Cambodia, Ceylon, Chile, China, Czechoslovakia, North Vietnam, Ethiopia, India, Indonesia, Laos, Nepal, Poland, Saudi Arabia, the Soviet Union, Yugoslavia. Mr. Krishna Menon claimed twenty in the United Nations debate, but the other four were not named.
2. Details given in *Panchsheel: its Meaning and History*, Lok Sabha Secretariat, New Delhi, 1958.
3. G. Stevens: 'Arab Neutralism and Bandung', *Middle East Journal*, Washington, spring 1957.
4. K. Tidmarsh has given a full account of 'The Soviet Re-assessment of Mahatma Gandhi' in *St. Antony's Papers, No. 8*, London, 1960. The change in Russia's attitude towards Afro-Asia is dealt with in such works as C. Sen's *Against the Cold War*, London, 1962; W. K. Kulski's *Peaceful Co-existence*, Chicago, 1959; J. W. Mackintosh's *Strategy and Tactics of Soviet Foreign Policy*, Oxford, 1962.
5. Letter of the Central Committee of the Communist Party of China dated 16th June 1963 replying to the letter of the CPSU of 30th Mar. 1963.
6. R. K. Karanjia: *The Mind of Mr. Nehru*, London, 1960.
7. Krylov and Durdenvsky: *Peaceful Coexistence of States and Nations and International Law*, Moscow, 1957; Mao Tse-tung: *People's Democratic Dictatorship*, Peking, 1948.
8. A speech of 20th Nov. 1956.

9. J. Smole: *Yugoslav Views of Coexistence*, Belgrade, 1961, p. 28.
10. *Op. cit.*, p. 41, a quotation from Edward Kardelj.
11. Text in Appendix B.1.
12. Nehru: *India's Foreign Policy*, p. 172.
13. *Op. cit.*, p. 102.
14. For excerpts from text see Appendix B.2.
15. In an interview with *Look*, June, 1957.
16. Nehru: *India's Foreign Policy*, p. 556.
17. Speeches of 10th Nov. 1956 and 12th Dec. 1956.
18. Given by F. O. Wilcox in the chapter entitled 'The Nonaligned States and the United Nations', *Neutralism and Nonalignment*, New York, 1962.

CHAPTER XI

The Parody and the Echo: The Afro-Asian Solidarity Movement and the Asian Socialist Conferences

The amplifying instrument through which the Communists trumpeted the Bandung Spirit to the four corners of the earth was an organisation of their own creation—the Afro-Asian Peoples Solidarity Movement (AAPSM). Succeeding where the Afro-Asian governments themselves had failed, Russia and China and their local supporters established and maintained what is, to date, the only permanent, continuing organisation that spans the two continents. Without the Solidarity Movement the Bandung Myth would have been infinitely less well known and would have had a shorter span of life: this noisy backing kept the myth alive for at least two years after the governments had recognised its mythical quality.

In the early years of the movement after its foundation in 1955, its originators used it to stress the Panchsheel and peaceful co-existence aspect of the Bandung Spirit; thereafter it was the anti-colonial content of Afro-Asianism that was played up, though this theme had never been absent from the movement's all-too-many proclamations.

It is strange that this most insistently vociferous of the Afro-Asian activities had its origin in Europe, for the hot ardour of the AAPSM was born in the cool architectural elegance of Stockholm. It was the 'peace' element in the movement's programme that produced this outlandish nativity.

The AAPSM was a metamorphosis of the World Peace Council. By 1954 that particular Trojan horse was showing signs of wear and tear: it had nearly succeeded in making 'peace' a derogatory word. The headquarters of the Council had been asked to move on from Paris to Prague, which imparted too obvious a label, and then to Vienna, where it was not especially welcome. Neutral Stockholm had already given its name to the first of the Council's 'peace' appeals, which is how the Solidarity Movement was first talked of at a con-

The Parody and the Echo

ference on 'the Relaxation of International Tension' that was held in June 1954 in the Swedish capital.

The skilful shifting of the Communist mass-appeal from the theme of peace to that of militant Afro-Asianism, which the Solidarity Movement facilitated, was part of the changed Communist attitude towards the Third Area that followed on Stalin's death. This change, as we have seen, was given its first formal expression in a speech by Malenkov in August 1953, but the real switch in the policy line came after Bandung. It is instructive to recall just how swift and complete a change this was. For example, in 1955 a Russian writer, I. I. Potekhin[1] described Nkrumah as 'representing the interests of the bourgeoisie and not the workers' and Azikwe of Nigeria as a follower of 'the policy of petty bourgeois national reform'. In 1956 the same I. I. Potekhin wrote: 'In every colony political leaders of ability and energy emerge: Nkrumah, Azikwe and Kenyatta.' The Solidarity Movement gave Russia entry into the new world of Afro-Asia to which she had been refused official entry at Bogor.

The new working alliance between one side in the Cold War and the peoples of countries whose governments were unaligned in that contest naturally had to be worked out with circumspection; otherwise the unaligned might have been frightened off. Hence in the activities and organisation of the Solidarity Movement, the Russians and Chinese have always been as careful to maintain a deep fringe of non-Communist sympathisers as they have been to keep, or try to keep, all real control and guidance in the hands of a hard core of Communists or pro-Communists.

Various Indians—Communist, pro-Communist and non-Communist—played a leading part in founding the movement, so its beginnings are best described in the words of Mrs. Rameshwari Nehru, who was to remain a key figure in the movement for many years. The chief functions of this lady, a direct, if somewhat distant, relative of the Indian Prime Minister, was to bring to the movement the prestige of the name of Nehru, which she had acquired through marriage.

Mrs. Nehru records[2] that the Asian countries represented at Stockholm were China, India, the Soviet Union, Vietnam, Korea, Japan, Syria and Lebanon. 'The delegates were all responsible persons but the delegations from Japan, China, the Soviet Union and Vietnam were particularly influential . . . a spirit of kinship tied the Asian delegates with one another. A general desire for a get-together was felt and on the initiative of the Indian delegation, a meeting of all the Asian delegates was held at Stockholm on the 23rd and 24th

251

June 1954.' In consultation with the Japanese, the Indians suggested a 'similar conference of Asian countries on non-party lines' which was approved 'with warm acclaim'. It was also agreed that the conference should be 'on the widest possible basis' to provide for discussion between peoples of various opinions.

With these impeccable references the Indian delegation, which had evidently been given the task of arranging the conference, had little difficulty in setting up in New Delhi a large Preparatory Committee 'including over a hundred members of Parliament'. Here was the façade; naturally, action could only be taken through a much smaller group. This was the international preparatory meeting that was held in New Delhi in February 1955, at which Burma, Japan, Korea and Syria were represented.

Mrs. Nehru writes of this conference as 'a little meeting composed of earnest young men and women who were althrough [*sic*] conscious of a sense of urgency of the present situation which calls for Asian Solidarity to protect the peace and freedom of our countries. A spirit of warm friendship prevailed'.

An Indian writer, somewhat more tough-minded that Mrs. Nehru, has stated[3] bluntly that the agency entrusted with the organisational responsibility for the conference was the Peace Liaison Committee of the Asian and Pacific Regions, a section of the World Peace Council based in Peking. One of the secretaries of the Indian Preparatory Committee was Deputy Secretary-General of the Peking Committee. Whatever the exact political affiliations of these 'earnest young men and women', they set up a secretariat to arrange the conference composed of representatives of Ceylon, China, India, Japan, the Soviet Union and the Arab countries. The big battalions were moving in.

By this time—February 1955—the Bogor Conference had been held and the world had been informed that a meeting of Asian and African governments was to be held at Bandung in April, to which Russia was not invited. An undignified race now developed between the official conference and 'The Conference of Asian Countries' at the popular level, that was also scheduled for April. Though the Solidarity Movement later became the parody of, and the parasite on, the Bandung Spirit, its founding conference was held in direct competition with Bandung, and twelve days before it.

The Indonesians understandably felt that another conference, to be held in one of the countries sponsoring Bandung, was an attempt by the Indians to steal the thunder of the official gathering. The same suspicions were entertained by the Indian Government. Mr. Nehru, who was embarrassed by the activity of his female namesake, stated officially that the government had nothing to do with the earlier meeting and that he personally did not much like the idea. A request was even made to the organisers to postpone their conference till after Bandung, but the Communists were having none of that. In response to the reserved attitude of some governments and the suspicions voiced, in the Indian press and elsewhere, of the conference's obvious Communist coloration, its organisers blandly replied that their meeting was meant to strengthen the hands of the official delegations at Bandung.

According to Mrs. Nehru the inaugural session of the conference, on the 6th June 1955, was attended by 'a couple of thousand persons including over two hundred delegates from fifteen participating Asian countries'. Her description of the scene is quoted because it exactly catches the mood of at least some, perhaps most, of the participants. The meeting was held in the open air and 'at one end of the lawn a big dais was constructed which was artistically decorated with beautiful yellow fresh marigold flowers. Red carpets were spread on the dais and in the background was displayed a big blue curtain on which in bold letters of gold and silver were embroidered in Hindi and English the inspiring words 'Long Live Friendship of the Asian Countries and the Peace of the World'. The traditional lotus flowers, the home of the goddess Lakshmi and a symbol of purity and spirituality, were embossed between. A couple of white lovely pigeons bringing the life-giving message of peace were also seen. On this dais, in the cool refreshing breeze of an April evening, sat the leaders of all the delegations in the colourful national costumes of different orient countries. A reverent *bhikku* (Buddhist priest) from Cambodia in his flowing yellow robes also sat amongst the rest and blessed the conference. The whole atmosphere was permeated with calm serenity, all-pervading love, peace and goodwill.'[4]

This piece of pure *Gemütlichkeit* does more than recall the similar naïve enthusiasm of the Asian Relations Conference, eight years earlier, it also indicates the quality of the popular feeling, in India at least, and perhaps elsewhere as well, during the Panchsheel period. This dewy innocence could be but a step to self-righteousness and from that to straightforward denunciation. But most of the time, at this stage of the Solidarity Movement's existence, sincere and simple-minded emotion served to sugar-coat the pill of propaganda: all else apart, the emotion was, in this way, of immense practical use.

Mrs. Nehru, who presided—a grey-haired grandmotherly figure—

was not above mingling political stricture with her peaceful bene-
dictions: 'Colonisation in all forms—open or covert, crude or subtle,
must go,' she said in her opening address; 'we want to extend the
area of peace; our political and economic affairs have had a bias in
favour of the West. All we want is to rectify that position, and develop more friendly co-operation with our immediate neighbours.'
Naturally Panchsheel was a major theme in almost every speech.

The conference may have had a gentle aura but its proceedings and
resolutions were precise and firm, and firmly anti-Western. On political issues the Western countries were naturally castigated over the
whole range of colonial problems, from Korea to Kenya. But even
on economic matters the conference called for the termination of
all preferential trade agreements with Western countries and un-
restricted trade with China, Russia and Eastern Europe: the embargo
on trade with China was condemned. The resolutions would have
satisfied even the most demanding Communist.

This patent anti-Western bias did not go unprotested. One Indian
cabinet minister walked out of the conference, and a press report that
members of the Indian Congress Party had dissociated themselves
from its proceedings had to be denied. The peace-loving respectability of the conference was, however, successfully maintained, so
that despite official suspicions, the President of India received the
delegates and Mr. Nehru invited them to tea.

At the closing plenary session, Mrs. Nehru reports that 'the whole
audience vibrated with a sense of unity'. The final function was a
public meeting 'attended by approximately twenty-five thousand persons. All sat in pin-drop silence giving cheers of welcome to the delegates'. Three Chinese girls sang a song in Hindi to the words 'Hindi
Cheeni bhai bhai—Indians and Chinese are brothers'.

So far so good. But in the weeks and months that followed it
seemed as if the Solidarity Conference would be, like the Asian Relations Conference, forgotten and unproductive of practical results.
For one thing the success of the Bandung Conference quite took the
wind out of the sails of the earlier meeting, and governmental agreement was obviously more significant than popular unity.

Again, the Solidarity Conference had established a continuing
permanent organisation called 'The Asian Solidarity Committee' in
New Delhi, with a secretariat under Dr. Anup Singh, a Congress
Party Member of Parliament. But for over a year the ASC secretariat
seemed as moribund as that of the Asian Relations Organisation
before it. The one positive development was that by October 1955

National Committees of the ASC had been set up in Russia, China, North Korea and North Vietnam.

From the first beginnings at Stockholm in June 1954 to the conference in New Delhi in April 1955, and for the immediately ensuing period, the Solidarity Movement was exclusively Asian in context. The only country represented at the conference with a claim to be called African was Egypt. It was late in 1956, at the height of the Suez crisis, that the Asian Solidarity Committee in New Delhi was subjected to a new and powerful Communist thrust which propelled the movement's headquarters out of India and settled it, as an Afro-Asian Organisation, in Cairo.

This decisive and drastic move had doubtless been brewing for several months but the actual decision to extend the scope of the Asian Solidarity Committee was taken in December 1956, at an Asian Writers' Conference held in New Delhi. As a first step its name was changed to the 'Afro-Asian Solidarity Committee'. In February 1957, a four-man delegation went to Cairo to talk to Colonel Nasser and his friend and collaborator Anwar Sadat. The four were Anup Singh, who can be described as a left-wing socialist, Yang Shou, a Chinese novelist, Anatoly Sofranov, a Russian writer, both Communists, and Masaharu Hatanaka, a Japanese journalist said to be a fellow-traveller. At this meeting it was agreed that a large Afro-Asian Solidarity Conference should be held in Cairo in December 1957.

At this point the question must be asked: Why did Egypt take over the leadership of the Solidarity Movement from India, or perhaps it would be more correct to ask, why was Egypt chosen as the successor to India by those who galvanised the Solidarity Movement?

From the beginning it must have been clear that an effective organisation would need full-scale governmental support: fine words and finer slogans butter no parsnips, and popular enthusiasm, for peace or anything else, does not of itself produce efficiently-run international organisations or conferences. If the Afro-Asian Solidarity Movement had been sited geographically in the area of its ideological base—that is in one of the Communist countries—it would immediately have become even more suspect than its predecessor, the World Peace Council. Clearly it had to be located in a country indubitably Afro-Asian and non-aligned.

Why then did it not continue in India itself? India had the necessary prestige and organising capacity, but by late 1956—in fact from

255

the very first conference—it was clear that Mr. Nehru and his government had seen through the movement, did not like what they saw, and were not, even in calculated cynicism, prepared to use it. Mr. Nehru's fastidiousness had already been repelled by the stridency of the World Council's campaign for peace: he did not take any more kindly to attempts to adopt the concepts of 'Afro-Asia' or 'non-alignment', especially the latter. Indonesia might have been chosen, if Russia had not been excluded from Bandung.

Egypt, then, became the logical choice, being geographically the hinge between Asia and Africa, and the northern gateway to the continent of Africa, which becoming of greater interest to the world Communist movement. The Russian and Chinese Communists may also have calculated that in 1957 President Nasser would be 'soft' on a 'progressive' movement out of gratitude for the arms deal concluded in September 1955 and for Russia's rocket threats during the Suez crisis. That crisis had also made Egypt a new and exciting symbol of successful resistance to Western imperialism.

Nevertheless, Egypt was an unexpected choice, for she had played an inconspicuous part in the origins of the Solidarity Movement. She came into the picture only when an Egyptian delegation took part in the New Delhi Conference. She could hardly have done otherwise, with her new military regime preoccupied with internal matters and with President Nasser keeping his Communists and left-wingers on a tight rein, if not behind prison bars.

Subsequent happenings make it clear that the Egyptian leader saw through the movement from the start but, unlike India, was prepared to use it. Why? It may be that in 1957 Egypt, still reeling from the effects of the tripartite aggression, remembered how useful Afro-Asian moral and propaganda support had been during the crisis, and that Egypt, too, was beginning to become interested in Africa. The shift to President Nasser's capital was of mutual benefit to both sides; but, in the event, the Communists discovered that they had caught a Tartar.

Seven months after the visit of the four-man delegation it was announced that a twenty-one-nation preparatory committee would meet in Cairo to discuss the agenda of the main conference and issue invitations. Of the twenty-one, four were Communist countries (Russia, China, Mongolia and North Vietnam), six were African (Egypt, Tunisia, Algeria, Libya, Sudan and Cameroon), and no less than eight were Arab (Egypt, Tunisia, Algeria, Libya, Sudan, Lebanon, Syria and Iraq). The preparatory secretariat was put under

Yusuf Sibai, an astute and competent Egyptian man of letters.

President Nasser took the precaution of sending a personal emissary to Tunisia, Morocco, Ethiopia and Ghana to assure them that the conference would be neutralist, and not dominated by the Communists—an expectation that was not wholly realised, perhaps because the conference was too large and unwieldy to be subject to his control.

The Cairo Solidarity Conference of December 1957 remains, to date, the biggest gathering of Afro-Asians that has ever been assembled; five hundred delegates represented forty-five countries or colonial territories. The arrangements made were on an elaborate scale and at considerable expense.

The large Soviet delegation was headed by an Uzbek Vice-President of the Supreme Soviet of the U.S.S.R., and the equally large Chinese group by the President of the Chinese Academy of the Sciences. At least a fifth of the delegates were members of the Communist Party. Russia asked and received permission for observers to attend from the World Peace Council, and delegations came from Rumania, Czechoslovakia, Yugoslavia, Britain, France, Canada and some Latin American countries. Jordan, Tunisia, Aden and Algeria were represented by exiles, and Togo, Madagascar, Zanzibar and Somaliland by nationalists groups that were supposed to be clandestine.

The most significant pointer to the future of the Solidarity Movement happened at the outset. Despite expectations, and contrary to practice at its first Afro-Asian conference, President Nasser did not address the gathering. Egypt was, of course, giving full support to the movement, but the Egyptian leader was evidently not prepared publicly to commit his prestige to it.

The two main opening speeches, by Anwar Sadat and Mrs. Nehru, made plain that henceforth the main emphasis of the Solidarity Movement was to be not on peaceful co-existence or Panchsheel or even non-alignment, but on Afro-Asian anti-colonialism. The personalities of the two speakers were symptomatic of the change—the Egyptian, young, vigorous and a bold and hardened conspirator taking over from the aged, ailing, pacific lady from India. Mrs. Nehru referred once to Panchsheel, but then went on to say that they were 'humble people come together from lowly huts and cottages without any trappings of power and authority' who were merely trying to 'divert erring humanity' into 'the path of righteousness, co-operation and inter-dependence in friendship and love'. But this Gandhian gentleness was not what the conference had met to hear. Mrs. Nehru said that she could make 'a solemn declaration from this platform, that we are not against any people or against any bloc'. But in his speech Mr. Sadat made it clear that in his opinion, all present were strongly against one of the major blocs—that of the West; he made one reference to non-alignment but at the end of his speech, and almost in passing.

Even more clearly anti-imperialist is the grandly styled Cairo Declaration issued by the conference in which, again, there is no reference to peaceful co-existence or non-alignment. The Ten Principles of Bandung are repeated but co-existence, as we have seen, was not one of them. After calling for disarmament the Declaration condemns 'imperialist domination, foreign exploitation and . . . other evils'.

The first Asian Solidarity Conference in 1955 had been a competitor to Bandung; by contrast, this first Afro-Asian Solidarity Conference of 1957 viewed itself as dedicated to completing Bandung's work. As Mr. Sadat put it 'this peoples' Conference of ours meets partly in honour of the spirit of Bandung and as a reminder of the principles and ideals it stands for, and partly to push it a step forward'.

That the Solidarity Movement represented a return to the earlier anti-colonial era of Afro-Asianism, by-passing the Panchsheel period, is evident, too, from the massive series of resolutions that it passed. These fill no less than thirty-seven printed pages in the official conference document,[4] subdivided into political, economic, social development, cultural and organisational sections.

Only the last were of any real importance. Yet it is worth mention that the political resolutions, after calling for nuclear disarmament and the admission of China and Mongolia to the United Nations went on to condemn 'imperialism in all its forms and manifestations' and specifically its activities in Cameroon, Kenya, Uganda, Chad, Togo, Madagascar, Yemen, the Arabian Gulf, West Irian, Okinawa, Cyprus, Goa, Korea, Vietnam, Morocco and Somaliland. There were separate resolutions on racial discrimination and Algeria, and a long report by the Palestine delegation was accepted *in toto*.

The only points of interest in the economic resolutions were that the conference had 'no objection to the investment of foreign capital' or to foreign loans, but without strings, and that it 'denounced' the European Common Market. Among a wealth of recommendations on cultural matters is one for the establishment of an international university for Afro-Asian studies—possibly the germinal idea for the Patrice Lumumba University in Moscow.

This mass of verbiage is of importance only because it set the pattern for all future solidarity meetings; wherever held, on whatever subject and whether general or specialised, large or small, the same anti-colonial sentiments on the same range of issues were to emerge.

The length and detail of these resolutions suggests that much thinking and planning had been devoted to them before the conference. This forethought is at its most evident in organisational resolutions, for from them, after a mere seven days of discussion, emerged a large and many-sided Afro-Asian permanent organisation.

At the centre of a complex pattern of specialised 'Movements' was the Afro-Asian Solidarity Organisation as such. The 1957 Cairo meeting decided that this should be based in that city and that it should have a council and a permanent secretariat. Later on an executive committee was added, standing between the council and the secretariat.

In its complete form, which it achieved only towards 1962, the Solidarity Movement's structure was shaped as follows: the sixty National Solidarity Committees appointed one representative each to the council. Some of these were, or have become, well-known personalities such as Oginga Odinga from Kenya, Dom Mintoff from Malta, Kenneth Kaunda and Joshua Nkomo from Northern and Southern Rhodesia respectively, Tanganyika's Oscar Kambona, Kamal Jumblatt from Lebanon, Mehdi Ben Barka of Morocco and Antoine Gizenga of the Congo. From these council members, twenty-seven were chosen to form the executive committee. The permanent secretariat consisted of eleven secretaries under an Egyptian Secretary-General, Mr. Yusuf Sibai.

The Asian countries had twenty-two out of the sixty places on the council, twelve of the twenty-seven seats on the executive committee, and six of the twelve posts in the secretariat.

Russia and China are represented on all three bodies, and they have a right to be so, for they hold the purse-strings. The organisation's budget is said to be of the order of £(Egyptian) 15 million a year of which Russia and China each contribute a third, and the other fifty-eight members the remaining third, with Egypt making a substantial contribution. The political influence of the Communists may have been decisive in the early years of the movement, but nowadays they are allotted only a minor role, at least on paper, within the secretariat: of the five sections into which it is divided, the

Russian secretary is allotted merely the 'Cultural Sub-Section' of 'Documents and Research', and China shares the 'Social Sub-Section' of the same not-very-vital operation. This modesty may, of course, be an example of stooping to conquer.

In orbit round this central body are a glaxy of so-called 'Friendly Movements and Bodies'. Most of these were the outcome of resolutions taken at the Cairo Conference. Such are the Afro-Asian Youth Movement that held its first gathering in Cairo in February 1959; the Afro-Asian Women's Movement, whose first conference was held also in Cairo in January 1961; the Afro-Asian Writers' Movement that held its first conference at Tashkent in November 1958 and now has a permanent bureau at Colombo; and the Jurists' Movement whose first meeting, at Damascus in November 1957, preceded the Cairo Conference, but whose later meetings have been held under the Solidarity Movement's auspices.

The Cairo Conference also gave its blessing to a projected Conference of Afro-Asian Trades Unions and Chambers of Commerce and this developed, as a separate and serious body, into the Afro-Asian Organisation for Economic Co-operation (AFRASEC), also based in Cairo.

Later additions to the Solidarity Movement proper were the Afro-Asian Solidarity Fund, set up in 1960 with headquarters in Guinea and the then intention of providing financial assistance to the Lumumba-Gizenga regime in the Congo, and the International Committee for Aid to Algeria and the Congo.

In 1961 it is recorded that the Solidarity Fund received from China a contribution of $40,000; from Indonesia, a financial contribution of $15,000 and scholarships for the Children of Freedom Fighters; from the United Arab Republic, a contribution of $20,000 and scholarships, and from Russia $20,000, materials to the value of Rs. 10,000, and scholarships to the Lumumba University.

Because of subsequent events in Algeria and the Congo these particular organisations have tended to fade away.

The many-sided activities of this wealth of Solidarity bodies have certain common characteristics: they reveal efficient, interlocking organisation and they all display much energy and industry. The Afro-Asian governments were neither willing nor able to produce anything remotely resembling this beehive. Obviously behind the Solidarity Movement was the hard, strong, well-aimed, carefully-directed thrust from an extraneous force—the Communist Party, and especially its Russian and Chinese centres.

The Parody and the Echo

What did all these 'bodies' and 'movements' do? They met in a variety of places, from Tokyo and Tashkent to Colombo and Conakry, they conferred, and they passed resolutions which recorded them as being 'revolted' by this fact and 'indignant' at that, as a consequence of which they 'vigorously denounced' or 'refused to tolerate' or 'resolutely warned'.

One special activity of the Movement was the holding of a 'day' (or even 'a week' or 'a fortnight') dedicated to some political question. Thus in 1959 fifteen of these days were observed with meetings or demonstrations, and by 1962 they had been increased to twenty-three; Laos, Military Pacts, Oman, Vietnam, Palestine, Mongolia and Nuclear Weapons were some of the issues thus publicised.

And what did all the meetings achieve? That is perhaps an unfair question; because while in some member countries, such as Russia or China, Egypt or Guinea, the movement had full official support, in others like India or Pakistan, Iraq or Morocco, the government was indifferent and in yet others, Mozambique and the Congo, positively hostile. As a self-professed peoples' movement it could scarcely exercise direct authority: it could merely try and apply pressure by agitation and propaganda, and these it produced in abundance.

The Solidarity machine has continued to produce its quota of verbal assaults on 'aggressive imperialism' or 'neo-colonialism', but these are becoming increasingly mechanical. The movement in fact had a very brief heyday, lasting little more than a few months after the 1957 conference, when genuine enthusiasm matched organising ability. Several reasons can be found for this slow, steady decline.

Like all too many international organisations, the Solidarity Movement has suffered from a lack of funds and a lack of interest. Its budget seems to have been adequate, but some of the money was doubtless syphoned off into financing nationalist movements, and the elaborate secretariat comfortably installed in a spacious villa on the banks of the Nile took a substantial slice. So that in 1963 the secretariat-general admitted that because of financial stringency and a lack of response, the Documentation and Research section could not function properly and the monthly bulletin had appeared only four times in the year. Earlier, Mr. Sibai had complained of difficulties in keeping in touch with the national committees and of the non-functioning of some of these committees. The Board of Secretaries was in being only between April 1961 and mid-1962.[5]

But these material difficulties were the symptoms, not the real causes, of the malaise that afflicted the Solidarity Movement soon

261

after its inception at the end of 1957. There were three such causes: the reserve, born of disillusionment, felt by Russia and China towards the Afro-Asians (which found expression in a sharp controversy between Russia and the host country, the United Arab Republic); the growing controversy between Russia and China; and the Sino-Indian conflict. The latter two will be examined later.

As we have seen, the Communist powers were discovering, as the Bandung Myth faded, that the Afro-Asian non-aligned were not prepared to be obedient satellites. The most striking proof of their independence was a blunt reproof to Russia uttered by President Nasser in a speech of December 1958; at the same time, he rounded-up and interned all known Communists and pro-Communists. At about this juncture, the Egyptians decided to break the grip of the Communists on the Solidarity secretariat. Initially, the ideological division of the eight section heads in the secretariat was five Communists or pro-Communists to three non-Communist nationalists. Among the five were the representatives of India and Japan. After the first Chinese aggression against India in 1959, the Indian vote shifted to the non-Communist side, but the guiding body of the organisation remained divided and at deadlock.

Because of this internal struggle the second main conference that was to have been held at Conakry in December 1959 was held only in April 1960. And at Conakry the nationalists were able to push through a resolution creating the twenty-seven member executive committee (standing between the full Council and the secretariat) and to see to it that the executive committee's membership included only eight Communists. The next step taken was to get this packed committee to decide, at Beirut in November 1960, and against the wishes of the Communist representatives, to confer relatively complete executive control on the Secretary-General.

At this Beirut meeting, senior Egyptian secretariat officials were congratulating themselves on having helped to weed out the Communists from the national committees of such countries as Lebanon, Ceylon and to some extent, Indonesia; they were of opinion that this still remained to be done in India and Japan. But their estimate was over-optimistic.

The shadow of serious divisions to come lay over this Beirut meeting, for the Chinese first strenuously opposed, and later abstained on a resolution approving the action of the United Nations General Assembly in putting on its agenda an item proposed by Mr. Khrushchev calling for an end to colonialism.

The Parody and the Echo

When the Solidarity Organisation proved an embarrassing guest, the United Arab Republic must at times have wondered whether its offer of hospitality had been a wise one. On balance, Egypt, and the Arabs generally, have drawn political benefits from the movement. It has helped to strengthen the Arab link with Africa and it has, on its own popular level, isolated Israel from Afro-Asia. In the formative days of 1955 in New Delhi, a message of goodwill was received from Israel, but that was the first and last connection between the Movement and the Jewish state. There has never been any question of Israel's becoming a member or being invited to any conference; quite the other way, innumerable resolutions from a variety of Solidarity meetings and demonstrations have supported the Arab case on Palestine and roundly denounced Israel. Yet, though the African members support these anti-Israel resolutions, the governments of many of these African states maintain most friendly relations with Israel.

The title of this chapter suggests that the Afro-Asian Peoples Solidarity Movement is a parody—a parody of what a genuine organisation of the peoples of Afro-Asia should be. The grounds for this judgement are that the movement has been an obvious attempt by one bloc in the Cold War to identify itself with the Afro-Asians and then to use their anti-colonial sentiment as a weapon for belabouring the Cold War adversary. Within the Afro-Asian world the Solidarity Movement never really achieved respectability or acceptance. This was so because of its Communist associations and its emphasis on negative anti-colonialism rather than the more positive attitude of non-alignment.

That Russia and China should be major members of the Organisation was in itself enough to give it a heavy pro-Communist bias. But there were other specific links—for example, that with the World Peace Council of which it was an avatar. The Peace Council offered to award the Solidarity Movement a gold medal in 1959. There were always numerous 'observers' from the Peace Council at its various conferences down to the last one, held at Moshi; and in 1961 the secretariat was ordered to bring together, along with the Solidarity Organisation itself, the Latin American Conference for National Sovereignty, Economic Emancipation and Peace, the All African People's Conference and the Peace Liaison Committee of the Asian and Pacific Regions—that same section of the Peace Council based in Peking that was, at least partly, responsible for the convening of the 1955 New Delhi Conference. The non-Communist Afro-Asian

263

nationalists have at best been unhappy with the Solidarity Movement's pinkish red tinge; at times they have actively tried to eliminate it.

At Moshi the Secretary-General, Mr. Sibai, spoke of the movement as one 'whose main task is the struggle against imperialism and colonialism'. His authoritative description is wholly accurate. Up to the present the Solidarity Organisation beats out at every one of its meetings the same insistently repetitive rhythm on the drum of anti-colonialism. And by doing so it roots itself in the past—in the period between 1945 and 1960. In the early 1960's the Afro-Asian peoples moved on from anti-colonialism, and centred their main political attention on the concept and policy of non-alignment, and on the economic disparities between the developed and the developing countries. The Solidarity Movement has shown only a half-hearted interest in these newer ideas.

Still suspect because of its Communist connections, embarrassed by the Sino-Indian dispute, confused and irritated by the bitter wrangling of the Russian and Chinese within its organisation, the Afro-Asian Peoples Solidarity Movement is today not merely a parody but a wan, old-fashioned one.

The Afro-Asian governments were both unwilling and unable to establish a permanent official organisation; the Communists were willing and able to set up an elaborate permanent body which, however, contained within itself the seeds of its own undoing; somewhere in between the two stood the impermanent organisation put together by the Asian Socialist Parties which after a brief, ineffective existence has collapsed into desuetude.

The only outcome of any real significance to this Socialist effort was that it enabled two outsiders, Yugoslavia and Israel, to make contact with the Afro-Asian non-aligned, with successful results for the Yugoslavs but with a very limited measure of success for the Israelis.

The idea of inter-continental co-operation between the Socialist parties was slow to develop. Once again the germinal idea was Indian: in August 1947 the Indian party thought of calling a world Socialist meeting in India, but changed this to a purely Asian conference after contacts with other Asian Socialists at an I.L.O. regional conference held in Delhi in December 1947.[6] Only in March 1952, over four years later, did a preparatory meeting of Indians, Indonesians and Burmese meet in Rangoon. One item on the agenda was the setting up of a permanent organisation.[7]

The Parody and the Echo

The First Asian Socialist Conference was held, also in Rangoon, in January 1953, and was attended by 177 delegates and observers. Invitations had been sent to parties in Indonesia, India, Burma, Malaya, Pakistan, Lebanon, Syria, Iraq, Egypt, to both the right and left wings of the Japanese Socialists, and to the centrist Mapai Party of Israel rather than to the leftist Mapam. Observers were invited from seven African freedom movements, showing that at this time the Asian Socialists were ahead of Asian governmental thinking on the matter of co-operation with Africa. Fraternal delegates attended from the Socialist International and from the Yugoslav League of Communists. The former were led by Lord Attlee, the latter by Milovan Djilas and Israel sent its Foreign Minister Moshe Sharett; the names indicate the importance ascribed to the event by these delegations. Because of Israel's presence, Syria and Iraq did not attend, and Egypt and Lebanon, after a brief appearance, walked out of the conference.

One of the two main topics of discussion was whether or not the Asian Socialist Conference should become a regional member of the Socialist International. The International itself wanted this, and as a member of that body Israel favoured the proposal, supported by the right-wing Japanese faction and by the Malayans. Strongly opposed to any such idea were the Socialists from India, Egypt and Lebanon, and, less strenuously, those from Pakistan, Indonesia and Burma. The basis of this opposition was straightforward Asian feeling, coupled with a belief that the Socialist International had not taken a strong enough line on anti-colonialism and neutralism.

Between the proposal for affiliation and the counter-proposal that members of the Asian body should be prohibited from joining the International, the meeting devised and adopted a compromise resolution that there should be liaison at all levels between the two large groups.

The second main subject discussed at Rangoon was neutralism. The Asian Socialists, or at least those from the South-Asian countries, have had their own distinctive approach to this issue: they have stood for aligned non-alignment, a Third Bloc organised on the lines of the other two.

Here again compromise prevailed. The suggestion that the conference formally declare itself in favour of non-alignment was opposed by Israel and the right-wing Japanese, so that the resolution merely said that the Asian countries should not identify themselves with 'so-called peace movements', or with any military system, but should strengthen themselves and make up their own minds on problems of world peace.

This Rangoon Conference established a permanent bureau to carry forward its work, such as it was. On this body were represented Burma, India, Indonesia, Israel, Japan, Malaya and Pakistan, with the delegates of the Socialist International and Yugoslavia in attendance. An Indonesian was made Secretary-General with joint secretaries from Burma and India.

A second meeting of the Bureau was held at Hyderabad in India in August 1953, where the decision was taken to create an Anti-Colonial Bureau with a heavily pro-African programme; this resolve, which was never implemented, had included the calling of an All-African Congress. But a representative of the Convention People's Party of Ghana was appointed as Secretary of the Bureau.

The third and fourth meetings of the Bureau were held in Burma in May 1954 and Japan in November 1954. No decisions of any consequence were taken, and, for lack of funds, there were no more meetings of the Bureau till November 1956, though it had wished to meet twice a year.

Inanition and lack of funds had by now overtaken the Socialist permanent organisation. Of sixty-three party reports, only thirteen had been received and its monthly, *Socialist Asia*, had only 190 subscribers. Its total collapse was postponed until the Second Asian Socialist Conference in Bombay in November 1956. The unprincipled compromises accepted by that meeting confirmed its demise.

A wholly spurious air of importance marked this meeting, for the Burmese delegation was led by its Prime Minister, the Indonesian and the Israeli by former Prime Ministers. There were new delegations from Cambodia, Ceylon and South Vietnam. The Nenni Socialists were represented, and even the Popular Socialist Party of Chile. The fraternal Yugoslavs were again present. This time the only Arab representative was from Algeria, possibly because the Suez crisis was at its height during the conference.

The tripartite aggression naturally dominated the session. But while the Afro-Asian governments at the United Nations, and their peoples in street demonstrations, were spontaneously condemning the aggressors, the Asian Socialists found themselves unable to do so. A draft resolution expressing condemnation was unacceptable to Israel and so had to be toned down; and on the weaker wording Israel was persuaded to abstain. The reason given for this weakness was that the Socialist organisation had come to lean heavily on Israel; of this more will be said.

The Socialists were, however, able to express condemnation of Britain and France and, in slightly less strong terms, of Russia's actions in Hungary. The wording on the latter issue was stronger than anything used till then by Mr. Nehru, and this lead given by the Socialists stiffened Indian popular opinion against its Government's timid attitude.

At this conference Ceylon, Nepal and Vietnam decided to join the permanent organisation, but the Cambodian delegation decided not to do so because the angry and irresponsible resolutions that were passed conflicted with 'respect for the Five Principles of Co-existence and the position of neutrality of our country'—a merited rebuke.

By the time of this Bombay Conference the secretariat of the Permanent Bureau had dwindled to a single Burmese acting Secretary-General; its budget was heavily in deficit. At this juncture Israel produced a plan for the organisation including special funds to promote party contacts. The Israel delegation assured a reluctant and sceptical gathering that these funds would be forthcoming from sources it did not choose to specify. The assurance, coupled with Israel's ability to veto the condemnatory resolution, suggests that the organisation had become financially dependent on her—that, in fact, she had tried to buy her way into Afro-Asia through this Socialist grouping. The gesture availed her little, for her plan was not accepted and the Asian Socialist Organisation, smitten with bankruptcy that was as much ideological as financial, faded into inaction and insignificance—a thin, forlorn echo.

These attempts by the Communists and Socialists to harness Afro-Asian feeling and non-alignment to their special party interests were both failures. The noisy hectoring of the Solidarity Movement, and the apologetic mumblings of the Socialists produced no more practical results than had meetings of the Afro-Asian governments. But in the 1950's Afro-Asianism and non-alignment were perhaps more vital and alive in the realm of emotion and ideals and aspiration than in the field of practical politics. In the sphere of intangibles even a parody and an echo may have played a useful part.

NOTES TO CHAPTER XI

1. I. I. Potekhin in an article in *Sovetskaya Ethnografia*, 1955, and in *Moscow News*, Oct. 1956.

2. In the Introduction to the official report on 'The Conference of Asian Countries', New Delhi, 1955.
3. D. S. Jhabvala: *Afro-Asian Solidarity*, Calcutta, 1957.
4. 'The First Afro-Asian Peoples Solidarity Conference', published by the Permanent Secretariat of the AAPSO, Cairo, 1958.
5. Report of the Secretary-General in the volume on 'The Third Afro-Asian Peoples Solidarity Conference', Cairo, 1963, pp. 53–5.
6. Report of the Foreign Affairs Department of the Socialist Party of India, Nasik, 1948.
7. The Asian Socialist Conferences are fully described by S. Rose in his *Socialism in Southern Asia*, Oxford, 1959.

The principles, structure and friendly organisations of the Afro-Asian Peoples Solidarity Movement are described at length in a 270-page handbook produced by the Permanent Secretariat in Cairo.

INTERLUDE II

The Two Years of Africa, 1960–1

Africa is the only wholly non-aligned continent in the world to-day. None of its thirty-two independent states has a formal treaty involving defence obligations with either side in the Cold War, or indeed with any country outside the continent.

That is the position on paper. The reality is rather different. While it was never divided by the Cold War, to the degree that Asia has been, into aligned and non-aligned groups, Africa felt that war's impact, and is divided into completely non-aligned, largely non-aligned and nearly aligned countries; in the last group are some states that are only a whisker's-width away from full alignment.

These divisions have come about because the salient fact about independent Africa today is that the nightmare of its nationalists has come true: it is balkanised. The weakness of division has exposed the new African states to associations, if not alliances, that united strength could have rendered unnecessary.

No less than thirty-two 'independent' states met at the African Summit at Addis Ababa in May 1963 and more were to follow: Africa already has more separate national entities than any other continent. A feeble giant, large in size but weak in human resources, in terms not only of population but of experience and education, Africa is additionally afflicted with a spastic twitch caused by antagonistic states and groupings.

This fragmentation might not have been expected in 1950 or even 1955, because Africa's nationalism always had a strong tendency towards continental unity, to a degree not found in Asia. Perhaps the nationalist leaders were overtaken by the speed of Europe's exit; the main process of decolonisation was completed in six years—between January 1956, when the Sudan became independent, and December 1961, when Tanganyika became the twenty-fourth new African state. In the last two years there was such a stampede for freedom by former colonies that no one had time to repair to a few protective corrals, each instead preferring to go its own way.

This impulse need not have prevailed, for there had been a great deal of co-operation between the nationalists in the period before,

271

and just after, the beginning of liberation. Five Pan-African congresses had been held, from Paris in 1919 to Manchester in 1945. The foreign ministers of the African states had met together at Accra in 1958 and at Addis Ababa in 1960. Two All African Peoples Congresses had been held, in Accra in 1958 and at Tunis in 1960. The Afro-Asian Solidarity Movement had also met twice in Africa, at Cairo in 1957 and at Conakry in 1960. And the Pan-African Freedom Movement had met annually from 1959 onwards. Yet despite all this unionist activity the forces of anti-continental separation won the day.

Especially in the vast expanses of French Africa, balkanisation could have been avoided, because the alternative to it had been created after World War II in the form of two large federations of West and Equatorial Africa. The nationalist parties in these two areas were conceived on regional lines and operated, as some still do, as single units ignoring what have become 'national' frontiers. But when the French Empire passed into the French Community, the French Government, presided over by de Gaulle, cold-bloodedly wrecked its own federal creations and insisted on transfers of power to the bits and pieces—one of the finest examples of the policy of lose, divide and leave. While some of the nationalist leaders protested the French succeeded because they were vigorously aided and abetted by other African leaders, notably President Houphouet-Boigny of the Ivory Coast. It is remarkable that federation plans were rejected both by the rich colonies, such as the Ivory Coast and Gabon, who did not want to share their wealth, and by the poor ones, like Niger, who did not want to be the neglected partner in a large group. For a variety of reasons, it was to a litter of micro-nations that Mother Africa gave birth in 1960.

This new, dismembered Africa had to grapple with the complicated, and prolonged Congo crisis which was at its height for about a year, from July 1960, when the Congolese Army mutinied, to August 1961, when Adoula became Prime Minister. In this period the Congo witnessed the secession of Katanga under Tshombe and the overthrow and murder of Lumumba. These events were, to African nationalists all over the continent, perfect examples of the policy of neo-colonialism—here was Western Europe using its economic power to set up puppet regimes and brutally eliminating those that challenged its authority. On the other hand the Lumumbists had set up a near-secessionist government under Gizenga at Stanleyville; this was strongly leftist in orientation and raised before the more conservative

African leaders the spectre of Russia and Communism planted in the heart of Africa.

Faced with these developments the new African states split into three groups, of Radicals, Moderates and Conservatives. The Radicals, comprising Ghana, Guinea, Mali, Morocco and the United Arab Republic, saw Western neo-colonialists and their puppets as the chief danger in the Congo; their objective was a strong centralist government under a genuinely nationalist and Pan-Africanist regime, to which the United Nations should be merely an adjunct. The Moderates included Nigeria, Togo, the Sudan, Somalia, Tunisia, Liberia, Ethiopia, and Libya and for them the Congo's difficulties were due to Belgian, African and non-African interventionists and to the irresponsibility of the Congolese leaders; their objective was to preserve the Congo's legal and territorial integrity by upholding such constitutional institutions as the President and the Parliament. They allotted a major role to the United Nations in the maintenance of law and order, in the training of the civil administration and the army, and as the sole channel of foreign aid. The Conservatives were Cameroon, Chad, Congo (Brazzaville), Dahomey, Gabon, Ivory Coast, Malagasy, Mauritania, Niger, Senegal and Upper Volta. For them the threat in the Congo came from Communist imperialists, and to their local henchmen the answer to this danger was a decentralised, federated Congo in which the United Nations would have a minor role limited to foreign intervention.[1]

The Asian states were divided along the same lines. Indonesia vigorously supported the Radicals (as did Yugoslavia and the Communist countries); India, Ceylon, Malaya and the other Asian non-aligned states backed the Moderates (along with the Scandinavian countries); the aligned nations in Asia and the West were behind the Conservatives.

Fortunately for the Congo it was the Moderates who prevailed, and after the withdrawal by Egypt and Morocco of their troops, it was the United Nations' forces drawn from India, Ethiopia, Malaya, Ireland and Scandinavia that finally baulked Katanga's secession.

The differences in approach to the Congo problem by the African states were not the result of any prior grouping; rather the groupings were produced by policy differences over the Congo. But it was not long before these differences in approach became formalised in official groupings.

The splitting process began at Abidjan in October 1960, when eleven ex-French states, all from the Conservative group, agreed to form a bloc the existence of which was confirmed, with the addition of Malagasy, at Brazzaville in December 1960. This group, plus other like-minded ex-British states, twenty-one in all,[2] assembled in Monrovia in May 1961 and drew up a Charter for an Organisation. The Charter called for the acceleration of development in the fields of economics, health and education, and for concerting political action 'as far as possible'. This was to be attained by means of an Assembly of Heads of States and Governments which was to meet once a year, a Council of Ministers meeting twice a year, and a General Secretariat.

The radical Africans had already formed a group on their own. As a retort to the Brazzaville meeting they had conferred at Casablanca in January 1961, and had produced their own Charter and Organisation. This conference was attended by the Heads of State of Ghana, Guinea, Mali, Morocco, the United Arab Republic, and the Algerian Provisional Government and by representatives of Libya and Ceylon. The incongruous presence of Ceylon is an indication that the conveners originally intended to call a larger Afro-Asian meeting. Those who decided not to attend were India and Indonesia from Asia and, from Africa, Ethiopia, Nigeria, Togo, Liberia and Tunisia. Had they attended, the Casablanca group might not have become, as it did, an association of angry and irresponsible states.

The Casablanca Charter was far more aggressively political than the mild Monrovia document. The former called for unity of action in international affairs and the adoption of a policy of non-alignment, the liquidation of colonialism and neo-colonialism, and an end to foreign military bases on the continent; the exploitation of the national wealth and its equitable distribution for the benefit of the people; and intensified efforts for African co-operation. Its organisation comprised an assembly of three committees, political, economic and cultural; a joint African High Command of Chiefs-of-Staff, to ensure common defence against aggression in any part of the continent; and a Liaison Office. The High Command idea was a grandiose notion suggested by Ghana; the United Arab Republic was especially unhappy about it because Ghana's armed forces were still officered by Britons and trained by Israelis, with whom Egypt could hardly be expected to co-operate and share military information.

Libya seems to have attended Casablanca by mistake, and made trouble over the clause on military bases, since she was host to a very large American installation near Tripoli. Ceylon was an obvious odd man out, and took no further part in the activities of the group.

274

The Two Years of Africa, 1960–1961

Apart from their existing differences over the Congo the Monrovia and Casablanca Charters drew new lines of division between the African groupings. In the latter document there was the suggestion of Socialism in its mention of 'the equitable distribution of wealth', which was anathema to the Conservatives. Its attack on colonialism, neo-colonialism and military bases put the Casablanca countries in clear opposition to the Western Powers with whom the Monrovia countries were, to say the least, very closely associated (France pays the twelve ex-French colonies $775 million a year).

And for the first time, non-alignment became a divisive element in Africa. When proclaimed as the policy of the Casablanca group, it automatically became suspect to the Monrovia countries. This was unfortunate, for among them were some moderates who were virtually non-aligned, or who could have been drawn into non-alignment if tactfully handled.

Two specific political issues also divided these two groupings. To please Morocco the Casablanca group denounced Mauritania, a member of the Monrovia alliance, against which Morocco has territorial claims; and to please the three Arab states the group denounced Israel, with whom many of the Monrovia states (and Ghana) have good relations.

Above all they were divided by President Nkrumah's favourite political concept of 'Pan-Africanism'. It is ironic that the slogans of African unity divided, and to some extent still divide, the African states—'Pan-Africanism', 'the African personality' and 'negritude' or negroness. The Casablanca states made these concepts the basis and driving power of their African policy while the others viewed them cautiously and even with suspicion. Whether the approach to these ideas was friendly or hostile, they dominated and divided political thinking in Africa in the early 1960's.

Try as one may, it is not easy, at least for a non-African, to understand what they mean, because they seem for the most part to be slogans without positive content; one sympathises with the Nigerian intellectual who describes them as 'trying to be profound about the obvious'. 'Pan-Africanism', and 'negritude' were concepts conceived by Negro exiles, the former in the United States and the latter in the French West Indies; understandably, therefore, they are full of nostalgic emotion that is powerful and evocative but not easy to define. While the three ideas seem to be interchangeable in meaning, 'Pan-Africanism' is more often applied to politics, and 'negritude' to the cultural sphere.

275

The Two Years of Africa, 1960–1961

Pan-Africanism says—to use the title of a book by President Nkrumah—that *Africa Must Unite*, as a single regenerated independent continent with a single government. To the Monrovia states, with their concept of loose African confederation, this is nothing short of 'black imperialism'. And if one asks why Africa, alone of all the continents, should have this unified destiny, the answer is because the continent is, and always has been, united through its essential 'negritude', because all aspects of life on it are expressions of a single 'African personality'. And that personality is distinctive in its love of life, of colour, of laughter; in the warmth of its tolerance and brotherhood, its devotion to peace, and so on. This romanticism apart, scholars have detected four positive strains in political Pan-Africanism today: Marxism, Gandhian non-violence (which few African leaders are large-minded enough or honest enough to admit to), a devotion to traditional African culture, and an eclecticism which makes it possible to combine the three. Perhaps Chief Enahoro of Nigeria has given the most comprehensive definition yet of Pan-Africanism: economic and cultural development, the avoidance of conflicts in Africa, and the promotion of African unity and of African influence in world affairs. By including everything this definition comes perilously close to meaning nothing. The negative content of Pan-Africanism is all too obvious and Africans themselves state it bluntly: colour-feeling, racial consciousness, and a common colonial history.

On the cultural plane, 'negritude' also seems a negative reaction rather than a positive assertion. It is significant that this idea came from the French colonies where the intellectuals had to fight hard against the process of assimilation aimed at making them into black Frenchmen. Cultural colonialism has always been more of a French than of a British speciality, and negritude is the reaction against it.

The most vigorous and comprehensive assertion of 'the African personality' is, simply, that 'Africans are Africans and nothing else'. To outsiders this seems obvious, but to Africans its reiteration has value because they feel that 'Africanness' was denied to them during the colonial period. One suspects that it is meaningful also because Africans have no continuity of history: when there are not blank century-wide gaps in the annals one finds what a scholar from Upper Volta has called 'the micropolitical history of pre-colonial Africa'. It was ideas such as these that lay beneath the divisions of the Casablanca and Monrovia groups—inspiring to the former, they seemed merely dangerous to the latter.

The Two Years of Africa, 1960–1961

Through participation in the Congo debates in the Security Council, or the active participation of their troops in the Congo operation, the Asian non-aligned countries had also been drawn into the divisions of ideas, of approach, and of policy that this African crisis produced among the new African states. The Congo crisis created divisions not only between the Asians themselves, but even between the non-aligned Asians and the other non-aligned governments. Thus, in the last quarter of 1960 and the first quarter of 1961, the United Arab Republic and Yugoslavia were most displeased with India because, unlike them, it had not recognised the Gizenga regime in Stanleyville nor withdrawn its troops from the Congo; indeed, India had even increased its contingent there.[3]

It was in this not-wholly-comradely atmosphere, as prevailing in the middle of 1961, that the non-aligned nations began discussing their next big conference.

NOTES TO INTERLUDE II

1. R. G. Good: 'The Congo Crisis', *Neutralism and Nonalignment*, New York, 1962.
2. Dahomey, Upper Volta, Congo (Brazzaville), Cameroon, Ivory Coast, Central African Republic, Gabon, Malagasy, Chad, Niger, Senegal, Mauritania, Liberia, Togo, Nigeria, Ethiopia, Libya, Somalia, Sierra Leone, Tunisia.
3. 'Thank God for India' was Mr. Hammarskjöld's reaction to this Indian support for the United Nations' operation.

CHAPTER XII

The Exclusive Club of the Non-Aligned: the Cairo Preparatory Conference for Belgrade, June 1961

The preparatory meeting held in Cairo to discuss the holding of a conference of the world's non-aligned countries acquired an importance of its own over and above the suggestions it made for the subsequent gathering. This was so because it framed the first and, to date, the only official definition of non-alignment and because it excluded the greater part of independent Africa from the non-aligned area.

Nineteen countries[1] were present on the 5th June 1961. Of these, seventeen were Afro-Asian, one—Cuba—was Latin American, and Yugoslavia represented Europe; a second Latin American country, Brazil, attended as an observer.

The meeting was held in an ornate hall that had once been the dining-room of the luxury hotel which had formerly occupied the building. Earlier, during World War II, the same hall had been the infectious diseases ward of the military hospital that had been billeted there. This memory had relevance, because non-alignment as a policy had certainly proved infectious. The non-aligned states at Cairo were twice as numerous as those present at Bandung, owing not only to a net addition of new states from Africa but to conversions from the ranks of those who had been aligned years earlier. There were five of these converts: Ceylon, Iraq, Ethiopia, the Sudan and Cambodia. And not two continents but four, the New World and the Old, were now represented.

For this reason, if no other, the Cairo meeting, and the Belgrade Conference to which it led, should have represented the high summer of non-alignment and co-existence and Panchsheel—a confident assertion of their importance in world affairs. Instead, these conferences were touched with a late autumnal feeling.

If they had been held in 1958, soon after the seventy-seven states at the United Nations had accepted the first Four Principles, they might have been fired with more zest, but too many daunting happenings had taken place in the intervening three years. The Communists and the non-aligned were not nearly as friendly as they had once been; Russia and China were at loggerheads; the first small Chinese attacks had taken place on India's borders, and the non-aligned had not seen eye-to-eye on the Congo. These events produced a failure of nerve, so that though the non-aligned were more numerous at Cairo, they were inward looking and positively against making any further converts.

In the preceding year the centre of non-aligned gravity and initiative had shifted markedly westward from India and Indonesia to the United Arab Republic and Yugoslavia, and it was these two countries, acting in concert, that had summoned the Cairo Conference. A close working alliance between the two was a distinctive feature of the politics of the non-aligned area following the meeting on Brioni in 1956 of Presidents Tito and Nasser and Mr. Nehru. It was Mr. Nehru who had helped to draw these two presidents into the non-aligned group but increasingly the two men found more in common with one another than between themselves and the Indian Premier. This was understandable, since Yugoslavia and Egypt are similar in size and in the type of their authoritarian regimes, both of which claim to be revolutionary; whereas India is large, and a parliamentary democracy, and by that fact is necessarily committed to gradualism. Yugoslavia found Egypt a useful link with the Arabs and Africa, as well as receptive of its ideas, while Egypt felt she had much to learn from Yugoslavia about industrial organisation. The two countries had co-operated closely on the Congo question and both had recognised the Gizenga regime there.

Something of the feeling of the Cairo Conference towards the rest of the non-aligned—its almost angrily exclusive approach—derived from its sponsors, especially from Egypt. President Nasser had no doubt been moved to call it because, as a dynamic leader, he felt himself frustratingly hemmed-in at this juncture, both in the Arab World and in Africa. He had suffered many disappointments. His union with Syria, that had produced the United Arab Republic, was now three years old and showed no signs of gaining new adherents. Tunisia had refused to attend the Casablanca meeting, and at a conference of Arab foreign ministers in Baghdad in January had opposed their endorsing the Casablanca resolution; it had then attended the Monrovia conference. Libya had attended Casablanca only to be obstructive and it, too, had then gone to Monrovia. The Sudan had likewise turned down the invitation to Casablanca, and had then refused transit facilities to Egypt and the Soviet Union when they wished to send supplies to the Gizenga government in Stanleyville. His relations with Iraq and Saudi Arabia were more cordial, but not those with Jordan; the Yemen was not being co-operative, while Lebanon was friendly, but too correctly neutral in these inter-Arab disputes for his taste.

In Africa his Congo policy was clearly not successful, and had been partially responsible for frightening off invitees from Casablanca. Nor were his relations with his ally Ghana too good. Ghana was the one Casablanca country that had promised, and then refused, to withdraw its troops from the Congo. And Ghana, in its turn, was aware of Egypt's coolness towards its ideas of the African High Command and the African Charter. Among the Moslem states, Egypt had cordial relations only with Indonesia, since Turkey, Iran and Pakistan were aligned, and Malaya was reckoned to be almost so.

Yugoslavia was probably not so constricted politically, but President Tito had for the past three or four years been in favour of a non-aligned conference wherein Yugoslavia would be officially accepted as a member of the uncommitted group. He had become particularly anxious for such a gathering after the failure at the United Nations of a five-nation resolution recommending a meeting between Mr. Khrushchev and President Eisenhower.

The two leaders probably also wanted to anticipate President Sukarno's continuing attempts to hold a Second Bandung. In March 1961 the Indonesian President had sent out letters suggesting this meeting, and in April, when Marshal Chen Yi, the Chinese Foreign Minister, visited Indonesia, their joint communiqué had said that it 'was very necessary to convene a Second Afro-Asian Conference in the shortest possible time'. By the standards of Egypt and Yugoslavia, if a conference was to be held, it was preferable that this should be among the like-minded non-aligned rather than among the varied Afro-Asians; such a gathering, moreover, would exclude European Yugoslavia.

The Egyptian and Yugoslav presidents were so anxious and so determined to hold this conference that they at length decided to ignore Mr. Nehru's reluctance. The Indian Premier had passed through Cairo in March 1961, and, once again and as usual, had turned down the proposal, made by President Nasser, for a large Bandung-type conference of the non-aligned. Indeed, the prevailing impression was that India had finally scotched the idea. But it had not; when President Tito arrived in Cairo in mid-April, at the end of a long tour of West and North Africa, the two presidents discussed the proposal and agreed to go ahead on their own, with or without India. They incorporated their decision, in veiled language, in their joint communiqué of the 22nd April 1961, which said that because of 'the unfavourable development of international relations' 'the two presidents held the view that consultations between the non-aligned countries are indispensable for the purpose of consolidating world peace'.

The invitations to a preparatory conference to arrange the main conference went out in the names of Presidents Tito and Nasser about a week later. It said that 'the time is opportune for the heads of non-aligned countries to convene in the greatest possible numbers', and 'at the nearest possible time'.

India, despite its known reluctance, was of necessity invited because a conference of the non-aligned without the first and largest non-aligned country would have been an oddity. Even had she not been faced with a *fait accompli*, India was under an obligation to accept because a refusal would have been interpreted either as an abandonment of non-alignment, or else as evidence of hostile feeling towards the sponsors. This uneasy, compulsory co-operation was the keynote of India's attitude to both the Cairo and Belgrade meetings.

The initial reaction of New Delhi to the idea of the Belgrade Conference was almost identical in terms with its first reaction to the idea of Bandung. The timing and preparation of the conference, it suggested, should be carefully thought out; and the objective should be practical results rather than mere condemnation. Above all there should be no suggestion that a Third Bloc was in process of formation. India took at their face value the words used by the sponsors in their invitation about non-aligned leaders meeting 'in the greatest possible number', and accordingly suggested the addition of about fifteen countries to those to be invited to the preparatory conference.

The sponsors were able to reassure India on the general points it had raised: neither the United Arab Republic nor Yugoslavia had any desire for a Third Bloc, or for vague condemnations. On membership, however, their ideas were different from India's: they were never prepared to consider adding more than three or four countries to the list of invitees.

On the 16th May an announcement and an invitation from Presidents Tito, Nasser and Sukarno stated that a preparatory meeting for a non-aligned conference would meet in Cairo on the 5th June to be followed by a main conference held sometime before the 16th

The Exclusive Club of the Non-Aligned

General Assembly of the United Nations. And, it added, 'Prime Minister Nehru has asked us to say that he is happy to join us in extending this invitation'. Prime Minister Nehru had done no such thing, and India merely underlined her reluctance when she sent a note to the other invitees, which found its way into the press, unconvincingly protesting that she was not unenthusiastic about the conference and that Mr. Nehru had authorised the sponsors to mention his name in their invitation.

The nineteen countries that met in Cairo in June were, therefore, all invitees of Presidents Tito and Nasser. On what basis had they made their selection? Indeed this very question was put to the sponsors, but the principles they had applied were never revealed to questioners. The question is prompted by the fact that 'non-alignment' did not seem equally applicable to the policies of all the invitees. By this time the general term 'neutralism' had come to cover a wide variety of policies.

It is proof of the living vitality of the idea, and of the varied multiplicity of national interests, that in 1961, the genus 'neutralism' englobed many species—progressive neutralism, positive neutralism, non-alignment, the uncommitted, the disengaged. These are not just different words, for they represent real shades of policy among the neutralist states. No one definitive, hard-and-fast classification can be laid down but Cuba, Yugoslavia and, Guinea (at this time) could be called 'progressive neutralists'; the 'positive neutralists' took in such countries as Ghana, Egypt, Mali, Indonesia and Algeria (and Finland); India, Burma, Ceylon and Afghanistan (along with Ireland and Sweden) could be classed as 'non-aligned'; Saudi Arabia, Sudan, Ethiopia, Tunisia and Lebanon as 'uncommitted', while Austria, Cambodia and Laos were 'disengaged' or should be so. These last represented the violet shades in the political spectrum of neutralism, with Cuba and Yugoslavia representing the reddish tints at the other end of the range.

Mr. Nehru and Presidents Nasser, Nkrumah and Sukarno were at one in being neutralist leaders, but a catalogue of some of the concepts that underlie this shared approach reveals differences as varied as the sects within Protestant Christianity. In short, their implementation of neutralism is as diverse as were their reasons for originally adopting this policy.

Mr. Nehru's concerns encompassed the world—too much so, very often; President Nkrumah's involvement is essentially with the African continent; President Nasser's performance is tied to the Arab

282

area, while President Sukarno's objective is the greater glory of his own country and of himself. For Mr. Nehru the enemy was no longer colonialism but the Cold War with its bitterness and its propaganda vulgarities; for President Nkrumah it was neo-colonialism; for President Nasser the main problem was old-fashioned colonialism exemplified by Israel, World Zionism and its Western supporters, while for President Sukarno it was, quite simply, the Dutch, and now is Malaysia. The bases of non-alignment for Mr. Nehru were cloudy, even woolly principles and his peaceful co-existence was more than a little pacifist; President Nkrumah's peaceful co-existence was (like President Tito's) merely a policy; and it is doubtful whether Presidents Nasser and Sukarno accept peaceful co-existence at all—certainly not with their immediate enemies. Neither Mr. Nehru nor President Nasser (nor Tito) wanted a neutralist Third Force; but President Nkrumah does so, as does President Sukarno, composed of what he calls 'the new emerging forces'. Even in the realm of practicalities we find that India and Ghana get their arms from Britain and Russia, the United Arab Republic from Russia, and Yugoslavia from America. Mr. Nehru permitted, and President Sukarno permits, political activity to the Communist Party; Presidents Nasser and Nkrumah do not; and President Tito is a Communist.

Because of this jostle and variety within the neutralist camp, the United Arab Republic and Yugoslavia were unable precisely to explain the principles that governed their selection of countries invited to Cairo. All those who were invited came within the wide scope of neutralism, but not all those entitled to inclusion within its ambit were invited; some were specially favoured merely because they happened to be the friends and neighbours of those issuing the invitations.

That Cuba should have been invited to this meeting of the non-aligned is now seen to have been a mistake, for it has since become aligned and was probably so even in 1961. But the ambition underlying the invitation was the far-sighted one of expanding the non-aligned area to Latin America. That continent is, like Asia and Africa, underdeveloped and primarily agricultural, which gives a similar texture to its life. Furthermore, some of the Latin American countries, such as Mexico, Bolivia, Ecuador and Brazil, had from time to time shown signs of following an independent foreign policy, despite their membership of the Organisation of American States and the firm grip of American capital on their economies.

The Exclusive Club of the Non-Aligned

Fidel Castro had met the non-aligned leaders of the 1960 General Assembly Session in New York, and in June 1961 he was a hero for surviving the American-backed attack on the Bay of Pigs—an act of criminal folly comparable to Suez. Yugoslavia and Egypt each now say that it was the other that was mainly responsible for inviting Cuba, but perhaps the Yugoslavs are the more accurate. Not wanting unduly to irritate the United States, they had not moved too close to Cuba; the Cuban Ambassador to Yugoslavia, after presenting his credentials, had left for a long period, and returned only just before the Belgrade Conference—hardly a sign of close relations.

There were two quite different concepts of the purpose of the preparatory conference. The principal items on its agenda as proposed by the sponsors were two: the place, date and duration of the main conference, and its agenda. The principal item on the agenda suggested by India, which was accepted, was 'Composition'. For the sponsors and their friends, all those present at Cairo would be present at the main conference, and no others, and they had now merely to decide where and when they should next meet. India went to Cairo not in the least committed to the main conference, which she said she would attend only if it conformed to her ideas. The Indian delegation, then, tried for three objectives: a generally-worded agenda eliminating local, bi-lateral squabbles; a new inviting body to consider afresh all invitations to the main conference, and the despatch of these invitations to countries of all shades and degrees of neutralism—a minimum of fifteen more with a possible maximum of twenty-five extra. India got what she wanted on the first point, completely failed on the second, and so achieved very little on the third. This time, the familiar, belated Indian take-over bid did not succeed.

The relatively unimportant issue that captured the headlines during the Cairo Conference was the question of granting admission to the Provisional Algerian Government and to the Stanleyville regime of Mr. Gizenga as the legal government of the Congo. After two whole days of heated debate, and in the teeth of opposition by a group of countries led by India, it was decided to admit Algeria as a member both of the preparatory conferences, whereas the Stanleyville administration was to be invited only to the latter. This decision was a considerable victory for the Casablanca group, but Ghana was enraged at the distinction drawn between Algeria and the Congo: it felt that it had been let down by the other Casablanca countries, and its reaction marked the beginning of the decline of this artificial grouping.

The Exclusive Club of the Non-Aligned

Only on the fifth day of the conference, when the question of membership was discussed, was the battle about non-alignment joined between those who wanted a larger grouping at the main conference and those who were quite content with their own close clique. Among the 'exclusives' were the Casablanca countries and Yugoslavia, for whom the non-aligned area was a closed society, an exclusive club to which they, the true-blue members, had the right to control admission. The 'inclusives' were mostly Asian—India, Burma, Afghanistan and Nepal, with support from the Sudan and Ethiopia. For them the non-aligned area was an open society, the central idea of which had a magnetic power capable of attracting other governments to it. Accordingly, they argued at Cairo, the conference of the non-aligned ought to represent all the diverse tendencies of neutralism, thus ensuring that it would not function as a bloc. A narrow definition of non-alignment would only create new divisions. In an attempt to broaden the basis, India was even prepared to draw a distinction between military alliances, which were objectionable, and agreements for military training concluded between ex-colonies and their former rulers, which could be condoned. The leader of the Indian delegation, Mr. R. K. Nehru, the then Secretary-General of the Indian Foreign Ministry, contested that if non-alignment was a good idea it ought obviously to extend its scope. At one point he challenged the courage of the Casablanca countries, adjuring them not to be afraid of meeting with the Monrovia countries which they affected to despise.

Through such arguments, and sheer persistence, the 'inclusives' gained their point, when it was agreed that a sub-committee should draw up the criteria of non-alignment and apply them to the countries of the world.

In two sessions, the non-aligned countries discussed the criteria of non-alignment presented by the sub-committee that had taken eleven hours of discussion to formulate them. These were:

1. A country should follow an independent policy based on peaceful co-existence and non-alignment, or should be showing a trend in favour of such a policy.
2. It should consistently have supported movements for national independence.
3. It should not be a member of multilateral military alliances concluded in the context of great power conflicts.
4. If it had conceded military bases these concessions should not have been made in the context of great power conflicts.

The Exclusive Club of the Non-Aligned

5. If it were a member of a bi-lateral or regional defence arrangement, this should not be in the context of great power conflicts.

This was the first time that the non-aligned peoples tried to define non-alignment. The elements in their definition relative to alliances and bases are negative prohibitions. The second item on their list is straightforward Afro-Asian anti-colonialism, and not an integral constituent of non-alignment. The first requirement—that of 'an independent policy based on peaceful co-existence'—confuses the essence of non-alignment, 'an independent policy', with the later parasitic outgrowth of 'peaceful co-existence'. This graft was made at India's suggestion, and ironically enough, was made when India's increasing difficulties with China had taught India, if not yet its government, that peaceful co-existence and non-alignment were two quite different concepts.

But when the conference reached its real task—that is, the interpretation of these criteria and the application of them to individual countries—it decided that it had already sat for so long that it could not tackle the assignment. This ticklish problem was then handed over to a committee of the ambassadors in Cairo of the participating states.

The sub-committee on 'time and place' reported on three proposed venues: Yugoslavia, Cuba and the United Arab Republic. Egypt, having played host to the preparatory conference, did not press its claim to house the main conference; the idea of Cuba was greeted in total silence; so Yugoslavia was accepted; as was the date of the 1st September 1961.

The conference accepted an omnibus agenda for the main meeting including the liquidation of colonialism and neo-colonialism, racial discrimination, disarmament and military bases, co-existence, the role and structure of the United Nations, and the problems of unequal economic development and of economic co-operation. The administration and arrangements for the conference were left to Yugoslavia.

The often angry discussions at Cairo afforded an accurate preview of Belgrade, where the older Asians and the younger Africans continued to do battle with each other. And at the end of it all the Cairo Conference, by its failure to decide on membership, left the better part of its work undone, unlike the Bogor preparatory meeting where aligned and non-aligned managed to reach quick and workmanlike conclusions. Evidently neutralism was no longer enough.

The Exclusive Club of the Non-Aligned

The Committee of Ambassadors that had been instructed to apply the criteria of non-alignment was not, of course, the new inviting body that India had wanted. In discussion, it had been said that the criteria should be applied equally to those present at Cairo and to prospective invitees. But it was difficult, if not impossible, out of diplomatic politeness if for no other reason, for the envoys to eliminate a country whose ambassador was present; nor could an ambassador accredited to Cairo easily say that in his opinion one of the United Arab Republic's close friends failed to qualify. Since eliminations were out of the question, and only additions could be considered, the process gave an unfortunate impression of first-class neutralists picking fastidiously from among second-class neutralists.

In the last resort the new invitations depended on how forceful or obstinate an ambassador was in the lengthy, argumentative sessions, or how many votes he could muster, or what bargain he could offer in this international horse-trading. The division was usually fifteen to five against the 'inclusives'.

India, leading the inclusive group, put forward fifteen countries; in Europe—Ireland, Sweden and Finland; from Latin America, Chile, the Argentine, Costa Rica and Paraguay (this was a mistake for Uruguay); in Asia—Lebanon, Jordan and Malaya and in Africa —Nigeria, Sierra Leone, Tunisia, Upper Volta, and Togo. Later India also suggested Tanganyika, Kenya and Uganda.

Ghana, Guinea and Mali judged the other possible African invitees according to their policy towards the Congo. The United Arab Republic's real criterion was the extent of co-operation extended by various states to the Casablanca group. And Cuba, who claimed and asserted her veto on the Latin American invitees, took her decisions according to the reaction nations had displayed to the Bay of Pigs invasion.

The 'exclusives' were also able to produce some general principles to justify their blackballing of new members. They objected, quite naturally, to members of multilateral military alliances and to those with bi-lateral agreements granting military bases to Western Powers. This, in principle, eliminated Nigeria, Libya, Tunisia, Malaya and, allegedly, Jordan. Saudi Arabia and Morocco, who were present, were not objectionable on this score because they had given notice to the United States to quit the bases it held on their territory. One criteria of non-alignment was that if bases had been granted, these should 'not be in the context of great power conflicts'. In the discussions in the ambassadors' committee a further escape clause was added: the willingness with which countries accepted bases should also be taken into consideration. This put a premium on hypocrisy by giving a higher rating of non-alignment to governments that took the revenue paid for the bases but did so with a guilty conscience. These contortions were necessary to justify the presence of Ethiopia and the invitation to Cyprus. The very large American base at Massawa in Ethiopia was allegedly only for telecommunications, and therefore not strictly in 'the context of great power rivalries'; and Cyprus, it could justifiably be said, had unwillingly had the British bases imposed on it.

But what of the Latin American countries whom both groups were eager to bring into the non-aligned fold? They were, through multilateral and bi-lateral treaties, the military allies of the United States; but since no one was anxious to publicise this fact no objection was raised to the Latin Americans on that score.

Other reasons for ruling out a country were easy to find. Thus objection was made to Lebanon because she had not voted for Communist China's admission to the United Nations, and had not supported the three-nation plea to Mr. Khrushchev and President Eisenhower.

The first obstruction devised by Ghana, Guinea, Mali was that only those non-aligned countries who were sufficiently interested to apply for invitations should be considered. After further acrimonious discussion Yugoslavia proposed that there should not be any further additions from Asia or Europe or Latin America, but perhaps some from Africa. Later, Egypt proposed that the discussion should be closed with the addition of one new country, Cyprus; Indonesia supported closure because, as its ambassador said, all of Afro-Asia was going to meet soon, anyway, at the Second Bandung Conference!

Finally it was decided to invite Bolivia, Ecuador, Lebanon, Nigeria, Togo, Upper Volta and Cyprus. Pan-Africanist Ghana and Mali abstained on the vote accepting the three other African countries, and India recorded its dissatisfaction on the failure to approve of including Tanganyika. Lebanon and Cyprus accepted the invitation, Bolivia and Ecuador agreed to send observers, and the three African states declined, probably because they felt it would be beneath their dignity to accept invitations so reluctantly extended. Thus India failed, as might have been expected, in its attempt to persuade the majority at Cairo to convert itself into a minority at Belgrade.

The attempt by the non-aligned countries to extend their area to Latin America was wrecked by the association of Cuba with these invitations. There would have been general approval for invitations to the Argentine, Chile and Mexico, but because acceptance would have meant sitting with Cuba at the main conference these governments let it be known in advance that they would rather not be asked.[2]

It was the choice of Belgrade as the venue that discouraged the European non-aligned countries. Here again Sweden, Finland, and Ireland would have had invitations but they too cried off in advance because attendance at a political conference in Marshal Tito's domain might compromise their neutrality. They might have been willing if the city suggested by India and others, Beirut, had been accepted. So on account of the choice of Belgrade there were no other European participants.

The great absentee from Belgrade was the new Africa. That continent had not really been adequately represented at Bandung, where its special problems had been rather overlooked. Since Bandung twenty-five independent African states had emerged, and of these only six were at Belgrade, two from Arab Africa—Tunisia and Morocco, and four from Equatorial Africa—Somalia, Congo, Guinea and Mali. The great fact that Africa had truly become part of Afro-Asia was ignored because a small clique of non-aligned Africans excluded the rest, on the pretext that their non-alignment was not pure enough. Thus a main influence on the membership of the Belgrade Conference was the Congo crisis, and the antagonistic alignments it had produced among the new African states.

India was not happy at the way the choice of countries had been made; and it was only on the 9th August, a mere three weeks before Belgrade, and three and a half months after receiving the invitation, that Mr. Nehru reluctantly accepted. He had no choice; for India to be absent from a non-aligned conference convened by its friends Yugoslavia and the United Arab Republic, however badly this had been put together, would have called for a degree of toughness and independence that India's non-alignment policy did not display, then or later.

The unfinished Cairo Conference, that was scheduled to last for four days and went on for eight, nevertheless produced two important results—a definition of non-alignment and a tendency.

The tendency that developed at Cairo was that of the new African states to find the Asians, and especially India, old and effete and lacking in anti-colonial ardour. In uncompromising terms the Africans, urged on by Cuba and Yugoslavia, denounced the Asians' preference for compromises. At the main conference, this polemic was to occur aimed directly at India. Yet it was good for India and for the conference that she was present at Belgrade.

NOTES TO CHAPTER XII

1. Afghanistan, Burma, Cambodia, Ceylon, Ethiopia, Ghana, Guinea, India, Indonesia, Iraq, Mali, Morocco, Nepal, Saudi Arabia, Somalia, Sudan, the United Arab Republic, Yugoslavia. The Provisional Government of Algeria was admitted during the conference.
2. There is something curious about Chile's position. According to press reports Yugoslavia invited Chile to attend as an observer on 30th Aug., two days before the conference was due to begin. Chile regretted that this did not give her enough time to get her observer to Belgrade.

CHAPTER XIII

The Belgrade Conference, September 1961

On the day before the Belgrade Conference began, on the 30th August, the Soviet Union exploded a nuclear device at its Arctic testing grounds and announced that this was the beginning of a new series of atomic tests. Never before had an international conference met so immediately or so directly under the shadow of the mushroom cloud, but few of the participants bothered to glance up at it.

This explosion, and the international events preceding it, forced the discussions at Belgrade on to the highest level where, for once, the gravity of the situation matched Mr. Nehru's usual apocalyptic gloom. At that high and serious level he succeeded in setting his stamp on the conference and, despite its partial failure on the moral plane, he got it to do what he wanted; for this, however, he and India paid a heavy price.

The spring and summer of 1961 were a period of unusual tension in world affairs. The Summit Meeting of the Big Two, for which the non-aligned had clamoured at the 1960 General Assembly, took place in May at Vienna, and produced little friendliness and less relaxation. This, a stern encounter between Mr. Khrushchev and President Kennedy, showed that there is not necessarily any virtue or magic in the mere act of a meeting between leaders.

Indeed it was perhaps because of this meeting that Russia revived its old threat to conclude a separate peace treaty with East Germany that would have given that regime the right to control, or deny, Western access to West Berlin. The Western Powers announced that they would never accept that right, and both blocs then began to mobilise. A flood of refugees from East Germany swept into West Berlin, and to stop this the East Germans erected the infamous Wall through the heart of the divided city. In August 1961 Berlin was the nodal point of all the accumulated tensions of the Cold War between East and West.

Trouble had also flared up in the older colonial struggle on the

North–South axis. In July, when President Bourguiba challenged France's title to her base at Bizerta, the French asserted their right in a bloody encounter between their paratroopers and brave but ill-equipped Tunisians. This action gained Tunisia so much sympathy among the Afro-Asians that, late in August, President Bourguiba was invited to the Belgrade Conference. Tunisia was propelled into the non-aligned camp by the French paratroopers, as Cuba had been by the emigrés landing at the Bay of Pigs.

The timing of the Russian test was so extraordinary that it may well have been a deliberate and massive snub to the non-aligned—a brutal reminder to them of where real power lay. Russia's action was indicative of her feeling of disenchantment with the non-aligned countries, which had largely replaced her earlier effusive friendship for them. During 1960–1, the non-aligned had not merely refused to follow the Russian lead over the Congo, but had actually rebuffed some of Russia's cruder propagandist moves. Further, they had already lined up in opposition to her 'troika' proposal for the tripartite control of the United Nations. Hence it was not surprising that news about the forthcoming conference of the non-aligned was almost completely blacked-out in the press of the Communist countries (except in Poland). *Pravda* broke the silence a week before the meeting, but only to give the non-aligned a lecture on what they should decide.

The Western Powers might have been expected to make capital out of the obvious coolness of the Communist bloc by expressing their approval of the conference. That, however, would have demanded too complete a reversal of roles. There were the traditional tremors of atavistic alarm at this gathering of the Afro-Asian hordes—this time neither too openly nor too vigorously expressed. The West, in fact, agreed with the Casablanca group and Yugoslavia in antipathy to any further expansion of membership of the non-aligned area. The West had, at long last, come to terms with the idea of non-alignment but did not wish to see it gain new recruits. So pressure was put on Lebanon and Cyprus not to accept the invitation to Belgrade, and the United States Ambassador in Brazil told that Government that while it was, naturally, free to consider itself non-aligned and to attend the conference, the United States would not consider it as non-aligned, especially in matters concerning the Western hemisphere. The British Foreign Secretary was of the opinion that the non-aligned should not form a bloc, and his American counterpart supposed that they 'could have a very useful conference', and said that

America would make no effort to influence it. Compared with Western reaction to earlier Afro-Asian conferences, even these luke-warm and equivocal statements added up to a modified welcome, slightly warmer in tone than the attitude of the Communist countries.

Outside opinion on the conference was that it was important. No longer was there any sneering at the Afro-Asians as youngsters talking out of turn. On the contrary, it was accepted on all sides that the non-aligned could, if they wished, make a considerable impact. After all there were twice as many non-aligned representatives present at Belgrade as at Bandung, and everyone knew that there could, and should, have been many more. Non-alignment was an idea on the march. Further, at the United Nations the non-aligned countries had shown on several issues that they could act with both independence and responsibility.

Once again at Belgrade, Mr. Nehru was able to point out that the course of events since the issue of the invitations had enhanced the conference's intrinsic importance. Like the meetings at Colombo, at the time of the Indo-China settlement, and at Bandung, during the offshore islands crisis, that at Belgrade happened to coincide with a period of international tension. This time the issues were more serious than ever before—the bomb, disarmament, Berlin and Germany, nothing less than peace itself, nothing less than the purity of the world's air and water: the leaders of the non-aligned had been raised to the status of conservators of nature. This was the challenge that faced them at Belgrade, and they faced it before an expectant and hopeful world.

The city of Belgrade has a very different texture and quality of life from that of the towns in which previous conferences had been held. The conferences at New Delhi met amidst the massive, enduring architectural affirmations of Moghul and British imperial rule. Colombo, Bogor and Bandung were in tropical Asia, where the seedy, mildewed works of man seem for ever to be on the point of sliding back into the humid jungle. Belgrade was Balkan-flavoured Europe, with cobbled streets and baroque green copper domes and big new buildings to replace those destroyed by German bombing. It had not had a chance to become blasé over international conferences, since the last one to which it had been host was a small, bitter Cold War wrangle over Danubian navigation, and had happened ten years earlier; its friendly, helpful citizens were out in their thousands in the beflagged streets, filled with genuine interest and excitement. One element in common between Belgrade and Bandung and New Delhi was the heat—here burning away yet another Yugoslav harvest.

The Yugoslavs had made superbly efficient arrangements for the conference, and even the difficult accommodation problem was solved by urging local people to go on holiday and leave their apartments to delegates and pressmen. There were 600 of the latter who had only one complaint. Severe, even excessive, security precautions kept them rigidly separated from the delegations and, since the press gallery in the conference hall was very small, most of them had to watch the proceedings through the cold and selective eye of television.

Though designated 'non-aligned', this meeting was in essence yet another of the Afro-Asian conferences, for only the two Communist countries came from outside that area. There were ten Asians, eleven Africans and a Mediterranean island; from them came an emperor, a king, three princes, an archbishop, a general and the world's only feminine head of government. The conference was lucky in its absentees, Dr. Castro and General Kassem of Iraq—both wordy orators.

Throughout August, the Berlin crisis impinged directly on events, with both sides in that dispute exerting a flattering amount of pressure on the participants. Mr. Khrushchev sent letters on the question to some of the prominent Afro-Asian leaders which Dr. Adenauer countered through personal messages to all the invitees. The East German regime clumsily asked to be present as an observer; the conference secretariat naturally refused this request. Mr. Nehru was the focus of much of the pressure for at this time he was saying much—even too much—on Berlin. In one lengthy speech on the subject a few days before the conference, he proposed 'non-engagement' for both Germanies, but seemed to cast doubt on Western rights of free access to West Berlin. A retraction on this latter point was issued, on his behalf, by the American Ambassador in New Delhi. This extraordinary procedure seemed to reflect a confusion in Mr. Nehru's thinking that served to diminish the influence he might otherwise have brought to bear.

The strongest waves of pressure on the conference were, naturally, those that emanated from the Soviet nuclear test. And the contrary responses it evoked from the participants were evident when Mr. Nehru arrived at Belgrade airport. He was informed of the news of the test by Indian journalists, and asked for his reaction, at which point President Tito tried physically to interpose himself between the pressmen and their Prime Minister with the words: 'Later, later'; Mr. Nehru did not wait, however, and replied that he was against such tests anywhere at any time.

The messages sent to the conference, and even more those that were not sent, revealed the sentiments towards the meeting of the two sides in the Cold War. As well as a fairly cordial greeting from President Kennedy, there were many from various unofficial groups in Western countries. From the Communist bloc came official messages from Mr. Khrushchev, Chou En-lai, Ho Chi Minh and the Bulgarian Premier; but there were no 'unofficial' greetings from Russia, one from Hungary (that arrived after the conference) and only one from China; this silence was notable on the part of an area that could, on occasion, 'hail' an event with thousands of telegrams.

Study of the two types of observers that were invited, or permitted to attend, the conference by its Yugoslav secretariat throws some light on Yugoslavia's motives in sponsoring this gathering. In one group were representatives from nineteen African nationalist movements (those in Angola, Northern and Southern Rhodesia, Uganda, Ruanda-Urundi, the Cape Verde Islands, Mozambique, Kenya, South Africa, South-West Africa, and Cameroon). Their presence established Yugoslavia's claim on the friendship of the new countries of Africa. In a second group were representatives of eleven Socialist or Labour parties and leftist splinter groups from Malta, Italy, France, Japan, Ceylon, Chile, Argentine, Venezuela, and West Germany; their presence emphasised Yugoslavia's aspiration to be an alternative world headquarters for Socialist ideology. The Yugoslav Socialist Union paid the expenses of all, or most, of these groups. And by bringing them in the Yugoslavs cast the conference net over an area far wider than that covered by its unfortunately limited membership.

In the form of its deliberations the Belgrade Conference was unlike any other Afro-Asian meeting. All others had followed the pattern of a plenary session of opening speeches, not always public, after which the chief delegates went into private committee to get down to the real business; this was usually the drafting of the final communiqué. At Belgrade the plenary meeting remained in open session throughout—for fifteen separate sittings covering a total of nearly forty hours; during all this time the heads of state or government had to listen to each other's oratory. In the meanwhile, the drafting of the communiqué was being discussed by their alternates; only when these reached deadlock did the chief representatives meet in closed session. This happened twice: once, on the 4th September, for three-and-a-half hours and again on the last night, the 5th to 6th September, for eight-and-a-half hours. The unusual length of the last session was due to the fact that all the real work of the conference had been compressed into these two sittings because chief delegates would not forgo their public speeches. Having tried and failed to stem the flood of words at Bandung, Mr. Nehru did not even make the attempt at Belgrade.

The real issue at Belgrade was a question of priorities. World peace and colonialism were both important, but which issue, at that particular time, was the more urgent? According to the first eight speakers, including Presidents Tito, Sukarno, Nasser and Nkrumah, it was colonialism. For the ninth speaker, Mr. Nehru, the conference's main task, almost its only task, was to do what it could to start negotiations to avert the immediate threat of war, 'for if war comes all else for the moment goes'. The Indian Prime Minister spoke *extempore* for thirty-five minutes, ten of which he spent on 'anti-colonialism, anti-imperialism, anti-racialism and all that', and the remaining twenty-five on stressing over and over again that it was the conference's 'duty and function' to tell the great powers 'that they must negotiate'. Here he thumped the rostrum. His repetitions were designed to get the conference, as he put it, 'out of the rut of meeting together, passing long resolutions and making brave declarations and then going home'. The conference should not try to tell 'proud nations' what they should or should not do, because, as he had said so often before, the solution of the world's problems lay essentially with the Big Two. But it should urge them to negotiate, and to do this through a special and separate declaration that should be 'put not only foremost but so that it catches every person's attention'.

After this trumpet call—by common consent the high-point of the conference—all else was anti-climax. In the drafting committee Mr. Nehru, by *force majeure*, ultimately got his way; but, judging by the seventeen speeches that followed his in plenary session, he made few converts, for these were little more than the usual shrillings on the anti-colonial penny-whistle. Only three speakers agreed with him that the question of peace was paramount. They were Archbishop Makarios, Mrs. Bandaranaike and King Hassan of Morocco. That was how the Afro-Asian non-aligned peoples responded to the main challenge with which they were faced.

The reaction to Mr. Nehru's speech showed that, in private at least, his thesis was accepted, but with feelings of embarrassment on the part of the sponsoring countries, who would have preferred to be the first to make the point. The Indonesians, for instance, said President Sukarno took the primacy of peace for granted; the United Arab Republic claimed that President Nasser had said the same thing, and in the opinion of the Yugoslavs, Mr. Nehru had said nothing new.

The second challenge, a moral one, that the Belgrade Conference had to meet, and over which it partially failed, was to condemn the Russian resumption of nuclear testing. Great indignation was expressed at the time, especially in America, at what was described as its cowardly silence; but a closer examination of the speeches shows that its record is somewhat better than it was first thought to be. That condemnation should have been expressed is obvious. The Afro-Asians were foremost in urging a continuation of the moratorium on tests that America and Britain had observed since October 1958. When the French set off their atomic fire-crackers in the Sahara (which was the Russian pretext for resuming the tests) the African countries, Ghana especially, protested vigorously.

In all, thirteen speakers referred to nuclear tests but only seven of them mentioned the Russian decision. Mr. Nehru's condemnation was the most forthright.[1] He said that the new explosion made the situation 'much more dangerous', and that he regretted it deeply. President Nasser also expressed 'deep regret' and 'shock',[2] and King Hassan 'serious concern'.[3] For the rest, President Nkrumah, Archbishop Makarios and Premier Salam of Lebanon said they were 'shocked' and Mrs. Bandaranaike described it as something 'worse'. This, admittedly, is no great show of moral indignation, but it is better than the Afro-Asian showing on Hungary, for this time at least two of the leading non-aligned countries, India and Egypt, expressed disapproval.

One non-aligned leader came near to expressing approval. President Tito said that he was 'not surprised' by the Russian announcement, 'because we can understand the reasons advanced by the Government of the Soviet Union'; only the timing of the test, just before the conference, was surprising. And to show that even this expression of surprise was an after-thought, these sentences were issued as an addendum to the speech, not only during the conference, but in the printed volume on the meeting that appeared months later.

A moral judgement on this deplorable lapse of the non-aligned countries is justified because at Belgrade speaker after speaker referred to the assembly as having 'moral strength', or as 'the conscience of mankind' or, in President Sukarno's words, 'a co-ordinated moral force'. Yet the Indonesian President, and the very people making these large claims, were those who were silent about the Russian tests. Mr. Nehru, who did speak out, warned the conference that 'we must not over-estimate our own importance'.[4]

Since non-alignment was the basis of the conference, and since the criteria for non-alignment had been laid down at Cairo, its meaning and content could well have been taken for granted. Yet most speakers tried to give their own definitions of it; none succeeded in saying anything really new. The main point was that it was not a passive doctrine despite the negative prefix to the word. President Nkrumah spoke of non-alignment as 'a moral force which should be a balancing force', while President Keita of Mali said that it would be undignified to perform 'a kind of balancing act between the Great Powers'.[5] President Osman of Somalia, after making a pointed reference to the 'non-aligned states not represented' at the conference, went on to say that the definition formulated at Cairo was an interim one. He said with pertinence that abstention from military alliances must not be the sole criterion of non-alignment: 'If we show where our sympathies lie by expressions of bitter and biased criticism motivated by hatred and constantly levelled against one side only, our professions of non-alignment will be worthless and hypocritical';[6] this precept, if followed, would have been a much-needed corrective. A measure of hypocrisy was shown by the President of Mali and King Hassan when they said that the non-aligned area ought to be extended 'by inviting other nations to join our ranks'; at Cairo, three months earlier, their delegations had prevented extension from being brought about. The dry comment of the Afghan Prime Minister, that his country's traditional policy 'of impartial judgement' 'far antedates' the use of the word 'non-alignment', is worth mention.[7]

A striking fact about Belgrade is that in the whole of Mr. Nehru's speech there is not a single reference to or use of the word 'co-existence'. That Panchsheel should not be mentioned by him, or by any other speaker, is understandable because the Chinese had buried the principles when they made their border forays on India in 1959. Since it was India that insisted at Cairo on intertwining co-existence and non-alignment, Mr. Nehru's silence is unusual. Eight other speakers tried to define this concept. President Sukarno admitted that, to a large extent, co-existence entailed accepting the *status quo*, though not for ever; as far as Indonesia was concerned, co-existence did not cover relations with the Dutch; for combating them, he found sanction in the Koran.[8] For President Nasser peaceful co-existence was not a mere armed truce (which is what the Arabs have with Israel), and for the Emperor Haile Selassie and Prince Norodom it was not meant to be a cover for subversion—a faint echo of the Bandung debates.[9] President Tito sadly and wisely remarked that 'the practice and theory of co-existence seems different in different areas'.

There were surprisingly few references to Bandung; only about half a dozen speakers recalling the earlier conference. In fact when he tried to trace the antecedents of Belgrade, President Sukarno confused the Asian Relations Conference of 1947 with that on Indonesia in 1949, and placed it in 1948![10]

On two points there was general agreement: that the non-aligned had not gathered to form a bloc, and that Russia's pattern of 'troika' control in the United Nations was inacceptable. Haile Selassie uttered the solemn warning that anyone who weakened the United Nations 'is the enemy of all of us'.[11]

Two other issues that caused much controversy in the drafting committee were the setting of a date for the ending of colonialism, and the problem of Germany; differing views on these questions were revealed in the public speeches. Leaders like Mr. Nehru, Haile Selassie and Prince Norodom were of the opinion that 'classical colonialism is gone and is dead',[12] but for others it remained so lively a danger that they wanted to fix a date for its demise. The President of Mali said this should be 'immediate'; President Nkrumah suggested 'the 31st December 1962', and King Hassan and President Sukarno fixed a maximum of two years.[13]

In contrast to Bandung, where the immediate problem—that of tension in the Formosa Strait—was discussed only in the lobbies and on the margin of the conference, at Belgrade the immediate problem—Berlin and Germany, was mentioned in plenary session by many speakers, each with his own solution. A few cautious souls, like President Nasser and the Afghan Premier, merely suggested a negotiated settlement. But even Mr. Nehru, after saying that 'it is not for us even to lay down what should be done in regard to Germany and Berlin, which are the immediate causes of this present tension',[14] went on to say what should be done; he advocated the recognition of the two German regimes and a guarantee of free access to West Berlin. This was also the opinion of President Sukarno. Ceylon and Cyprus suggested self-determination for the German people; Ghana, Iraq and Ceylon proposed the recognition and neutralisation of the two Germanies; Cambodia advocated the neutralisation of a reunified

Germany, and Ethiopia merely unification. This multiplicity of ideas left the drafting committee without any firm guidance.

It was President Nasser who proposed, on the second day of the conference, that the drafting committee should begin its labours; these, he accurately prophesied, would be long and difficult. The committee in question was not a selected group but a committee of the whole conference, on which most of the representatives were foreign ministers. Its first meeting, on the 2nd September, discussed Mr. Nehru's proposal for a special appeal for urgent summit negotiations. After a long session the idea was accepted; it was ratified at the first working session of the heads of delegations meeting next day. In the debate the idea was supported by the Asian countries, but was questioned and even opposed by the Casablanca countries, minus Morocco and plus Yugoslavia. No one had the temerity to oppose a separate declaration on the need for peace, but it was received without enthusiasm; reception was lukewarm firstly because it was an idea put forward by a single delegation, and secondly because it was likely to attract special attention, as it was meant to do, thereby implying that other subjects, such as the anti-colonial question, were not important.

A compromise was worked out. Mr. Nehru got his separate declaration 'on the danger of war and an appeal for peace'.[15] But to it was added an idea suggested by President Nasser. He had said in his public speech that 'a mere appeal' was not enough, and that the conference should evolve 'a plan which can drive the negotiations between the two blocs into the domain of practical application'. This suggestion took shape in the form of letters addressed to Mr. Khrushchev and President Kennedy, to be delivered to them by two groups of emissaries. Mr. Nehru did not care for this idea, which seemed to him too dramatic, and though he went to Moscow from Belgrade he strenuously denied to the end that he was going there as a messenger from the conference. The heads of delegations finished their real work on the night of the 4th September; they listened to more speeches on the last day of the conference—a day that was to end in a marathon all-night drafting session.

While the leaders were putting the finishing touches to the appeal for peace, the drafting committee had been meeting separately, to pursue the task of drawing up the communiqué covering all the less important items on the agenda. Its second session on the night of the 4th September lasted from 10 p.m. to 5 a.m. on the following day, and produced no agreement.

The committee had before it, as working papers, drafts proposed by Ghana and Yugoslavia—the latter of thirty-four pages—in which the conference expressed its opinion on all the issues referred to by speakers in the plenary session. This provoked a difference of opinion (to which Mr. Nehru had referred in the course of the conference), between those who wanted a brief generally-worded communiqué and those who wanted specific references and proposals on all issues. As before, and as at Cairo, India and the Asians were in the first group and Indonesia and the West Africans in the second; the latter demanded their *quid pro quo* for prior agreement to India's principal demand on the special declaration. If all the colonial issues were to be referred to, the wording to be used gave rise to differences between the moderate Asians and the angry Africans. The question of fixing a time limit for the ending of colonialism had come up in many speeches; accordingly the Africans wanted a date to be incorporated in the communiqué. This point touched off a lively exchange: India did not want any precise date to be fixed on the grounds that this would be unreal and demagogic. Mr. Krishna Menon, who represented India on the committee, got round this difficulty by suggesting a return to the wording of the United Nations resolution on the ending of colonialism. That had suggested a 'speedy' ending, but he went one better by suggesting 'immediate'. In contrast to the similar occasion at Bandung, the other delegations knew this time that they had been out-smarted but, as at Bandung, they did not grasp how this had come about; for they could hardly resist Mr. Krishna Menon's mock-serious reproach that they were 'losing their sense of urgency'. This was almost the only point of substance on which the committee reached agreement.

As might have been expected, the plethora of proposals on Berlin and Germany precluded agreement on anything substantial. Israel could likewise have been expected to be a disturbing element at Belgrade, as she had been at all previous Afro-Asian conferences; this she was. The two Socialist countries, Burma and Yugoslavia, were opposed to the strong Arab condemnation of their Socialist friend, Israel, and for the first time India, or at least Mr. Krishna Menon, supported the soft line on this issue. (On the previous night, Mr. Nehru had reiterated to Indian correspondents that India would continue to refrain from establishing diplomatic relations with Israel.) Menon's attitude greatly angered the Arabs; India also succeeded in antagonising the Indonesians, the Yugoslavs and the West Africans. Even disarmament, surprisingly, provoked differences between the majority, who felt that definite proposals from the non-aligned could help to break the deadlock that had paralysed the negotiations at Geneva, and the minority—including India—who believed that disarmament should be left to those who had arms.

Much of the friction in these debates was due to Mr. Krishna Menon personally; he was at his most acerbic throughout the conference. He thought that India should not have been present at Belgrade; he himself did not want to be there (and he made no great secret of either of these opinions); he was a sick man at the time. Sitting behind Mr. Nehru, he slept conspicuously through most of the speeches in the open plenary sessions more, perhaps, because of the latter than the former handicap; but his manners did not sweeten the feelings of other delegations towards him, or towards India. In the all-night session of the 4th September, his tactic of picking holes in the syntax and grammar of the English used by the other delegates angered even one of his old admirers, Dr. Subandrio, the Foreign Minister of Indonesia, who had worked for him in the India Institute in London twenty years earlier.

For one or other of these reasons, the drafting committee, when it broke up on the dawning of the last day of the conference, the 5th September, was stalemated on every important issue that it should have dealt with—whether the conference communiqué should be long and detailed or brief and general; whether it should refer to all or only to some colonial questions and if so which; the language to be used in making these references; disarmament; Germany; Palestine.

On the last day of the conference the Indian journalists, mingling with the 600 others in the Press Centre got the true measure of India's isolation from most of Afro-Asia. It was manifest in the stories put about by the quasi-official pressmen of Indonesia, Yugoslavia and Egypt. India, one heard, was trying to sabotage the conference; she was threatening to walk out; and Mr. Nehru no longer understood non-alignment. The official Indonesian news-agency reported that there were differences between President Sukarno and the Indian Premier, and the official Yugoslav news-agency reported this back from Jakarta in a bulletin distributed, gratis, to every journalist in Belgrade. Here was the shape of things to come a year later.

The morning session of the plenary meeting on the 5th was marked by the recognition, publicly announced, of the Provisional Algerian Government by Cambodia, Ghana and Yugoslavia (this last was the first European country to do so). It was also the occasion of speeches from two late arrivals, Messrs. Adoula and Gizenga, both representing a united Congo. (Soon after, Mr. Adoula imprisoned Mr. Gizenga.)

The Belgrade Conference, September 1961

This was all very well, but since some of the leaders were determined to leave Belgrade on the 6th—Mr. Nehru's arrival in Moscow on that day had been fixed three months earlier—they must have sat through these euphoric proceedings with some impatience.

It can be said, without fear of contradiction, that never before have so many heads of state and governments devoted themselves with such single-minded devotion to high affairs of policy as did the leaders at Belgrade, from 5 p.m. on the 5th September, to 1.15 a.m. on the 6th, without any break for rest or refreshment. The occasion was a fine example of the impact of physiology on politics.

The results of their deliberations were published in the final communiqué. This constituted a victory for India and the Asians on every important issue, and it was secured through a simple tactic. The Indian elephant simply sat down and was discovered to be a singularly immovable object. Perhaps some of those present recalled the statistical statement, made earlier by Haile Selassie, that India's population was larger than that of all the other countries put together.

On the issue of Palestine, President Nasser was of great help to Mr. Nehru, who had been committed by Mr. Krishna Menon to supporting the mild Burmese–Yugoslav draft. The Egyptian President personally intervened with the Arab delegations to persuade them to accept stronger wording, but nevertheless weaker than the paragraph in the Bandung resolution. Since President Nasser had described even that satisfactory formula as 'just a resolution', so just another resolution was not of great concern to that Egyptian realist, whatever it may have been to the more excitable Arabs.

In its clumsily-worded way, the Belgrade communiqué is an interesting document. It is not at all the long post-mortem-cum-diagnosis-cum-prognosis that Yugoslavia and Ghana wanted; it is not much longer than the Bandung communiqué. It is less parochial than that more famous document, for the preamble and the first two sections are concerned with general world issues. In a last crusade on behalf of co-existence, it asserts that this is 'the only alternative to the Cold War' and 'must be the only basis of all international relations'. In view of what was happening between the two biggest Asian countries, India and China, this was whistling to keep co-existent courage up. A notorious formula reappeared in an omnibus condemnation of 'colonialism-imperialism and neo-colonialism in all their manifestations'.

The conference was constrained by the Asian group to say that it was 'not making concrete proposals for the solution of all international disputes', and surprised many with the flat statement that the non-aligned 'do not wish to form a new bloc and cannot be a bloc'. Supporting Yugoslavia and Russia in one of their doctrinal disputes with China, the conference rejected the view that war is inevitable.

Only three colonial issues were mentioned—Algeria, Angola and Bizerta. Despite African protests, all other colonial topics were lumped together in a call for the 'immediate termination' of colonialism. Notably, this meant that President Sukarno did not get any overt support on West Irian, though Cuba managed to insert a reference to the United States base at Guantanamo.

On disarmament, the non-aligned countries conceded the principle of inspection, and then asked to be represented at future discussions —a request which was contrary to Indian ideas.

On Germany, the most important immediate problem of the day, the conference in effect said nothing. Proponents of contrary views fought each other to a standstill and, finally, cancelled each other out. All they could agree on, after a long discussion, was an appeal for a peaceful solution.

The communiqué is interesting for its omissions. In what it said there is little new, because the non-aligned had already expressed similar ideas at the United Nations and elsewhere. It is clearer and less ambiguous, but also less interesting, than the Bandung Declaration; it avoids the obliquities and self-contradictions of that document.

As for a permanent or continuing organisation, there was at Belgrade no reference to it anywhere, either in the speeches or in the communiqué. That particular Afro-Asia idea had been finally buried.

When the weary delegates left the conference at 3 a.m., the only further action it had agreed on (as some sort of private understanding rather than a conference decision), was that the letters to President Kennedy and Mr. Khruschchev should be delivered personally in Washington and Moscow by two teams of leaders from the conference, each consisting of an Asian and an African. The team sent to Washington, Presidents Sukarno and Keita (of Mali), were a well-matched tandem, but a poor choice, because their strongly pro-Eastern policies secured them a politely frigid reception in America.

The mission to Moscow was a comedy. It was supposed to consist of President Nkrumah and Mr. Nehru. But the Indian Premier steadily refused any such task. He was, in any case, going to Moscow in the course of a previously arranged tour and if President Nkrumah was also travelling there, that was Nkrumah's concern. This concept of high-powered missions was in truth ill-conceived: the emissaries were not expected to report the results back to anyone, and hence were merely glorified messenger-boys—a role that Mr. Nehru refused to accept. (It will be remembered that at Colombo in 1954, U Nu had had much the same idea of sending an emissary, uninvited, to the Geneva Conference.)

The Ghanaian President took off for Moscow some time before Mr. Nehru but, using a slower plane, arrived there just before the Indian party. In the meantime the airport and streets of Moscow had been decorated with Indian flags and with portraits of Mr. Nehru and crowds had begun to gather to greet him. Since it would have been awkward to receive President Nkrumah with a show of Indian flags, these were hurriedly removed, and Mr. Nehru's portraits were turned face to the wall. Seeing this the crowds, which did not know the real reason, suspected that it denoted some sudden drastic change in Indo-Soviet relations, and began to melt away. There was no time to replace the Indian flags and the portraits and to reassemble the crowds before Mr. Nehru followed President Nkrumah into Moscow.

The following morning Mr. Nehru began his talks with Mr. Khrushchev and naturally referred to the Belgrade deliberations. The Russian leader then asked if President Nkrumah could join them, to which Mr. Nehru could scarcely object. This is how they delivered the good news to the Kremlin.

The reactions of America and Russia after the conference were almost the exact opposite of their attitude before it. The West was bitter, even enraged, that the Afro-Asian non-aligned areas had failed to denounce the Russian resumption of nuclear testing. For those two reasons—the absence of non-aligned condemnation and Western anger at it—Russian reporting on the conference, though mendacious, was approving in tone. Indeed, the meeting was presented to the Russians as an endorsement of their government's policy. Thus Belgrade delayed, though only for a time, the process by which the non-aligned countries in general came to be regarded with equal friendliness, or hostility, by both sides in the Cold War.

Yugoslav relations with America never quite recovered from President Tito's speech, and he was soon angrily accusing America of withholding wheat from his drought-stricken country to punish it for his remarks at the conference on Germany and the Russian atomic test.

Belgrade was singularly unproductive of concrete results. Its appeal to the Big Two fell flat, and they have not met since. But it met at a time of crisis when it was right and necessary to make declarations about peace and negotiation; the conference redeemed most of its self-respect by making them, even if pushed into doing so. It also served to introduce the new African leaders to the Asian leaders. In addition, by making it clear that Afro-Asia opposed the 'troika' proposal for the United Nations, it may have helped towards gaining Russian approval for the appointment of U Thant, who was in the Burmese delegation at Belgrade.

One issue of long-term significance was debated at Belgrade without a word being said directly on the subject; this was the future of relations between independent Africa and independent Asia. At Belgrade these relations were not happy, most policy differences being on continental lines. The Asians found the Africans jejune and over-emotional, and the Africans found the Asians hide-bound and patronising. This incompatability derived from a difference in political maturity. The Asian states have nearly ten more years of independence behind them than do the new African states, and each year of independent responsibility should probably count as two. The human parallel is pertinent here: the gap between 5- and 15-year-olds is enormous, that between 25 and 35 is bridgeable; that between the 55's and 65's is non-existent. In time this difference in emotional approach between Asia and Africa should lessen, but at Belgrade it was marked, and still is so. And the focus of this difference at the conference was the difficult position in which Mr. Nehru and India found themselves.

At Belgrade, India burst out of the Afro-Asian chrysalis, to which there could be no return, however hard Mr. Nehru might try. Apart from the question of political maturity, India is separated from the other Afro-Asians by its sheer size. An official Yugoslav publication said that Belgrade 'will be a conference of small and medium-sized countries'; the sole exception to that statement was India. This difference of itself produces inescapable policy differences: a leader responsible for 400 million people cannot have the same approach to problems as a leader of seven million, as is President Nkrumah. Another cause of difference was India's absorption, to an almost unique degree in Afro-Asia, in the unexciting task of planning and internal development. For these reasons, and not least for his personal qualities, Mr. Nehru got his way at Belgrade, grasped the essentials, and made many other leaders look small. Reduction to scale is difficult to forgive, the more so when it is done without deliberate intent.

Mr. Nehru would have been better advised to follow his instincts, and to have stayed away from Belgrade. But he on one side, and

Presidents Tito and Nasser on the other, were caught in the toils of their non-alignment. He rightly said that non-alignment had spread because the peoples of Afro-Asian countries wanted it. An idea for which the time has come will irresistibly make its way in the world. Since non-alignment is based on this fundamental force it does not need to be decked out in fair words of love and friendship; often enough, these are not there. India was not forced, but was embarrassed, into going to Belgrade.

Belgrade would have been useful to India if she had taken note of the way in which the Afro-Asians reacted, or rather failed to react, to the Russian atom test; of how a brutal display of strength produced a revision of values, even of the most obvious humanitarian ones. India should have been warned. But she was not.

NOTES TO CHAPTER XIII

All references, unless otherwise specified, are to the volume *The Conference of Heads of State or Government of Non-Aligned Countries* produced by the Yugoslav Government; this contains the full text of all speeches made and of the final declaration and communiqué, as well as other useful data on the conference.

1. Yugoslav Government: *The Conference of Heads of State or Government of Non-Aligned Countries*, pp. 113–14.
2. *Op. cit.*, p. 47.
3. *Op. cit.*, p. 202.
4. *Op. cit.*, p. 113.
5. *Op. cit.*, pp. 99, 212.
6. *Op. cit.*, pp. 227.
7. *Op. cit.*, p. 80.
8. *Op. cit.*, pp. 34, 35, 36.
9. *Op. cit.*, pp. 47, 95, 192.
10. *Op. cit.*, p. 38.
11. *Op. cit.*, p. 89.
12. *Op. cit.*, pp. 90, 107, 185
13. *Op. cit.*, pp. 31, 104, 208, 224.
14. *Op. cit.*, pp. 111–12.
15. *Op. cit.*, see Appendix A.5.

CHAPTER XIV

Non-Alignment in the Market-Place: The Cairo Economic Conference, July 1962

The romantic belief that the peoples of the Orient are particularly spiritual and other-worldly would seem to be given substance by the length of time it took the Afro-Asian non-aligned peoples to awaken to the very real economic problems they had in common. Strong external pressure was needed to break through over fifteeen years of indifference to these vital issues.

Perhaps this was so because most of the nationalist leaders came from bourgeois backgrounds to whom 'the starving millions' was a valid but lifeless abstraction, and who thought of 'exploitation' mainly in political terms. Perhaps the passage of time was necessary for these leaders to feel the pressure of 'the revolution of rising expectations' among their own peoples. Whatever the reason for this neglect, even in the Marxian intellectual atmosphere of the Afro-Asian Solidarity Movement it was admitted, by the Secretary-General in 1959, that overmuch attention had been devoted to political matters and not enough to economic problems.[1]

At the Asian Relations Conference in 1947, the distinguished economists present were content merely to describe the formidable economic problems facing the newly-independent countries and to list the difficulties in the way of their solution. At that early stage, awe and modesty were understandable. But even seven years later the five prime ministers, meeting at Colombo, spared little time from political matters to consider 'certain proposals relating to economic co-operation and mutual aid' and merely referred these back to their governments.[2] An Indonesian suggestion that an Afro-Asian conference on economic questions should be held was not even accorded mention in the final communiqué.

A year later, at Bandung, economic realities were given some of their proper importance. One of the three committees of the conference dealt exclusively with economic questions and its findings, as embodied in the communiqué, mention the desirability of increasing trade within the Afro-Asian area, and the thorny problem of stabilising the prices of, and demand for, primary products. The fact that the artificial inflation of the prices of such products caused by the Korean War was beginning to fade may account for this greater degree of realism. Yet none of the leaders of delegations attended any of the meetings of the Economic Committee; this was the preserve of officials and experts; these last reached an agreed resolution in record time, and the heads of delegations approved it without question. The only issue that occasioned any debate in the committee was the suggestion that there might be a continuing technical organisation for economic co-operation. This was accepted, and the communiqué states firmly that the countries present at Bandung were not in favour of a regional economic bloc; they merely approved the appointment of liaison officers for economic questions in the various countries; nowhere was this suggestion followed up.

The years of the waning of the Bandung Myth—1958 and 1959—were also years of growing realisation by the Afro-Asian non-aligned peoples that they could no longer postpone tackling their numerous and urgent, even desperate, economic problems.

The salient fact of the world economic situation was that the poor countries were getting poorer and the rich richer. Within this grim prognosis was the dawning realisation of general propositions such as that the 112 countries listed by the United Nations as underdeveloped held 72 per cent of the world's population with 15 per cent of the world's production; and that while the estimated average per capita income in these underdeveloped countries was about $90 in 1950, it had only risen to about $100 in 1959—an annual rate of increase, in money terms, of 1 per cent: even if this were doubled to 2 per cent per annum, the underdeveloped areas would still take 150 years to catch up with the current level of income in the United States.

The complete disappearance of the Korean War boom had brought home to the Afro-Asians, aligned and non-aligned alike, the extreme vulnerability of their economic position as producers of primary commodities. It is agreed on all hands that the losses suffered by them because of the drop in prices of their primary products exceed the total public and private capital imports of the underdeveloped countries: in the 1950's, it is estimated, the price of raw materials fell by 20 per cent, while the price of industrial products rose by 6 per cent. In direct monetary terms this loss to the underdeveloped countries has been estimated at $1,600 million annually: the 'price scissors' were progressively opening wider and the fear was that, having opened to their widest, they would one day snap shut.

In addition, about 80 per cent of all the goods exported by some half of the underdeveloped countries were concentrated in about five products: the economic vulnerability of the Afro-Asians is truly frightening.[3]

By the early 1960's it had become apparent that the underdeveloped countries had failed in their attempt to reduce their dependence on all developed areas by increasing their trade with one another. Despite all their efforts, 75 per cent to 80 per cent of their total exports and imports were to and from the developed countries.

The final turn of the economic screw came in 1957 and 1958 when the developed countries of Europe, Eastern and Western, began organising themselves into closed markets—the Council for Mutual Economic Assistance (COMECON) and the European Common Market (ECM). With little more to sell, even at lower prices, underdeveloped producers now found their principal and traditional customers pulling down the iron shutters of their shops.

The various ways in which the tightening ECM system threatened the trade of the underdeveloped countries were all too obvious: tariff discrimination, quantitative restrictions on the import of certain commodities, and additional internal discriminatory fiscal measures such as the imposition of luxury taxes. It has been estimated that during the first three years of West European integration the share of the non-aligned countries in the Common Market dropped from 38 per cent in 1957 to 35·5 per cent in 1960. This decline caused the underdeveloped countries a dollar loss of $1·26 billion in export earnings per annum—that is, double the amount of bi-lateral financial aid allocated by the ECM countries to the underdeveloped ones. Here is yet another example of publicised giving failing to offset unpublicised taking.

At first glance, the economic policies of the Communist countries of COMECON seem to impinge less adversely on the underdeveloped countries than those of the ECM group. For one thing, after Bandung, the Eastern bloc became the new and generous donor (or promiser) of aid, at least to a selected number of Afro-Asians. For another, there was a rapid increase in the volume of exports from Afro-Asia to the Communist states. But these encouraging trends did not affect the basic Communist plan to achieve self-sufficiency in those products—rice, cotton, rubber, tea—that they principally imported from Afro-Asia. Moreover, in world terms the quantities they imported were not large; further, these imports were mainly primary products. Lastly, the volume of trade with the Eastern bloc was singularly erratic; in 1959 Soviet trade with the non-aligned countries dropped by 11·8 per cent to rise again by 18·5 per cent in 1960.[4]

With this increase of crushing external pressures on the economies of the Afro-Asian countries had come increased awareness within these countries of their economic needs and of the means to meet them.

Even from the vague discussions of economic questions at the Asian Relations Conference, in 1947, it was clear that planning and socialism would become the normal, accepted pattern for the economic life of the new Afro-Asian countries. This came about; by 1960 the levers of economic control were firmly in the hands of the government in several such states, from India to the United Arab Republic to Ghana.

By the early 1960's, most Afro-Asian governments had realised the weakness of the economies that they now controlled; they were aware of the increasing external pressures on them, and they knew what had to be done to achieve a degree of economic independence that would match their political freedom. They also knew that they had to act in concert. But what could they do to achieve their goals? To find the answer to this question was the objective of the conference on the problems of economic development held in Cairo in 1962.

This meeting was largely the result of Yugoslav initiative and it is to the credit of the Yugoslavs that, over a period of time, they brought home to their new non-aligned Afro-Asian friends the growing importance and urgency of their own similar economic problems. Their Communist background predisposed the Yugoslavs to analysis based on the economic approach. They were certainly among the first, if not the very first, to propound the theory that the really important, the really dangerous, division in the world was not the east-west line dividing the Communists from the anti-Communists, but rather the north-south line between the mass of coloured have-nots and the minority of non-coloured haves.[5]

Unlike the former French colonies in Africa, or the Commonwealth countries, whose case was pleaded with ECM by France and Britain, Yugoslavia had no friend-at-court at Brussels to speak for her. In this respect she was in the same boat as, for instance, Egypt. It was natural, therefore, for Yugoslavia and the United Arab Republic to adopt a similar attitude towards the Common Market and towards the need for economic precautions, or counter-measures, to be taken by the non-aligned have-nots.

The Cairo Economic Conference, July 1962

The first real chance that the Yugoslavs had of publicising their point of view on the economic problems of the non-aligned came at the Belgrade Conference. President Tito devoted a substantial section of his speech to a reasoned and effective statement of Yugoslav opposition to the new exclusive economic groupings, such as ECM and COMECON, which he mentioned by name. He called for economic co-operation among all the less developed countries, not only the non-aligned, but said that this must not lead to yet another regional grouping or 'a new closed market'. He suggested the calling of 'a world conference' on 'all the most important economic questions', which might be convened by the United Nations. This, as is well known, has since come about.

The Yugoslavs were successful in obtaining a specific reference to their pet project in paragraphs 21 and 22 of the final communiqué. In these sections reference was made to the adverse effects of 'excessive fluctuations in primary commodity trade' and of 'restrictive measures and practices'; nothing more specific was said, but all countries concerned were invited to consider the convening of an international conference 'as soon as possible'.[6]

In retrospect, these two paragraphs on economic questions may well prove to be the real, long-term achievement of the Belgrade Conference: they may be remembered as the starting point of other useful conferences long after the short-term excitement over political declarations on world peace have been forgotten.

Yet it was the political consequence of President Tito's speech at Belgrade that spurred Yugoslavia into pressing for a non-aligned economic conference. The United States, as has been noted, was much displeased at President Tito's complaisant reference to the Russian resumption of atomic tests. Tito, for his part, believed that, as a punishment, America withheld wheat supplies from his drought-stricken country. (In a speech of November 1962 he directly linked this alleged economic reprisal against Yugoslavia with a renewed request for an economic conference.)

It was a sense of urgency springing from the needs of his own country that impelled him to force himself on the meeting between President Nasser and Mr. Nehru that took place in Cairo in November 1962. Mr. Nehru, who was on his way back from a cordial meeting with President Kennedy, was unwilling to believe that America was deliberately trying to starve Yugoslavia. Partly because of this disbelief, but more because of his consistent doubt of the usefulness of large conferences, Mr. Nehru was not impressed with the need for an economic conference, though the two presidents more than once returned to the charge. The Indian Premier felt that the non-aligned countries could give each other little support economically because their principal markets, both for sale and purchase, were (and are) outside their area. All that emerged from this Cairo meeting was his vague proposal that the subject of non-aligned economic co-operation should be referred to the experts who had been sent to watch the current discussions within the Common Market at Brussels.

Again, and for the second time, Presidents Tito and Nasser decided to go ahead with the project of a non-aligned conference despite the reluctance of the remaining non-aligned triumvir. In the first week of February 1962, Finance Minister Kaissouni made the formal announcement that Egypt and Yugoslavia had decided to call a conference of the developing countries to be held in Cairo later that year. For ten weeks New Delhi remained indifferent, and even opposed to the idea, and only agreed to it, rather suddenly, on the 22nd April. It would not be unduly cynical to see in this sudden shift of position a reflection of India's anxiety about a forthcoming debate on Kashmir in the Security Council, of which the United Arab Republic was then a member: the *quid pro quo* is a recognised element in the conduct of foreign affairs.

India, having resisted the idea of holding this conference for as long as she could, began the familiar process of taking it over; this she did quite successfully. The Cairo Economic Conference was largely cast in the moderate Indian mould.

Its general form was decided by Yugoslavia, the United Arab Republic and India, which presented several memoranda explaining their views of what the conference should try to do.[7] Later, the ambassadors of the three countries were joined by the representatives of eight others that expressed the wish to become co-sponsors.[8] This preparatory committee of eleven did not agree to the Indian suggestion, made with a view to minimising the significance of the conference, that it should take place at the level of experts: instead it accepted the United Arab Republic's proposal that the meeting should be at the level of ministers of finance or economy.

Since the type of membership would pre-determine the type of resolutions to be passed, the number and type of countries to be invited was all-important. India, as at Belgrade, wanted a large, inclusive membership; Egypt still favoured exclusivity to the point of wanting only the eleven original sponsoring countries to attend; but Yugoslavia was now in favour of an inclusive group of all the developing countries. Her view tipped the scales in favour of a large membership.

India had wanted some forty-five countries to be invited to Belgrade, and according to the official record, it was to forty-nine countries that invitations were sent for the Cairo meeting. In fact, feelers were probably put out to two or three others, even though invitations were not sent to them. All of the twenty-five non-aligned countries present at Belgrade were invited to Cairo and all attended except Iraq and Nepal. To these were added twenty-three newcomers to the invitation list. Of these nine may be listed as non-aligned—Sweden, Finland, Austria, Switzerland, Ireland, Kuwait, Nigeria, Togo and Tanganyika; the rest were aligned—Japan, Argentina, Uruguay, Bolivia and Ecuador. It seems that Australia and New Zealand were sounded out; there were no great objections from anyone to their inclusion.

Obviously all the sponsors had finally accepted the idea that economic needs cut across political dividing lines, and that countries that were committed politically need not necessarily be as completely committed economically.

The invitation list reveals that the objective was a three-continent, perhaps even a four-continent conference, but the acceptances did not fulfil this grand design. Apart from Yugoslavia, no country from Europe attended; nor did the Australasians. Latin America was more adequately represented; Bolivia and Brazil were full members, instead of observers as at Belgrade, and Chile, Uruguay and Venezuela joined Ecuador as observers. Possibly this larger attendance was due to the fact that, this time, the Latin Americans were consulted as to whether or not Cuba should be invited (which she was), instead of the other way about, as before Belgrade.

Once again the principal absentee was Africa; of the four new African states proposed, only one attended. The massive Monrovia–Brazzaville group was conspicuously absent, because its members were, economically, so strongly integrated with Western Europe as to make nonsense of an invitation.

The only real newcomers present at Cairo were Malaya, Kuwait, Libya, Mexico, Pakistan and Tanganyika, giving an attendance of thirty-one in all, compared with twenty-five at Belgrade. The attempt to produce an impressive line-up of developing countries of all varieties had not wholly succeeded, but at least the attempt had been made. This Cairo Economic Conference was, as the Belgrade Conference had been, basically an Afro-Asian gathering: only the three

Latin Americans and Yugoslavia came from outside the area. It was also, basically, a gathering of the non-aligned countries, the aligned being represented by seven countries—Bolivia, Brazil, Mexico, Cuba, Malaya, Libya and Pakistan.

This non-exclusive membership, in fact, determined the outcome of the conference. Obviously the main issue before the meeting, the one that attracted the most publicity, was the attitude it would adopt towards the trade blocs of ECM and COMECON; this was expected to be critical. The three main sponsors differed on this question. Yugoslavia would have liked to reiterate the disapproval expressed by President Tito at Belgrade, with mention of the blocs by name, and would have welcomed even more strongly-worded condemnation, especially of ECM; though it favoured the setting up of a permanent organisation, it was not in favour of forming a counter-bloc. The United Arab Republic was also opposed to ECM, but was more enthusiastic for the establishment of a permanent organisation as a first step towards a counter-bloc. India was not in favour of any specific or strongly-worded condemnation, nor did she support the proposal for a permanent organisation.

Despite the decision that the conference was to entail representation at ministerial level, only nine of the thirty-one participants were sufficiently interested or impressed to send ministers to Cairo. (Though she had been so reluctant at the outset, India was one of them.) Fourteen countries were represented by ambassadors or chargés d'affaires, mostly those posted to Cairo who were bound to humour their host country. Thus, despite the increased awareness among the Afro-Asians of the importance of economic questions, their discussion, as seven years earlier at Bandung, failed to attract the presence of the leaders with real power.

In that they dealt with the same group of set economic themes the speeches in plenary session[9] were, inescapably, repetitious.

As well as numerous references to the deleterious effect of the drop in prices of primary products, preference was expressed for the granting of aid through the United Nations, and there were numerous references to its 'Decade of Development' idea; also to resolutions that requested countries to set aside 1 per cent of their national income, or savings from disarmament, for international development.

The dire need for population control hardly received the attention it deserved. The speech of the United Arab Republic representative gave it prominence and the Pakistan delegate, with languid cynicism, draped it in airy phrases: 'Sex is the only poetry known to the poor;

he procreates when he is happy, he procreates when he is un-happy, and he procreates when he is indifferent.'

Perhaps the most encouraging theme stressed was that while the developing countries admitted their need for aid from the developed countries, they must pay their way.

Attention was concentrated on what was said about international trade groupings, for the general expectation was that the conference would launch a sharp attack on the European Common Market, be-cause of the known attitudes of such leading sponsors as Yugoslavia and Egypt. These fears proved largely unfounded. The Yugoslav delegate criticised ECM at some length, but the Egyptian spokesman was cautious and referred to 'trade blocs and common markets' only in brief and general terms.

As might have been expected, the strongest attacks on ECM came from Cuba, and also from Ghana and Indonesia. Commonwealth countries such as India, Pakistan and Tanganyika also expressed con-cern, especially because of Britain's anticipated entry into that group. All these speeches were, in backhand fashion, a tribute to the eco-nomic power generated by ECM.

The European Common Market found one outspoken defender in the Brazilian delegate who said, frankly, that his country was 'tied economically' to some of the ECM members; it received some im-plied support from the Pakistan spokesman who said that he 'sus-pected' the phrase 'poverty anywhere is a danger to prosperity every-where'.

The Western trade group fared badly only by contrast with the lack of specific critical reference to COMECON, which was never once mentioned by name; its existence was acknowledged only in oblique references to 'two economic blocs' or to 'certain economic group-ings'. This silence is attributable either to the leftist bias of the non-aligned countries, or to the comparative weakness of the Communist economic bloc, or to both.

Despite the sheer verbal bulk of thirty-one speeches and the techni-cal details listed in the agenda, only one practical proposal was put forward as to how the developed countries could help the developing ones to pay their way. This was the suggestion, made in similar terms by India and the United Arab Republic, that the advanced countries should turn to 'the more complicated manufacture of capital goods', 'which need substantial investment and scarce technical experience' leaving to the developing countries 'primary and secondary indus-tries producing consumer goods'.

The only other positive suggestion of great future significance was the urgent demand by several delegations that the proposed United Nations Conference on International Trade should be held as soon as possible. The final communiqué called for 'an early date in 1963', but that conference was not convened until early in 1964.

Perhaps as proof of their 'maturity', none of the Afro-Asians reckoned that they could protect themselves by forming a third economic bloc: even the activitists—Ghana, Guinea, the United Arab Republic and Yugoslavia—rejected the idea in so many words.

These countries were, however, much more vocal on this, and other ideas, in the drafting committee and in its sub-committee, where the discussions were at times really vigorous. However, the Cubans were told that a resolution declaring that compensation need not be paid for nationalised assets would not be acceptable; and the African activists were able to obtain only an oblique warning to the African associates of ECM.

The formulation of the conference's views on ECM naturally produced controversy. Ghana led the attack, supported by Guinea, Mali and Algeria, but achieved only limited success. These African countries were particularly insistent that the association of other African territories with the Common Market should be condemned. Most delegations were, however, of the opinion that sovereign governments should not be criticised by a conference at which they were not present because they had not been invited.

In the lengthy final communiqué the proposal for a permanent organisation was fragmented into six 'recommendations for further co-operation': in order 'to keep continuously in touch with each other' the participants 'agreed to call meetings, seminars, expert groups and conferences'—everything short of a permanent organisation.[10]

The conference expressed its 'apprehension' of the adverse effects of groupings of industrialised countries, 'if conceived and operated in a restrictive or discriminatory manner'. It was resolved 'that action should be taken to minimise' their consequences and the industrialised countries were asked to show understanding. The five paragraphs of this section do not mention either ECM or COMECON by name.

The population explosion, the root cause of most of the economic problems of the developing countries, received surprisingly casual attention—no more than a reference to the need for 'appropriate legitimate measures'.[11]

The Cairo Economic Conference, July 1962

On non-controversial issues the communiqué made the expected pleas for the stabilisation of primary commodity markets and for increases in inter-regional trade, and of international aid. It stated that 'the establishment of an international compensatory financing system' was a matter of 'great urgency', and this subject was subsequently raised at the Geneva Conference.

The Cairo Declaration is a solid, serious document, a statement in unexciting terms of the approach of the have-not countries to the problems they face as part of the world's economic structure; with some indication, modestly worded, of what they thought should be done to help them and what they could do to help themselves.

Does this mean that the conference was a polite failure? No: because it showed that, as a group, the Afro-Asians were now well-informed on the economic questions affecting them. And the Afro-Asian governments were reasonable in their approach because they recognised that, in economic matters, the irresponsible and heroic ardours of politics not only count for nothing but are a positive hindrance.

The moderation shown by the Cairo Conference actually enhanced its long-term impact. Its recommendations maintained the pressure for the United Nations Conference on World Trade, of which, after their meeting in Cairo, the Afro-Asians became the chief proponents. The have-not countries played a decisive, even a dominant role at this conference at Geneva, and their solidarity and the effectiveness of their attack can be attributed in large measure to the unanimity they reached, not without difficulty, at the earlier meeting. In a way, Cairo was for the Afro-Asians a preliminary briefing session for Geneva.

At Geneva, 'the Seventy-Seven' underdeveloped countries of Asia, Africa and Latin America emerged as a potent new factor in world economics; but for the solidly reasonable agreements reached by the thirty-one countries present at Cairo this later momentous development might not have come about. At Bandung the Afro-Asians, and at Belgrade the non-aligned, saw just how numerous they were and thereby gained confidence; the Cairo Conference did the same for the have-nots.

A second question that may be asked is whether the conference was really a manifestation of non-alignment in the market-place. Speeches made a few references to non-alignment and not many to Bandung. Was it then merely a grouping of the have-not countries with non-alignment impinging only indirectly on their discussions of economics? The absence of the non-aligned European countries would seem to favour this interpretation: they were not present, perhaps because of pressure, but more probably because they belong to the group of the haves; and the presence of such aligned countries as Pakistan and the South Americans was obviously due to the fact that they are among the have-nots.

It is true that the large majority of the countries present at Cairo were officially listed as non-aligned, and this conference was an essential expression of non-alignment in its economic aspect. The non-aligned reject both the CENTO–SEATO grouping and the Warsaw Pact; at Cairo they sought to free themselves from the more harmful and far-reaching effects of ECM and COMECON. They wished to achieve freedom of action, which is the essence of non-alignment, in the economic field, in an open market-place, as they had earlier done in the realm of politics. And within the narrow limits permitted to them by the operation of the iron laws of economics, that is what they began trying to do at the Cairo Conference, and carried further at Geneva.

The Cairo meeting was significant on two other counts. It drew more Latin American governments into co-operation with the Afro-Asians than did any previous conference. And it was the last occasion for some time on which an assured and self-confident India, despite original misgivings, took over and shaped a conference in its own image: for just three months after Cairo the Chinese attacked south across the Himalayas.

NOTES TO CHAPTER XIV

1. In his report contained in the volume on 'The Second Afro-Asian Peoples Solidarity Conference', Cairo, 1959.
2. Appendix A.2.
3. A vast body of statistical material is available on the economic problems of the underdeveloped countries, much of it in the form of reports of various United Nations bodies and conferences. One good general survey of part of the field is S. Dell's *Trade Blocs and Common Markets*, London, 1963. The Yugoslav point of view is given in J. Stanovnik: *World Economic Blocs*, Belgrade, 1962. See also B. Ward: *The Rich Nations and the Poor Nations*, London, 1962.
4. D. Jerkovic: *On the Eve of the Cairo Consultation*, Yugoslav Information Service, Belgrade, 1962.
5. The official volume on 'The Belgrade Conference', pp. 259–60.
6. The official volume on 'The Conference on the Problems of Economic Development', Government Printing Offices, Cairo, 1962, p. 5.
7. These eight were: Ceylon, Ethiopia, Ghana, Guinea, Indonesia, Libya, Mali and the Sudan.

8. These are given in the official volume which is a poorly-edited work; at times the language used, allegedly, by speakers is so ungrammatical as to be unintelligible. One assumes that this is due to incorrect translation.
9. *Op. cit.*, paragraphs 64–9, pp. 364–5.
10. *Op. cit.*, paragraph 37, p. 359.
11. *Op. cit.*, paragraph 13, p. 354.

CHAPTER XV

Afro-Asia Fails the Test: the India–China Dispute

For a certain type of Afro-Asian leader the itch to meet at conferences is a chronic affliction. When leaders do meet they squabble; but no sooner have they stopped meeting than these confirmed conferenciers want to meet again. These are the flamboyants. They are great orators, experienced world-travellers and dashing riders of hobby horses. Among them can be counted Presidents Sukarno and Nkrumah and Tito. Juxtaposed to them are leaders like U Nu, and President Nasser and Premiers Nehru and Tafawa Balewa. The pushing and pulling between them on whether or not there should be a Second Bandung and, later, a Second Belgrade was one of the main forms of Afro-Asian activity in the twelve months after the Belgrade Conference. President Tito was a fairly recent recruit to the group and what he wanted was not so much a continuation of, as a counter to, Belgrade.

On his return from a visit to President Kennedy in November 1961, Mr. Nehru broke his journey for a day in Cairo; he intended this stop to be a gesture of support for President Nasser after the secession of Syria from the United Arab Republic, which had taken place in the preceding month. President Tito asked if he could join their talks and Mr. Nehru, repeating what he had said about President Nkrumah at Moscow, replied that that was for Tito to decide. This casual meeting was then represented by the Yugoslavs as 'a neutralist summit', to Mr. Nehru's considerable irritation.

The United Arab Republic and Yugoslav Presidents conferred for over five hours on the day before the meeting, and drew up a long agenda, including an item on 'resisting what seems to be an attempt to weaken the bonds binding the non-aligned countries'. The meeting, the Cairo Press said, would be a non-aligned riposte to the hard blows dealt by the imperialists at states that went to Belgrade as punishment for their stand there. The reference was to the alleged foreign inspiration behind Syria's secession, and to the delay in the grant of American wheat to Yugoslavia.

X   321

When, in this context, President Tito suggested the possibility of a Second Belgrade, Mr. Nehru spoke uninterruptedly for an hour and a quarter (out of a total three-and-a-half hours of talks) on the need for clarifying the ideals and objectives of non-alignment; he worked in references to Mahatma Gandhi, Jefferson, Lincoln and other political idealists. Clearly he had not forgotten the exclusive approach to the idea of non-alignment earlier displayed by the Belgrade sponsors. His speech was the advance epitaph, valid for some time to come, of a Second Belgrade.

President Tito's reference to the need for a non-aligned Common Market was countered by Mr. Nehru's statement that the economies of Afro-Asian countries were competitive not complementary. But on this subject, as we have seen, India had had to change its mind.

As for a non-aligned counter-attack, Mr. Nehru firmly but gently put it aside. His visit to Washington had generated much goodwill for India in America, which he was not prepared to dissipate on Yugoslavia's behalf. In the communiqué, he succeeded in diverting the flood of indignation into the placid shoals of platitude.

After Belgrade, India's isolation from Afro-Asia began to worry the Indian Foreign Ministry. There was no real reason why she should have seemed so, because 400 million people can hardly be 'isolated' from 300 million, but having been a member of the Afro-Asian family, Indians were not yet tough enough to do without this cosy feeling of companionship. As Chinese pressure on the Indian border increased in 1962, the Indian desire to find protection or strength, however illusory, in the Afro-Asian group likewise increased. Accordingly, when President Sukarno yet again revived the Second Bandung idea, India shifted from her position of consistent opposition to one of virtual approval. By September 1962 she had agreed, albeit reluctantly, to attend a preparatory meeting that was destined to be held in December. Apart from weak good nature, and a desire to please Indonesia, India probably calculated that such conferences might provide opportunities for impromptu talks with the Chinese leaders who would have been present.

It was President Nasser who stiffened Mr. Nehru's backbone on the subject of development. Egypt had for long felt that another Afro-Asian conference was unnecessary, and it expressed this critical view following a meeting between President Nasser and Mr. Nehru in Cairo in September 1962. Having for years said 'no', India had then said 'perhaps', but now said 'perhaps not'; the United Arab Republic agreed. Their reluctance was shared by Nigeria, Lebanon,

Afro-Asia Fails the Test: the India-China Dispute

Burma and Ceylon: in short, three of the five original sponsors of Bandung were now against a repeat performance. On the other hand Pakistan and China were most anxious for a repetition. All this manœuvring was swept into insignificance by the Chinese attack on India in October—one of the many good results of that aggression.

This military action was the culmination of a long process in which, step by step, China had pressed forward as India retreated, both in the disputed territory and in diplomatic argument. The first Chinese claim on Indian territory was made in July 1954, forty-eight days after the signing of the agreement on Tibet that established the Five Principles of Peaceful Co-existence. When Mr. Nehru visited China later that year, he received the first of many Chinese assurances that maps showing parts of Indian territory as Chinese were old copies that the Chinese had had no time to revise. In 1955, the year of Bandung, and in 1956, the Chinese nibbles and probes continued, despite an undertaking given by Chou En-lai that China was prepared to accept the traditional frontier of the McMahon line.

The switch in China's foreign policy to an openly aggressive line is usually dated from the middle of 1957. The launching of Russia's first *sputnik*, and of her first inter-continental ballistic missiles in late August, were the direct causes. These developments gave Russia a feeling of strength and assurance. They had the opposite effect on the Chinese, who argued that the Communist world should now move confidently forward into the kill. In a speech at Moscow University in November of that year, Mao Tse-tung said that the east wind now prevailed over the west wind, and that the *sputnik* marked 'a new turning point' in world affairs.

Perhaps because of this new feeling of Communist power, the Chinese Government blatantly announced in the Peking press in September 1957 that it had completed a road linking Western Tibet with Sinkiang. The map it obligingly published clearly showed that the road ran across Indian territory in northern Ladakh.

Not until a full year later, in September 1958, did Indian patrols verify the road's existence; the first Indian protest against this intrusion was despatched the following month. The planning of this road must have begun not long after Bandung.

In January 1959 Chou En-lai made formal claim to 50,000 square miles of Indian territory, saying that the frontier issue had not been raised earlier because conditions were then 'not ripe' for its settlement. And in May 1959 China equally formally abandoned the Five Principles; she said that she would respect them at her convenience.

This abandonment of Panchsheel may have been due to Chinese anger with India for giving asylum to the Dalai Lama after his flight from Tibet in March of that year.

The Chinese had already arrested and ill-treated Indian soldiers and frontier guards; but the first real, if small-scale, fighting began in August 1959, when they attacked and overran the frontier post of Longju on the eastern sector of the frontier.

Here we must note a remarkable circumstance. Up to this time the Indian people, press and parliament had been kept completely in the dark by the Indian Government on the political events underlying the frontier incidents. Only in September 1959, when his hand was forced by popular indignation over Longju, did Mr. Nehru own up and tell his people of the Chinese road, the Chinese claim to 50,000 square miles of Indian territory, and Chinese repudiation of Panchscheel.

In November the Indian Government submitted a compromise offer, whereby Indian troops were to withdraw south, behind the line claimed by China, while Chinese troops moved north, beyond the line of the Indian claim. The creation of a buffer zone would eliminate the risk of border clashes, it said. This plan was rejected by the Chinese who advanced farther, building more roads.

On India's invitation, Chou En-lai visited Delhi in April 1960. The talks then held came to nothing, beyond agreement that officials from both sides would jointly study all the relevant documents. While Chinese patrols continued to probe, the officials studied the documents and produced a massive report in February 1961, which the Chinese first referred to only three months later: nothing came of this effort. Since the Chinese were consolidating their hold on the 12,000 square miles of territory that they now actually occupied, further discussion was pointless. Nevertheless, after still more border incidents the Indian Government, in May 1962, renewed its suggestion of mutual withdrawals and, going further, declared its willingness to permit use of the road in Ladakh by Chinese civilian traffic. There was no Chinese reply to this offer. The military build-up on both sides continued till the Chinese crossed the frontier in strength on the 20th October. After heavy fighting, they advanced southwards to a point overlooking the plains of Assam until, on the 21st November 1962, they unilaterally proclaimed a cease-fire.

Before examining the Afro-Asian reaction to this armed conflict between the two biggest Asian countries, two aspects of this chain of events deserve attention.

The first is Mr. Nehru's extraordinary reluctance to bring the dispute out into the open. The reason for this is clear, if insufficient to justify his conduct. The Chinese action shattered the very basis of his entire Afro-Asian policy. That policy had been based on the assumption that Asia ought to be a continent of friendliness and co-operation, that peaceful relations ought to obtain between its governments, and that the most important example of this was the friend-ship between India and China. Now it had become clear that China rated territorial expansion into areas of very minor value more highly than the friendship that India had shown her. Mr. Nehru had asserted, over and over again, that there was 'something', which he never precisely defined, that drew the Asian countries together—an Asian fellow-feeling. Clearly that feeling did not obtain among the rulers of China's 700 millions. What is more, the Chinese action not merely shattered, it buried his own particular brain-child and special addition to non-alignment—Panchsheel. The very country with which Panchsheel had first been agreed now stated baldly that it had been using these principles to suit its own convenience. The attempt to curb China's expansion by getting her to pledge herself publicly to friendship had been turned against India to lull her into a sense of security. To have to admit to failure on two counts was a course from which Mr. Nehru shrank for two whole years. Even in the speeches in September 1959 in which he confessed his mistakes, he said that it would be 'amazing folly' for countries like India and China 'to get into a major conflict and war for the possession of a few mountain peaks'; it would be 'a tragedy for Asia and the world'. A year later he was still so strongly under the influence of Panchsheel that he averred, in April 1960, that 'you either have war or you have some kind of talks. You cannot have something between the two'. This is fallacious. For twelve years all the Arab countries and Israel had shown that, if circumstances and policies so willed, there could be something between the two: no peace, no war, no talks.

His last-ditch defence of the tattered remnants of Panchsheel only serves the more strongly to emphasise the second important aspect of the events leading up to the Chinese attack—that, throughout, India was looking, almost desperately, for a peaceful solution, since she had not the slightest desire to advance into Chinese territory. Her ignorance of what was happening along her frontiers, her repeated offers of negotiation even after Chinese attacks, above all Mr. Nehru's concealment of the facts (which, he said, was partly due to his fear of Indian popular reaction)—all these were proof that India was not aggressively disposed, and that she was not merely passive but even neglectful of her own interests. Mr. Nehru said then, and maintained to the end of his life, that India must not cultivate a war psychosis and must be prepared to negotiate, despite the un-popularity of these views in India. Indeeed, no one who knows the facts doubts for one minute that on the 20th October 1962 China was the aggressor and India the victim.

What was the Afro-Asian reaction to this attack by China on India? In the first seven days after it Tunku Abdul Rahman, the Prime Minister of Malaya, and Archbishop Makarios, the President of Cyprus, expressed their sympathy and support for India; and with-in a few hours of the Chinese move President Nasser sent a message to Mr. Nehru suggesting that he might be of use by keeping in touch with both sides and putting forward mediatory and compromise proposals. The rest was silence.

The United States, Britain and countries in other continents were prompt and generous with offers not merely of sympathy but of help. But in the wide zone of silence that surrounded India only two small voices and one suggestion of mediation were to be heard. Five days later the Soviet Union urged India to accept China's 'constructive' proposals for a 'peaceful settlement'.

A week after the first Chinese offensive Mr. Nehru, swallowing his pride, sent a circular message to all the governments of the world asking for their sympathy and support. Seven days after this appeal eight of the remaining Afro-Asians had answered affirmatively: Jordan, Lebanon, Ethiopia, Nigeria, Uganda, Thailand, South Korea and the Philippines. Thus, fourteen days after the attack, coun-tries recognized as non-aligned by the sponsors of Belgrade gave their support to India. In a second category were half a dozen Afro-Asians who merely expressed concern that Indian official circles wish-fully identified with support. Among these were Ceylon, Tunisia, Libya and Israel.

A third group offered mediation: besides the United Arab Repub-lic it contained Syria, Iraq, Liberia and Tanganyika. Lastly, a special group composed of Pakistan and Ghana tried to prevent India from getting aid.

Two months later, and according to the inflated figures of the Indian Government, forty-five out of sixty Afro-Asians had replied. Of these twenty-six had supported India, thirteen of them non-aligned; nine had expressed concern; seven had hoped for a peaceful settlement and three were non-committal. Despite persistent ques-tioning in Parliament (and, incidentally, enquiries made by the author) the Indian Foreign Ministry refused to give details as to how the groups were comprised. Mr. Nehru himself was not certain whether any Afro-Asian country had condemned China as an aggressor.[1]

The attitude of the Communist countries of Eastern Europe reflected that of the Soviet Union, which continued to express hope for a peaceful settlement through negotiation, without pre-conditions; this was what the Chinese had offered.

Despite its bitter dispute with Communist China and despite its non-aligned friendship with India, Yugoslavia's reaction was curiously muted. No spontaneous response was forthcoming in the first week and then, by an oversight, Mr. Nehru's appeal was delayed in transmission to Belgrade. Sticking to protocol, the Yugoslavs waited for its arrival—a pause of another week—and President Tito then said that he hoped for a peaceful settlement. Yugoslavia may be a heretical Communist, but her umbilical link with the Communist world was considered more important than her association with her oldest friend among the Afro-Asian non-aligned countries.

As for President Nkrumah, he declared himself 'distressed and saddened' at the prospect that Britain should supply arms to India, and hoped that she would refrain 'from any action that may aggravate the unfortunate situation'.

Thus when the final count was made one Afro-Asian non-aligned country spontaneously supported India; and twelve other non-aligned countries—half of the Belgrade Conference membership—did so upon request and after some delay. None of the silent or non-committal non-aligned countries supported China, or said that it was in the right: had they done so, their attitude would have been more understandable. They merely kept quiet. Such was the end-product, for India, of twelve years of Afro-Asian policy and non-alignment, and seven years of Panchsheel.

No one, Indian or otherwise, would be justified in holding the Afro-Asian non-aligned countries as morally accountable if, during those seven years of the Panchsheel period, they had not, as India did, claimed for themselves moral superiority in international affairs. Yet when aggression was committed in their area by an Asian they revealed themselves as moral weaklings.

The principal reason for this lapse was that, for each, national interest and traditional attitudes were more important than Afro-Asian brotherliness, or non-aligned solidarity or moral principles. Examination of their motives affords a case-study of the many and varying causes that may outweigh the pull of Afro-Asianism, or that of non-alignment of the Panchsheel variety.

The strongest of these was inhibition about Russia. Russia was lukewarm on this issue, and China was Russia's ally, and countries did not want to offend Russia—important to them as a source of economic aid, military assistance or political counterweight to the West. This consideration applied to many countries from Indonesia and Cambodia in the east to the United Arab Republic, Algeria, and Ghana in the west. If Russia's attitude towards China in October 1962 had been as critical as it is today, far more Afro-Asian sympathy for India would have been forthcoming. A second cause for silence was, quite simply, the fear of a belligerent China, or of Chinese-controlled local Communists; these were a factor in Indonesia, Cambodia, Laos, Burma, Nepal and even Ceylon. A third motive in some South-East Asian and East African countries was traditional dislike and jealousy of India, combined with the presence of unpopular local Indian communities.

Some countries underestimated the importance of the event because of a lack of clarity and firmness in the presentation of the Indian case. India deliberately underplayed the attacks as mere border incidents. Ironically enough India—prototype of the non-aligned—was let down by other non-aligned countries because of their differing concepts of non-alignment. Some misinterpreted it as a mere playing-off of one side against the other—of maintaining a rigid equidistance between contending parties—and saw no reason why they should not remain equidistant as between India and China. Strictly personal feelings also played their part: in the recent past Mr. Nehru had been somewhat offhand in his dealings with Presidents Sukarno, Tito and Nkrumah; in addition, members of the Afro-Asian group at the United Nations remembered Mr. Krishna Menon's handling of them as if they were retarded children. Bilateral misunderstandings also had their effect. Indonesia, for instance, was piqued over India's long-standing opposition to a Second Bandung conference, and at the fact that an Indian official had happened to mar the *éclat* of the Asian Games recently held in Jakarta; (the Indian Embassy there was attacked in revenge). India's support for the popular opposition party in Nepal against the monarchy had alienated that regime. And India's refusal to recognise Iraq's claim to Kuwait or Morocco's to Mauritania hardly predisposed them in her favour.

An inter-Arab quarrel played its part in determining the Arab attitude. Some of these countries, such as Iraq, Syria, Saudi Arabia and Tunisia might, in general, have been more friendly to India, and might have supported her now, if India had been less friendly with their antagonist, the United Arab Republic. On the other hand, about half a dozen Arab countries that were friendly to Egypt, and might have been inclined to follow her lead, remained silent because India's best Arab friend was merely offering mediation. Thus President Nasser's offer determined reaction in the whole Arab area. And not in that area alone, because from it flowed the non-aligned attempt at mediation: a confused and murky episode. In short, any or every national interest or prejudice or hobby-horse counted for more than the moral tinge that the Panchsheel theory had so unfortunately imparted to non-alignment.

India, it has been said, outgrew the Afro-Asians at Belgrade. So there need be no real cause for surprise or hurt feelings because these nations failed to rally to her side in her struggle with another big country. What the Afro-Asian non-aligned peoples betrayed was not India but the moral standing that they claimed to possess. The other large countries, the United States immediately and the Soviet Union ultimately, supported India. In material terms this was all that mattered. But India, unsure of herself at this point, made the mistake of stepping back into the Afro-Asian arena, which she had quitted by promoting Afro-Asian mediation and by submitting herself to it. Because Mr. Nehru was determined to prove that his Afro-Asian policy and his Panchsheel theory had not failed, India tried, unsuccessfully, to squeeze herself back into the Afro-Asian chrysalis.

NOTE TO CHAPTER XV

1. Questions and answers in the Lok Sabha on 22nd Jan. 1963.

CHAPTER XVI

Twilight: the Second Colombo Conference, December 1962, and the Failure of Non-Aligned Mediation, 1963-4

Having failed to meet the initial test—the test of courage—presented by the Chinese attack on India, the Afro-Asian non-aligned were confronted with a second, political test, rendered difficult because of the first failure.

This second challenge was the product of three converging lines of policy. The Afro-Asians could not ignore the conflict between the two biggest Asian countries; they had to try and do something to assert their presence and help towards a solution, and they had to do so without taking sides or passing moral judgement. They resolved this dilemma by means of a conference of six non-aligned countries held in Colombo in December 1962.

The Colombo Conference was unable to produce a solution acceptable to both sides, and the compromises incorporated in its resolution, coupled with the subsequent unwillingness of the six governments to stand resolutely thereby, dissipated whatever moral capital the Afro-Asians had left.

The six countries cannot be held wholly to blame for this unsatisfactory outcome. They would probably never have attempted mediation had not the Indian Government, or more precisely Mr. Nehru and a 'China lobby' of senior civil servants in the Foreign Ministry, still been looking for a negotiated compromise with China. The instrument they chose for this dubious endeavour was President Nasser.

The first large-scale Chinese move south was made on the 8th September 1962 when Chinese troops for the first time crossed the international frontier, known as the McMahon Line, on one portion of its eastern sector. The full-scale, massive, attack on the eastern, central and western sectors followed on the 20th October.

Within a few hours of this second attack, on the 21st October,

President Nasser cabled to Mr. Nehru and to Chou En-lai suggesting that he might help by keeping in touch with both sides and putting forward compromise proposals. New Delhi promptly accepted and so, after a lapse of time, did Peking.

The crucial factor was that Mr. Nehru did more than merely accept the Egyptian President's offer. Indian officials actually suggested to the United Arab Republic that it should not take a firm, denunciatory line against China, lest this jeopardise its role as a future mediator. Thus while the officers and men of the Indian Army, taken by surprise, inadequately clothed, badly armed, and led by a couple of defeatist generals were, with their customary gallantry, fighting the Chinese 'border guards' in the snow and ice of the high Himalayas, Indian officials were desperately trying, through secret back-door negotiations, to salvage something from the wreck of Mr. Nehru's unreal China policy.

Indians are likely to ask themselves for some time to come which was the more deplorable: the underhand initiative of their own diplomats, or the fact that President Nasser's first response was a proposal of mediation, and not a spontaneous offer of support such as Mr. Nehru had offered Egypt at the time of the Suez crisis.

On receiving affirmative answers from India and China, President Nasser communicated with the governments of Afghanistan, Indonesia, Algeria, Sudan, Morocco, Ceylon, Ghana, Guinea, Cambodia, and Mali, inviting them to join in a common effort by the Casablanca Charter countries and the Afro-Asian non-aligned nations to ward off the dangers of war in Asia. On the 26th October President Nasser proposed a four-point solution suggesting a cease-fire, the demarcation of a demilitarised buffer zone, negotiations, and the withdrawal of troops 'to the positions they held prior to the recent clashes which began on the 20th October, that is, behind the line where their forces stood on the 8th September last'.

India accepted this United Arab Republic proposal, after obtaining clarification of the operative clause on withdrawals (the Arabic original seemed to offer a choice between the 8th September line 'or' that of the 20th October). The Chinese, as might have been expected, rejected the plan on the 2nd November, because by their standards it came too close to India's wishes. Such was the unsuccessful end of the United Arab Republic's first attempt at mediation.[1]

India's acceptance represented her first failure, her first withdrawal from a firm stand, in this process of mediation by the non-aligned countries. An official Egyptian publication[2] admits that 'in actual details the United Arab Republic's resolution did not fully conform to the Indian minimum demand for a complete restoration of the before-the-invasion border; but it came very near to it'. Yet Mr. Nehru bestowed unusually high praise on President Nasser for making this proposal—an indication that it was in line with his own thinking.

The United Arab Republic's suggestion to the ten Afro-Asians that they should meet in conference to discuss the issue on the basis of its four-point proposal received a lukewarm response. President Sukarno did not even trouble to acknowledge it, and 'few countries were prepared to meet on the basis of the resolution';[3] it was too clear-cut and too pro-Indian for them.

While Egypt adopted an attitude friendly towards India in her diplomacy, her public position was highly equivocal. Indian newspaper correspondents in Cairo, and through them the world, were informed that President Nasser had bluntly told the Chinese chargé d'affaires in Cairo that China had committed aggression and should withdraw, but not one word of this appeared in the United Arab Republic's Press. In private the Egyptian Government was insistent on certain boundaries and geographic lines, while in public it said that the Arab people were not even ready to discuss the arguments of the two sides, since differences over the McMahon Line were no concern of theirs. With the same ambivalence the Egyptians allowed an arms deal with India, concluded earlier, to go through, so as to reduce her dependence on the West for military supplies, but at the same time expressed hope that the dispute would be settled before the arms reached India.[4]

The United Arab Republic's proposal for a mediatory conference of the non-aligned peoples provoked similar suggestions from other countries equally eager to be at the centre of affairs, from Ceylon and Cambodia to Tanganyika, Syria and Guinea. The Ceylonese proposal for a six-nation meeting matured first merely because one of the invitees, Burma, accepted quickly and so set matters going. Egyptian diplomats did not hesitate to say, with asperity, that the Ceylonese idea had been filched from them and then truncated; while Ghana, having accepted Ceylon's invitation, at once suggested that the conference be transferred from Colombo to Accra. Thus India's 'funeral bak'd meats did coldly furnish forth the marriage tables' of neutralist non-alignment.

The list of ten countries approached by the United Arab Republic and that of the six invited by Ceylon differed not only in number but

Twilight: the Second Colombo Conference

in political quality. The ten were a representative selection of the Belgrade non-aligned, spanning not only all Afro-Asia from the South China Sea to the Atlantic, but also covering regimes ranging from right-wing monarchies and parliamentary democracies to left-wing authoritarian governments. The Ceylon Government selected five from the United Arab Republic's list—Egypt, Ghana, Cambodia, Indonesia and Ceylon itself, and added Burma. The countries omitted—Morocco, Algeria, Sudan, Afghanistan, Guinea, Mali— had in common the fact that they were Islamic and were, in greater or lesser degree, likely to follow the United Arab Republic's lead, which was already known to be close to the Indian viewpoint.

When Ceylon was asked why it had dropped them, the answer given was that it wanted to restrict the membership, more or less, to the area of the dispute itself—that is to South and South-East Asia—but that Afghanistan had been omitted because it was a neighbour to the disputants. This last argument was, conveniently, not applied to Burma which is in exactly the same geographic position.

There was, however, an unspoken political assessment underlying Ceylon's selection. By the time the invitations were extended, in the second week of November, it was clear that, with the exception of the United Arab Republic, the five countries had decided to sit on the fence, refusing to take sides or to pass judgement. This politically amoral attitude was reflected in Ceylon's stipulation that the conference should meet without an advance agenda and solely for purposes of mediation; an agenda-less meeting was something new in the history of Afro-Asian conferences.

The host, or rather hostess, of this conference was also a newcomer to Afro-Asian affairs, and a worthy addition to the colourful gallery of Afro-Asian leaders. Mrs. Sirimavo Bandaranaike was not only the world's sole woman head of government, but had reached that station without any previous experience of government whatsoever. She had succeeded her husband, whose assassination had made him a victim—unfortunately neither the first nor the last—of the malign forces of religious, racial and linguistic reaction that he had himself deliberately released from their Pandora's box.[5] In power, his wife proved an adroit politician, shrewd and stubborn. But it is still not known how much of her policy derives from herself and how much from her chief adviser, her late husband's nephew, Mr. Felix Bandaranaike, who is by way of being a lesser Krishna Menon. At home her government was facing a difficult situation: the economy

333

was running down and governmental power was based on a precarious parliamentary colition; prestige accruing from initiative in the field of foreign affairs would have been welcome to her.

From the start India was, understandably and wholly correctly, not at all enthusiastic about the Colombo Conference. She could hardly be expected to relish mediation by a group containing four countries—Ceylon, Burma, Cambodia and Indonesia—whose relations with China were those of uneasy friendship; they had a dragon close behind them and it was treading on their tail. Nor did the six countries carry the weight of numbers and size that President Nasser's larger selection might have done; they consisted of one fairly large, two medium-sized and three small countries, with a total population of about 175 million people, out to solve a conflict involving 1,000 million people. Their endeavour might have been gallant if they had regarded their very smallness as a challenge to moral greatness. But their moral stature turned out to be even smaller than their physical size. India in her hesitation at first tried to scuttle, and then to delay, the holding of the conference. In this she was aided by the United Arab Republic—also most reluctant to attend. Egypt managed, by requests for clarification, to delay the opening from the 1st December until the 10th, but on or about the 6th, an indignant Ceylon issued a scarcely-veiled threat to the United Arab Republic that the conference would be held with or without her.

The United Arab Republic seems finally to have agreed to attend mainly in order to be of assistance to India, whose resistance to the conference had broken already. On the 26th November two teams headed by Indian cabinet ministers had travelled eastwards and westwards to explain to the six governments the Indian position on the border problem.

They had made no converts anywhere, except in the already-converted United Arab Republic, and in the process India had sacrificed her dignity because the Indian missions were either immediately preceded or followed by Chinese explanatory teams.

The Chinese were able to look forward to the Colombo Conference with confidence, in view of its composition. India can have had no such hopes. Why then did she not dissociate herself from it, for instance, by advising the United Arab Republic not to attend? At this stage those conducting Indian foreign policy were thoroughly flustered; the failure of the attempt to befriend China through Panchsheel, the lack of support from the Afro-Asian non-aligned countries, and the capital being made of both these developments by a vigorous internal opposition, had combined to knock India's Foreign Ministry off balance. For no good reason the Indian Government felt that it was 'isolated', and in an access of humility began trying to ingratiate itself with its neighbours. This mood was not shared by the Indian people who, roused to nationalist fervour, were quite prepared to stand on their own. Mr. Nehru found their naïve enthusiasm slightly vulgar and dismaying.

Not long before the Colombo Conference was due to meet, one more attempt was made to widen its membership. The Yugoslavs, realising too late that sulking does not pay, plunged abruptly into the fray. The Yugoslav Foreign Minister paid an unexpected visit to Cairo and tried to persuade the Egyptians of the desirability of a second Belgrade, another neutralist summit. For once the Egyptians were not prepared to support their Yugoslav friends, and bluntly declared that there was no urgency for such a meeting.[6]

In the days immediately before the beginning of the conference India made one more attempt to strike a bargain with China through the United Arab Republic. Despite China's earlier rejection of Egypt's four-point plan, India suggested to President Nasser that he might sound the visiting Chinese mission as to whether they would be prepared to accept the idea of the demilitarised zone as proposed by the United Arab Republic, but on the western sector of the front only. If this extended to the 8th September line, India was prepared to discuss whether control in this area should be through civilian or military posts. This issue became important later, but for the time being nothing came of it.

President Nasser decided not to go to Colombo because of a promised visit to Morocco; but, oddly enough, the postponement of his North African visit was announced at the same time as his inability to attend the Colombo Conference. Two other Heads of State were present however—Prince Norodom Sihanouk of Cambodia and General Ne Win of Burma; Ceylon and the United Arab Republic were represented by their Prime Ministers, Mrs. Bandaranaike and Mr. Ali Sabry; Indonesia sent its Foreign Minister, Mr. Subandrio, and Ghana its Minister of Justice, Mr. Ofori Atta. This level of representation hardly matched the conference's unique and momentous task—unique because never before had the Afro-Asian non-aligned countries tried to settle a dispute within their own area, and momentous because it involved the two Asian colossi.

It is significant that the Ceylon Government officially designated the meeting as 'The Conference of Non-Aligned Countries, Colombo,

Twilight: the Second Colombo Conference

December 1962', even though only six of the non-aligned were represented, though one of the parties to the dispute under discussion, China, was not non-aligned, and despite the fact that in its proposals the conference was much more Afro-Asian than non-aligned. At Colombo we can, in fact, discern the first sign of the new confrontation of the concepts of Afro-Asia and of non-alignment, of Bandung versus Belgrade. In this preliminary skirmish Bandung won.

In purely human terms the six delegation leaders were a fascinating selection: a housewife turned politician; two professional politicans, from Indonesia and Ghana; two former military conspirators, in the persons of Wing Commander Ali Sabry and General Ne Win (whose mother is Chinese); and a former playboy prince who, following the advice given by Bernard Shaw in *The Apple Cart*, had also become a singularly successful politician.

Seven, not six, delegations were actually present at the conference because at the last minute India hurriedly despatched a group of its Chinese experts to Colombo, headed by the secretary-general of its Foreign Ministry, the topmost civil servant of the Government of India. They were meant to be available for consultation and the provision of technical data. The experts did something of the latter but only the United Arab Republic's representatives bothered to consult the Indians. Explanation on behalf of the Chinese was given by the head of the Colombo office of the New China News Agency. This difference in level of representation accords with the pertinent remark made by Chou En-lai to the French at the first Geneva Conference on Indo-China: 'You will not get at the conference table more than you got on the field of battle.' India learnt this lesson at Colombo.

The six opening speeches offered a rich confusion of themes, but the note most commonly struck was that this conference was immensely important, so important as to be apocalyptic.

For Mrs. Bandaranaike the India-China dispute was 'a threat to our very existence, and to non-alignment itself', 'to our way of life and the future of mankind'. Both Prince Norodom and Mr. Sabry claimed that the conference represented all of Asia and Africa (the Prince threw in Latin America for good measure) and that Afro-Asian unity and solidarity were at stake. While Dr. Subandrio more realistically remarked 'if we cannot solve this problem between India and China, let us not have any illusions that we can solve other great problems which may have to be faced by the countries of Asia and Africa'. The delegations were aware of the daunting challenge that they faced.

They were unanimously of the opinion that they had to face it without going into the merits of the case, without passing judgement and without taking sides. On no other issue was there such total agreement. In six speeches this washing of hands took place at least sixteen times. At its mildest this equating of aggressor and victim took the form of references to 'our great friends', 'our brothers', or 'these two sister countries'. More usually it was expressed in anodyne terms, with references to the fact that the conference was not a court and that its task was to mediate not arbitrate. The most arrant evader of responsibility was General Ne Win, who, five times in the course of a ten-minute speech, contrived to shelter behind the smoke-screen of the phrase 'friendly third powers', used to describe the neutralist six. Close behind him were Mr. Ali Sabry and Dr. Subandrio; the latter saw to it that in the official text of his speech there was underlining beneath the words in which he declared that the conference was 'certainly not' intervening 'in the substance of the conflict between India and China'.

How was such a conference to get to grips with the problems before it? According to the communiqué issued after the first day of deliberations 'the conference decided that its purpose was not to consider the merits and demerits of the dispute but to provide for an exchange of views in order to assist the two countries to resume negotiations with a view to arriving at a peaceful settlement'.

Ignoring the fact that India and China had been discussing this issue, in the most minute detail, over a period not of weeks or months but of years, Prince Norodom nevertheless implored them 'to resume their discussions' and Mr. Ofori Atta asserted President Nkrumah's belief that 'the sole purpose of the conference is to establish the conditions for peaceful direct negotiations between the two parties'.

The other general principle of action agreed upon was that the unilateral cease-fire declared by the Chinese on the 21st November should be strengthened and confirmed.

When it came to making specific and positive recommendations, some delegations were obsessed with the cease-fire and seemed to regard it as an end in itself. Two of the delegates thought that the conference should merely promote the resumption of negotiations and confirm the cease-fire.

These two negativists were Prince Norodom and General Ne Win.

Twilight: the Second Colombo Conference

With what amounted to a Gallic shrug of the shoulders the Prince's attitude was *je m'en fiche*. He did not think the conference could do much in any case, and least of all in producing a compromise because of the gap between the known positions of the two parties. His pessimism was well-founded. The General's hesitations were the product less of cynicism than of fear of compromising his strictly neutral position: all he suggested was the possibility of good offices committees.

Mrs. Bandaranaike, in more positive vein, said that the task of the conference was to suggest an equitable basis for a cease-fire line and perhaps also 'joint action which our countries can propose to ensure the continuance of a cease-fire'—an obvious reference to contributing a border force. The Indonesian proposal was simpler: 'If it is a matter of face saving', said Dr. Subandrio, 'I think it may be possible to find a solution. On the other hand if we cannot find a solution through this conference I think we will be later able to judge, without touching on the substance of the conflict, who is the aggressor and who is the expansionist.' This approach, presumably, anticipated rejection by one side or the other of the conference's resolution. But when this happened, the conference members refused to fulfil the intention to say who was in the wrong.

To everyone's surprise, Ghana was the author of detailed proposals at the opening session. These were couched in peremptory terms: India and China 'must' accept a cease-fire; they 'must' withdraw their forces from a zone of 'disengagement' between them, which would be neutralised and maintained 'only by unarmed police on both sides'; this area 'must' be determined as soon as possible through direct negotiations; if these failed India and China 'must' agree to the 'conference determining the area of disengagement'. The representative of Ghana's Redeemer was not overawed by the immensity of the task.

There was in these exordiums just one gleam of hope for India. This pierced the gloom when Mr. Ali Sabry enunciated two basic principles; the necessity for a peaceful settlement and 'that there must not be any territorial gain on account of military operations. This principle is in conformity with the spirit of the Bandung Conference'.

Here was one of several references to Bandung: the word rang through the speeches like the toll of a funeral bell. The conference, though described as 'non-aligned', obviously saw itself far more as a successor to the Afro-Asian meeting than to Belgrade. Non-alignment was seldom mentioned except by Mrs. Bandaranaike and Mr. Ofori Atta, who declared it to be the same thing as Afro-Asian solidarity, which can only mean that they did not understand the true significance of either.

Only once did India receive special mention from a speaker. The Ceylon Premier paid tribute to her as 'the foremost champion of non-alignment' and to Mr. Nehru's 'tireless efforts' to promote the idea. But Mrs. Bandaranaike had immediately preceded this remark with a reference to India's quest for arms from the Western Powers; her conclusion therefore was that 'this kind of entanglement with power blocs would be contrary to the cardinal principles of non-alignment'. India had fallen from her state of non-aligned grace, when even a statement of her obvious, special connection with non-alignment had to be offset by critical comment.

When the conference went into secret session on the evening of the 10th December, it set aside the proposal that it should not make a detailed study of the issue and applied itself to studying the maps of the disputed border. The Burma–Cambodia approach thus gave way to a more general feeling that the conference must not be content with a mere peace appeal. Indeed this would have contrasted strangely with the alarm and despondency expressed in the opening speeches.

The United Arab Republic's delegation immediately presented a proposal for a demilitarised zone on the western sector of the frontier, in Ladakh—an idea that had been discussed by President Nasser with the Chinese mission in Cairo a few days earlier. The suggestion was generally welcomed, especially by Indonesia; Burma, however, questioned the wisdom of any formula that was not acceptable to both sides. And this particular proposal, it was already known, was not acceptable to China.

Thus from the start of the discussions the two chief protagonists emerged: Mr. Ali Sabry trying to maintain the no-reward-for-aggression principle, favourable to India, and General Ne Win apprehensively insisting that nothing should be proposed that was inacceptable to China. In the event neither the United Arab Republic nor Burma received satisfaction.

It is curious that the General and Mr. Sabry were insistent, in their public speeches, that the secrecy of the secret sessions should be preserved. To this end, even the shorthand reporters were excluded from the discussions. Consequently what the delegates thought they were saying in private became ever more different from what they said publicly. But these security precautions were vain; the first item on the second day of the conference was an apology from the Ceylon delegation that the substance of the previous evening's 'secret' sessions should have been spread across the front pages of that morning's Colombo newspapers. As during the conference of 1954, Colombo in 1962 maintained its reputation for being a city without secrets.

The second day of the conference, the 11th December, was a day of deadlock, with the United Arab Republic and Burma standing squarely in each other's way. In the 'secret' sessions, Egypt reiterated its suggestion that, in Ladakh, a demilitarised zone should have as its northern and eastern boundary the line of the 8th September from which the Chinese began their first lunge forward. To the Burmese argument that China would not accept this proposal, the United Arab Republic replied that the conference must feel free to make suggestions *ab initio*, irrespective of the positions that the two parties might have taken earlier.

The Burmese counter-suggestion on Ladakh was that the northern-eastern boundary of the demilitarised zone should be the line to which the Chinese promised to withdraw in their cease-fire offer: this line only partly coincided with the 8th September line and thus did not amount to a total deprivation of the fruits of aggression.

The type of 'administration' for this zone on the western sector also produced much energetic though cordial discussion, without any direct bi-lateral confrontation. Three ideas were discussed, inconclusively: whether the 'administration' should be civil or military; whether there should be any 'administration' in a zone that would be a real no-man's-land; whether the conference should undertake to fill the vacuum with a boundary force of its own.

Since this demilitarised zone in Ladakh was the stumbling-block over which the Colombo Conference countries subsequently tripped and fell, it is necessary to examine what sort of area they were arguing about. With commendable thoroughness the neutralist Six pored over the large-scale maps obligingly provided by the Indian and Chinese experts. Unfortunately these maps were, as usual, two-dimensional; they did not indicate, except to the trained eye, that this area of Ladakh was a bare, icy plateau, well over 10,000 feet high, scourged by the savage winds of Central Asia, and normally totally devoid of habitation or life, human or animal. Its only current inhabitants were the long-suffering soldiers of the Indian and Chinese Armies. To talk of the 'administration' of such forbidding terrain was unreal; even to consider the improbable prospect of frozen Indo-

340

nesian, Ceylonese or Ghanaian troops patrolling these barren wastes was nothing short of comic.

Yet the conference was right to concentrate attention on the area, for it was, and is, Ladakh that the Chinese want to hold, and across which they secretly built their strategic highway from western Tibet to the developing areas of Sinkiang. For India the crucial area lay 1,500 miles eastward in north-eastern Assam, along the McMahon Line—territory that dominates the plains of the Brahmaputra and the Ganges.

Throughout the second day, deadlock between the United Arab Republic and Burma reduced the tactical prospects to a plain issue: one side or the other must achieve a 'breakthrough' by winning over to its side the largest country present, Indonesia. Sheer weight might then pull Ceylon or Cambodia on to the same side.

This breakthrough came on the morning of the third day and was due to personal inadequacy. Mr. Ali Sabry is an able administrator, but this was the first important international conference at which he was the chief representative of his country—he had been listed ninth in his delegation at Bandung and third at Belgrade—and he was unaccustomed to the interplay of pressures through which conferences normally reach decisions.

On the morning of the 12th December there was a discernible shift of the Indonesians and Ceylonese towards the Burmese position. President Nasser had earlier expressed the fear that the United Arab Republic would be 'lonely' at Colombo, and this loneliness was now apparent. Sensing his opponents' weakening position the Burmese delegate struck: with a deplorable use of the *argumentum ad hominem* he 'accused' Mr. Sabry of being the spokesman for India. Instead of countering that Burma was the advocate for China, the United Arab Republic's delegate backed away from the charge and gave ground. Indonesia thereupon seized its chance to put forward its compromise proposals, licked into shape by Mr. Felix Bandaranaike.

Technically the Colombo proposals were supposed to be secret till they were transmitted to the two parties by emissaries deputed by the conference who, when doing their job a month later, also provided certain clarifications. The proposals in their original form were, however, known in Colombo within a matter of hours after the conclusion of the conference.

In substance these proposals aimed at consolidating the cease-fire as a prelude to the resumption of direct negotiations. Accordingly in the western sector—Ladakh—the Chinese were asked to carry out the withdrawal of twenty kilometres that they had promised in their cease-fire order of the 21st November, which took them back, at points, across the 8th September line. The Indian Army was to stand where it stood and, according to the clarification, 'the demilitarised zone of twenty kilometres created by Chinese military withdrawals will be administered by civilian posts of both sides. This is a substantive part of the Colombo Conference proposals'. India and China were to decide on the location, number and composition of these posts. In the unimportant central sector the *status quo* was to be maintained.

In the eastern sector of Assam, according to the clarification, the Indian Army was permitted to return right up to the old frontier of the McMahon Line, to which the Chinese had already withdrawn under the cease-fire, except for the two disputed areas of Longju and the Thagla Ridge, arrangements for which were to be discussed later.

Thus the proposals, as far as the position of troops on the ground went, did not require the Chinese to do anything which they had not already promised to do; they also did not require the Indian Army to make any withdrawals and, in the east, permitted it to return to the old frontier.

Did this mean that aggression was deprived of its fruits? Not wholly. In Ladakh the area overrun was not to be handed back to India but merely demilitarised under partial Chinese civilian control, nor did the Chinese Army move completely back across the 8th September line. And in Assam the fate of the two most controversial areas was left open for future settlement. The proposals sought to give China what she wanted in the western sector—that she considered important—and to satisfy India in the east, which was the vital area for her.

An official United Arab Republic publication admits that though Mr. Sabry 'could not get [his] proposals fully adopted by the Colombo Conference he succeeded to a very large extent in giving the Colombo proposals a realistic content. These proposals do not give India all she wants; but essentially they call for . . . a return of the Chinese forces beyond the pre-invasion line'.

The fatal defect of the Colombo proposals was the refusal of their authors to make a judgement on the real merits of the case. From their speeches it is clear that these leaders knew that the dispute had aroused passions, that pride and prestige were involved, that India was aggrieved. Yet they deliberately set this knowledge aside and tried to deal with the dispute aseptically, as if it were an exercise in diplomatic abstractions, as if the moving of frontiers on the maps was a staff college problem. This approach was wrong in principle and in practice, and was directly responsible for the failure of the subsequent efforts at mediation by the conference countries. When one of the disputants remained obdurate there was nothing more they could do, because they stood on no firm base but only on the shifting sands of technicalities.

Yet within its own amoral framework, and judged by the goals it set for itself, the Colombo Conference achieved a result that justified the mood of modest self-congratulation, displayed at its closing session by a richly but discreetly jewelled Mrs. Bandaranaike. More gratifying perhaps than the proposals themselves was the fact that the conference had deputed Mrs. Bandaranaike to present them to the antagonists at New Delhi and Peking. The mission conferred on her the prestige and responsibility of a messenger of peace from all of Afro-Asia to the quarrelling giants. But insufficient heed was paid to the cautious realism of one passage in Prince Norodom's closing speech: he continued to express 'pessimism' about the outcome of their efforts for 'no "technical" or diplomatic arrangement can make up for an absence of goodwill on the part of the adversaries'. But the proposals were a 'technical arrangement' and there was no goodwill to be had.

Although Mrs. Bandaranaike alone had been officially authorised to convey the proposals to India and China, all the delegation leaders, except General Ne Win, visited New Delhi and Peking, as a group or singly, in January 1963 or in the immediately succeeding months. Mrs. Bandaranaike and Dr. Subandrio were together in Peking, and a few days later she presented the proposals, with clarifications, to Mr. Nehru in the company of Mr. Ali Sabry and Mr. Ofori Atta.

The Indian Prime Minister himself admitted that the proposals did not fully meet the Indian viewpoint, but the Indian Government, speaking from a position that it thought to be weak, accepted them tamely and with an air of conscious rectitude. A motion to reject them, tabled by the Socialist Party in the Indian Parliament, was defeated by 349 votes to 59, cast by the stern majority of the Congress Party. Mr. Nehru made only one condition for acceptance: he stipulated that negotiations with China on the basis of the proposals could begin only if China accepted them *in toto*, together with the clarifications, as India had done; 'any attempt to accept them in part will mean a rejection of them as a whole'. These words were uttered on the 25th January 1963.

Twilight: the Second Colombo Conference

Unknown to the Indian Government, but with the full knowledge of the Colombo Conference emissaries who had come to New Delhi from Peking, the Chinese Government was trying to do precisely what Mr. Nehru said would not be acceptable—to make piecemeal adjustments to the proposals.

While keeping these Chinese reservations secret, the Colombo powers were, even if reluctantly, permitting China to give the false impression that she had accepted the proposals. After Mrs. Bandaranaike's visit to Peking the official communiqué stated that China had given 'a positive response', and even after her return to Colombo from her journey to Peking and New Delhi, Mrs. Bandaranaike was still asserting, without any concrete evidence, that 'a positive response' was 'an accurate description' of the Chinese reaction: 'I feel confident that both India and China will accept' she concluded on the 21st February; it was even announced that China had accepted 'in principle'.

This wishful thinking fitted in exactly with the Chinese policy of toying with the Colombo powers, half-promising, half withdrawing, cajoling and bullying by turns. China could afford to act thus for she, and her interlocutors, well knew that she was talking from strength.

What, in fact, Chou En-lai had done was to ask for more. China's response has been described, especially in India, as a 'rejection' of the proposals: this description is not strictly accurate. Peking accepted and implemented the conference proposals as they applied to China: what China demanded was that the Colombo powers should deny to India the most vital concessions that had been made to her. It is to the credit of these countries that they did not really press India to make these concessions for some time, and shamefacedly, they had not even the courage to reveal to India the full extent of the Chinese demands.

The basic Chinese stipulation was that, in the western sector in Ladakh, India should not have the right to introduce even unarmed civilian posts in the demilitarised zone; but that if India accepted this China, as a concession, would refrain from establishing its own civilian posts; in the eastern sector, in Assam, the stipulation was that the Indian Army should not advance to the McMahon Line; only armed civilian personnel were to move into the territory vacated by the Chinese frontier guards. From these two demands China has not budged an inch.

When, by the second week of February, it had become clear that the Colombo powers had not succeeded in obtaining—had not even

344

attempted to obtain—India's acceptance of these further concessions, China turned against the neutralist Six. In a speech at a banquet given on the 12th February to Prince Norodom, the Chinese President, Liu Shao-chi, went so far as to describe the Colombo proposals as an obstacle in the way of direct negotiations between India and China. China then announced that the concession she had been prepared to make towards maintaining the demilitarised zone as a no-man's-land no longer applied, and that she had established seven civilian posts in that area. Behind this stiffening of the Chinese position lay a battle of wills between Peking and the Colombo powers that had been going on secretly during January and February 1963.

When Mrs. Bandaranaike and Dr. Subandrio met Chou En-lai in Peking early in January, they together handed to him a two-page document entitled 'Principles underlying the proposals of the Six' which were far more explicit than the 250-word clarification given to Mr. Nehru in New Delhi a few days later by Mrs. Bandaranaike, Mr. Ali Sabry and Mr. Ofori Atta. Based on the principle that 'neither side should be in a position to derive benefit from military operations', it made five points for the western sector, in Ladakh, leading to the conclusion 'this [demilitarised] zone should be administered by civilian posts of both sides'. For the eastern sector the principle was that 'whether the McMahon Line is considered to be illegal or not it has in fact become the line of actual control', and therefore come to be accepted as some sort of frontier.

In this document we see the neutralist Six trying, in private dialogue with the Chinese, to clarify, emphasise and strengthen those particular points which they thought the Chinese might not accept and which, in fact, the Chinese did not and have not accepted. But because this line was taken secretly—this particular document was given to India only two months later, in March—Peking gained a propaganda advantage over the Colombo powers themselves, permitting China, for some time, to adopt the pose of having accepted the proposals 'in principle'.

When in February 1963 China showed no signs of accepting the proposals, and began attacking them, the neutralist Six began to close their ranks. On the 16th February General Ne Win sent Mrs. Bandaranaike a letter specifically endorsing her line of action in Peking and New Delhi, and Prince Norodom did so later in the month.

During March 1963 the exchanges between Peking and the Six became somewhat more venomous. On the 7th March Mrs. Bandaranaike sent Chou En-lai a letter in which she wrote: 'I should like to disabuse your mind of any erroneous impression you have formed that the Colombo Conference proposals have not been clearly and consistently explained to India and China.' A week later, on the 15th, the Chinese Foreign Minister, Chen Yi, retorted that there was 'a great discrepancy' between the clarifications given in Peking and New Delhi, and he made the valid point that the Colombo Conference had accepted only the proposals, and not the clarifications.

Thus the Chinese Government openly accused the Colombo powers of dishonesty and bad faith—of saying one thing in New Delhi and another in Peking. The 'goodwill' desired by Prince Norodom between the disputants did not even exist between one of the antagonists and the mediators. In its attempts to calumniate and split the Six, Peking was aided by two circumstances. In the first crucial exchanges of view in mid-January, only Mrs. Bandaranaike went directly from Peking to New Delhi; thus she alone knew at first hand what both sides were saying, and she had shown herself to be a temporiser. Though the Six as a group told India that joint civilian administration in the western demilitarised zone in Ladakh was 'a substantive part' of the proposals and though they, collectively, stressed this point to China, Mrs. Bandaranaike wrote, about this time, to Chou En-lai that 'it would not be contrary to the spirit of the Colombo proposals if the area remained unoccupied'. This, she added, was 'her personal view' and not that of the conference as a whole. In the confusion one detects one or other of the Six trying, on its own, to edge nearer to the Chinese position of strength. Little wonder that the Chinese thought they could divide and browbeat them. Only a relic of moral scruple, or final twitch of guilty conscience, held the Six back from submission to Peking's bullying.

In fairness to Mrs. Bandaranaike, it must be said that she had perhaps been encouraged towards moral obliquity by the tactical suppleness of Mr. Nehru himself. As has been said, the vital sector for India of the long India-China border was in the east. Here the Colombo powers, backing India, had said that the Indian Army ought to return to the traditional frontier of the McMahon Line. Peking had refused this, and behind the refusal lay the threat of a resumption of hostilities. In January 1963 Indian newspapers reported that Mr. Nehru had authorised Mrs. Bandaranaike to tell Chou En-lai that India would not send its troops up to the McMahon Line once China accepted India's right to do so in principle. Subsequently this Indian offer has frequently been queried in the Indian Parliament, but Mr.

Nehru never confirmed or denied it. China, in any case, has ignored this sophistry and India has had to do likewise and refrain from moving its troops forward.

If India was unprepared to take advantage of the stand taken on her behalf by the Colombo powers on the eastern sector, which she considered vital, is it any wonder that these countries should try and accommodate Peking on the western sector, which was of prime importance to China?

In April China pressed home the advantage that it had gained thanks to the wavering Colombo powers. In a speech during the visit to Peking of Mr. Ali Sabry, Chou En-lai stated flatly that there were different interpretations of the Colombo proposals, which there were not; that these differences themselves could be discussed at another conference; and that India was trying to set 'preconditions' which, as we have seen, was what China was attempting to do. India, the Chinese Premier went on, was trying to turn the Colombo proposals into a verdict—a shrewd thrust because he knew that any appearance of taking a decision on behalf of one side was what the Six feared most.

Having failed to gain acceptance of their original proposals from China, having connived without avail at a temporary pretence that China had accepted, and having then been browbeaten by China for not obtaining India's consent to Peking's further demands, the neutralist Six prudently said and did nothing more for six months.

A brief spurt of mediatory activity took place in October 1963, when President Nasser suggested that the Colombo powers should make another effort, but reiterated that this must be on the basis of a return to the 8th September line. He seemed to think that results might be obtained, because six months earlier Chou En-lai had told Mr. Ali Sabry that China would 'forget' its reservations to the proposals. But by October China had not, officially, forgotten them. Thus even President Nasser entered into the cat-and-mouse game that China was playing with the Six. Nothing came of his suggestion.

Also in October President Nkrumah proposed another session of the conference (which presumably would have been held in Accra) with India and China attending. China, of course, was only too willing to accept his idea, but Mr. Nehru's somewhat angry reaction was that the Colombo powers must stand by their resolution, and that there was no question of bringing India to the negotiating table with China till the latter accepted the Colombo proposals.

At this moment Peking made it plain that she had no intention of doing anything of the sort. A muffled, one-sided conversation had been going on between India and China since April. In that month, Mr. Nehru had suggested a negotiated settlement of the boundary question after the acceptance, 'without reservations' of the proposals; officials could then meet to decide on matters left undefined by the conference and these meetings could be followed by high-level talks; if these failed the dispute could be referred to the World Court or to international arbitration. Meeting blank silence from Peking, India sent a reminder in September and was given the answer 'no' in October.

A final rejection of the Indian offer could have been anticipated; what was unexpected was a renewal of China's attacks on the honesty of the Six. The Chinese note stated categorically that 'the clarifications furnished by Ceylon, Ghana, and the United Arab Republic were drafted in New Delhi and are India's interpretations of the Colombo proposals'. Thus, this time, the Colombo powers were not only accused of duplicity but of subservience to India. Here was a direct slap at these countries, and through them at the large majority of the Afro-Asian non-aligned peoples who, in the months following the Colombo Conference, had accepted the proposals as a fair basis for negotiation. No reply was made to this Chinese accusation.

Following this rebuff the Colombo powers lapsed into silent inactivity, except for Ceylon. In February and March of 1964 Chou En-lai visited Burma, Ceylon, Egypt and Ghana and, doubtless, the proposals were discussed with the leaders of all four countries, but only the talks in Colombo produced any result.

After Chou En-lai's visit Mrs. Bandaranaike informed Mr. Nehru that the Chinese position now was that they were prepared to withdraw their civilian posts in the demilitarised zone in the western sector if India agreed to discussions. In Parliament on the 13th April 1964, Mr. Nehru, abandoning Indian insistence that the proposals must first be accepted *in toto*, stated that India would be prepared to enter into negotiations if China agreed to withdraw her posts first. This withdrawal would convert the demilitarised zone into a no-man's land, an idea that had been considered and rejected by the Colombo Conference, but which, as we have seen, had first been mooted, privately, by Mrs. Bandaranaike more than a year earlier.

China had received this Indian reply, through Mrs. Bandaranaike, more than a month before Mr. Nehru announced it publicly, but there was no sign that Peking was prepared to make what was for it only a minor concession—one of timing. The Chinese may well have been earlier aware of this major modification in the Indian position, for the suggestion of a no-man's-land had been put forward in New Delhi late in 1963 by two emissaries of a well-meaning busybody, Lord Russell; Mr. Nehru had accepted and the envoys had then gone on to Peking.[7] The only conclusion to be drawn from Peking's failure to respond is that, determined to retain the fruits of aggression, she was not interested in negotiations or in the well-meaning efforts of quixotic liberal philosophers or deferential Afro-Asian leaders.

It is one of the ironies of history that if the Colombo Conference had been held a week or two later its proposals would have been rather different, and far more just to India. For a change in the Russian attitude towards the dispute was just becoming apparent while the conference was being held.

As was said in the preceding chapter, the lukewarm response of many of the Afro-Asian countries was attributable to 'the Russian veto'—the fear of displeasing Russia which, under the stress of the Cuban crisis, had temporarily dropped its neutrality on the Indo-Chinese dispute and moved nearer to the Chinese position. When, say the Chinese, these 'considerations of expediency' no longer applied, Russia reverted to her original position of 'support to India'. The Soviet line was hardly that, but on the 12th December 1962—the day the Colombo Conference ended—Mr. Khrushchev uttered a first faint, veiled criticism of China. But to the Chinese dogmatists even these cautionary words amounted to treachery: on the 15th December the Peking *People's Daily*, in a front-page editorial, attacked Russia for criticising China on the border issue, the gravamen of the charge being that while Russia called China 'a brother' she treated India like 'a kinsman'. Had this editorial appeared a few days earlier, the positive line advocated by the United Arab Republic at Colombo might have gained some supporters.

Subsequently, as is well known, Russia has come out openly and said that 'China attacked India' and that when she did so she gave up party principles and was, instead, actuated by 'blind arrogance'.

At least one non-aligned country was prepared to analyse what had gone wrong: this was Egypt. In the official publication earlier quoted, it asked, with astonishing frankness and lack of diplomatic tact: 'Why, among the non-aligned countries, has the United Arab Republic alone stood firmly behind India in her gallant fight against Chinese aggression? Why, at the Colombo Conference, did the United Arab Republic alone come out with clear-cut proposals for the vacation [*sic*] of Chinese aggression?'[8] These are brave words, but they probably came too late to save the United Arab Republic from the charge that she had herself deeply comprised her own principle of 'no reward for aggression'—of especial importance to her after Suez, and because she has in Israel a hostile and belligerent neighbour.

The United Arab Republic publication tries to answer its own questions. It says that 'the Asian neighbours of China were apprehensive of China's wrath' and India's diplomacy and public relations work had been 'poor'. These are only partial explanations. The real reason for the failure is to be found in the concept of non-alignment as a policy of mere equidistance, and in a special variety of neutralist ethics.

At least five of the countries that a Colombo newspaper described as 'the inconsequential Six' belonged to the neutralist species of the non-aligned genus. Their concept of non-alignment was, it happens, clearly expressed in an article in the same newspaper during the conference.[9] The author wrote: 'Dynamic neutralism is not an absolute, it is not an abstract immutable principle. It is contingent on the protracted conflict between East and West. Outside the contest of the Cold War non-alignment has no functional status or meaning. For non-alignment is only a *modus vivendi* forced upon certain nations by the unpleasant actualities of contemporary politics.' The Colombo proposals were a fine example of this tactic of balance and equidistance but, accordingly, had little connection with independent judgement of the case on its own merits, which is the essence of non-alignment.

At Colombo the neutralist non-aligned countries were determined to remain rigidly neutral between the antagonists even though one of them, India, was non-aligned and China was not, and even though India was the founder of the policy of non-alignment according to which, allegedly, they were acting.

The ethical 'principle' underlying the policy was explained thus: 'A time-honoured habit of the neutralist community—that is, to suspend *moral* judgements, or the public declaration of such opinions, in order to serve the more *urgent* (and more important?) *political* necessities of negotiation and peaceful settlement of international disputes.'[10] This 'principle' was all too evident at the Colombo meeting; it also produced evidence of a strange, sliding scale of values, according to which when a government stops some action that it should not have started, it performs an act of positive virtue. Likewise there is positive gain if a country is not obliged to do something which it should never have been asked to do in the first place.

This is pure neutralism, not non-alignment, but since the Six described themselves as non-aligned, that concept and that policy have, quite incorrectly, been described as failures. The saying 'what's in a name' does not apply in politics.

The conference was a meeting of the Afro-Asian non-aligned countries, but at it Afro-Asianism and the Bandung Spirit betrayed non-alignment and the principles of Belgrade: the first of many subsequent skirmishes.

The Colombo powers, however mixed their motives and however dubious their manœuvrings, did try to make a start towards settling the India-China dispute. Nothing has come of their efforts because they did not try hard enough. Was this because they were too small and weak, or merely because they were too frightened and too clever and too selfish? The moral of the story seems to be that when the small get caught up in the conflicts of the great they get crushed unless they dare to be very brave.

NOTES TO CHAPTER XVI

1. Details of the United Arab Republic's mediation are given in several Indian Government publications and also in the issue on 'Chinese Aggression and India' of *International Studies*, July–Oct. 1963, Indian School of International Studies, New Delhi. This issue contains useful surveys of international reaction to the Chinese attack.
2. *The United Arab Republic Magazine*, United Arab Republic Embassy, New Delhi, Jan. 1963.
3. *Op. cit.*
4. An article in *Al Ahram* (newspaper), Cairo, 9th Nov. 1962, by Hassanein Heikal, who is recognised to be President Nasser's authoritative if unofficial spokesman.
5. For a condign indictment of the politics of Solomon West Ridgeway Dias Bandaranaike, see Tarzie Vittachi: *Emergency '58: The Story of the Ceylon Race Riots*, London, 1958.
6. *Al Ahram*, Cairo, 29th Nov. 1962.
7. For a self-laudatory, and at least partially self-deluded, account of Lord Russell's intervention in the India-China and Cuban crises, see his *Unarmed Victory*, Penguin Special, London, 1963.
8. *The United Arab Republic Magazine*, New Delhi, Jan. 1963.
9. 'Focus on Colombo', by M. de Silva, the *Ceylon Observer*, 9th Dec. 1962.
10. *Ceylon Observer, ibid.*

INTERLUDE III

Africa Moves Off on its Own: The First Two African Summit Meetings

I t is difficult to see the First and Second African Summit Conferences, held at Addis Ababa in May 1963 and at Cairo in July 1964, in proper prospective not only because they are near in time but also because they are of such towering significance. However, even an initial estimate of these meetings and of the forces that produced them leads to the conclusion that they represent a major shift in the world's political geology—a movement in geo-politics so vast that one would have expected it to be almost imperceptibly slow, which it was not.

In essence what happened at Addis Ababa and Cairo is that, within the space of fourteen months, all the independent countries of a continent, a new continent in political terms, drew together, gave themselves a single, comprehensive co-ordinating organisation and launched themselves on a political course of their own choosing. This African continental unity was achieved, however, at the expense of bi-continental Afro-Asian solidarity.

When the thirty-two African heads of state met at Addis Ababa they were impelled, even compelled, to reach agreement by both negative and positive factors. In the course of the preceding two years people had come to recognise that the division of Africa into the two antagonistic 'Monrovia-Lagos' and 'Casablanca' groups had done a great disservice to the continent. This split had diminished Africa's prestige and injured its interests at the United Nations and in international gatherings; it had also led to attempts at subversion and assassination and to the revival or exacerbation of frontier disputes.

These developments ran counter to the positive elements in African political thought and feeling, foremost of these being the widespread belief that Africa, a single compact geographic unit, should also be a single compact political unit. Apart from recent concepts such as 'Pan-Africanism' or 'negritude', African continental feeling was greatly strengthened by the fact that throughout its vast expanse Africa had only two main religions, three principal languages and two 'peoples'—the pinko-grey Mediterranean Arab and the black sub-Saharan African. Hence it is that while one may well ask what unites a Pole and a Portuguese or a Thai and a Syrian, the question for Africa is what in essence divides a Senegalese from a Kenyan.

On the plane of practical politics African governments were united in a vigorous pursuit of anti-colonialism and a widespread adoption of the one-party state structure. There could be only one cheer for democracy at Addis Ababa because only one in three of the assembled states had anything approaching parliamentary government.

Sensing that the undertow pulling towards unity had more strength behind it than any surface agitations, the Emperor of Ethiopia placed himself in the forefront of the Pan-African movement. He made his first attempt at a meeting of the Monrovia group at Lagos in May 1962, a gathering which almost succeeded in reconciling the Monrovia and Casablanca groupings. Dissensions that began to appear within these two groups later that year made their members more amenable to reason, so that even the most reluctant could raise no objection to accepting the Emperor's invitation to the first all-African summit meeting. Thus one witnesses the strange spectacle of an often gorgeously-clad septuagenarian Emperor, an emperor in fact and title, leading a movement composed for the most part of shirt-sleeved young anti-imperialist agitators, trade unionists and partisans.

Two large issues dominated the Addis Ababa Conference—whether independent Africa should abandon its divisions and unite, and if so in what form? The first, and by far the more important, question was not really debated by the heads of state; the second by contrast was so. However, the possibility of African unity was debated at great length by the African foreign ministers who held a preparatory meeting before the summit. After a week-long session, all that they could agree on was that after further work on a charter of African Unity by experts and by themselves, the resultant document should be submitted to yet another summit conference. Set against the enthusiasm that the Addis Ababa meeting had generated throughout Africa, such a decision was a total anti-climax.

The heads of state, being political leaders, were naturally more responsive to popular feeling than the professional diplomats. They simply brushed aside the cautious, laborious hesitations of their ministers because, in the words of one president, 'we have not met here merely to decide to meet again'. There was almost a note of desperation in the insistence of some of the leaders on the necessity for a charter. 'We must have a charter,' said Sir Abubakar Tafawa; President Nasser's words were 'let there be anything so long as it is something real'; and President Nyerere stated boldly: 'the people of Africa want any charter'. With speaker after speaker repeating the same general desire for a single continental structure, its establishment became not so much a decision as a taken-for-granted assumption.

It was the form of the organisation that produced genuine debate between the heads of state—fourteen hours of continuous discussion on the conference's final day. They faced two utterly opposed theses. On the one hand the Ghanaian delegation, and one or two others, called for a unitary continental government with a single constitution, parliament, citizenship, currency and defence system, and with just one vote in the United Nations: all this to be established in the shortest possible time. On the other hand the much larger Monrovia group would not accept anything more than a loose federal structure.

As at Bandung and Belgrade, there were sharp differences of opinion between the two groups—in this case the activists, who were neutralist and Pan-African, and the gradualists, who were moderately unionist and pro-Western. As before, the latter, who at Addis Ababa were centred on the thirteen ex-French colonies, were well organised and voted as a close caucus. So while at Bandung and Belgrade the clash resulted, more or less, in a draw, at Addis Ababa there was a clear-cut victory for the well-drilled and more numerous moderates.

The picture of a united Africa, as drawn by President Nkrumah, was a glittering, tempting prospect. He based his call for total, immediate unity not only on a calculation of its practical advantages, which are obvious and impressive, but also on a fear which he expressed in the phrase: unite now or become like Latin America.

The main defect in the Ghanaian thesis was that it was altogether too feverish and apocalyptic, and its time-table too desperately urgent. The alternatives it offered of 'unite or perish' were obviously so unreal that they sent no shudders of fear down any African spine. Its opponents had no great difficulty in disposing of it—Sir Abubakar with heavy scorn; and President Nyerere with savage personal sarcasm.

In the charter the heads of state did better than seemed possible but less well than had originally been expected. The document provides for an annual meeting of the heads of state, a bi-annual meeting of ministers, and a secretariat provisionally located at Addis Ababa; and also for the establishment of various specialised commissions, including a defence commission and a separate one for mediation, conciliation and arbitration. All this amounts to little more than an elaboration of machinery for consultation based on the Lagos Charter of January 1962, which, in its turn, was founded on the Monrovia Charter of May 1961. Yet the fact remained, and it was a massive fact, that there was now just this single charter accepted by the whole of independent Africa: 'We renounce the Casablanca and Monrovia Charters,' as Prime Minister Obote put it.

More important was the adoption of seven principles that included the acceptance of the separate and equal sovereignties and the territorial integrity of all existing states, the condemnation of assassination and subversion, the dedication to the total emancipation of Africa, and non-alignment.

In the speeches there was little mention of non-alignment, which is not to be wondered at. It was thanks to preliminary spade-work by President Sékou Touré of Guinea that the aligned ex-French colonies accepted this reference to a principle they did not practise. The Guinean President would have been well-advised to desist, for his insistence merely meant that so much (aligned) water was added to the (non-aligned) milk as to leave the latter diluted beyond recognition. Fortunately several African states soon made clear that their 'acceptance' of non-alignment was limited to the euphoric atmosphere at Addis Ababa itself.

On colonial issues the Charter was, naturally, forthright and specific. The boycotting of South Africa was accepted, as also the establishment of an air and sea blockade. A freedom fund to help nationalist movements, composed of a contribution by each state of 1 per cent of its national income, was agreed to, and a nine-nation committee to co-ordinate and finance the nationalist struggle in the remaining dependent territories was established at Dar-es-Salaam.

These agreements and decisions added up to a very substantial achievement; yet the Addis Ababa Conference should be judged not merely by the Charter and the Organisation it produced but by subsequent agreements that the Charter and Organisation made possible.

The fourteen months between the two summits was certainly a busy enough period. It witnessed meetings of the committees on defence, economics, scientific and technical affairs, education and culture, and law, as also conferences of ministers of finance, health and labour.

Africa Moves Off on Its Own

The African foreign ministers were kept particularly busy: not only did they hold two regular bi-annual conferences but also two other extraordinary sessions.

The latter were in connection with challenges that the Organisation of African Unity had to meet soon after its inception. When fighting broke out on the borders between Algeria and Morocco, and Ethiopia and Somalia, the OAU was at least able to bring the hostilities to an end and, in the former case, to promote a reasonably permanent settlement. And when army mutinies broke out in Tanganyika, Kenya and Uganda, military aid to the first two countries was pledged by Nigeria and Ethiopia. On a suggestion from the foreign ministers, Tanganyika accepted and resettled refugees from Ruanda, and Uganda some from the Sudan. West African states surrounding Lake Chad agreed on the common exploitation of its waters, and accord seems likely on a trans-Sahara highway.

Strangely enough the OAU did not accomplish as much on the anti-colonial front, where one might have expected quick results. African air-space, it is true, was effectively closed to South Africa, but the committee in Dar-es-Salaam that was meant to spearhead the attack on the colonialists, got bogged down in internecine squabbles between its more and its less activist members.

Nevertheless the second African summit conference in Cairo could, and did, meet in a mood of modest self-congratulation. It was, in fact, restrained to the point of dullness, President Nasser setting the tone with a declaration that unity of thought and approach was what mattered, while resounding resolutions were not important.

That four of the governments represented at Cairo owed their presence there, and perhaps their very existence, to the prompt and vigorous intervention of British commandos and French paratroopers was in itself a great incentive to the sober approach.

In a session mainly devoted to workaday housekeeping details of organisation, the OAU fixed on Addis Ababa as the site of its head-quarters and appointed a Guinean as its Secretary-General.

The debate on an immediate unitary government for Africa was once again revived by President Nkrumah, but though it was more hotly argued than at Addis Ababa, this second round of discussions was not as real as the first since the issue had in fact been decided, at least for some time to come. Once again it was President Nyerere who led the assault on the idea of unitary government which he described as 'a curious animal', 'a series of absurdities' and 'a product of mere propaganda'. The conference made a small bow

359

in the direction of the Pan-Africanist ideal when it appointed a committee to study the Ghanaian plan, while at the same time commending President Nyerere's suggestion of a step-by-step approach to continental unity.

Yet one cannot help feeling that the last word on this matter will be with the Pan-African unitarians rather than with the comfortable and cautious Black Sahibs who happened to sway the votes at Addis Ababa and Cairo: but this may not be for another generation.

Another issue, a product of genuine political idealism, became a casualty at Cairo. The Addis Ababa summit conference had affirmed 'the principle of declaring Africa a denuclearised zone', and opposed the manufacture and testing of all nuclear weapons. A year later the host government to the second summit, the United Arab Republic, had to confess that it was in a serious dilemma on this question because of its fears that Israel was proceeding with a plan to build an atom bomb. Accordingly the Egyptian delegation suggested that one or other of two escape clauses should be added to the declaration on denuclearisation: either a specific exemption should be made in favour of the United Arab Republic, or the ban on acquiring and testing nuclear weapons in Africa should be said to refer only to non-African powers—an obvious reference to France's tests in the Algerian Sahara.

Since neither of these exceptions was acceptable to the other delegations, the conference, in some embarrassment, removed the item on denuclearisation from its agenda altogether. But, since this item was of general humanitarian concern, and could hardly be ignored, a separate declaration on denuclearisation was issued a day after the conference ended, almost as an afterthought. This text made no specific reference to the concept of Africa as a denuclearised zone but submerged it in a general call for world nuclear disarmament. Since the African states adopted such an indecisive and pusillanimous attitude towards the nuclear threat to their own continent, it is little wonder that they showed indifference to this challenge when it was again issued to them, in slightly different form, at the second nonaligned conference three months later.

Though Israel's representation in, and penetration of Africa, had become one of the outstanding features of the African scene, and though this had become a major point at issue between the Arab Africans and the sub-Saharan Africans, the latter, at both summit meetings, refused to give public support to the Arabs against their enemy, despite Arab arguments that Israel was as much a racialist state as

South Africa. Here politics was conforming, honestly, to the geographic and human fact that there is, at bottom, as much or as little sympathy and understanding between the Arabs north of the Sahara and the Africans south of it as there is between the Chinese north of the Himalayas and the Indians south of that other great natural barrier.

A further evidence of honesty was that the Cairo summit conference made no mention of non-alignment in its communiqué, not even in the form of reiterating the reference made to this policy at Addis Ababa. It could hardly do so when several governments before the conference, and at least one head of state at the meeting, declared that they did not accept non-alignment.

And more by default than by deliberate choice Algeria was selected as the site of the Second Afro-Asian Conference.

At the second summit meeting in Cairo the Congo was once again beginning to throw its clammy shadow over the OAU. Subsequently, the organisation tried and failed to get to grips with the troubles of that tortured country. It might yet happen that, despite the promising beginnings made by the OAU, events in the Congo will revive the contest between groups of African states that the Charter of African Unity seemed to have obliterated.

When the African states, through these two conferences and the organisation they produced, set about organising the affairs of their continent, Africa turned inwards on itself and, to some extent, turned its back on the other continents. President Nyerere summed up the distinction when he said at Addis Ababa that the symbols of the greatness of Europe, America and Asia were the symbols of Africa's humiliation.

Certainly the Addis Ababa summit meeting was only too successful in placing Africa at a certain distance from Asia, whether it intended this result or not. It had recommended that the African states at the United Nations 'without prejudice to their membership in and collaboration with the Afro-Asian Group' should 'constitute a more effective African Group'. The result was seen at the following General Assembly Session in the winter of 1963. An African group or sub-group had already been in existence for some years, but the Asian states had hitherto refrained from forming a separate caucus of their own. The manner in which the thirty-four Africans now acted independently in pursuit of their own interests, negotiating—according to the Iraqi representative—with everyone but the Asians, forced fourteen Asian states to form their own sub-group within the

Africa Moves Off on Its Own

Afro-Asian group on the 4th December 1963. To all intents and purposes this was the effective end of the body established by Sir B. N. Rau, on the 5th December 1950—a body that had subsequently, on several occasions, worthily and successfully carried the banners of Africa and Asia before the world. This desire of Africa to move off on its own is neither to be wondered at nor deplored. It corresponds to a deep feeling in African politics.

A growing-apart of Africa from Asia was bound to happen, and should even be welcomed as a sign that each continent, becoming more self-centred, is addressing itself to the essential tasks of internal development. It might even be greeted with relief, for when Asian and African leaders try and work closely together, as at Belgrade, then the impetuosity of the African irritates the Asian and the Asian's caution frustrates the African. The maintenance of a respectful distance is often the best basis for friendship.

The determination of Africa to go its own way and the shedding of its deep inferiority complex—so evident at these summits—and its consequent moving apart from Asia, is a major development in world affairs—a happening of tremendous import.

It needed the piercing, prophetic eye of the poet to discern this possibility years before it became evident. As a young man in Europe Arthur Rimbaud, still a long way in space and time from his residence in the mud-walled city of Harar in Ethiopia, wrote:

> . . . To all you emperors
> Regiments, peoples, colonists, we say: have done! . . .
> Europe, America and Asia, you are doomed
> Before our march of vengeance everything must yield . . .
> Ah, friends! Tis sure, O heart, these are our kin by birth,
> Strange Negro folk, when once we start! Quick, quick, begin![1]

NOTE TO INTERLUDE III

1. Arthur Rimbaud in his 'What do they mean to us?', *Illuminations*, trans. J. N. Cameron, London, 1947.

CHAPTER XVII

Bandung Versus Belgrade

Last scene of all, so far, in the strange eventful history of the independent countries of Asia and Africa is a new contest between those that give primacy to the general principles of non-alignment, symbolised by the Belgrade Conference, and those that are still rooted in the anti-colonial feelings expressed at Bandung.

This antagonism dominated the foreign affairs of Asia and Africa in 1964–5, but it was discernible earlier in differences, not so much of policies as between the styles of operation of individual Afro-Asian leaders. On the one hand were the modest moderates, not over-fond of conferences or of rhetoric; and on the other the ambitious flamboyants, restlessly promoting and attending international gatherings where they could strike grandiose attitudes. Since Afro-Asia's politics in large part turned on the characteristic quirks of a few dominating personalities, these differences of public image were of some importance.

As we have seen, President Sukarno began asking for a repeat performance of Bandung four months after that conference which, from his point of view, had been most successful in drawing world attention to himself and his country. Thereafter the Indonesians emitted their cuckoo-call for a Second Bandung with monotonous regularity, about once every six months, and whenever any international crisis arose. Since the Indonesian leaders knew what had really happened at Bandung, they can have had no illusions as to the suitability of another such conference for solving any particular problem, or generating any volume of real Afro-Asian goodwill. These Indonesian attempts failed time after time, because Mr. Nehru took a realistic view of the potentialities of any such gathering, and in this somewhat sceptical opinion he was, after a time, joined by President Nasser. It was primarily these two leaders who, wisely, prevented the holding of another Bandung for a full ten years. Since this was the attitude of these leading Afro-Asians, why did President Sukarno so persistently seek to hold another conference? With the best will in the world, one can find no reason other than that which prompted Indonesia's sponsorship of First Bandung—a consuming passion for publicity.

President Tito was even quicker to begin his campaign for a repetition of the Belgrade Conference: he made the first such proposal a mere two months after it. At the time, his motives were easily understandable. As a consequence of the stand he had taken at the Belgrade Conference, the Western Powers were not so friendly to him as before; his act of balancing East against West was therefore threatened with disequilibrium; and he reckoned that this unbalance could perhaps be righted by a reaffirmation of his ties with the third group of countries. Only after a lapse of time, in 1963, did Yugoslavia's motives become more general and esoteric.

By sheer dint of repetition, Indonesia succeeded in building up effective pressure behind its demands for a Second Bandung, and it nearly had its way in 1962. In the late summer of that year, Indian opposition to the idea slackened and this, for Indonesia, was a real 'breakthrough'. Apart from India's weak good-nature—an inability to say 'no' firmly was a large and sometimes important element in Mr. Nehru's policy both at home and abroad—there were two other possible reasons for this change in Indian policy. India was already beginning to sense the lack of Afro-Asian backing for her stand against the Chinese thrust; and the Indian Foreign Ministry perhaps thought that such a conference would provide the opportunity for quiet talks with China without the embarrassing necessity of laying down advance conditions. Whatever the reasons, New Delhi all but agreed to attend a preparatory meeting in December 1962.

President Nasser, despite this defection by his Indian friend and mentor, did not slacken his opposition to a meeting. He bluntly told the Indonesians that he felt such a conference to be unnecessary. His misgivings can but have been increased when, in reply to a query from Cairo, Jakarta listed the following items on its proposed agenda—Kashmir, the India-China dispute, the division between the Monrovia and Casablanca groups in Africa, the differences between the aligned and the non-aligned Afro-Asians, economic co-operation and the co-ordination of policy at the United Nations. President Sukarno obviously saw himself as the Great Conciliator.

One of the happy results of the Chinese attack on India was that it rendered impossible any further moves towards the holding of this Afro-Asian meeting; with the two largest Afro-Asian countries in bitter opposition such a gathering would have been inappropriate and inadvisable. Even President Sukarno saw as much when he announced, in November 1962, that he was dropping the idea. At the same time, nothing daunted, he announced that he was considering calling a second non-aligned Summit, and thus began poaching President Tito's preserves.

Sukarno's shift of objective soon took on an ironic aspect, because from the middle of 1963 a real tussle developed between the Indonesian proposal for a Second Bandung and the Yugoslav suggestion for a Second Belgrade. The two conferences might have been complementary to each other, but they had in fact become competitive.

In June 1963 Indonesia, perhaps because it felt that the Afro-Asians had redeemed their honour by evolving the Colombo proposals, even though they had not gained China's acceptance of these, resumed its drive for a second Afro-Asian gathering. The campaign gained a new and, useful, if rather unexpected recruit in Pakistan. One consequence of the Chinese attack on India had been a swift blossoming of friendship between Pakistan—a member of the two anti-Communist alliances CENTO and SEATO—and Communist China, begun when they discovered that in their mutual antagonism for India they had a new and powerful reason for co-operation. Consequently when China supported Indonesia's move for a Second Bandung, and when during the Indonesian President's visit to Karachi in June 1963 his Foreign Minister complained of India's 'selfish and heartless attitude' towards Indonesia's pet project, Pakistan had a twofold reason for warmly supporting the idea of Second Bandung. Thereafter this idea became the focal point of this strange, ill-assorted, tripartite alliance.

One other consequence of Chinese support for Indonesia was that India's equivocal attitude towards an Afro-Asian conference shifted to opposition and, this time, to resolute antagonism. The Indian Government—or rather Indian public opinion imposing its sense of outrage on its government—had no desire to see India at the same table as China, nor attending a meeting at which China could swagger before the rest of an unduly impressed and intimidated Afro-Asia. But a shaken and demoralised Indian Foreign Ministry was not, at this stage, capable of mounting an attack, or a diversionary movement, against a Second Bandung. This task fell to those governments who, for a variety of reasons, positively preferred a Second Belgrade.

This counter-movement developed, in open, formal fashion when Mrs. Bandaranaike conferred with President Nasser in Cairo in mid-

October 1963. Their joint communiqué mentioned 'the necessity' of holding a non-aligned conference some time in 1964, because they had 'the profound conviction that the conference would create a better understanding between states and help towards easing world tension'.

Since by October 1963 world tensions were satisfactorily easing of themselves, one must look behind their words for the real reasons that prompted this particular sponsorship. (Incidentally, combination between the United Arab Republic and Ceylon in this new move showed that any coolness produced by their differing approaches to and at, the Colombo Conference had now been forgotten.)

Ceylon having, for reasons of prestige, taken the lead once in summoning a small conference of small powers was understandably keen to be associated as an original sponsor with an important fellow-member in calling for a full meeting of the non-aligned club.

For the United Arab Republic, a Second Belgrade was desirable if only in contrast to a Second Bandung, which President Nasser still thought was unnecessary and which with its wider membership was likely to give grounds for controversy. Egypt also wished to please its close friend Yugoslavia, who actively wanted another non-aligned Summit (she would be excluded, as a European, from an Afro-Asian gathering, at which, moreover, her arch-enemy China would be present). At a guess, Egypt also reckoned that a non-aligned conference would offer her an escape in the direction of Africa from the disappointing frustrations of Arab policy. The United Arab Republic (and Yugoslavia) were this time as anxious to see the maximum number of African states attend as they had been determined to have the minimum number present at Belgrade.

In the two months that followed the United Arab Republic-Ceylon communiqué, the proposal for a Second Belgrade gathered support more rapidly and in greater volume than did that for a Second Bandung. By mid-December all the leading non-aligned countries (including even Indonesia) had agreed that it should be held in the autumn of 1964.

But Pakistan and China did not by any means give up their efforts for an Afro-Asian conference, not only to be held first, but to eliminate the need for a non-aligned meeting. Visiting Ceylon in December 1963, President Ayub Khan of Pakistan said that a non-aligned conference would be 'a waste of time. What did the last (one) achieve?' Upon this frontal assault, even Mrs. Bandaranaike went so far as to say that a Second Bandung 'would serve a useful purpose'.

Bandung Versus Belgrade

Simultaneously, a far more formidable pro-Bandung assault was being launched by Chou En-lai in Cairo, at the beginning of a tour of Africa. His best efforts failed to get President Nasser's endorsement for an Afro-Asian conference, but he did manage to extract another half-admission that the first Bandung Conference had been a good thing and that there was 'need to safeguard the spirit of the conference'. Armed with this faint praise, Chou En-lai was able to obtain a measure of support from some of the smaller and more gullible non-Arab African states.

What, it may be asked, was the significance of all this high-level pother, toing-and-froing, conferring and lobbying? Clearly Bandung versus Belgrade had come to mean something more than a preference for one selection or group of states over another. The old names of these conferences had come to be labels for new political concepts.

Appropriately, the new connotation of 'Belgrade' is essentially of Yugoslav inspiration. For the Yugoslavs, 'Belgrade' has come to stand for a whole cluster of political ideas and hopes and policies. These it is easy to explore because the Yugoslavs, being political theoreticians, have already produced a considerable body of writing on the subject;[1] unfortunately their output, despite its volume, does not always make meanings or causal connections as clear as they should be. It is mystic, and mysticism, political or otherwise, is by its very nature difficult to define.

The basic premises of the Yugoslav assessment are solid and factual enough. These are that there is a general *détente* in international affairs—a thaw in the Cold War, and some progress towards disarmament. Whether as cause or result, the rigid organisation of the World Powers into two tightly disciplined groups is breaking down and bi-polarisation is giving way to polycentrism.[2] There are rifts in the West European as well as in the Eastern camps, between Russia and China and within the Communist parties the world over, and (the Yugoslavs fail to mention) between the Afro-Asian non-aligned also. So far so good. Next comes the leap into causeless irrationality.

As a consequence of all these welcome developments, the Yugoslavs go on to argue, there must be a recognition of non-alignment as the sole, or principal, path to world peace; there must also be a new codification of the principles of peaceful co-existence. A close reading of the Yugoslav writings on this subject fails to reveal why a world moving slowly towards peaceful conditions needs to be lectured on peaceful behaviour.

Of the two ideas the first—*Non-alignment, a Universal Movement for Peace* (to quote the title of President Tito's address to the 1963 General Assembly), is the more nebulous. All that various Yugoslav writers can do is to repeat their leader's slogan as if it were some religious incantation, which perhaps it is for them. It need not detain us further.

The second Yugoslav idea is more solidly based. Yugoslavs see the movement for the codification of the principles of peaceful co-existence as part of the process of imposing on the lawless nation-state certain moral and legal obligations. They claim to have been fighting for this in the United Nations General Assembly since the session of 1960, and they achieved a measure of success in the session of 1963. The item was then accepted for the agenda, and was discussed. It was agreed that a special committee should examine the possibilities of codification, and inform the 1964 session of the results achieved, in the hope that a declaration on the codification of the principles of co-existence would be passed at the jubilee Twentieth General Assembly session in 1965.

Within this movement the Yugoslavs embrace a Mexican suggestion for the conclusion of a convention on non-intervention, and Mr. Khrushchev's proposal made in January 1964 on the renunciation of force in the solution of territorial disputes.

For the Yugoslavs it is these ideas and proposals that are embodied in the word 'Belgrade', and the adoption and propagation thereof by the largest number of countries possible would be the main purpose of a second Belgrade Conference. Hence they battled for this conference under a 'banner with a strange device—Excelsior!' —stranger still because it was borne by such normally hard-headed people.

In setting up its Committee on Codification the General Assembly listed seven basic principles of co-existence: the ban on the use of force in international relations, solution of disputes by peaceful means, non-intervention, sovereign equality of states, the right of nations to self-determination, international co-operation, a respect for international obligations. If this highly moral stuff tastes familiar, it is because these seven principles are a watered-down version of the four principles (which were, it will be recalled, an edited version of the Five Principles of Panchsheel) that the tolerant General Assembly passed on the 14th December 1957. Yugoslavia was one of the three co-sponsors of that resolution but why, in 1964, she should wish to hark back to the palmy days of Panchsheel, which had proved such a failure, it is not easy to see. The most charitable explanation is that the Yugoslavs are victims of the logical fallacy 'after it and therefore because of it'; there has been a relaxation of international tensions since the 1958 resolution, and since the Belgrade Conference, and therefore they must be its cause.

Fortunately, by no means all the countries that preferred a Second Belgrade to a Second Bandung did so for the mystical-moral reasons of the Yugoslavs. There were some who based their choice on a preference for the non-aligned and realistic optimism of Belgrade over the denunciatory Afro-Asian fervours of Bandung. For them Belgrade signified the broad principle that anti-colonialism was now secondary to such real, contemporary problems as disarmament and the attainment of economic equality between the northern and southern halves of the globe—an idea for which the Yugoslavs can justly claim much credit.

If, at the end of 1963, the Indian Government had been capable of thinking in such broad terms it would certainly have subscribed to this order of ideas. But, India, instead of accepting the special, hard lesson that First Belgrade had taught her—that she had outgrown the Afro-Asian chrysalis—returned, clumsy and unsure, to the Afro-Asian arena at the Colombo Conference. At that meeting, and from subsequent developments, India had discovered that she could expect no justice from the Afro-Asian non-aligned. Accordingly she was not anxious for a Second Belgrade and, by now, was actively opposed to a Second Bandung. But she had also learnt from past experience that if she behaved coyly, Presidents Nasser and Tito were quite capable of going ahead without her in calling a conference. This time, therefore, she promptly supported the idea of Second Belgrade, not because she believed in it, but because she (and Cairo and Belgrade too) hoped that such a meeting (at which China, and Pakistan, would not be present) would at least postpone a Second Bandung and might even render an Afro-Asian gathering unnecessary. For the second time—the first being over the Cairo Economic Conference—India gave appproval to a conference for tactical reasons.

Here it should be noted that Peking, briefly and mischievously, floated the idea that since she was no longer friendly with Russia she was no longer aligned with Moscow and might accordingly be considered eligible for attendance at the non-aligned meeting. Reaction to this suggestion was so incredulous that Chou En-lai, sensibly, foreswore it in Cairo at the start of his African tour.

'Belgrade' had come to mean something more than non-alignment for its original host country; 'Bandung', by contrast, had come to mean something less, something narrower in scope than Afro-Asia for its original host, Indonesia. For some time President Sukarno had been toying with the idea of 'the new emergent forces'; he had used these words several times in his speech at Belgrade, and in 1963, the concept became an active element in Indonesian foreign policy. At Belgrade, he had drawn a distinction between the non-aligned and the newly emerging forces; in a speech in August 1963 he distinguished between them and Afro-Asia, for while he hoped that another Afro-Asian conference would be held, he expressed the further hope that this would be followed by a conference of the New Emerging Forces.

What are these forces and which countries embody them? According to his August speech they are 'all nations in Asia, Africa and Latin America, Socialist countries and the progressive groups in capitalist countries', 'a mighty power composed of two billion people'.

This definition would seem to give the forces a wider, not a narrower geographic range than Afro-Asia, but in practice Sukarno's concept is more restrictive. The key element therein is 'turmoil'. Here the Indonesians project their own condition: their reasons are as follows: Indonesia is in turmoil (the President described the history of Indonesian independence as consisting of two difficult periods, from 1945 to 1950 and from 1950 to 1962); and because it is in turmoil, turmoil in itself is a valuable condition; therefore other countries in turmoil are vital and emergent.

The first concrete expression given to the idea of this new selective grouping was the holding of the games of the New Emerging Forces (GANEFO) in Jakarta in November 1963. Many of the countries that attended the games were not aware of the political category into which they were putting themselves, but the selection made by Indonesia of countries to attend the preparatory meeting for the games indicates who she thinks the New Emerging Forces really are. These countries were Cambodia, China, Guinea, Mali, Iraq, Pakistan, North Vietnam, the United Arab Republic, and Russia, with observers from Yugoslavia and Ceylon. This unusual selection includes both non-Afro-Asians and the aligned. What the countries chosen seem to have in common is an activist attitude towards imperialism and neo-colonialism. When, subsequently, China, Indonesia and Pakistan constituted themselves the core of the new emergent Bandung, what they had in common was anti-Indian feeling. This found expression when in July 1963, by order of President

Sukarno, the Indian Ocean was renamed the Indonesian Ocean.

Behind Second Belgrade lay a new dogma of world peace and behind Second Bandung lay an old dogma of anti-colonialism. But what really gave force and pungency to the competition between the two conferences was that they became identified with one side and the other in the struggle between Russia and China.

Afro-Asia and the Bandung Myth had been vested with worldwide importance thanks to the combined support of Russia and China and the world Communist movement. Now Afro-Asia was in danger of being torn apart by internal Communist splits and by the fact that both Russia and China had decided upon it as their battleground. Their first big campaign against each other, in which battle was joined early in 1964, was fought on the issue of Bandung versus Belgrade.

China had already indicated its full support for Indonesia's proposal for a Second Bandung and for its idea of the New Emerging Forces. Indonesia had also been chosen as China's stalking-horse in South-East Asia, and had, in fact, become a hostage to China's goodwill and support. One of the two principal political elements in Indonesia was its large, strong, well-organised Communist Party that gave allegiance to Peking. President Sukarno could not afford to antagonise this menacing domestic element, and China could but support this all-too-co-operative friend.

Russia then had to be for Belgrade. She could but support the idea of a non-aligned conference. In February 1964, *Pravda* remarked that such a meeting would help the struggle of peace-loving forces against imperialism 'without dividing them on a geographical or any other basis'.

This mention of divisions on other bases is a reference to the attack, on racial and colour lines, that China had mounted on Russia within that most Afro-Asian of all Afro-Asian organisations—the so-called People's Solidarity Movement. This inter-Communist struggle has ended by reducing the Movement to virtual impotence, but in the process it not only had side-effects on the Bandung versus Belgrade tussle; it also helped to define the issues involved.

The first shots against Russian pale-faces were fired by the Chinese at a Conference of Afro-Asian Journalists held in Jakarta in April 1963. (The Solidarity Movement itself disowned this meeting, for it sensed that this was, perhaps, the beginning of a move by the Chinese, and their Indonesian satellites, to set up a rival organisation.) At this Jakarta meeting, attended by thirty-four Afro-Asian

371

countries, Russia and India were excluded from the 'presidium' and the Russians were accorded only observer status since, it was said, they were not really Afro-Asians; and nor they were, in the geographical, or race, or colour sense.

China by now had reason to think that she might not be able to bend the Afro-Asian Solidarity Movement to her will because of what had happened two months earlier, at the Third Conference of the Movement held at Moshi in Tanganyika. To begin with, neither Russia nor China could take much comfort from the opening remarks of President Nyerere of Tanganyika nor the closing remarks of Mr. Jomo Kenyatta. Mr. Nyerere had said that he was going to talk of 'the imperialists old and new' and then went on 'I wish I could honestly say that the second scramble for Africa is going to be a scramble only between the capitalist powers'. The Socialist countries, he went on, seemed to be committing the same crimes as the old capitalist ones, they were using their wealth for capitalist purposes—the acquisition of power and prestige. Marx's class distinction had been transferred to the international plane, to the struggle between the rich nations and the poor nations. 'This is the coming division of the world—a class not an ideological division—with capitalist and socialist countries on both sides of the conflict.' Mr. Kenyatta was almost as explicit when he remarked: 'We must not be too concerned with a fixation about imperialism.' Russia later objected to these sentiments,[3] but the more supple Chinese maintained a clever and discreet silence.

At Moshi China chalked-up two partial successes. She could hardly exclude Russia from a conference of a movement one-third of whose budget was being paid by Moscow; but, despite Russian protest, she obtained a ruling that representatives from East European countries should not be admitted, even as observers, because, as her representative said, there was no place for whites at an Afro-Asian conference.

The other Chinese semi-success was over the India-China dispute. The item that was originally on the agenda was removed by the Tanganyikan chairman of the Political Committee. When the Indians threatened to walk out the item was restored, and the United Arab Republic tabled a resolution asking for the acceptance by both sides of the Colombo proposals 'without reservations'. The Indian delegates, having been assured that this would be passed, unwarily left the conference which then, under Chinese pressure, removed the words 'without reservations' and approved what was left as a 'recommendation' not 'a resolution'. This is a fair example of the level of political integrity obtaining in this movement.

The Moshi Conference marked the peak of Chinese influence in this organisation. At its next meeting, held at Nicosia in September 1963, China sustained a crushing defeat on a new and truly important issue. This was whether or not the conference should express approval of the Moscow Test Ban Treaty which every Afro-Asian government had endorsed, except China. On this question even China's most devoted followers, Indonesia, Japan, Guinea and Algeria, could not support her. The conference officially expressed its approval, but the secretariat was partially successful in concealing the fact that the Chinese delegation had asked for its dissent to be recorded.

The Chinese representatives could hardly have adopted any other line, however unpopular their own position, because their leader, almost in tears, said that if they expressed approval they would be shot when they returned home.[4]

China's loss of influence within the Solidarity Movement continued apace at the Council meeting at Algiers in March 1964. Despite hand-picked delegations from such clients as Cameroon and Ceylon, and despite bribery, China lost friends because of her rigid, dogmatic and pugnacious attacks on Russia and India, and against peaceful co-existence, disarmament and the United Nations. Several times her delegation was shouted down and she gained none of her points in the resolutions. Over her protests the conference welcomed the Geneva Conference on World Trade and the idea of a Second Belgrade; it repeated its endorsement of the Test Ban Treaty; and it rejected a Chinese resolution condemning Mr. Khrushchev's proposal for the peaceful settlement of frontier and territorial disputes. When the Chinese reproached Russia for supplying helicopters to India that had been used against China, the Russian retort was that some of them had been shot down by the Chinese with guns supplied to them by Russia. The end result is that within the Solidarity Movement, and especially within its secretariat at Cairo, China is on the defensive and isolated; she might yet attempt to wreck it from within and resume her efforts at establishing a rival group.

These polemics between the Communists served the Afro-Asians well. It forced them into adopting non-alignment as between Russia and China, with most of them leaning to the former, and it encouraged many of their representatives to speak out and say openly that they were weary of an ideological conflict in which they were not interested. More important was their exasperated insistence that

Russia and China should not make Afro-Asia the scene of their struggle for power. The Afro-Asians were also spurred into saying that colonialism was not necessarily the monopoly of one group of countries, nor any longer the most urgent and important question to be dealt with. In their eyes, the problems of disarmament, and especially of economic development, had become at least equally important, if not more so; and if most of them favoured Russia over China it was because they shrewdly realised that Russia could deliver them substantial aid, while China could only promise it. The racialist basis of the Chinese attack on Russia entailed a revaluation of Afro-Asian attitudes towards this problem also: it was seen that there could be a colour-bar in reverse, and most agreed with the Russian speaker at Algiers when he said 'anyone who tries to set against one another people with a white, black or yellow skin, to cause quarrels between countries and even continents, adheres to the very same imperialist principles of "divide and rule" which have long been condemned'.

Thus China unwittingly prompted the Afro-Asians to define the forward-looking non-aligned policies associated with a Second Belgrade, and to express a preference for these over those regressive, agitatory attitudes that the Chinese had linked to a Second Bandung.

In February 1964 a real race, and a rather undignified one, developed between the non-aligned and the Afro-Asian sponsors. India propelled the non-aligned. Recovering, belatedly, from the shock produced by the disastrous diplomatic results of the Chinese attack, the Indian Foreign Ministry realised that if prompt action were not taken Chou En-lai, then touring Africa, might pick up enough support to bring off a Second Bandung, and to do so in advance of a Second Belgrade. An Indian emissary was despatched hot-foot to Cairo and Belgrade to speed-up the preparatory arrangements and at the same time, with a touch of its former coyness, New Delhi let it be known that it would be prepared to play host to the conference if someone else suggested this. Understandably, Ceylon viewed these maladroit efforts as the latest example of the Indian practice of taking over a conference about which India had, initially, not been enthusiastic. Accordingly a Ceylonese emissary was rushed to Cairo and Belgrade to register protest and to make the valid point that Ceylon, after all, had been one of the two original sponsors. To mollify the indignant Ceylonese it was agreed that the preparatory conference, at ambassadorial level, should be held in Colombo in March 1965.

Bandung Versus Belgrade

The non-aligned barely won the race for primacy for the preparatory conference, because it was soon announced that the initial
meeting for the Second Bandung would be held in Jakarta, a mere
seventeen days after the Colombo Conference. But, thanks to the
United Arab Republic's announcements, the non-aligned did not
really have to worry as to which of the main conferences would be
held first. The Nasser-Bandaranaike communiqué had stated that
the Second Belgrade would be held in 1964 and, early in that year,
Egypt had informed Indonesia that since the second Summit Conference of African Heads of State was being held in Egypt in July and
the Second Conference of Arab Heads of State was also being held
there, in August, it could not fit a Second Afro-Asian meeting into its
programme for that year. This intimation amounted to a veto on
any possibility of holding the Second Bandung before the Second
Belgrade.

Here was a bitter pill for Indonesia to swallow. In a fit of pique
the Indonesian Information Minister said, in February, that his
country was not keen 'on attending the non-aligned summit since his
country considered an Afro-Asian meeting' more urgent. In the
event Indonesia had to swallow its resentment.

The main debate at the Colombo Preparatory Conference for the
Second Belgrade turned on the procedural question of just how much
power of decision delegates possessed. All the twenty-five countries
present at Belgrade had been invited and only Burma and Mali
stayed away; the rest were represented by ambassadors ,and they had
to make up their minds whether they should limit themselves to deciding only on the time, place and agenda of the main conference or
whether they should also lay down its membership which was, of
course, by far the most important aspect of a Second Belgrade.

On membership there were two points of view. Both agreed that
the Second Belgrade should have a larger membership than its
eponymous predecessor. India, it will be recalled, had wanted forty
to forty-five countries to be invited to that first conference and she
still felt that to be the ideal number. Non-alignment, she argued, had
made its way in the world and gained new adherents, but an indis-
criminately large membership would merely devalue the policy and
blur its distinctiveness.

Yugoslavia, with some support from the United Arab Republic,
had completely reversed its pre-Belgrade attitude on membership.
Then, both these countries had fought hard and successfully to maintain the exclusivity of the non-aligned club. Now, the United Arab

Bandung Versus Belgrade

Republic, in view of the success of the Addis Ababa summit, wanted to bring in all the independent African states and Yugoslavia, in addition, wanted to draw in as many Latin Americans as possible. She was thinking in terms of thirty or even forty extra members. As we have seen, enlarged membership was part of her campaign to propagate non-alignment and co-existence as universal panaceas for peace.

Yugoslavia felt that this question of membership was so important that it could not be decided by ambassadors but should be handled at least by foreign ministers, and President Tito signified that he himself would be prepared to attend and address any such gathering. India also favoured a foreign minister's conference, but for different reasons. She hoped to play host to such an intermediate-level gathering, if not to the main conference, and so once again to assert New Delhi's position as a leading non-aligned capital. She also felt that this intermediate conference would so fill up the conference calendar for the latter half of 1964 that there would be no time left for a Second Bandung. To such trivia had India's non-alignment descended.

The argument for and against a separate Foreign Ministers' Conference was the usual topical and controversial question that dominates such conferences, to be forgotten a month later. Ceylon was bitterly opposed to the idea because she felt it was an Indian attempt to belittle the importance of the current meeting. To get around this anti-Indian suspicion, Yugoslavia at one point proposed that the foreign ministers should meet at Accra instead of New Delhi. It was finally decided that the foreign ministers should meet separately, but immediately before and in conjunction with the main conference.

Ultimately, it was agreed that the conference as a whole should decide on membership, rejecting a Ceylonese suggestion that this be handled by a committee on which she did not include India! After all these lengthy procedural discussions, agreement on membership was quickly reached by the simple process of inviting all and sundry.

It will be recalled that the Cairo Preparatory Meeting of June 1961 had drawn up criteria of membership which, however, had not been applied when additional invitations to Belgrade were discussed. It was voting power and bargaining power that had counted then. The same was true at Colombo. There was no attempt to define the precise principles or limits of non-alignment, still less to apply them to individual invitees.

Consequently about sixty-five countries were accepted as invitees to the Second Belgrade, forty more than before. These included the

376

twenty-five original members; all thirty-two members of the Organisation of African Unity (OAU) plus Kenya, Zanzibar, Nyasaland
and Northern Rhodesia; the Provisional Government of Angola,
and any other such government approved by the OAU; the thirteen
Arab states; in Asia, Laos; from the Caribbean, Trinidad and Tobago
and Jamaica; from Europe, Finland, Sweden, and Austria; and,
from Latin America, Argentine, Bolivia, Brazil, Chile, Mexico, Uruguay and Venezuela.

In her opening speech Mrs. Bandaranaike had warned her hearers
against a watering down of the concept of non-alignment but that
is precisely what came about.

The blanket invitation to the thirty-two OAU states was particularly unprincipled. It is true that at Addis Ababa they had accepted
non-alignment as a constituent of the continent's foreign policy, but
at a subsequent meeting in Lagos of foreign ministers several of
them—those from Liberia, Sierra Leone, and Malagasy, for instance
—had specifically repudiated non-alignment.

Again, the defence commitments of the Latin Americans to the
Organisation of American States preclude non-alignment, but once
again the non-aligned decided to ignore this fact.

Apart from Yugoslavia's propagandising missionary zeal, the most
likely reason for this large invitation list was an attempt by the non-
aligned to outbid the Second Bandung, to which, of course, they
knew all the Africans would automatically be invited.

Having taken this step backward because of their uncertainty, it
is not surprising that the non-aligned were pushed even further back
during the main conference. Having reached agreement on membership the ambassadors quickly disposed of the questions of time and
place—the first week of October at Cairo—and of the agenda.

Yugoslavia managed to get its theme of 'peaceful co-existence and
the codification of its principles by the United Nations' on to the
agenda. And Indonesia was given a consolation prize with a reference
to 'the promotion of positive trends and new emerging nationalist
forces in international affairs'. Led by India the preparatory conference had flatly turned down an Indonesian proposal that it endorse
the idea of a separate conference of the New Emerging Forces (a
Trojan horse of the Second Bandung within the walls of the Second
Belgrade!). The Indonesians failed largely because they could not
give concrete shape to their idea, which is hardly surprising: most of
the countries in the grouping of that name are neither new, nor
emergent nor forceful.

377

Not that non-alignment as a policy emerged in any way strengthened by the deliberations at Colombo. By sacrificing quality to
quantity, non-alignment was, in fact, gravely weakened.

At Colombo the principles underlying the concept and policy of
non-alignment could and should have been discussed. At the Jakarta
preparatory meeting for a Second Bandung in April 1965 there was
never any doubt that the main concern was tactics, pure and simple—
or rather, impure and complicated.

Indonesia, from the start, imparted this devious quality to the
conference by tampering with the invitation list so as to produce a
packed membership of countries she believed favourable to her ideas.
Hence, in contrast to what had happened at Colombo, the twenty-
nine countries that had been present at Bandung were not all invited;
eleven of them were dropped and nine new countries were added. Of
the twenty-seven governments asked, twenty-two were represented at
Jakarta, and more than half were African—a decisive change in
composition.

For some obscure reason Indonesia chose to be devious on the
question of China's attendance. First it was officially stated that she
would not be present, though as a member at Bandung she had
every right to be there; next, three days before the conference began,
it was announced that she would attend; finally, a large Chinese
delegation arrived headed by no less a person than Chen Yi, the
Foreign Minister.

Since India's delegation was also headed by a cabinet minister, this
meeting developed into the first direct confrontation at high level
between India and China since the Chinese attack. Their antagonisms, this time, were played in a minor key, and India achieved a substantial diplomatic triumph over China through a display of toughness and frankness that was a novelty in Indian diplomatic practice.

From the first China was thrown on to the defensive, and the anti-
Indian group consisting of China-Pakistan-Indonesia into confusion,
by an early and unexpected two-pronged Indian attack.

This the Indian representative launched in an opening speech that
simultaneously put forward a minor and sensible idea, and a major
but questionable one: on time and place India suggested that the
Second Bandung should be held in Africa in April 1965, the tenth
anniversary of the first conference, and on membership she suggested
invitations to Russia and Malaysia.

The first of these proposals was a vicious thrust at Indonesia. By
now the whole world knew that Indonesia had been persistently ask-

ing for a Second Bandung Conference only in order that it should be held in Bandung and thus bring publicity and prestige to Indonesia once again.

The Indian thrust was the more vicious because it was at once clever and plausible. There was a certain emotional correctness about the idea of a tenth anniversary, which could not be denied. And the suggestion that the venue should be Africa had merely to be made to be seen as inevitable. It rightly accorded recognition to the 'Afro' half of Afro-Asia, a half that had emerged into independence subsequent to the first conference. There had, in truth, been some vague suggestion at Bandung itself that its successor should be held in the other continent. But what carried the day was that the pleased and flattered African representatives were in a majority at Jakarta. Indonesia had tried to pack the membership, but in the end was hoist with her own petard.

She and Pakistan did not, however, give in without a struggle. For four days they insisted that an Afro-Asian conference was more urgent than that of the non-aligned; but they could hardly oppose Africa as a site, and the only African capital that was in a position to play host to such a conference at short notice was Cairo, which had already said it was not available for 1964. Hence in the end, and to Indonesia's bitter disappointment, the dual Indian suggestion as to both time and place had to be accepted. It was left to the Organisation of African Unity to fix the meeting place, and Pakistan managed to bring the time forward by a month, from April to March, so that it should not clash with her presidential 'elections'.

On the issue of venue, China unceremoniously abandoned her two allies. She was gathering strength to do battle on the question of Russian membership and she did not wish to antagonise the Africans whose support she needed on what was, for her, a more important question.

Before examining India's motives in proposing Russian membership the point must be made that Moscow very much wanted to be invited. This wish represents consistent policy. Before the First Bandung Conference, when it was clear that no states of the Soviet Union were going to be asked, Mr. Molotov, it will be recalled, put out a feeler when he told an Indian visitor that the Asian states of the Soviet Union attached great importance to the conference, which the Soviet Government welcomed also. The Russians, in 1955, were still drawing a distinction between their Asian Republics and the Central Government in Moscow. In 1964, however, they said that they wanted to attend only as the Soviet Union, and thereby weakened their case.

The Indian proposal at Jakarta represented a second change in Indian thinking on Russia as an Asian country. In 1947 the Central Asian Republics had, of course, all been invited to the Asian Relations Conference; but before the Bogor preparatory meeting in 1954 Mr. Nehru sent a note to the four other sponsoring prime ministers saying: 'I would not invite the Soviet Asian Republics. We should consider the Soviet Union as a unit. It can hardly be described as an Asian power.' Now a reversal of policy, approved by Mr. Nehru himself, led India to say that Russia was an Asian power, or perhaps, by its actions had become an Asian power.

The Indian delegate at Jakarta argued that Russia was an Asian country because, geographically, the greater part of its territory lay in Asia, and that it had ancient links of culture and civilisation with the rest of Asia. And it had become an Asian power by its support of Asian causes—as during the Suez crisis—by its loyalty to the Spirit of Bandung, and by its participation in such organisations as the Afro-Asian Solidarity Movement and attendance at the Afro-Asian Games. Its absence from the Bandung Conference was described as 'an unfortunate omission'.

None of these arguments carry conviction. The fact remains that the Soviet Union is a single political entity with its centre in Moscow, which is a city in Europe. If most of its territory is in Asia, most of its population lives in Europe. Above all, on two very important counts Russia is wholly different from the Afro-Asians. She has no recent history of imperial domination or of an anti-colonial struggle; and she is a developed not an underdeveloped or developing country—she lies to the north of the line separating these two groups. These two characteristics were to be found in the Soviet Central Asian Republics but, for obvious reasons, Moscow did not want them to be considered for membership.

Nor did India herself abide by her inclusive geographic principle, because she declared herself 'opposed' to inviting Israel, South Africa and Southern Rhodesia, presumably because all three are founded on a racialist base.

Even more significant is the fact that the Indian suggestion ran counter to the basic principle that the Big Two should be kept out of inter-Afro-Asian affairs. This idea, largely of Indian origin, was after all the germinal concept which produced non-alignment from within the body of Afro-Asia.

380

Bandung Versus Belgrade

The reasons that moved India thus to repudiate its own past principles and practice should have been of compelling importance, but
they are not. It needs no great political acumen to discern that India
wants Russia at the Second Bandung Conference in order to please
Russia, to keep China on the defensive beneath a barrage of heavy
Russian artillery and, perhaps, to provoke China into another of its
immoderately-worded attacks that the Afro-Asians find distasteful.
These reasons explain the Indian move; they do not justify it.

The justifiable doubts felt by the other Afro-Asians about the
wisdom of India's suggestion became painfully apparent when the
subject came up for discussion at Jakarta. China and its henchmen
naturally strongly opposed the idea but, of the fifteen-odd delegations
from which some support could have been expected for Russia's
admission, only one, Ceylon, actually spoke out. This silence may
have been due to a desire not to get embroiled in what was really an
extension of the Russia-China dispute, or to a recognition of the
force of the arguments against Russia's attendance, which delegates
did not wish to express so as not to embarrass her or her Indian
sponsor. Not even the United Arab Republic, to which Russia had
given and is still giving massive military and economic assistance,
said a word in her favour. Russia has always claimed that her aid is
given without 'strings' attached; the United Arab Republic proved
this at Jakarta.

Both India and China were excluded from the sub-committee set
up to decide on membership, but at 10 p.m. on the last night of the
meeting, they had to be called in. Their face-to-face confrontation
lasted till 2 a.m. and the result was a draw. India first secured
majority support for a resolution saying that there had been differences of opinion on membership and that the matter should be referred for final decision to the heads of states themselves. The
Chinese Foreign Minister threatened to walk out of the conference
if this was accepted. So, with some assistance from the Indonesian
chairman, the Chinese were able to obtain a re-wording to the effect
that there were further differences of opinion on whether or not the
matter should be referred to the heads of state.

For the first time the unanimity rule or the consensus procedure
was not followed at an Afro-Asian conference. The unusual double
reservation described above left the door slightly ajar for Russia's
possible entrance, but in itself was hurtful to Russia's prestige.

At Colombo, India had made a tentative effort to cause Malaysia
to be invited to the non-aligned conference, but had been inhibited

381

by the fact that no Malaysian leader had ever said that that country was non-aligned. At Jakarta, India was on surer ground and insisted on this invitation, despite strong Indonesian opposition. The resolution on this question said that the matter should be deferred pending resolution of the Malaysia-Indonesian dispute, but it also recorded the support of several countries for Malaysia's immediate admission.

A comparison of the agendas produced by the Colombo and Jakarta preparatory conferences reveals something of a reversal of roles. The non-aligned conference was to discuss imperialism, colonialism and neo-colonialism which were relegated to a position of secondary importance at Belgrade. On the other hand the Afro-Asian meeting was instructed to pay special attention to problems of economic development which, normally, would have been of greater interest to the non-aligned states.

It has been said that 'Bandung' and 'Belgrade' stand for broadly different approaches to the problems of the world. It has also been said that they could complement one another because they are not necessarily competitive. For example, thanks to the dilution of non-alignment, the lists of the invitees to the two conferences are not very different. Yet these policy differences have become the subject of controversy and open competition between the Afro-Asian non-aligned, because certain governments are trying to use these conferences merely to serve their own narrow national interests; and this line is being pursued more by the Afro-Asians than by the non-aligned.

This misuse of the 'Bandung' and 'Belgrade' concepts for individual ends, and the splits that it could produce, would all be greatly accentuated if and when China were definitely and exclusively to be associated with Bandung, and Russia with Belgrade. The latter identification is less likely, for Russia could hardly claim to be non-aligned unless she were to slip into this group under the broad Yugoslav categorisation of 'non-aligned because practising peaceful co-existence'. But, since Jakarta, Russia has concentrated her efforts on proving that she is Asian; in an official diplomatic note to all Asian governments she has argued that geographically, socially, culturally, ethnically and otherwise she is linked more with Asia than with Europe. It is difficult to decide whether this statement should be taken as a serious policy statement or whether it is merely, on a national scale, an expression of the impulse to return to the womb. There is every indication that Russia herself considers the matter most seriously. She is determined to be present at the Second Bandung Conference, so as to prevent China from dominating the Afro-

Bandung Versus Belgrade

Asians on its own. She will do what she can to force them out of a position of non-alignment as between herself and China. Such external pressures, firmly applied, suggest that Afro-Asia rather than the non-aligned will be rent asunder by the Russia-China feud. India would have done the Afro-Asian non-aligned a grave disservice if she, the principal organiser of the Afro-Asian feeling, had been in any way responsible for such a division within Afro-Asia.

NOTES TO CHAPTER XVII

1. A series of articles on this subject has appeared in the monthly publication *Review of Internal Affairs*, Belgrade.
2. *Polycentrism*, ed. by W. Laqueur and L. Labedz, New York, 1962. The term was coined by Togliatti, the Italian Communist leader.
3. V. Kudryavtsev: article in *Mezhdunarodnaya Zhizn*, no. 5, 1963, Moscow.
4. From a source in the Solidarity Movement Secretariat.

CHAPTER XVIII

The Second Non-Aligned Summit, Cairo, October 1964

The second conference of the non-aligned nations marked the return of non-alignment to the parent body of Afro-Asianism, both because of the scope of its membership and the type of its recommendations. The tussle between 'Bandung' and 'Belgrade' ended in a merger—Belgrade merging itself with Bandung, not because of a congruence of political ideas or attitudes, which remain distinct if not necessarily antagonistic, but because of the timidity of the non-aligned in the face of the steadily-growing cohorts of the Afro-Asians. For non-alignment, the Cairo Conference was a retrogressive return to a state of mind it had outgrown.

Apart from two unexpected and unfortunate developments during the conference this meeting in Cairo, while the largest, was perhaps because of that, also the least remarkable of all the Afro-Asian conferences held since 1947: and those two developments confirmed not just the failure, but the refusal of the non-aligned states to assume moral responsibility in world affairs.

The Cairo Summit did, however, help to bring one very significant trend into the open. At this conference of the non-aligned who had mistakenly confused peaceful co-existence with non-alignment, the first public attempt was made by an organised group of countries to diminish the importance and the urgency of peaceful co-existence, almost to the point of repudiating the idea.

It was, in a way, unfortunate, that this conference did not coincide with a dangerous political crisis, as had been the case with both those at Bandung and Belgrade. This circumstance not merely robbed the meeting of urgent topicality; it also deprived it of a focus and even of a valid *raison d'être*. The conference was presented with a challenge, the prospect of Chinese acquisition of the atom bomb, but it was able to turn its back on that challenge, on the pretext that the possibility was just below the horizon.

The non-aligned leaders at the Second Belgrade faced a very differ-

ent international scene from that which confronted them at the time
of the First Belgrade, because of three momentous developments that
had taken place in the intervening three years.

Thanks to the East–West *détente*, that had been greatly helped by
the Cuban crisis, polycentrism had made such progress within the
two blocs that it was becoming difficult to talk, in the simplistic terms
of former years, of 'East' and 'West'. To most of the non-aligned
peoples, who practised non-alignment as a game of playing-off one
side against the other, the proliferation of power centres seemed to
put them out of business.

The second development is the nuclear stalemate that has reduced
the Great Powers to virtual impotence. The two nuclear giants are
so muscle-bound that they can take no really drastic action, military
or political, against even the most impertinently minute antagonist.
This means that for the non-aligned the area of choice is both wider
and freer than before.

Thirdly, at the Geneva Conference on Trade and Development, the
North–South division between the haves and the have-nots has been
formalised, and 'the Seventy-Seven' delegations from the three
underdeveloped continents have functioned effectively as the new
and powerful bloc.

From the speeches of the non-aligned at Cairo, and from the communiqué they issued, one gathers that only the Geneva Conference
had made any real impact on their political thinking. A polycentric
independence of choice in foreign affairs was something that almost
all the leaders found too new and too daring for their peace of mind.

The huge auditorium of Cairo University in which fifty-seven delegations[1] met, forty-seven as full members with ten observers, was
indicative of the elephantiasis that now afflicted non-aligned membership. This over-large gathering was, of course, the result of sacrificing
quality to quantity. If any sort of criteria had been applied, no more
than forty countries, if that, should have been invited. The twenty-
eight delegations at Belgrade met as members of a fairly exclusive
club; the Cairo conference resembled the general meeting of a public
institution.

If the limits of the definition of non-alignment still have any clarity
and sharpness, however blurred by the indiscriminate hospitality of
the non-aligned countries, this is due to the refusal of invitations to
Cairo by those African states honest and courageous enough to say
that they were aligned.

Despite this gross inflation in numbers, the character of the membership remained overwhelmingly Afro-Asian. No less than forty-five of the forty-seven members were from that area, twenty-nine from Africa alone. The new geographic extension took place in the Western Hemisphere from which there were now nine observer countries instead of three: only one new recruit came from Europe—Finland, as an observer.

The Asians were obviously so overawed by the fact that the Africans outnumbered them by two to one, that they meekly acquiesced in the African mishandling of the question of permitting Mr. Tshombe, the Prime Minister of the Congo, to represent his country. This thoroughly undignified episode—Mr. Tshombe's arrest on his arrival in Cairo and his subsequent virtual expulsion—was the topical, irrelevant issue that, as so often before, dominated the news headlines during the conference. It not merely lowered the tone of the gathering; it also established the dangerous precedent that a conference can pick and choose between a country's leaders as to who should or should not represent it. Most of the Asians and some African delegations disapproved of the conference decision to exclude Mr. Tshombe, but they nevertheless accepted it in silence.

The United Arab Republic's leading editorialist, on the eve of the conference, wrote that many people were asking sceptically, 'What have the non-aligned to add to what they said at Belgrade?' and he answered: 'Many new things'—things which certainly could have been said at Cairo but were not. One head of state, truthfully, described the forty-seven speeches as 'one long soliloquy'. In almost all of them one found the same set themes: a review of events since Belgrade, self-congratulation on the growth of non-alignment, support for the United Nations and for the group of the Seventy-Seven at Geneva.

From many speakers, mainly those not invited to Belgrade, came rather patronising references to the earlier conference on the score that it had only dealt with the general principles of non-alignment. This criticism was coupled with frequent definitions of non-alignment, along the usual lines, and equally frequent references to the need for non-alignment to find a new role and a new purpose in international affairs. Despite this feeling, entirely justified, that non-alignment, as normally practised, had reached a dead-end, no concrete suggestions on its new role were forthcoming: the non-aligned soul searched restlessly but in vain for a new political body.

Fairly numerous references were made to the horrors of a nuclear holocaust and, for some leaders, merely mentioning them justified the claim that the non-aligned constituted a moral force. Events in the conference itself soon disproved this assertion.

As with its predecessors, the real battles were fought, and the real work was done, in the committees and sub-committees of the conference, which had gone into session even during the foreign ministers' meeting that preceded the main conference. The principal issue debated was the same that had preoccupied First Belgrade: this was the question of priorities—which is more important and urgent, world peace or decolonisation? The battle was fought all over again at Second Belgrade, but this time the outcome was rather different.

Indications of this division were given in the public speeches. There were the all-too-numerous and all-too-lengthy discourses of the African leaders in which they belaboured imperialism and colonialism and neo-colonialism. When they talked of the Cold War it was to say, with the President of Mali, that 'the cooling of the Cold War has led to the hotting up of the hot war'. The larger international *détente* was something in which they did not seem interested or did not want.

The lines of division were most clearly drawn in speeches from the leaders of three of the old-established non-aligned countries. President Sukarno made a frontal assault on the policy of peaceful co-existence when he said that there could be no real co-existence as long as colonialism existed anywhere in the world: therefore the anti-colonial struggle came first. President Tito, in a lengthy defence of peaceful co-existence, gave it primacy not only over anti-colonialism but even over non-alignment; though, as if in partial answer to President Sukarno, he said that peaceful co-existence did not mean an acceptance of the *status quo*. Prime Minister Shastri of India added fuel to the fire when, as Mr. Nehru had done before him at First Belgrade, he declared that nuclear disarmament came 'first and foremost'. He even put 'the peaceful settlement of border disputes' before anti-colonialism. And, quite deliberately, he set himself against the whole approach of President Sukarno when, in a quietly controversial aside, he declared that the non-aligned must strive 'to resolve all differences through peaceful methods by conciliation as distinct from confrontation'.

At First Belgrade the debate in committee had been between the Asians and the Africans. At Second Belgrade it was between on the one hand the group of the New Emerging Forces led by Indonesia, and on the other India, supported by a few Asians. Besides Indonesia, the NEF clique contained Cambodia, Tanganyika, Burundi, Guinea,

Mali, Cuba, Congo (Brazzaville) and, often, Algeria and Ghana. Ceylon gave fairly consistent backing to India; the United Arab Republic followed a wavering line in between. Yugoslavia agreed with India on most issues but kept silent in debate: the solitary white-skinned Yugoslavs seemed inhibited when they met the browns and the blacks and the yellows *en masse*.

The NEF group was well-drilled and co-ordinated in its attack. Hence the somewhat improbable intervention of the representative of the small, remote kingdom of Burundi who spoke at great length on the plight of Cambodia. The Chinese sponsors had clearly put in a lot of preparatory spadework, whereas the non-aligned group were non-aligned with one another.

In the prolonged debates on peaceful co-existence, the attack on it was led by Indonesia which had submitted an angrily-worded fifteen-page memorandum on the subject. The Indonesian representative even went so far as to say that peaceful co-existence was impossible between states of differing political and social systems, and that war was preferable to co-existence of that type. This, of course, is the Chinese thesis in its purest form. The NEF approach to the anti-colonial struggle was presented by Burundi, which claimed that healthy prophylactic interference in another country's affairs was not real interference.

The other issue that produced much discussion concerned the inviolability of traditional frontiers, which India sought to have re-affirmed in an obvious attempt to put China in the wrong. Differences of opinion on these issues were so sharp that, for the first time in such a conference, votes were taken in the committees.

Because at Cairo there was no one of the stature of Mr. Nehru to oppose the propagandist approach of the New Emerging Forces group, and because the group made effective use of the organisational weapon, it succeeded in setting its stamp on the final communiqué. This was twice as long as the Bandung declaration and three times the length of the Belgrade communiqué to which, however, it added nothing new or significant. The difference is to be found in style and emphasis.

While the Belgrade document dealt briefly and eloquently with the major problems of world peace in large general terms, the Cairo statement referred in detail and in declamatory language to numerous specific problems. The biggest difference is that while, however reluctantly, First Belgrade accepted the Nehru thesis that 'imperialism is weakening' and colonialism 'disappearing', Second Belgrade emphatically asserted the continuing and dangerous vitality of these two policies.

This was a very considerable victory for the NEF group: it is hardly accidental that the section on colonialism came first in the communiqué, a long way ahead of that on co-existence. The 'Bandung' idea thus unfortunately asserted its primacy over that of 'Belgrade'.

The communiqué showed that India made some modest gains. There are several references to the sanctity of frontiers, which are as relevant to the substance of the India-China conflict, and as efficacious, as the words on the Lamaist prayer-flags that flutter in the cold winds of the Himalayan passes through which the Chinese army attacked.

Still bemused with peaceful co-existence, India presented a new set of ten principles. Nine principles are embodied in the communiqué, six and a half from the Indian draft. Yugoslavia's favourite idea that the principles should be codified by the United Nations was also accepted. Thus there are now in existence, apart from the one, single Golden Rule of real peaceful co-existence, the Two Principles of the preamble to the United Nations Charter, the Four Principles accepted by the General Assembly, the Five Principles of Panchsheel, the Nine Principles of Cairo and the Ten Principles of Bandung. One small orange is shredded into ever-increasing quantities of moralistic marmalade.

The Cairo communiqué is, for two reasons, a puzzling document. Like the Bandung declaration it is not a compromise between, but a compendium of, self-contradictory political positions. Thus, while declaring that imperialism and neo-colonialism are 'a basic source of international tension', to be fought by force of arms, it also states that peaceful co-existence is 'the only way to strengthen world peace'. The puzzlement deepens because of the announcement, made on the day after the conference, that certain delegations maintained 'reservations' on the communiqué and that these would be kept secret. India, more or less publicly, declared her reservation to the principle of self-determination being applied to 'peoples'. But no one, evidently, will ever know what part of the communiqué each country accepts or rejects.

On two issues the Cairo Conference descended to earth with a hollow thud from the cloudy heights of peaceful co-existence.

The first concerned the attempt made by the non-aligned to mediate between India and China. A somewhat impatient Mr. Shastri pointed out to President Nasser that the Colombo proposals, now over two years old, had produced no results. In reply the United Arab Republic President said that since all six countries that sponsored them were present at Cairo, he would try to revive the proposals. It is doubtful whether the attempt was ever really made. The fact remains that only one leader, Mrs. Bandaranaike herself, made the briefest of references to the India-China dispute and to the non-aligned mediation. This non-aligned conference could have thrown its full moral weight behind these proposals; by not doing so it gave them a decent non-aligned burial.

The second challenge to the conference as a whole also originated with the Indian Prime Minister. Following persistent reports that China was about to explode a nuclear device, Mr. Shastri proposed that the conference should send a mission to China to ask her to stop making atomic weapons. This idea was inserted into his speech at the last minute, and other delegations were not sounded beforehand. However, it was not for lack of preparation that the idea fell flat. Several leaders told Mr. Shastri in private that his suggestion was a good one and that the conference should 'do something' about it. The United Arab Republic was among those who thought that such a mission 'was unnecessary', and only one speaker, President Makarios, gave public support to the Indian idea. In the event the conference did nothing about it; it did not call for a special mission; it did not issue a special peaceful plea (as at Belgrade), or even insert a special paragraph in the communiqué.

All that India got was a single, interpolated sentence calling on countries without nuclear arms to refrain from making them. In return India proposed, and the conference accepted, the proposal that the forty-seven signatories should renounce any idea of making atomic weapons. India can make the atomic bomb: the other forty-six cannot. Thus, jeopardising its country's national security, the Indian Government has tied its hands in return for a worthless non-aligned moral interdiction on China.

Just how worthless was this interdiction became apparent when, a mere six days after the conference, China detonated its nuclear device. Its act can only be interpreted as a deliberate slap in the face for the non-aligned. Apart from India, of the other forty-six some six countries, including Ghana, Cyprus, Uganda and Zambia, criticised the Chinese action. Two countries, Cambodia and Indonesia, went so far as to praise it, and a few weeks later Indonesia, despite its recent pledge at Cairo, announced that it would soon be manufacturing its own atomic bombs; this claim is wholly incredible but is revealing of how a country can aspire, vainly, to a horrific wickedness.

The non-aligned countries refused to act on the two proposals made by Mr. Shastri because they were afraid of displeasing China. Though it was absent, China's ominous shadow lay heavy across the assembled non-aligned peoples. Thus the Shastri proposals stripped the non-aligned lands of their moral pretentions, showed them to be a group of countries like any other, and revealed that if they wish to be a real group they must find a similarity of policy and not depend on the geographic accident that almost all of them come from Africa and Asia.

Lest this should seem too harsh a judgement perhaps this point needs to be added: there is necessarily a gap between the counsels of perfection of the revealed religions and daily human practice. But when counsels of perfection do not descend from heaven, but are framed by ordinary mortal politicians and diplomats, then the existence of not merely a gap but a contradiction between the counsels and the conduct of the states those diplomats represent amounts either to deliberate hypocrisy on the part of the states, or to an amiable hypocrisy on the part of the diplomats.

Second Belgrade might have achieved the level of First Belgrade if a second Nehru had emerged.[2] He was much missed at Cairo, and there were many moving tributes to his memory. There was also much speculation as to who would succeed him as the unacknowledged leader of the non-aligned world. Though this occasioned some sidewards glancing between the main contenders for the role, the large void left by Jawaharlal Nehru is still empty.

Three tendencies, of interest for the future, emerged somewhat obliquely from the Second Belgrade. The first was the importance ascribed to the Geneva Conference on World Trade. This perhaps indicates that the non-aligned have at last awakened to where, in the future, their real interests lie. It would not be too daring a prediction that, in the years ahead, the only non-aligned or Afro-Asian conferences that will have any real value will be those dealing with economic questions.

Secondly, at Cairo some of the so-called non-aligned countries sought, violently almost, to distinguish between non-alignment and peaceful co-existence. Those who did so were the wrong sort of people, for the wrong reasons, and in the wrong context; for anti-colonialism is not more urgent or important than the problems of peace. But to detach, in whatever manner, the moralistic excrescence of peaceful co-existence from non-alignment, and that this should be done by some of the non-aligned themselves, is a great service to the principle of independent choice in world affairs.

Thirdly, under the impulsion of the small but vocal New Emerging Forces group, Afro-Asian sentiment seemed to swamp the quieter, wiser counsels of non-alignment. This triumph can only be temporary, for anti-colonialism is, by its very nature, a wasting asset. It was a victory gained by default, because the non-aligned countries were un-organised and leaderless at Cairo.

Some of the past conferences of the Afro-Asian non-aligned peoples had practical results, however modest and indirect. Such were the New Delhi Conference on Indonesia, the First Colombo Conference, the Cairo Economic Conference and the two African Summits. Others, like Bandung and Belgrade, had no direct practical results but were symbols of new ideas; their very names have a historic resonance. But that can only happen once. At the second non-aligned Summit all the various streams and rivulets of non-alignment seemed to flow back into the sea of Afro-Asia. And the sea is vast and hospitable and salty and indifferently uncomprehending.

NOTES TO CHAPTER XVIII

1. The following countries were present at Cairo as full members: Afghanistan, Algeria, Angola, Burma, Burundi, Cambodia, Cameroon, Central African Republic, Ceylon, Chad, Congo (Brazzaville), Cuba, Cyprus, Dahomey, Ethiopia, Ghana, Guinea, India, Indonesia, Iraq, Mauritania, Jordan, Kenya, Kuwait, Laos, Lebanon, Liberia, Libya, Malawi, Mali, Morocco, Nepal, Nigeria, Saudi Arabia, Senegal, Sierra Leone, Somalia, Sudan, Syria, Togo, Tunisia, Uganda, United Arab Republic, United Republic of Tanganyika and Zanzibar, Yemen, Yugoslavia and Zambia.
   The observers were: Argentine, Bolivia, Brazil, Chile, Finland, Jamaica, Mexico, Trinidad and Tobago, Uruguay and Venezuela.
2. Mr. Nehru died on the 27th May 1964.

CHAPTER XIX

The Darkling Plain:
the Preparatory Second Bandung Meetings,
Algiers, June and October 1965

It had a dying fall, the spirit of Afro-Asia, at the two abortive meetings in Algiers, and in the splendid new conference building there it found a magnificent mausoleum. But it was an indecent burial: hurried and furtive, and conducted in the early hours of the morning by weary, angry participants who were only anxious to be gone their separate ways.

The executioners of Afro-Asia were India and China; the gravediggers were the Africans, both Arab and non-Arab; and they accomplished their ends by insisting on being negatively neutralist rather than actively non-aligned in the disputes between Russia and China and India.

In the main conference hall the green-coloured roof and carpets and the greenish lighting created the pallid subaqueous effect of an aquarium. Equally unusual was the form of these two meetings. In June the full assembly met for a total time of just one minute; both meetings discussed little else apart from whether they should go on meeting; both ended in decisions to adjourn forthwith and to postpone the summit conference of the heads of state. After the second adjournment in October everyone knew that, for the sake of Afro-Asia, the postponed Second Bandung would not and should not ever be held.

From the start—when the invitations were issued in April 1965 for a meeting of the Afro-Asian foreign ministers who would prepare the details of a summit conference—even then a group of at least nine French-speaking African states expressed their disinclination to attend. Their reluctance was largely due to the fact that the meeting was being held in and organised by Algeria, which had been giving military aid to the anti-Government rebels in the Congo. Furthermore, China was very anxious for the conference to be held, and Chou En-lai, on a tour of Africa, had said that the prospects for revolution were excellent in that continent, revolution that could only be

393

against existing national governments. These governments, therefore, were not anxious to sit at the same table as a China that was eagerly awaiting their downfall. In the event, about thirty delegations attended the June meeting: slightly less than half of those invited.

The *coup* in Algeria that overthrew Mr. Ben Bella a mere five days before the foreign ministers were due to meet was not the real cause of the postponement; it merely provided a providential pretext. A few small demonstrations by students in the streets of Algiers did not present any real security threat to the visiting dignitaries.

The first direct blow against the Second Bandung was struck not in Algiers but in London. This came in the form of a suggestion or appeal for postponement by thirteen of the Afro-Asian leaders attending a Commonwealth Prime Ministers Conference. They gave no reason, and they were not really aware of what was happening in Algiers. Their move was simply an expression of their reluctance to attend the conference.

In Algiers the new government was divided in its attitude towards the conference. The President, Colonel Boumédienne, was indifferent, but his young and ebullient Foreign Minister, Mr. Abdel Aziz Bouteflika, was determined to use the meeting to gain quick international recognition for the regime. The strongest card in the Algerian hand was that the twelve other Arab states were pledged to follow its lead. This was true even for a wavering and uncertain United Arab Republic delegation that was not at all happy at the overthrow of President Nasser's personal friend, Mr. Ben Bella. However, as it became increasingly clear that the Boumédienne Government was firmly in the saddle, the United Arab Republic swung more definitely behind the Algerian demand for the conference.

By the evening of Friday, 25th June, it seemed certain that a foreign ministers' meeting would be held the next day. Arab solidarity added thirteen votes to the four countries (China, Indonesia, North Korea and North Vietnam) who were already in favour, thus giving a majority of the thirty odd delegations. This spelled defeat for India which, supported by Ceylon, Thailand, Japan and Laos, was proposing postponement in the hope that delay would slowly kill a conference she had never wanted.

Fortunately for India the supporters of Mr. Ben Bella, who did not want the Boumédienne government to gain credit or respectability from the conference, exploded a small bomb inside the main conference building in the early hours of Saturday. That was sufficient to swing a reluctant United Arab Republic, and the other equally doubtful African states, back in favour of postponement. On Saturday afternoon the eleven African states present at Algiers, speaking through the Secretary-General of the Organisation of African Unity, announced that if the foreign ministers' meeting were held no African state would attend: the Asians, they said, were free to meet on their own. The two halves of Afro-Asia were thus placed in unfriendly confrontation.

This decision was the *coup de grâce* and a contest then developed between those striving to claim credit for the postponement. In a deplorable display of diplomatic bad manners the Algerians permitted the delegations—several foreign ministers included—to foregather at the conference hall, twenty kilometres from the city, for the opening session, while at the same time a group consisting of Algeria, the United Arab Republic, China, Pakistan, Indonesia, Mali and Syria was meeting in Algiers drawing up the resolution for its postponement. Co-operating with the inevitable, those delegations that had hitherto opposed postponement had made an abrupt and total reversal of policy and now supported the idea.

When the resolution was ready the delegates were called into session in the conference hall for one minute and were asked to return to the city for a meeting of the Standing Preparatory Committee of fifteen ambassadors, of whom only eleven were actually present. To this truncated body the announcement was made, as a *fait accompli*, that the summit was postponed and the foreign ministers' meeting adjourned. The Guinean delegate described this arbitrary procedure as 'illegal'.

At the October meeting there were even more tortuous behind-the-scenes manoeuvrings, largely as a result of the contortions of Indian and Chinese policy. Like acrobats in a circus the two countries had somersaulted past each other. The last-minute change made in June, from opposition to support for the postponement of Second Bandung, remained China's policy. India, however, who had hitherto been strongly opposed to the conference, was now equally strongly in favour of its being held. These reversals of policy reflected a change in the power balance between the two main Asian antagonists.

In the intervening three months India had achieved a small but definite success in a limited 'war' against Pakistan, in the course of which China, supporting Pakistan, had presented India with an ultimatum and had then failed to execute her threats when India ignored the challenge. Furthermore, China's continuing inability to do anything to help her other ally, North Vietnam, now subjected to direct

American air attacks, had called forth jibes that she was 'a paper tiger'. A more self-confident India looked forward to giving the lead once again at an Afro-Asian Conference from which a sulky China stayed away because she feared defeat.

And China feared defeat on an issue that to her was all-important —the admission of Russia to a conference of Afro-Asia that had become, it must be remembered, the main battle-ground and the main prize in the Sino-Soviet dispute. In June it had been by no means certain that there were sufficient votes in Russia's favour, and it was not even certain whether Russia wanted to attend. Prodded by India and provoked by Chinese sneers, Russia resolved to attend, and used its considerable pressure to gain enough votes to make that possible. By October it was certain that Russia would be accepted as an Afro-Asian.

Faced with sure defeat, China announced that she was so opposed to the conference that she would boycott not only the heads of state summit but also the foreign ministers' preparatory meeting. The issue became the subject of prolonged and bitter debate between the Indian and Chinese ambassadors in the Standing Committee. In the end a harassed Algeria polled the invitees a week before the meeting and just over forty, two-thirds of Afro-Asia, declared themselves in favour of the meeting being held.

After a two-day postponement, to give time for laggards to arrive, the foreign ministers' meeting opened in full formal session on the 30th October with forty-five delegations attending, including about fifteen foreign ministers, though not, curiously enough, the Indian Foreign Minister. That this meeting should be held at all, in the face of strong Chinese objections, was in itself a serious setback to that country.

At this time the Algerian Government was once again divided on the issue of whether or not to hold Second Bandung. The conference chairman, Mr. Bouteflika, was in favour, but something of the doubts still being expressed in the ruling Revolution Council on having to choose between Russia and China came through in the chairman's opening speech, in which he had fair words for Russia's support to anti-colonial causes but also spoke of China's absence being 'cruelly felt'.

After that one welcoming speech and the election of officers, the meeting went into secret session, and re-emerged in public only to hear the chairman's closing address. At the start of the first closed session the Indian representative, Mr. C. S. Jha, with adroit alacrity, seized the earliest opportunity to propose formally the immediate admission of Russia, Malaysia and Singapore: there could be, he said, 'no escape' from this basic issue of membership and in support produced the same specious, unconvincing arguments about Russia being an Afro-Asian power and its heart being in the right Afro-Asian place.

The counter-attack came from Uganda, which proposed consideration of the report of the ambassadorial Standing Committee that would, indirectly, have opened the door to a debate on whether or not the conference should be held in the absence of a quarter of the Afro-Asian countries. The next day Indonesia brought the issue right out into the open by formally proposing postponement. The remaining closed sessions were nothing but one long rearguard action in which India and her friends abandoned the idea of a summit but fought for Russia's admission to the foreign ministers' meeting. Fundamentally India still remained opposed to Second Bandung.

In these sessions the speakers addressed themselves in confused fashion simultaneously to the two themes facing the meeting, the invitation to Russia and the postponement of the conference. Of those who spoke, no less than nineteen were in favour of Russia being present—among them such key states as the United Arab Republic, Japan, Nigeria, Mali, Kenya, Ethiopia and the Sudan. No one spoke against this and only Nepal clearly abstained.[1] Unfortunately for India there were still more favouring postponement, many of which were also advocates of Russian membership. In short, these Afro-Asians were having the best of both worlds by saying in effect: 'We think that Russia should attend our conference but at the present time our conference should not be held.'

Both the Arab and the African blocs were split on the issue. While most of the Africans wanted postponement, Nigeria, Chad and Malawi spoke forcibly against it; and Tunisia and Morocco, who wanted the conference to be held, were not in line with the general Arab position which, following the United Arab Republic, was prudently equivocal.

Arab equivocation clarified into opposition when, two days after the conference had opened, and after prolonged debate within the Algerian Revolution Council spread over three days, that body decided against the conference being held. Once the position of the host country became clear, with the Arab bloc equally clearly supporting it, there was no chance for the Indian thesis to prevail. In very quick succession twenty-three countries were found prepared to co-sponsor a resolution favouring postponement. A dozen of the signatories had, ten days earlier, been against any such thing.

The infection of collective timidity apart, the main reason for the majority agreement on postponement was the Afro-Asians' desire for equidistant neutrality between the two contending blocs. China had opposed the foreign ministers' meeting and the summit as well as the invitation to Russia; but the foreign ministers had met and, according to the chairman, the 'general consensus' approved the invitation to Russia. China had thus been rebuffed on two counts and therefore, to maintain the neutralist balance, it was necessary not to have the summit with Russia actually present; and it was so decided. The Afro-Asians thus indicated that they were not prepared to give a clear advantage to Russia and India in their struggle with China and Pakistan.

Various reasons may be advanced why, on the major issue, the Afro-Asians were prepared to accept what was virtually a Chinese veto. They did not wish to offend unduly a country that was potentially a Great Power and already a member of the exclusive nuclear club. There was the consideration of the material aid that could be forthcoming from China, even though that country had not fulfilled a tenth of the promises that it had made. Ideological affinities also played their part. China was still militantly anti-colonial, and those similarly inclined did not wish to forfeit her support in favour of that of the conservatives. Algeria, for instance, was not happy with the backing of Saudi Arabia and the Sudan, or of Nigeria and Malawi, as against that of her 'progressive' friends like Syria, Guinea and Mali.

Above all the decision to postpone was an expression of the protest of the small and medium-sized Afro-Asian countries against the attempts of the bigger countries to force them into line. This feeling was best expressed by the Philippines delegate, Mr. Lopez Salvador, who said that at Bandung China, in its capabilities, had been still akin to the other underdeveloped Afro-Asian states. Since then it had become a giant with all the vices of a giant. Either China should quit the Afro-Asian forum and leave the smaller Afro-Asians to go their own very different way, or the latter would be forced to bring Russia in as a counter-balance to China; and that they did not want to do.

This quit notice from the small and medium-sized Afro-Asians should, and eventually will, be served on India too. It is her dispute with China that broke the back of Afro-Asia across the ridges of the

Himalayas. A hesitant Russia only intruded on the conference because India tried to bring her in to annoy and neutralise China.

The abrupt changes in policy could be transformed into conference decisions only because the meeting was bullied and browbeaten in ruthlessly undemocratic fashion by the chairman, Mr. Bouteflika. If he suspected that a delegation would oppose the Algerian position he quite simply refused to give it the floor. Here one saw in action the new generation of Afro-Asian leaders bred in a harsher, more revolutionary, more dogmatic school, that had little time and less respect for the diplomatic niceties of its elders.

For the governments of Afro-Asia it was a good thing that they did not meet for a second time at the summit because if they had they would have savaged each other. It was equally a good thing that Russia did not become one of their number for Russia should have no place in Asia.

As the weary and disillusioned delegates moved out from the conference building into the forecourt above the softly soughing Mediterranean they were agreed on just one thing: there must be no more Afro-Asian conferences. The political process begun eighteen years earlier, and in another continent, beneath the dusty, crumbling walls of the Old Fort in Delhi, had here found its end. From now on the spirit of Afro-Asia would be best expressed politically through the organ that first gave it formal expression—the Afro-Asian group at the United Nations. For the militant malcontents there would always be the so-called Afro-Asian Solidarity Movement, which was moving away from its original bi-continental base into a new tri-continental grouping comprising Latin America: an ingathering of the wretched of the earth—not merely of those of this race or that colour or the other continent. The seventy-seven developing countries in the United Nations Commission on Trade and Development were a similar grouping that had a useful future before it.

The conference building, it was said, was built over the grave of a Muslim saint. Perhaps his protesting spirit lay like a curse over the meetings and helped make them fail. His ghost and the Afro-Asian spirit can now both be laid to rest.

Non-alignment remained intact and untouched, for it is the moral deficiency of neutralism that has completed the swift cycle of the Afro-Asian movement: dawn at Delhi, high noon at Bandung, the onset of twilight at Colombo, and at Algiers the darkling plain on which ignorant armies clashed by night.

The Darkling Plain: the Preparatory Second Bandung

NOTE TO CHAPTER XIX

1. The countries favouring the admission of Russia were: India, Mongolia, Nigeria, Malawi, United Arab Republic, Tunisia, Somalia, Laos, Jordan, Japan, Mali, Kenya, Ruanda, Turkey, Lebanon, Iran, Morocco, Ethiopia, Sudan. The following made no mention of the subject: Indonesia, Syria and Senegal. Nepal stated that it was abstaining on the issue.

Epilogue

The twenty years covered by this book is only a short time in the long history of Afro-Asia, yet for several reasons this span has a special significance.

For one thing, into it were compressed developments that might have occupied decades, or even centuries, in more spacious and leisurely times. The history of Afro-Asia now has a tension, a new density, that gives it a heightened quality more significant than considerations of quantity.

For another, this score of years covered a unique and crucial happening—the re-emergence of the two continents into freedom from foreign rule. Today, on the mainland of Asia, the only areas under European influence or control are Aden and its hinterland, Kowloon opposite Hong Kong, Macao, and the surrogate-European enclave of Israel. To find a comparable period of self-rule in Afro-Asia one has to go back to the years between 1291, when Asian power expelled the Crusader Kingdoms from the Levant, and 1415, when Prince Henry the Navigator seized Ceuta in Morocco in a resurgence of European power. The span of time, however brief, that witnessed the swift and total reversal of an historical trend begun five centuries earlier is, on any score, bound to be memorable.

It is now necessary to cast a backward glance over these twenty years to see to what extent the three themes mentioned in the Prologue have emerged intact or been moulded by the turbulent events of the period.

The attempt by some Afro-Asian countries to base their foreign policies on the commandments of morality has not been successful. However sincere and well-intentioned the motives behind this endeavour, it only ended by proving that Afro-Asian governments are, in the conduct of their foreign affairs, no better and no worse than any other governments. The pressure of events stripped Afro-Asian non-alignment of the crypto Gandhian excrescences in which India sought to enwrap this policy. It is now clear that countries can believe

c2

in and practise non-alignment without need to believe in or practise peaceful co-existence over the whole range of their foreign policies. The Arabs in relation to Israel, India in relation to China, and India and Pakistan in relation to each other, have accepted temporary, enforced co-existence—no war but no real peace.

Another moralistic outgrowth that has had to be abandoned is the theory that all disputes must be settled by negotiation. The Arabs have never negotiated with Israel, India has been unable to negotiate with China despite non-aligned mediation, and negotiation between Indonesia and Malaysia produced no results. It was significant that at Belgrade the appeals from the non-aligned for negotiations were addressed to the Great Powers; they were not applied to problems involving the non-aligned themselves.

These pious beliefs have been described as crypto-Gandhian because, during the Chinese attack on India, the propaganda organs of the Indian Government, that had for years equated non-alignment with the Five Principles and with non-violence, had no difficulty in producing a profusion of quotations from the Mahatma to the effect that the worst sin was cowardice, that sometimes one had to fight and die rather than surrender, that sometimes it is too late for negotiation.[1]

Non-alignment, even when interpreted in its narrow neutralist sense as merely independence of the two blocs, has emerged as something simple, realistic and pragmatic. One can now see that it is a policy, not a creed; a tactic, even a weapon, but not a gospel; for whatever else gospels may do, they do not establish or preserve the national self-interest of newly and fiercely independent states.

On the clash between illusion and reality, the illusion of continental brotherliness and the reality of separate national interests, in which reality was bound to prevail, the happenings in Afro-Asia prompt one startling reflection. It is surprising that the predominance of national interests took some years to assert itself; yet this is understandable. Nationalist struggles in Afro-Asia have not only had to assert and defend a national feeling; they have frequently had to create this nationalism in countries where it ought to exist, where, eventually, it has come to exist and where, in some cases, it had never existed before. Only after fully realising their new identity can emerging states define and comprehend the national interests which that identity calls into existence in order to sustain and protect itself. Hence when, in their early years, some of the Afro-Asian states, and even countries like India, pursued policies that were quixotic, they did so not merely out of piety or romanticism, but often because of a lack of self-awareness born of the newness of their national selves.

The various intertwinings and interactions of Afro-Asian feeling and non-alignment in this twenty-year period have finally made clear that the two sentiments are not identical and can even be antagonistic. What is not so clear is whether, because of what has happened and is happening in the world at large, the Afro-Asian impulse and the policy of non-alignment are going to endure, or whether, like the Marxist state, they are going to wither away after fulfilling their purpose.

The more likely of the two to meet this fate is the Afro-Asian movement because its essential ingredient is negative anti-colonialism; now that the long trek back to Europe of the colonial powers is wellnigh completed, there will be fewer targets for the attacks on which the movement sustains itself; it seems dead already.

The moving apart of Africa and Asia—its two constituent elements —is another reason why the Afro-Asian concept is likely to lose strength. This divergence has happened not only because of differences in historical background, in temperament, and in political maturity, but because in Africa there is a sense of continental solidarity, whereas in Asia there has been no such thing. This particular difference has now been formalised and institutionalised, Africa giving itself a single co-ordinating organisation; this Asia was never able to do, because the smaller Asian countries feared that any such grouping would be dominated by one or other of the continents' two colossi, India and China, while neither of these two countries would let the other take first place.

Above all Afro-Asia has already been rent by the antagonisms injected into it by the extraneous conflict between Russia and China, which has already reduced to deadlock the work of the Afro-Asian Solidarity Movement. But because the Afro-Asians are no longer passive objects, but are growing and changing all the time, whoever is victorious in the inter-Communist struggle will discover that the prize is not two complete continental entities but perhaps, and at most, bits of one or the other. The most likely combination of these oddments will be that grouped in the New Emerging Forces, the regressively anti-colonialist rump of Afro-Asia that may well function within the Chinese sphere of influence.

Will non-alignment as an attribute or function of the Cold War between East and West melt in the thawing of the antagonisms between these blocs? The answer depends on the definition given to non-alignment, which has been a prime victim of the tyranny of words. If it is viewed in its neutralist aspect, as a policy of equidistance between two sides that are to be played off against each other and bargained with, then naturally cordiality between the contestants would rob non-alignment of all scope for action.[2]

Were a coming-together of the Big Two to limit the field of manœuvre of neutralist bargainers, the development of polycentrism within the two blocs, and within Afro-Asia itself, would tend to increase the possibilities of calculated choice. Whereas hitherto the choice, or non-choice, lay only between Russia and America, alternatives are now offered—between Russia and China, America and France, India and China, to say nothing of choices involving the Arabs and Israel and Indonesia and Malaysia. In the future, neutralist playing-off, far from withering away, may become a more complicated, many-sided game.

But will non-alignment as truly defined—the desire of an independent country, or of a country that feels itself to be independent, to practise an independent foreign policy—will this type of non-alignment fade away because of Cold War relaxations? Obviously not, for every foreign policy issue that demands a choice presents an opportunity for a display of independence.

Despite appearances to the contrary, and the temporary upsurge of the Afro-Asians at the expense of the non-aligned, the policy of non-alignment will outlive the Afro-Asian feeling because it is based on a solid and useful principle and not merely on geography.

The events of our twenty-year period have demonstrated that even this true form of independence has full reality only if it is armed non-alignment, as is the case with Sweden, and armed from an independent, indigenous armament industry. Unarmed non-alignment does not always serve as a buffer but often, as in Laos, as an incitement to aggression. Hence the independence of the unarmed Afro-Asian non-aligned is more a state of mind than a state of fact. But it is not illusory, for in politics it is foolish to underestimate the solid reality of states of mind. If several hundred million people feel that they are independent, then they are so. But possession of one's own self-sufficient armament industry certainly helps to give this reality positive content. Both elements, the mental and the factual, are necessary; for a country can run its own armament industry and yet neither feel nor want to be independent.

The search for armed backing for their non-alignment has often compelled the non-aligned countries to accept military aid exclusively from one side in the Cold War. Even this vital commitment has not always adversely affected an uncommitted foreign policy, if the will to maintain that policy is there. This has been proven true by India, Yugoslavia and the United Arab Republic. And the same is true of economic aid from one side only.

Following the failure of the Afro-Asian non-aligned peoples to support India after the Chinese attack, there was much bitter comment, in India and elsewhere, that the policy of non-alignment had been fatally weakened by this moral weakness. This criticism is not wholly justified. What had been destroyed were the moral pretensions of many of the non-aligned countries. The attack only served to show that non-alignment calls not only for armed support but for courage of a kind that some of the smaller non-aligned countries displayed on this particular occasion.

No one country can claim to have practised true non-alignment all the time, though some countries may have done so more steadily than others. In the early 1950's, India's record in this respect was good, but Burma's was probably better. A close analysis of the United Nations voting record may well show that, in recent years, one of the smaller African states, far-removed from direct Cold War pressures, has applied non-alignment most of the time.

In any summing-up of the Afro-Asian movement and the policy of non-alignment the crucial question must be: have they justified themselves in terms of moral and material benefits achieved for those within the movement and the policy, and also for the world at large.

The Afro-Asians have undoubtedly pushed forward and speeded up the necessary policy of decolonisation—necessary because all continents, like all countries, must learn to live contentedly at home. And by and large the Afro-Asians have done this without in any way justifying Europe's guilty fears of a vast retaliatory race war. There has been no tremendous surge of avenging hordes out of steppe or jungle.

It is equally incontestable that the non-aligned peoples have served and saved the peace. Perhaps they did so most decisively during the years 1949 to 1953—the last years of Stalin—when that irascible old man was pressing the West hard in Berlin and Korea. Fortunately his own contemptuous hostility towards the new Afro-Asian states repelled them. If, in anger at the West for past wrongs, countries such as India or Indonesia or the Arab states had thrown in their lot vigorously with the Communist East in 1950, the result could have been catastrophic. At the very least the Cold War would have reached a lasting, freezing intensity. On Korea, on Indo-China and later on disarmament, the weight of the non-aligned countries, such as it was and is, was flung decisively on to the side of peaceful agreements.

In more than one harsh crisis the policy of the non-aligned has presented itself as an attempt to break out of the stale, arid rigidities of Cold War attitudes and judgements, to offer something fresh and new, like the piping voice of the clear-eyed child saying that the emperor wears no clothes.

Both the Afro-Asian movement and the group of the non-aligned peoples served their turn by gathering the new countries into protective corrals wherein they had time to learn the techniques of foreign policy and diplomacy before exercising the right to independent choice. They made the world a less lonely and more friendly place for these newcomers.

And bi-continental Afro-Asianism helped to launch independent Africa on a steadier, surer course towards continental unity than Asia on its own had been able or willing to follow.

These solid achievements provide the answer that Afro-Asia and the non-aligned have justified themselves.

There are perhaps a few lessons to be drawn from this survey.

The first is that there is increasing congruence between two sorts of map—the geographic map and the map of political power. On the geographic map peninsular India and peninsular Arabia are as large as peninsular Europe; but on the other type of map the first two shrink while the third expands into a large land-mass. The process may be slow and long-drawn-out, but nevertheless will end in both maps looking approximately the same.

There is also a foreshadowing of 'regional' affiliations that will assert themselves. Similarities of geography, religion, language and culture have tended to draw into distinct groups the South Asians or the Arabs as also the Sub-Saharan Africans; and peering into the cloudy future, one sees the possibility that Russia and the rest of Europe will find themselves nearer to the Indo-European Asians than to the Mongolian Asians.

If these smaller groupings do not materialise it will be because the poor countries set their present economic needs above their past heritage of religion and language and culture. The unity displayed by the seventy-seven poor countries of Asia, Africa and Latin America at the Geneva Conference on Trade and Development suggests that economics may have the last word. The moderation and compromise displayed by these countries, and by the rich, offers a heartening, tantalising glimpse of the rich and the poor, the coloured and the non-coloured, joining together in a new assemblage to launch mankind into a real battle against its ancient foes—poverty, ignorance and disease.

Lastly, this brief period in the history of the Afro-Asians and the non-aligned teaches the lesson that there can be no friendship without frankness. That new and inexperienced nations should be carried away by emotionalism is understandable, but not that they should succumb to such sentimentalism as 'the Asian feeling' or Panchsheel. In their dealings with each other the Afro-Asian non-aligned have shown too much friendliness in public and too much frankness in private—attitudes that may have been due to the sentimental feeling that public disagreements would amount to a betrayal of the cause. The opposite proved to be the case. When private frankness was forced to emerge as realistic policy, it presented a shocking contrast to the unrealistic verbiage of overmuch public friendliness.

If this book, in however small a measure, helps to bring about this identity of friendship and frankness between the Afro-Asian non-aligned peoples it will have served its purpose.

NOTES TO EPILOGUE

1. The rejection of peaceful co-existence by Hinduism, and its very tenuous links with Buddhism, were mentioned in chap. 6. Dr. Fayez Sayegh has proved conclusively that there is no link between Islam and Neutralism in a paper so entitled, submitted to the Conference on Islam and International Relations held at Duke University in June 1963. See *Islam and International Relations*, ed. J. Harris Proctor, London, 1965, pp. 61–93.
2. The consequences of complete accord between the United States and Russia are delineated in Bertrand Russell's *Nightmares of Eminent Persons*, London, 1954. Asia is allotted to Russia, Africa to America, while Europe is divided. The nightmare is that of President Eisenhower, but such a prospect is a very real and continuing worry for the presidents of such countries as Indonesia, or the United Arab Republic or Ghana.

BIBLIOGRAPHICAL NOTE

There has of late been a small flood of books on the subject of Afro-Asia and non-alignment. Most of them come from the United States. One among them escapes the pitfall of trying to deal in detail with a subject that the authors, necessarily, can only write about at second hand. This is M. Rossi's *The Third World*, New York, 1963. From now on the history of Afro-Asia will not only be made but must also be written by Afro-Asians.

The Conference on Indonesia, 1949

Resolution I Adopted on 22nd January 1949

This Conference of representatives of the Governments of Afghanistan, Australia, Burma, Ceylon, Egypt, Ethiopia, India, Iran, Iraq, Lebanon, Pakistan, Philippines, Saudi Arabia, Syria and Yemen.

Affirming their support of the purposes and principles of the United Nations and the obligation of all member states to accept and carry out the decision of the Security Council in accordance with the Charter;

Having considered the situation in Indonesia in the light of all available data and, in particular, the reports submitted by the Good Offices Committee of the Security Council;

Being of the opinion that the Dutch military action launched on the 18th December 1948, constitutes a flagrant breach of the Charter of the United Nations and defiance of the efforts of the Security Council and its Good Offices Committee to bring about a peaceful settlement;

Noting that the Netherlands authorities have failed to give full effect to the resolutions of the Security Council adopted after that date;

Finding that this action is directed against the very existence of the Republican Government which the Security Council and several member Governments of the United Nations, including the Netherlands Government itself, have recognised;

Conscious of the danger to the peace of South-East Asia and of the world through the continuance of hostilities in Indonesia;

Recognising that the people of Indonesia are entitled, according to the principles of the Charter, to independence and the exercise of full sovereign rights;

Recognising further that the maintenance of international peace and security and the development of friendly relations among nations based on respect for the principles of equal rights and self-determination of peoples constitute the high and steadfast purpose of the United Nations;

Firmly convinced that the Security Council is properly seized of the Indonesian question, as a breach of the peace and an act of aggression, under Article 39 of the United Nations Charter;

RECOMMENDS to the Security Council of the United Nations:

A. (1) That members of the Republican Government, other Republican leaders and all political prisoners in Indonesia, be immediately restored to complete freedom;

(2) That the Republican Government be enabled to function freely and, to this end,

  (i) the Residency of Jogjakarta be handed back immediately to the Republic and the Netherlands authorities refrain from taking any action that may interfere with the effective functioning of the Government of the Republic. That Government should also have facilities for communication and freedom of consultation throughout Indonesia;

  (ii) such areas of the Island of Java, Sumatra and Madura as were held by the Government of the Republic on the 18th December 1948, be restored to the Republic not later than the 15th March 1949;

  (iii) Dutch forces be withdrawn (a) immediately from the Residency of Jogjakarta, and (b) progressively from the rest of the Republican territory mentioned in (ii). Such withdrawal to be effected in stages and under conditions to be prescribed by the Good Offices Committee or any other body to be appointed by the Security Council and to be completed not later than the 15th March 1949;

  (iv) All restrictions imposed by the Netherlands authorities on the trade of the Republic be immediately removed;

  (v) Pending the formation of the Interim Government referred to in (3), the Republican Government be afforded facilities for communication with the outside world.

(3) That an Interim Government composed of representatives of the Republic, and representatives of territories in Indonesia other than those under the authority of the Republic, commanding the confidence of the Indonesian people, be formed not later than 15th March, 1949, with the approval

and assistance of the Good Offices Committee, or any other body that may be appointed by the Security Council. Pending the results of the deliberations for the Constituent Assembly referred to in paragraph (6) below, no new regional governments shall be formed or recognised.

(4) That, subject to the provisions of paragraph (5), such Interim Government shall enjoy full powers of government including control over its armed forces. To ensure these, all Dutch troops shall be withdrawn from the whole of Indonesia on a date to be determined by the Good Offices Committee, or any other body appointed by the Security Council. Pending such withdrawal, Dutch forces shall not be used for the maintainance of law and order except at the request of the interim Government and with the approval of the Good Offices Committee or any other body that may be appointed by the Security Council.

(5) That the Interim Government shall have such freedom in external affairs as may be determined, in consultation with the Interim Government and the Netherlands authorities, by the Good Offices Committee or any other body that may be appointed by the Security Council.

(6) That elections for the Constituent Assembly of Indonesia be completed by 1st October 1949;

(7) That power over the whole of Indonesia be completely transferred, by the 1st January 1950, to the United States of Indonesia whose relationship with the Netherlands shall be settled by negotiation between the Governments of the United States of Indonesia and the Netherlands;

(8) That the Good Offices Committee, or any other body appointed by the Security Council, be given authority to secure the application of the foregoing recommendations under the supervision of the Security Council to whom it shall report as frequently as may be necessary.

B. That, in the event of either party to the dispute not complying with the recommendations of the Security Council, the Council shall take effective action under the wide powers conferred upon it by the Charter, to enforce the said recommendations. Member States of the United Nations represented at this Conference pledge their full support to the Council in the application of any of these measures.

C. That the Security Council be pleased to report, for consideration by the United Nations General Assembly at its adjourned session commencing in April 1949, the measures taken or recommended by the council for a solution of the Indonesian problem and the action taken by the parties concerned to give effect to these measures.

Resolution II Adopted on 22nd January 1949

In order to ensure close co-operation among themselves on matters dealt with in Resolution I, this Conference recommends to the participating Governments, whether member States of the United Nations or not:

(a) That they should keep in touch with one another through normal diplomatic channels;

(b) That they should instruct their representatives at the Headquarters of the United Nations or their diplomatic representatives to consult among themselves.

Resolution III Adopted on 22nd January 1949

The Conference expresses the opinion that participating Governments should consult among themselves in order to explore ways and means of establishing suitable machinery, having regard to the areas concerned, for promoting consultation and co-operation within the framework of the United Nations.

Joint Communiqué by the Prime Ministers of Burma, Ceylon, India, Indonesia and Pakistan, Colombo, 1954

The Prime Ministers of Burma, Ceylon, India, Indonesia and Pakistan met in Colombo on 28th, 29th, and 30th April, and in Kandy on 1st and 2nd May 1954, and exchanged views and discussed problems of common interest and concern to them all. This was the first occasion on which the Prime Ministers of these countries had met together. The informal and cordial atmosphere of the conference enabled them not merely to get better acquainted with one another's views, but also to come to know one another better.

While it was not expected there would be complete unanimity of approach to the variety of problems they discussed, the conference made it evident that there was substantial community of outlook on many of these problems. It was a happy coincidence that the Prime Ministers of these countries should have met together when problems vital to the stability and peace of the Far Eastern and Asian region were being considered by the Geneva Conference.

The Prime Ministers reviewed the situation in Indo-China, where a long and tragic war threatens the establishment of the freedom and independence of the peoples of Indo-China, as well as the security of the peace of Asia and of the world as a whole. They welcomed the earnest attempt being made at Geneva to find a solution to the problem of Indo-China by negotiation, and hoped the deliberations by the Geneva Conference would bring about a speedy termination of the conflict and restoration of peace in Indo-China.

They considered that the solution of the problem of Indo-China required that agreement on a cease-fire should be reached without delay.

The Prime Ministers felt that a solution of the problem required direct negotiations between the parties directly concerned—namely France, the three Associated States of Indo-China and the Vietminh, as well as other parties invited by agreement. The success of such direct negotiations will be greatly helped by agreement on the part of all countries concerned, particularly China, the United Kingdom, United States, and Soviet Union, on steps necessary to prevent a recurrence or resumption of hostilities. The Prime Ministers contemplated that this negotiating group would report to the Geneva Conference for a final decision.

They proposed that France should declare at the Geneva Conference that she is irrevocably committed to the complete independence of Indo-China. In order that the good offices and machinery of the United Nations might be utilised for furtherance of the purposes of the Geneva Conference and implementation of its decisions on Indo-China, the Prime Ministers were of the opinion that the conference should keep the United Nations informed of the progress of the deliberations on Indo-China.

The Prime Ministers viewed with grave concern developments in regard to the hydrogen bomb and other weapons of mass destruction. They welcomed the current efforts of the United Nations Disarmament Commission to bring about the elimination and prohibition of such weapons and hoped that the commission would be able to reach an agreed solution of this problem urgently.

The Prime Ministers were of the opinion that pending such an agreement no further explosions of hydrogen bombs should take place and that the United Nations and the Powers principally concerned should take steps to publish authoritative information regarding the destructive capabilities and the known and probable disastrous effect of these weapons. They believe that such publication by rousing the conscience of the world would help in the search for an agreed solution of the grave problem that threatens humanity.

The Prime Ministers were concerned by the question of the representation of China in the United Nations by the Government of the Peoples' Republic of China. They felt that such representation would help to promote stability in Asia, ease world tension and assist in bringing about a more realistic approach to problems concerning the world, particularly in the Far East.

The Prime Ministers discussed the problem of colonialism, which they regretted still existed in various parts of the world. They were of the view that the continuance of such a state of affairs was a violation of fundamental human rights and a threat to the peace of the world.

The Prime Ministers also considered particularly the problem of

Tunisia and Morocco. They were of the view that national sovereignties and the demands of their peoples for independence should be recognised and that they should be enabled to exercise the right to self-determination.

Communism: This subject, in its national and international aspects, was generally discussed, and the Prime Ministers made known to each other their respective views on and attitudes towards Communist ideologies.

The Prime Ministers affirmed their faith in democracy and democratic institutions, and being resolved to preserve in their respective countries the freedoms inherent in the democratic system declared their unshakable determination to resist interference in the affairs of their countries by external Communist, anti-Communist, or other agencies.

They were convinced that such interference threatened the sovereignty, security, and political independence of their respective states, and the right of each country to develop and progress in accordance with the conceptions and desires of its own peoples.

In considering the situation in the Middle East the Prime Ministers indicated grave concern over the sufferings of Arab refugees in Palestine. They urged the United Nations to bring about and expedite the rehabilitation of these refugees in their original homes. The Prime Ministers expressed deep sympathy with the Arabs of Palestine in their sufferings and affirmed their desire to see a just and early settlement of the Palestine problem.

The Prime Ministers considered certain proposals relating to economic co-operation and mutual aid and decided that these proposals should be referred to the Governments represented at the conference for their consideration.

In their relations with one another, the Prime Ministers affirmed adherence to the principles of respecting the sovereignty of each country and of not intervening in the domestic affairs of others.

The Prime Ministers discussed the desirability of holding a conference of African-Asian nations and favoured a proposal that the Prime Minister of Indonesia should explore the possibility of such a conference.

The Prime Ministers expressed their satisfaction that the conference had paved the way for similar meetings in the future.

APPENDIX A.3

Joint Communiqué by the Prime Ministers of Burma, Ceylon, India, Indonesia and Pakistan, Bogor, 1954

The Prime Ministers of Burma, Ceylon, India, Indonesia and Pakistan met at Bogor on the 28th and 29th December 1954. The main object of their meeting was to consider matters concerning the proposed Asian-African Conference suggested at the first meeting of the Prime Ministers at Colombo last April.

2. The Prime Ministers took advantage of the opportunity of their present meeting to review briefly, and in general terms, problems and issues of common interest and concern to them all.

3. The Prime Ministers agreed that an Asian-African Conference be held under their joint sponsorship. They also reached agreement on all consequential matters.

4. The purposes of the Asian-African Conference would be:

    (a) to promote goodwill and co-operation among the nations of Asia and Africa, to explore and advance their mutual as well as common interests and to establish and further friendliness and neighbourly relations;

    (b) to consider social, economic and cultural problems and relations of the countries represented;

    (c) to consider problems of special interest to Asian and African peoples, e.g. problems affecting national sovereignty and of racialism and colonialism;

    (d) to view the position of Asia and Africa and their peoples in the world of today and the contribution they make to the promotion of the world peace and co-operation.

5. The Conference will meet in Indonesia in the last week of April 1955. The Government of Indonesia has agreed to make the necessary arrangements for this Conference on behalf of the sponsoring countries. A Conference secretariat representing the sponsoring countries will be set up in Indonesia.

415

Joint Communiqué by Prime Ministers, Bogor, 1954

6. The Prime Ministers agreed that the Conference should have a broad and geographical basis, and that all countries in Asia and Africa, which have independent governments, should be invited. With minor variations and modifications of this basic principle, they decided to invite the following countries:

1. Afghanistan	13. Lebanon
2. Cambodia	14. Liberia
3. Central African Federation	15. Libya
4. China	16. Nepal
5. Egypt	17. Philippines
6. Ethiopia	18. Sudan
7. Gold Coast	19. Syria
8. Iran	20. Thailand
9. Iraq	21. Turkey
10. Japan	22. Vietnam (North)
11. Jordan	23. Vietnam (South)
12. Laos	24. Yemen

The above twenty-four countries, together with the five sponsoring countries, namely, Burma, Ceylon, India, Indonesia and Pakistan, will, it is hoped, participate in the Conference.

7. Representatives at the Conference will be at Ministerial level and it is hoped that each country invited will be represented by her Prime Minister and/or Foreign Minister, together with such other representatives as each government might wish to include in its delegation.

8. The Conference will determine its own procedure and agenda, the general scope of which is set out in the purposes of the Conference.

9. The Prime Ministers wished to point out that acceptance of the invitation by any one country would in no way involve or even imply any change in its views of the status of any other country. It implied only that the country invited was in general agreement with the purposes of the Conference. They had also borne in mind the principle that the form of government and the way of life of any one country should in no way be subject to interference by any other. Any view expressed at the Conference by one or more participating country would not be binding on or be regarded as accepted by any other, unless the latter so desired. The basic purpose of the Conference was that the countries concerned should become better acquainted with one another's point of view. The Prime Ministers hoped that

416

this clarification would enable all the invited countries to accept their invitation.

10. The Prime Ministers wished to state that in seeking to convene an Afro-Asian Conference, they were not actuated by any desire for exclusiveness in respect of the membership of the Conference. They did not desire, either, that the participating countries should build themselves into a regional bloc.

11. The Prime Ministers expressed gratification at the results of the Geneva Conference on Indo-China and the cessation of hostilities. They expressed the hope that the Geneva Agreements would be fully respected and implemented by all concerned and that there would be no outside interference which would hinder their successful implementation.

12. The Prime Ministers, in the context of their well-known attitude towards colonialism, took note of the case of West Irian. The Prime Ministers of Burma, Ceylon, India and Pakistan supported the position of Indonesia in this matter. They expressed the earnest hope that the Netherlands Government would reopen negotiations to implement their obligations under the solemn agreements concluded by them with Indonesia.

13. The Prime Ministers expressed their continual support of the demand of the peoples of Tunisia and Morocco for their national independence and their legitimate right to self-determination.

14. The Prime Ministers reiterated their grave concern in respect of the destructive potential of nuclear and thermo-nuclear explosions for experimental purposes which threaten not only their countries, but the world, and their far-reaching and yet unascertained effects which may do permanent damage to human life and civilisation. They earnestly requested all concerned to bring about a cessation of such experiments. They also requested the Disarmament Commission to take this matter into immediate consideration.

15. The economic development of Asian countries, which is so urgently necessary for the happiness and well-being of their peoples, required the planned approach with a view to the utilisation, in the most effective manner of the available resources. An essential prerequisite of such an approach is full knowledge of these resources.

Surveys of physical resources, particularly of the mineral and subsoil wealth of each country, should therefore be conducted, and cooperation in the supply of technical personnel and in other ways should be made available.

16. The Prime Ministers considered that co-operation in the eco-

Joint Communiqué by Prime Ministers, Bogor, 1954

nomic sphere for the supply of technical personnel and in all other ways should engage the attention of their Governments. They considered that a committee of experts should set up to consider economic questions of common interest to their countries.

17. The Prime Ministers, meeting on the Eve of the New Year, expressed their earnest hope that the year 1955 would witness a further growth in the friendly co-operation of the countries represented in the Conference as well as other countries and further the cause of world peace.

BOGOR, the 29th of December 1954

APPENDIX A.4

The Bandung Conference, 1955

The preceding sections have been omitted since they are of no special importance.

G. *Declaration on the Promotion of World Peace and Co-operation:*

The Asian-African Conference gave anxious thought to the question of world peace and co-operation. It viewed with deep concern the present state of international tension with its danger of an atomic world war. The problem of peace is correlative with the problem of international security. In this connection, all states should co-operate, especially through the United Nations, in bringing about the reduction of armaments and the elimination of nuclear weapons under effective international control. In this way, international peace can be promoted and nuclear energy may be used exclusively for peaceful purposes. This would help answer the needs particularly of Asia and Africa, for what they urgently require are social progress and better standards of life in larger freedom. Freedom and peace are interdependent. The right of self-determination must be enjoyed by all peoples, and freedom and independence must be granted with the least possible delay to those who are still dependent peoples. Indeed, all nations have the right freely to choose their own political and economic systems and their own way of life, in conformity with the purposes and principles of the Charter of the United Nations.

Free from mistrust and fear, and with confidence and goodwill towards each other, nations should practise tolerance and live together in peace with one another as good neighbours and develop friendly co-operation on the basis of the following principles:

1. Respect for fundamental human rights and for the purposes and principles of the Charter of the United Nations.
2. Respect for the sovereignty and territorial integrity of all nations.

419

3. Recognition of the equality of all races and of the equality of all nations large and small.

4. Abstention from intervention or interference in the internal affairs of another country.

5. Respect for the right of each nation to defend itself singly or collectively, in conformity with the Charter of the United Nations.

6. (a) Abstention from the use of arrangement of collective defence to serve the particular interests of any of the big powers.

    (b) Abstention by any country from exerting pressures on other countries.

7. Refraining from acts or threats or aggression or the use of force against the territorial integrity or political independence of any country.

8. Settlement of all international disputes by peaceful means, such as negotiation, conciliation, arbitration or judicial settlement as well as other peaceful means of the parties' own choice, in conformity with the Charter of the United Nations.

9. Promotion of mutual interests and co-operation.

10. Respect for justice and international obligations.

The Asian-African Conference declared its conviction that friendly co-operation in accordance with these principles would effectively contribute to the maintenance and promotion of international peace and security, while co-operation in the economic, social and cultural fields would help bring about the common prosperity and well-being of all.

The Asian-African Conference recommended that the five sponsoring countries consider the convening of the next meeting of the Conference, in consultation with the participating countries.

APPENDIX A.5

Statement on the Danger of War and an Appeal for Peace Issued by the Belgrade Conference 1961

This Conference of the Heads of State or Government of Non-Aligned Countries is deeply concerned that even apart from already existing tension the grave and critical situation which, as never before, threatens the world with the imminent and ominous prospect of conflict which would almost certainly later develop into a World War. In this age of nuclear weapons and the accumulation of the power of mass destruction, such conflict and war would inevitably lead to devastation on a scale hitherto unknown, if not to world annihilation.

2. This Conference considers that this calamity must be avoided, and it is therefore urgent and imperative that the parties concerned, and more particularly the United States of America and the U.S.S.R., should immediately suspend their recent war preparations and approaches, take no steps that would aggravate or contribute to further deterioration in the situation, and resume negotiations for a peaceful settlement of any outstanding differences between them with due regard to the principles of the United Nations Charter and should continue negotiating until both they and the rest of the world achieve total disarmament and enduring peace.

3. While decisions leading to war or peace at present rest with these Great Powers, the consequences affect the entire world. All nations and peoples have, therefore, an abiding concern and interest that the approaches and actions of the Great Powers should be such as to enable mankind to move forward to peace and prosperity and not to the doom of extinction. In the certain knowledge that they seek peace, this Conference appeals to the President of the United States of America and the Chairman of the Council of Ministers of the U.S.S.R. to make most immediate and direct approaches to each other to avert the imminent conflict and establish peace.

4. This Conference expresses the earnest hope that all nations not represented here, conscious of the extreme gravity of the situation

will make a similar appeal to the leaders of the Powers concerned thereby proclaiming and promoting the desire and determination of all mankind to see the achievement of lasting peace and security for all nations.

United Nations Resolution on Peaceful and Neighbourly Relations among States (1236 (XII), 14 December 1957)

The General Assembly considering the urgency and the importance of strengthening international peace and of developing peaceful and neighbourly relations among states irrespective of their divergencies or the relative stages and nature of their political, economic and social development, Recalling that among the fundamental objectives of the Charter of the United Nations are the maintenance of international peace and security and friendly co-operation among states, Realizing the need to promote these objectives and to develop peaceful and tolerant relations among states, in conformity with the Charter, based on mutual respect and benefit, non-aggression, respect for each other's sovereignty, equality and territorial integrity and non-intervention in one another's internal affairs, and to fulfil the purposes and principles of the Charter, Recognising the need to broaden international co-operation, to reduce tensions and to settle differences and disputes among states by peaceful means, Calls upon all states to make every effort to strengthen international peace, and to develop friendly and co-operative relations and settle disputes by peaceful means as enjoined in the Charter of the United Nations and as set forth in the present resolution.

APPENDIX B.2

Excerpts from the United Nations Resolution on the Ending of Colonialism (1514 (XV), 14 December 1960)

Recognising that the people of the world ardently desire the end of colonialism in all its manifestations . . . Convinced that the process of liberation is irresistible and irreversible and that, to avoid grave crises, it is necessary to put an end to colonialism and to the practices of segregation and discrimination that accompany it . . . Convinced that all peoples have an inalienable right to complete freedom, the exercise of their sovereignity and the integrity of their national territory . . . Solemnly proclaims the necessity of putting an end rapidly and unconditionally to colonialism in all its forms and manifestations.

Index

425

Index

Index

Index

Index